CW01646664

"Dear Painter, paint me..."

Painting the Figure since late Picabia

Centre Pompidou
KUNSTHALLE wien
SCHIRN KUNSTHALLE FRANKFURT

The exhibition "*Dear Painter, paint me ...*" has been co-organized and co-produced by the Centre Pompidou, the Kunsthalle Wien and the Schirn Kunsthalle Frankfurt

12 June – 2 September 2002, Centre Pompidou
20 September 2002 – 1 January 2003, Kunsthalle Wien
15 January 2003 – 6 April 2003, Schirn Kunsthalle Frankfurt

Centre national d'Art et de Culture Georges Pompidou
Bruno Maquart, Chief Financial Officer
Alfred Pacquement, Director, Musée national d'art moderne-Centre de création industrielle
Jean-Paul Ollivier, Head Administrator, Musée national d'art moderne-Centre de création industrielle

Kunsthalle Wien
Gerald Matt, Director

Schirn Kunsthalle Frankfurt
Max Hollein, Director

EXHIBITION

Exhibition Curators
Alison M. Gingeras, Curator, Musée national d'art moderne-Centre de création industrielle, Paris
Sabine Folie, Chief Curator, Kunsthalle Wien
Blaženka Perica, Curator, Schirn Kunsthalle Frankfurt

Curatorial Assistants
Birgit Eusterschulte, Kunsthalle Wien
Martina Weinhart, Schirn Kunsthalle Frankfurt

Exhibition Coordinators
Claire Blanchon, Centre Pompidou
Patrick Peternader, Kunsthalle Wien
Karin Grüning, Schirn Kunsthalle Frankfurt

Exhibition Designers
Jasmine Oezcebi, Centre Pompidou
Pauhof, Wien/Berlin
Ronald Kammer, Schirn Kunsthalle Frankfurt

Exhibition Registrars
Anne-Sophie Royer, Centre Pompidou
Patrick Peternader, Kunsthalle Wien
Karin Grüning, Schirn Kunsthalle Frankfurt

Chief Exhibition Technicians
André Toutcheff, Centre Pompidou
Ramón Villalobos Kröll, Kunsthalle Wien
Andreas Gundermann, Schirn Kunsthalle Frankfurt

Exhibition Intern
Kate Benson

CATALOGUE
Alison M. Gingeras, Editor
Alison M. Gingeras, Sabine Folie, Blaženka Perica, Editorial Conception
Laurent Fétis, Graphic Designer
Jemima Montagu, Gabriele Mackert, Coordinating Editors for the English language edition
Dominique Moyen, Coordinating Editor for the French language edition
Gabriele Mackert, Coordinating Editor for the German language edition

Production Supervisor
Martial Lhuillery

Translators
Tom Appleton (also additional English proofreading), *Joan Clough, Charles Penwarden, Susan Schwartz, Stewart Spencer, Jean Torrent, Gene Zibowkski*

Publications Department
Emmanuel Fessy, Director
Philippe Bidaine, Associate Director
Françoise Marquet, Head of Editorial Services
Benoît Collier, Head of Sales
Matthias Battestini, Claudine Guillon, Contract and Copyright Services
Nicole Parmentier, Administrator

French version ISBN 2-84426-124-8
English version ISBN 2-84426-138-8
German version ISBN 3-85247-037-4
Publication number: 1184
Legal deposition: September 2002

On the cover:
Elizabeth Peyton
Jarvis, 1996
Oil on board, 28 x 35.6 cm
Collection Susan & Michael Hort, New York

Directors' Preface

Over the past few years, a number of museum exhibitions have addressed the "renewal" of painting, even going so far as to claim its "renaissance". As this terminology implies, painting's "death" has often been proclaimed, or even definitively confirmed by the very same institutions that have thought it necessary to see it reborn on the occasion of an exhibition.

There is either a healthy dose of hypocrisy or deliberate blindness in the assumption that pictorial art practices have been rejected by some of the century's most pertinent artists. A swift, retrospective examination of the past twenty or thirty years of art history radically contradicts such assertions—one does not even dare to enumerate a list of such artists' names as their importance seems so evident. A certain number of these historical figures introduce *Dear Painter, paint me* ... Their presence underscores the point that the main themes of this exhibition are not limited to a purely contemporary context. Instead, this exhibition attempts to trace a particular artistic lineage that is firmly rooted in generation after generation of figurative painters.

Dear Painter, paint me ... is not limited to a simple affirmation of the importance of pictorial art practice today—a curatorial approach that does not offer any real depth or critical argument. Through a rigorous selection of artists, the exhibition has adopted a tightly focused approach to examine painters that have chosen to represent the human figure through the lens of mass media images. Francis Picabia—whose controversial nudes from the 1940s have recently been resuscitated through recent developments in art historical research—opens this genealogical introduction to the exhibition. This predominately European family tree continues with Bernard Buffet's erratic portraits—detested for so long by modern art museums—as well as the work of Sigmar Polke, Alex Katz, and Martin Kippenberger (from whom the exhibition borrows its playful title). The twelve contemporary artists that sustain the legacy of these historical figures share an antagonistic position that has driven each artist to question the loaded historical and political assumptions about figurative painting. This critical spirit has enthusiastically motivated our three European institutions to collaborate together in exploring this aspect of contemporary figurative painting.

We would like to take this opportunity to thank our curators—Alison M. Gingeras, Sabine Folie, Blaženka Perica—as well as their respective teams who worked in collaboration so diligently to organize this important exhibition.

Alfred Pacquement
Director
Musée national d'art moderne
Centre Pompidou, Paris

Gerald Matt
Director
Kunsthalle Wien

Max Hollein
Director
Schirn Kunsthalle Frankfurt

We would like to express our gratitude to the following individuals and institutions who so generously agreed to lend us their works for the duration of the exhibition.

Lenders to the exhibition

Sammlung Peter & Heidi Aaen, Neustadt
ACME, Los Angeles
Kai Althoff, Cologne
Monsieur & Madame Agostini, Paris
Lorinda Ash Fine Art, New York
Carole Benzaken, Paris
Laura & Stafford Broumand, New York
Annabel Buffet, Paris
Joanna Chevalier-Sèvres, Paris
Douglas S. Cramer, New York
Contemporary Fine Arts, Berlin
Corvi-Mora Gallery, London
Thomas Dane, London
Deitch Projects, New York
Collection Jeffrey Deitch, New York
De Pont stichting voor hedendaagse kunst, Tilburg
Galerie EIGEN + ART, Leipzig/Berlin
Flick Collection
Marc Foxx, Los Angeles
Gilles Fuchs, Paris
Kenneth L. Freed, Boston
Sammlung Goetz, Munich
Sammlung Karola Grässlin, Cologne
Sammlung Grässlin, St. Georgen
Fondation Guerlain, Paris
Sammlung Hauser & Wirth, St. Gallen
Galerie Max Hetzler, Berlin
Collection Susan & Michael Hort, New York
Collection Debra-Houtsaeger, De Panne
Galerie In Situ, Paris
Galerie Michael Janssen, Cologne
The Dakis Joannou Collection, Athens
Jean-Paul Jungo, Genève
Alex Katz, New York
Anton Kern Gallery, New York
Estate of Martin Kippenberger, Galerie Gisela Capitain, Cologne
Kunstmuseum Wolfsburg, Wolfsburg
Stephan Landwehr, Berlin
Fabienne Leclerc, Paris
Ninah & Michael Lynne, New York
Marlborough Gallery Inc., New York
Collection Byron Meyer, San Francisco
Warren & Victoria Miro, London
Musée d'art moderne de la Ville de Paris
Museum of Contemporary Art, San Diego
Museum of Fine Arts, Boston
The Museum of Modern Art, New York
Galerie Christian Nagel, Cologne
Patrick Painter, Los Angeles
Enoc Perez, New York
Elizabeth Peyton, New York
Karin Polke, Berlin
Centre Pompidou, Musée national d'art moderne, Paris
Collection Bob Rennie, Vancouver
Collection Ivelin and Craig Robins, Miami Beach
Galerie Thaddaeus Ropac
Sammlung Ruth
The Saatchi Gallery, London
Sammlung Scharpff, Stuttgart
Sammlung Alexander Schröder, Berlin
Robert Harshorn Shimshak & Marion Brenner, Berkeley
Sammlung Speck, Cologne
Collection David Teiger
Collection Dean Valentine and Amy Adelson, Los Angeles
Collection van Cauwenberghe-De Man, Bachte Maria Lerne
Leopold Villareal Fernandez
Walker Art Gallery, Liverpool
Dianne Wallace, New York
Zeno X Gallery, Antwerp
Collection Bobbi & Walter Zifkin, Los Angeles
Collection David & Monica Zwirner, New York

And all the lenders that wish to remain anonymous.

Curatorial Acknowledgements

Dear Painter, paint me ... has greatly benefited from the generous contribution of time and energy of all of the artists. We would like to take this opportunity to sincerely thank each one of them for their participation and feedback. We are deeply grateful to the authors for their texts and comments. It also goes without saying that a project of this scope could not be organized without the assistance of many persons. We would like to deeply thank the following persons for their contribution to the success of this exhibition:

Geoffrey Batchen, Kirsty Bell, Gavin Brown, Daniel Buchholz, Gisela Capitain, Guillaume Cerutti, Yan Chateigné, Wendy Chang, Sarah Cohen, Sadie Coles, Tommaso Corvi-Mora, Bice Curriger, Yasmine Dabiens, Frank Damaegd, Jeffrey Deitch, Corinne Durland, Jennifer Flay, Flick Collection, Friedrich Christian Flick, Marc Foxx, Maurice Garnier, Cornelia Grassi, Francesca Grassi, Bärbel Grässlin, Katerina Gregos, Catherine Grenier, Robert Gunderman, Galerie Hauser & Wirth, Max Hetzler, Laura Hoptman, Bellatrix Hubert, Nigel Hurst, Stéphanie Hussonnois, Michael Janssen, Kathrin Jentjens, Anton Kern, Laurent Le Bon, Fabienne Leclerc, Gerd Harry Lybke, Christine Macel, Laura Mackall, Victoria Miro, Laura Mitterand, Christopher Müller, Christian Nagel, Galerie Neu, Nathalie Obadia, Anthony d'Offay, PaceWildenstein, Patrick Painter, Wim Peeters, Jean-Pierre Piton, Shaun Regen, James Rondeau, Thaddaeus Ropac, Andrea Rosen, Clare Rowe, Charles Saatchi, Samia Saouma, Regina Schultz-Möller, Randy Sommer, Reiner Speck, Iwan Wirth, Sachi Yoshimoto, David Zwirner.

Very special thanks to the following people whose advice, assistance, and continuing support was a precious element in the conception and elaboration of this project:

Françoise Bertaux, Martin Bethenod, Bernard Blistène, Patrice Blouin, Samuel Bourdin, Jennifer Bornstein, Marcel & Marie Brient, Maurizio Cattelan, Louis Clayeux, Chivas Clem, Meghan Dailey, Dedee & Tom Gingeras, Massimiliano Gioni, Morad Koufane, Didier Krezentowski, Germaine de Liancourt, Dietmar Lutz, Arnaud Macé, Hachimi Nait-Saïd, Julie Pellegrin, Laurent Perreau, Rémy Poirson, David Riminelli, Alexander Roob, Myriam Salomon, Sam Stourdzé, Ali Subotnik, Véronique Terrier-Hermann, Aude Tincelin, Eric Troncy, Markus Vater, Alexi Villedrouin, Ursula Walbröl, Franz West.

Table of Contents

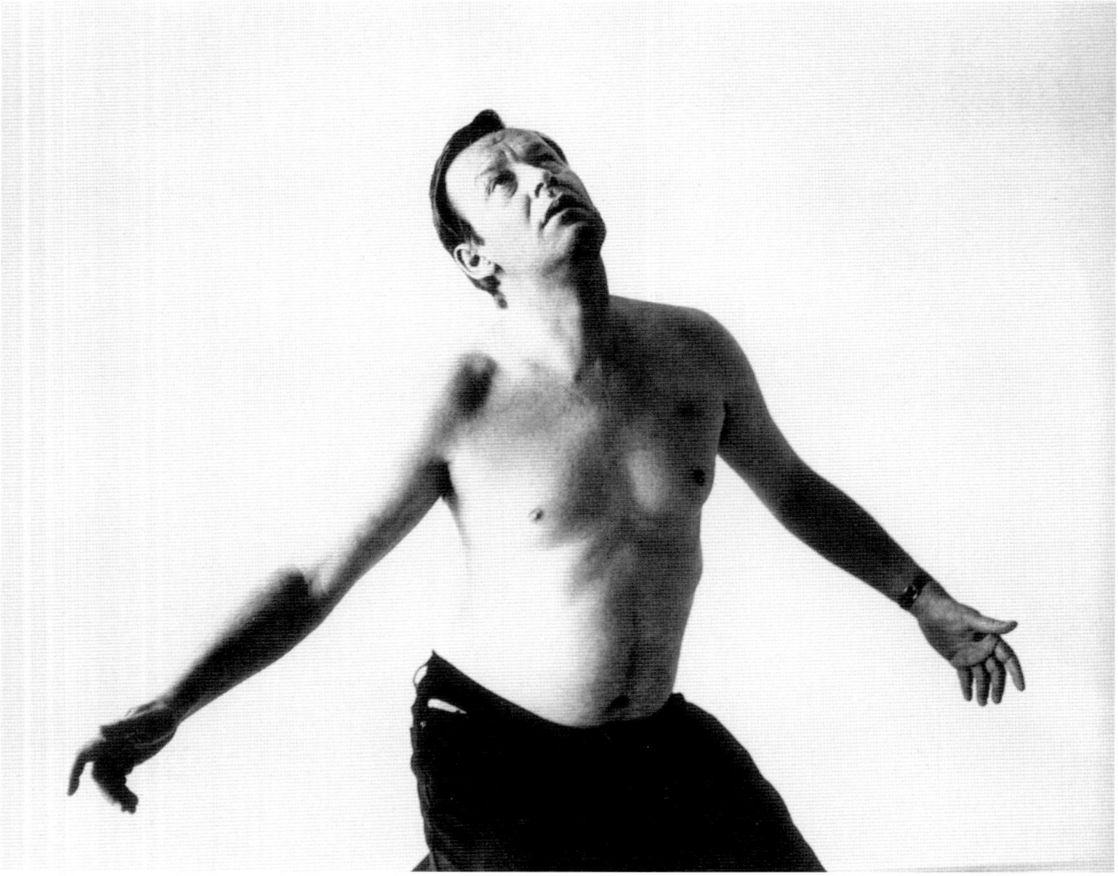

Martin Kippenberger miming a pose of one of the shipwrecked
passengers depicted in Théodore Géricault's painting *Radeau de La Méduse* ("Raft of the Medusa", 1818-19). Photo taken from a series of 17 photographic studies for a series of self portraits executed in 1996. Photograph taken by Elfie Semotan.

"Lieber Maler, male mir..."

Learning from Kippenberger: Figurative painting as provocative and sincere, critical and sentimental

Alison M. Gingeras

Lesson One: A good title is everything
Giving a title is always a delicate affair, especially in the domain of art. While the ubiquitous and delightfully neutral "untitled" offers an easy escape route for the naming of an individual artwork, it is not an option for the titling of an exhibition. A good title should encapsulate a complex set of ideas succinctly; it should be witty without being a one-liner; it should be conceptually compelling, but readily legible. And when finding a new, original title seems impossible, some creative thievery may be order.

Among his many talents, artist Martin Kippenberger was a master of bestowing the perfect title on his works. He used his titles-cum-slogans to incite provocation and show off his knack for self-promotion, his gift for creating hilarious misunderstandings, and his distinctive brand of laconic irony that teetered between raw sarcasm and pathetic self–exposure [1]. Kippenberger was always able to encapsulate his densely layered critical art practice in a catchy title. *Lieber Maler, male mir ...* was the name of his first one-person exhibition at Berlin's Neue Gesellschaft für Bildende Kunst (New Society for Fine Arts) in 1981.

Kippenberger's title *Lieber Maler, male mir ...* articulates a radical statement about the contemporary status of the painter. His directive should taken at face value: "Dear Painter, Paint me", "Dear Painter, paint for me" or "Dear Painter, paint me something". Kippenberger is not only making a sarcastic delegation of artistic responsibility but he is clearly confirming that the "dear" figure of the painter has lost his cultural currency. This biting title is in fact an act of self–exposure: the figure of the painter has become interchangeable, empty, and untrustworthy in exactly same way that the (mass-media) images he draws upon are ambivalent, malleable, and deceptive. The contemporary alliance between the painter and the image explodes traditional humanist expectation for truth in representation.

For his *Lieber Maler, male mir ...* exhibition, Kippenberger commissioned the professional advertising company, Werner, who specialized in painting cinema posters to execute a series of highly realistic paintings from sources of his choice. Of the twelve canvases, a number of "self portraits" punctuate otherwise banal, nondescript scenes. One shows Kippenberger from behind, arm and arm with a friend as he (drunkenly?) totters down a busy Düsseldorf street. Another depicts the artist as "urban cowboy"–hands on his hips, staring off into the distance, complete with hat and five o'clock shadow. The posters that are glued onto the facade of the souvenir stand behind him ironically celebrate "30 Years of East Germany". The last and most obviously ridiculous portrayal of the artist shows him slouching in profile, wearing swim trunks with an inner tube around his waist. The caption at the top of the painting reads: "Refined extras program, better than as[th]ma group".

Forever the *agent provocateur*, Kippenberger fanned the flames of ambivalence that surrounded his initial reception. When speaking of his cheeky deferral of the paintbrush to a commercial artist, he quipped "With this, I'm also contributing to employment in Berlin, the city of Expressionism" [2]. As historian Daniel Baumann recalls, the *Lieber Maler, male mir ...* series was immediately read as an attack on a range of ideals still operating in contemporary Germany. Kippenberger addressed the notion of artistic authenticity through his attack of "the Romantic image of the autonomous artist creating entirely out of his inner depths". He opposed "the emotional overload of paintings by the Neue Wilden (Transavanguardia)" with his fluid mixing of 'hyper-realism, poster advertising, and East German art".

Kippenberger committed patricide by breaking with "Gerhard Richter's brand of Realism" while simultaneously announcing "a return to painting through the hand of someone else".[3] Like all of his subsequent works and gestures, each layer of meaning is designed to produce a misunderstanding; his real intentions are always obscured beneath layers of conceptual and formal play, antagonism, irreverence–toward everything, himself included.

Lesson Two: Form is strategy
Taking the title *Lieber Maler, male mir ...* for an exhibition of contemporary figurative painting is itself a Kippenbergian gesture, recalling without too much hubris his own strategies of creative "borrowings". In reference to the fiery launch of Kippenberger's influential career, the *Lieber Maler, male mir ...* title exudes a critical aura that could be used to dispel a number of negative assumptions about figurative painting practice today. In fact, a similar set of questions that loomed over Kippenberger's début continues to haunt the practice of figurative painting today. Is figurative painting intrinsically traditional, politically reactive, and anti avant-garde? Is painting the human figure a practice that necessarily embraces a return to humanistic themes such as the truthful representation of human experience and emotion? Can figurative painting be simultaneously provocative and sincere, critical and sentimental?

Using Kippenberger as a key conceptual alibi, this exhibition *Dear Painter, paint me ...* stakes the claim that the figurative painting is not necessarily a "return to order"–a regressive retreat into traditional forms of mimetic representation[4]. While all the artists in this exhibition offer different, sometimes conflicting responses to these questions, they each stake an antagonistic position for their work. The conventions of figuration, the weight of painting's history and the orthodoxy of Modernism are issues up for re-evaluation.

John Currin–one of the more prominent figures in the "revival" of figurative painting in the 1990s–has articulated an important nuance in the usual "birth and death" narrative of figurative painting. When asked why painting has come to hold such an antagonistic edge today, Currin conjectures that painting has never died as a practice, but that *painting as a culture* has long been dead. He elaborates,

> *The comfort of painting—painting as a culture, that is what pisses people off. What I am generally referring to is the guilt about painting, about pictures—this is part of the death of painting culture. There is still this feeling of shame in the late twentieth century about painting, pictures, and visual pleasure; these are still off limits.*[5]

Currin's comments acknowledge an obvious shift: painting is no longer the primary form of image making in contemporary western culture having been displaced by various forms of mass media. Unlike a century ago when even amateur viewers were familiar with the formal, iconographic, and historical language of painting and were able to decode their meaning, figurative painting today has lost its legibility as well as its general visibility. Painterly style and technical skill have become devalued and outmoded. In the realm of art historical discourse, figuration has become synonymous with a reactionary political agenda–an idea inherited from the Frankfurt School debates pitting "Realism versus Modernism" during the Second World War[6]. Yet despite these condemnations, it is possible to trace a distinct strain of figurative painting that has transformed these negative judgments into an antagonistic force, embracing painting's loss of mainstream currency as a source of freedom from the dogmas of art history, taste, and authenticity.

This shift in the cultural status of painting has had an important impact on the figurative painting's capacity to convey conceptual content, without sacrificing its ability to be a source of visual pleasure. The field is open for painters to play off a range of different pictorial styles. Realism, naturalism, kitsch, academicism, expressionism, as well as vernacular forms can be freely wielded or interchanged according to the artist's conceptual agenda. In the same manner, artists are no longer hindered by traditional criteria in regards to skill or craft. Instead, there is a sense of fluidity between the conventional poles of technical virtuosity and deliberately bad painting. In short, style and technique have become a set of conceptual tools for artists to utilize in the treatment of their chosen subjects.

Yet in order to understand how this string of painterly "isms" have been transformed into conceptual tools, it is important to underscore that they have not been completely flushed of the historical values and ideological agendas that they once represented. Devaluation of style or technique does not mean a complete evaporation of its history. In order for the notion of "style-as-conceptual tool" to operate, it must still retain a vestige of its weighty past. What follows is a rather tricky aesthetic game: on one hand, artists must "actively forget" the historical and ideological agenda attached to a given style in order to transform it into a strategic or critical element of their work. While on the other hand, artists willfully enlist the latent cultural "guilt" attached to the stylistic codes of figurative painting order to harness its (antagonistic) affect.

This double game is manifest in the example of Kippenberger's oeuvre and finds a contemporary echo in the words of Glenn Brown. Speaking about his highly skilled technique that blends styles and pictorial sources from different centuries in a single painting, Brown humbly chalks up his strategy to simply being "bad Modernist":

> *High Modernism turned the hand of the artist into a cliché. However, I like clichés. I like portraits and flowers and still lifes and trompe l'oeil and the story of van Gogh cutting off his ear. These things involve*

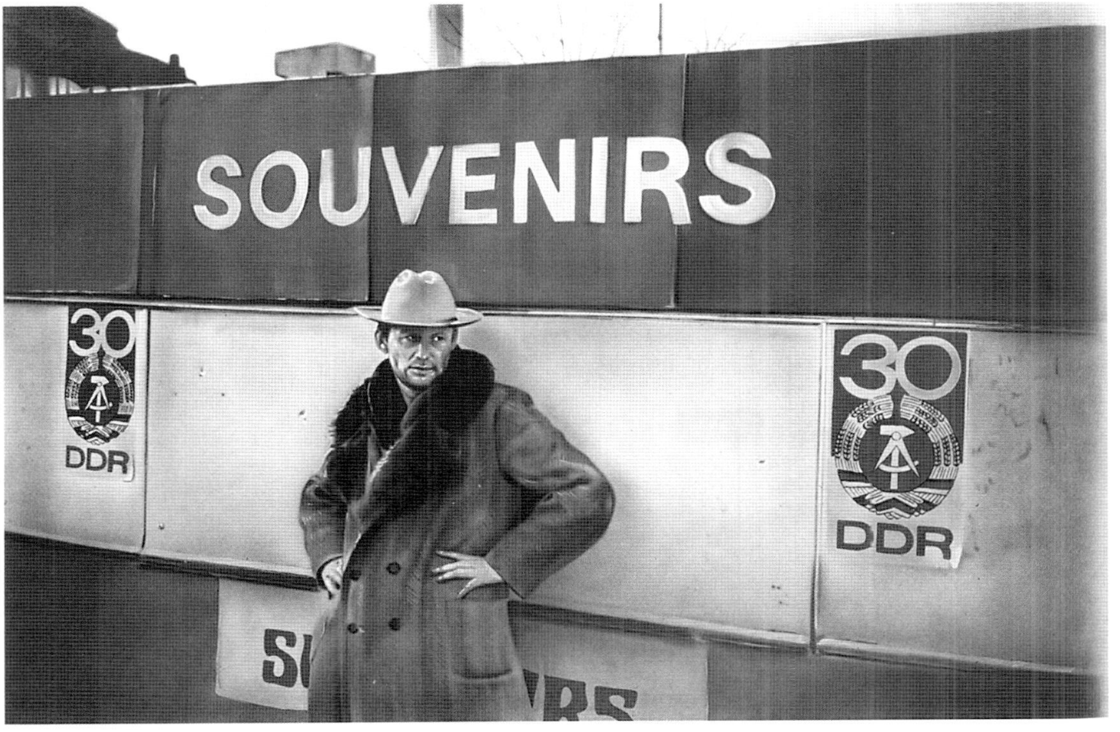

Martin Kippenberger
Ohne Titel, (aus der serie *Lieber Maler, male mir ...*), 1981
["Untitled", from the series "Dear Painter, paint me ..."]
Acrylic on canvas, 200 x 300 cm
Private Collection

> *sentiment, and sentiment, like Steven Spielberg movies, makes me cry. For some strange reason along with the 80 percent of the population these things make me feel real; genuine brush marks generally don't. (...) The enigma [of my work] being, why do I fall for clichés when I know how bad they are?*[7]

The common thread shared by the artists in this exhibition might be found in Brown's adolescent admission. While the transformation of style and technique into a field of critical intervention has become the hallmark of a certain vein of figurative painting being traced by this exhibition, this "criticality" does take a negative form.

Like Brown, Kippenberger and many other artists in this exhibition attest, despite their use of irony, sarcasm or other antagonistic strategies, figurative painting can also be a vehicle for the expression of more generous emotions as well as question of the canon of Modernism. As curator Laura Hoptman argued in her groundbreaking exhibition of John Currin, Elizabeth Peyton and Luc Tuymans in 1997,

> *Figurative painting for these artists is more than an act of conceptual art. It is also an act of love. It is this passion that makes their work seem so direct and so shameless, and what ultimately sets their work apart from their forerunners and their less adventurous contemporaries.*[8]

Lesson Three: Beyond the portrait
The outmoded genre of portrait painting is the main point of continuity in terms of content of the exhibition but like the aforementioned self-portraits in the *Lieber Maler, male mir ...* series, the works chosen for this show mark a strong departure from the conventions of traditional portraiture. Many of the artists take an *image*

of the human form as their starting point–almost never is a subject painted directly from life. Rather, their source material is taken from photographs, cinema, television, printed media, the canon of art history, or fictive figures based on existing visual and social codes. This adds an intermediary step or additional layer of distance in the relationship between artist and sitter. It immediately perturbs the humanist model of portraiture: the authentic translation of a human subject's physical or psychological likeness into paint.

Lesson Four: Genealogy versus hagiography
While the motivations for painting images of the human figure are as numerous as they are diverse, several tropes tend to emerge. Accordingly, the exhibition has been organized in the form of a loose genealogy, suggesting conceptual and formal affinities between the ways the artists approach their subjects. The exhibition begins with five artists from the post war period: Francis Picabia, Bernard Buffet, Sigmar Polke, Alex Katz, and Martin Kippenberger. This improbable family tree hardly suggests a pure bloodline, but prevents any hagiographic narrative that would privilege a single father figure for the contemporary artists in the exhibition. The diversity and divergence in these five artists' work define a series of radical moments in the practice of figuration since the Second World War.

Beginning with Francis Picabia's late nudes from the early 1940s, the question of painting as a filter of mass media's impact on both individual and collective sense of identity has emerged as a key preoccupation of the artists in the exhibition. These notorious paintings–shunned for their "regression" into realism and their embrace of kitsch–drew their pictorial source from tawdry black and white photographs culled from soft-core pornography magazines such as *Mon Paris* and *Paris Magazine*.[9] While the invention of photo-illustrated magazines did not occur in tandem with Picabia's late realist paintings, their infiltration of everyday life coincided with the post-war years. The increased circulation of these magazines served not only as an anesthetizing agent to numb wartime suffering, but actively shaped the identity construction of a new social corpus. As social historian Kristen Ross discusses in her study of the reconstruction of French society in the immediate post-war period, an emerging, new middle class used popular magazines both as "a script and a blueprint" for conformity. The "repetitive, secular ceremony of magazine reading" coupled with the growing popularity of narrative cinema were the primary agents of collective identity formation during the post war period.[10]

These historical observations provide a context to examine the various shifts in the way such media imagery has been digested by artists since late Picabia. Perhaps more than any American Pop artist, Sigmar Polke can easily claim his place as the heir to Picabia's radicality. This observation is based not only in terms of Polke's parodic engagement with mass media–seen in his early appropriation of advertising images such as the smiling bourgeois couples and faceless sausage eaters–but in his ambivalence towards the bankruptcy of painting itself. Like Picabia's flirtation with low-brow color palettes, black-outline technique, and other kitsch stylistic effects, Polke gravitated in the early part of his career toward ball-point pens, rubber stamps, children's poster paint and cheap paper in a campaign to systematically de-skill and cheapen his pictorial endeavors. Polke has served both as model and counter-model for subsequent generations of artists who continue to broker a relationship between painting, popular media images, and identity-based issues–whether it be critical engagement or a more personal, intimate act of appropriation.

As a representative of the 1950s–a period highly contested both in terms of aesthetics and politics–Bernard Buffet introduces the first moment of rupture in this exercise of genealogical speculation. Shunned by the majority of mainstream museums and critics, Buffet still remains an antagonistic thorn in the side of European post war art history even today. The Parisian outsider artist who was firmly rooted in figuration, Buffet stood in defiance to the École de Paris whose dogmatic espousal of abstraction still persists to a certain extent as the valid model of avant-garde painting in France today. While his kitsch appeal has earned him geographically isolated "revivals" (most notably in Japan), the presence of Buffet in this exhibition raises the twin specters of academicism and authenticity in figurative painting. Buffet also embodies a vision of figuration based in emotional realism that are almost considered to be historical documentation of the austerity of post-war reconstruction in France. For subsequent generations of artists such as Kippenberger and Currin, Buffet has also served as a counter-model because of the antagonistic power of his so-called "bad painting" and his unabashed embrace of ugliness.

Across the Atlantic, Alex Katz asserted an equally obstinate and singular position in the field of contemporary American painting, by founding his practice outside the dominant poles of Abstract Expressionism and Pop Art. Resistant to easy categorization, Katz's unique brand of figuration is characterized by an extreme pictorial economy, a minimal sense of narrative and a flattened application of color coming from a highly personal palette. As for his subject matter, Katz implicitly rejects the conventional vision of the bohemian or impov-erished artist. He affirms his bourgeois, cosmopolitan surroundings by painting the privileged and polished people that surround him. A subtle trace of popular culture emerges in Katz's large-scale group portraits from the early 1970s. His portrayals of banal social scenes recall the cool lens of French cinema that also was emerging at the same moment–especially the kind of insider examination of the *bourgeoisie* in the films of Eric Rohmer or Claude Chabrol. Katz's portraits of New York's elite social matrix maintain a calculated sense of distance or emotional detachment while simultaneously staking an independent vision of figurative painting. Despite his long exhibition history, the artistic vanguard continues to harbor a per-

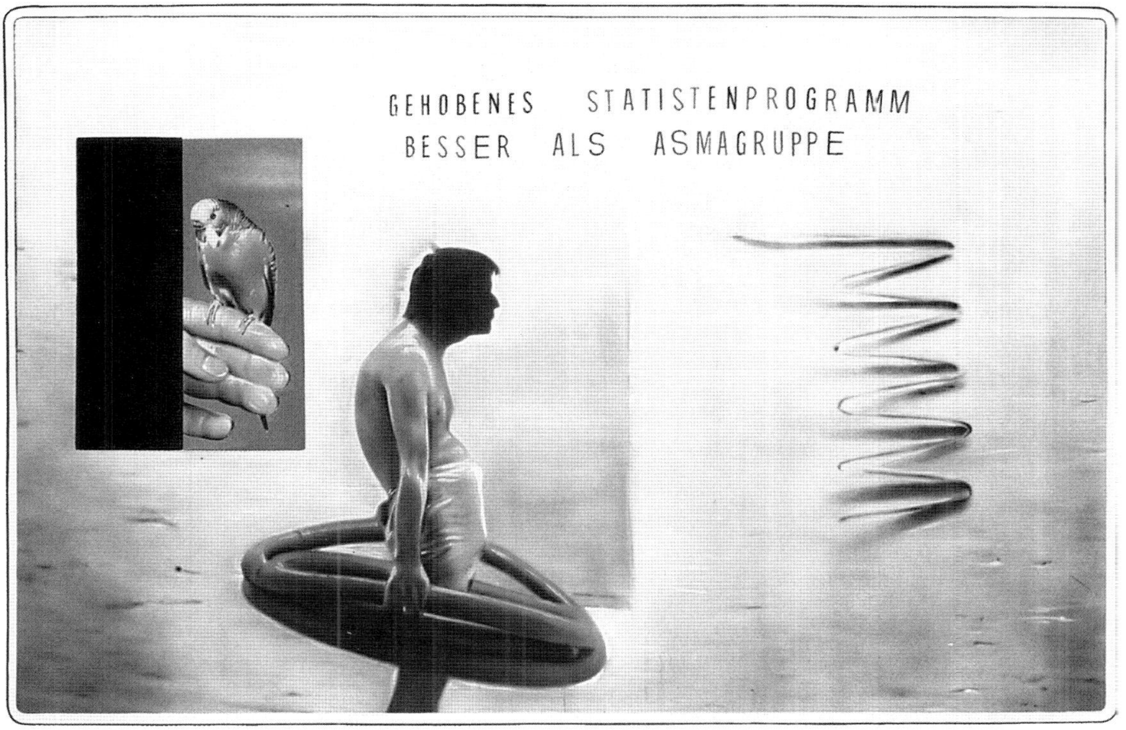

Martin Kippenberger
Ohne Titel, (aus der Serie *Lieber Maler, male mir ...*), 1981
["Untitled", from the series "Dear Painter, paint me ..."]
Acrylic on canvas, 200 x 300 cm
Estate of Martin Kippenberger, courtesy Galerie Gisela Capitan, Cologne

sistent sense of skepticism about the validity of Katz's work. His deceptively simple style along with his radical embrace of the middle-class has allowed Katz to retain an antagonistic edge that continues to influence younger artists while continuing to disturb aesthetic consensus.

With Kippenberger, these five figures offer a historical framework for an in depth examination of the contemporary practices of figurative painting in the monographic essays and artist interviews that follow in this catalogue. Although there are other figures who could be included in this speculative genealogy, this exhibition has been conceived as provisional map that plots out distinctive conceptual and formal coordinates without attempting to record every square centimeter of artistic terrain. In the very least, this exhibition hopes to disturb consensus and open up a space for the reception of contemporary figurative painting that simultaneously embraces provocation, criticality and visual pleasure.

Endnotes

1 Following are a few examples of Kippenberger's titles, which also served as personal maxims: "Fiffen, Faufen und Ferfaufen" ("Fuck, Booze and Sell" or "Smoke Pot, Buy and Get Drunk"?); "Ich hab' kein Alibi, höchstens mal ein Bier, hör auf zu mosern, so geht's nicht nur Dir" (I have no alibi, only a beer at best, why don't you stop whining, you're not worse off than the rest); Nicht zu Hause schlafen müssen" (Don't have to sleep at home); "Nieder mit der Inflation"/"Nieder mit der Bourgeoisie" (Down with Inflation Down with the Bourgeoisie); "Martin, ab in die Ecke und schäm dich" (Martin, Go in the corner, shame on you).

2 Newspaper clipping reprinted in *Kippenberger: Through Puberty to Success*, exh. cat. Berlin: Neue Gesellschaft für bildende Kunst (1981), n.p.

3 Excerpted from Daniel Baumann, "The Way You Wear Your Hat," in *Martin Kippenberger*, exh. cat. Basel: Kunsthalle Basel (1998), p. 64.

4 The most salient example of this negative historicization of figurative painting can be found in Benjamin H. D. Buchloh, “Figures of Authority, Ciphers of Regression: Notes on the Return of Representation in European Painting,” *October* (no. 16, Spring 1981), pp. 39-68.

5 The author in conversation with the artist for this catalogue, pp. 74-78.

6 Frederic Jameson, ed., *Aesthetics and Politics: The Key Texts of the Classic Debate within German Marxism.* (London: Verso, 1977), p. 198.

7 Glenn Brown interviewed by Sabine Folie in this catalogue, pp. 86-89.

8 Laura Hoptman. *Projects 60: John Currin, Elizabeth Peyton, Luc Tuymans.* (exhibition pamphlet). Museum of Modern Art, New York, (June 24 – September 8, 1997) n.p.

9 Sara Cochran “Francis Picabia's Painting during the Second World War and his Use of Photography”, in *Francis Picabia: The Late Works 1933-1953*, (exh. cat.) Rotterdam: Museum Boijmans Van Beuningen (1998).

10 Kristen Ross. *Fast Cars, Clean Bodies: Decolonization and the Reordering of French Culture.* Cambridge: MIT Press (1995), pp. 141-42.

Meta-Trash

or The Grotesque Love of Painting

Sabine Folie

"My concept of painting? It consists in forgetting about it; I view it merely as optical pleasure since in my opinion it's all decorative." Or again, in response to the question: "Are you a skeptic? Is there anything you believe in?"–"I'm always convinced of everything I do. But basically, I only rarely need to be convinced since those who understand my activity, I mean other people, are convinced in my place." And finally, in answer to the question: "Why do you write? Why do you paint?"–"Because I get bored, and in my opinion I bore other people. When I was young, I copied my father's paintings. Then I sold the originals and substituted the copies. Since no one saw any difference, I had discovered my calling." [1]

Francis Picabia's thoughts on the practice of painting are revealed by the following observation: it is decorative and arbitrary. To regard it with even a skeptical eye is almost according it too much consideration. Nonetheless, Picabia does not seem to have totally given up on art, because when he was asked: "Do you believe art has gone bankrupt?"–he replied: "No, people are always going to want to occupy themselves artistically. But they'll be able to disavow art without being accused of blasphemy. People aren't going to believe in God any more. Art, for example, will outlast militarism. In fact, art will be there precisely in order to replace militarism. People are used to seeing art as a kind of alchemy. Every artist a casting mold. I try to be several molds. I even hope to be able to write 'jack of all arts' on the side of my house some day." [2]

Picabia contaminated several generations of painters with these declarations of dilettantism and pluralism. He expressed his philosophy of spurning "talent", taste, and seriousness in his series of *Transparencies*–drawings and paintings that are layered one on top of the other, like photographic fades, that he started in 1933. These *Transparencies* hedonistically run the gamut of art history without regard to hierarchy or preference except for the recurring subject matter of female nudes and amorous couples. The real high point of what became associated with Picabia's flirtation with kitsch and eclecticism came in the early 1940s, in his paintings of nudes after original images found in pornographic and fashion magazines. Painted with extreme amateurishness, the composition of these nudes was often deformed. Picabia made frivolous additions and omissions to his source photographs. To borrow from Martin Kippenberger, these nudes would probably have been called a "joke".

Sigmar Polke consciously made reference to this series of *Transparencies*. Using a mixture of references, quotes and techniques, he concocted something in his witch's cauldron that Peter Schjeldahl once labeled demonic: "Polke's tastelessness (never bad taste, which is still taste) is an earnest example of his daemonic seriousness, his sense of permanent emergency at the core of all cultural conventions. For him, aesthetic decorum appears to be roughly as important in the present state of civilisation as table manners during an air raid ..." [3]. Miles Carpenter saw Polke's insolent, sneering manner as the expression of a "hackneyed joke that has been ridden to death".

In both the case of Picabia and Polke, the source of this pluralism of meanings–which is simultaneously sensual and skeptical–is rooted in a dandyish reflection on the Modernist spirit and the assumption that art is useless by its very nature. And yet, a kind of metaphysical helplessness that goes hand in hand with the creation of new myths, is expressed through the use of pastiche of style and technique, travesties, idiocies, and jokes. "The whole thing is borne by a kind of radical 'courage to filth'" or "There is only filth and beauty in filth", as Martin Kippenberger said. And this "beauty" cannot be attained somewhere beyond life as it is lived, but only smack in the middle of life, in the middle of the filth of truth, the filth that truth–"one of the filthiest birds in the world"–leaves beneath it. [4]

The liberating blow that comes from violating taboos cannot be reduced to academic activity in the studio, which, whenever possible, is destroyed again and again. Instead, it invades everyday life and the entire social domain of habits, friendships, and networks–at least this is what can be observed in the group around Kippenberger, Albert Oehlen and Walter Büttner, and among the younger artistic circles such as around Michael Krebber, Kai Althoff, and Cosima von Bonin. "I want to influence the way this period is discussed," Kippenberger has said with regard to his concept of the artist, whose work–while difficult to grasp, owing to its lack of artistic criteria, its political incorrectness, and a tendency to flaunt bad taste and provocation–is nonetheless linked to a radical, subjectivist, antiidealistic and anti-aesthetic attitude.[5] This attitude functions subversively, cynically, and yet in an explicitly non-ideological way as a "style that lacks any style". In the 1920s, cultural philosopher Egon Friedell celebrated absolute subjectivity by totally snubbing the history of ideas–modernism is also a history of ideas–as a substitute for the heroes and individuals who make history. Instead, he disqualified history as being anaemic, dull, and pitiful. Friedell described history as a mythology of concepts: "The 'least enlightened' superstition has more life in it than this desktop wisdom. This is probably where the whole danger of this theory lies: its purpose is to sterilize our entire life along with all our thoughts and feelings."[6]

In this case, the practice of painting–a syncretic mosaic of decors–stretches out its tentacles into the realms of fashion, music and poetry, and other painters of the younger generation, such as Glenn Brown, Peter Doig, and Neo Rauch, draw their energy from mastery of technique and the production of those atmospheric vapors which arise in the thickness of the confined space of a painter's studio.

Brown's affinity with dilettantism and his fascination with what is hackneyed or common place is consequently less hallucinatory and destructive than it is melancholic and romantic. Yet here, too, a devilish dose of destruction is present, appearing in the guise of punk attire and running the gamut from the snotty, saucy, and revolutionary to the opposite extremes of the introverted, suicidal and sentimentally pessimistic.

While for one artist language becomes a determining medium for spewing political, social, or other nonsense tidings into the world without rhyme or reason, other artists lay out their work like puzzles (that can range from the ultra-realistic to the fuzzy) in a precise and considered manner.

For both camps of artists, the introduction of trash, garbage and kitsch into their work is a legitimate practice. Sifted-through using a great love for detail and cherished for its touching sense of the everyday, garbage is of fundamental utility for both groups. What emerges here are two rival teams. Yet paradoxically, they both want to do the same thing in the end: to paint. As a consequence, trash has become a legitimate and necessary partner in reflection on painting. Trash has become a transcendental necessity. Even though no one can stand to hear the phrase about the end of painting any longer, we have to accept the fact that there can no longer be any painting without trash. This observation does not exclude seriousness of intent. Quite on the contrary. Whether as models, as the backdrop to our imagination, or as images that have been infinitely reproduced, the more everyday "trash" invades and contaminates our pictorial worlds, the greater is the potential for the "magical" quality of a work to emerge (cf. Doig, Tuymans, and Brown). The tone of these paintings may be emotional, erotic, fantastic, dark, heavy with history, mighty with memory, mystical, or intellectual–yet trash remains a fairly essential matrix for undertaking a meta-pictorial practice. It also shifts the point of departure for the reception of the work by the viewer.

Trash is thus the limit of an uninspired illusionism that "always and exclusively pursues the wrong goal, that is, making one temporarily forget the kind of representation and medium, in order to raise the picture's claim to validity above and beyond its claim to art."[7] Trash hangs over our heads like a sword of Damocles.

As a precautionary measure, Oehlen, Kippenberger and their circle have employed a sort of "strategic dilettantism" that uses language, the absence of perspective, or other deformations in order to block any communication of "truth." As early as 1918, Egon Friedell described this strategy in the following way: "In a word, human activities only have a real life force as long as they are practiced by dilettantes. Basically, there is nothing unnatural about this. The opposite is paradoxical for two reasons. First, in the case of the dilettante or amateur, none of his activities at that precise moment is alienated; rather, his activity coincides with his whole being. The second reason lies in the fact that the dilettante knows next to nothing of his capacities or even of his whole activity. He creates in a completely unconscious way, like a tree producing fruit. It would never occur to him to wonder about his 'ability' ... "[8]

This is the starting point for the connection to the trivial, the everyday, and the universal claim of linking everything with everything and therefore generating the best ideas. This is also where one is always walking the razor's edge along the limits of good taste. These are the limits of what can be barely tolerated and that will consequently go down in the history of art. One day, these inherent contradictions will be resolved or diluted. Admittedly, Friedell's dilettantism is genuine, intrinsic, and is stimulated by the energy of discovery and understanding. On the other hand–at least in Germany–the dilettantism of painting in the 1980s, sought instead to fight against satisfying the growing narrow-mindedness and philistinism that accompanied the aftermath of the "Leaden Years". It fought using strategies that always defeat the petit bourgeois, but which, simultaneously, they always struggle against.

Punk was the way out, and not just in Germany. In England as well, the desolate political depression sought to make itself heard in the dark and harsh melancholy of the music of the Sex Pistols, Joy Division, and the Cure.

Reality breaks into everyday life. To reflect upon the manner in which empty values become reified demands a return to the Romantic roots of escapism as well as a return to the annoying presence of the "Here and Now" (as well as its rejection). The combination of the sublime, dense legacy of the past and the desolate, pluralistic and empty-but-overfed pictorial world of the present, pretended–and continues to pretend–to multiply into focused intensities, shadings and concealments, means of enlightenment, disquieting dream worlds and states of exaltation. All of these, in turn, take possession of our bodies, while maintaining the distance that makes enjoyment possible.

While noone other than Picabia has made vulgarity and taboo-breaking presentable again (not at least in the current re-reading of his work), it is astonishing that the artists of the younger generation wind up once again under the spell of painting. This "return" has occurred despite all the discussion of Modernism and anti-Modernism. Even in spite of an acute awareness of the "pictorial legacy," these artists return to painting emphatically and seriously, embracing its brittle nature, its contradictions, as well as the melancholy and impudence that is on offer. It is no longer necessary to abide by Picabia's rejection of genuine painting in order for us to love it.

(translated from the German by Susan Schwartz)

Endnotes

1 Francis Picabia, *Poetische Aktion, Schriften in zwei Bänden*, Vol. 2, Edition Nautilus, pp. 33–37.

2 *Ibid.*

3 Peter Schjeldahl, "The Daemon and Sigmar Polke", *The Hydrogen Jukebox. Selected Writings. 1978-1990*, Berkeley, Los Angeles and London, 1991. p. 253.

4 Wilfried Dickhoff, "I N.P. oder Meinen Sie es auch gut mit den Menschen? ", *Die I.N.P.-Bilder*, p. 65. Quoted in Roland Schappert, *Martin Kippenberger. Die Organisation des Scheiterns*, Cologne 1998, p. [65 Galerie Max Hetzler, Cologne, 1984]

5 *Ibid.* p. 107.

6 Egon Friedell, "Abschaffung des Genies" ("Doing Away with Genius"), *Abschaffung des Genies*, Vienna 1993, p. 224.

7 Schappert, *op.cit.* p. 54.

8 Friedell, "Über Dilettantismus' (1918). See note 6, Friedell, p. 268.

Kitsch in the Age of Painterly Reproduction

or A Short History of Kitsch

Blaženka Perica

"Don't cry! And don't give me any kitsch," says the brothel madam Celestine to the girl Miranda in Max Frisch's play *Don Juan, or Love of Geometry.* Celestine explains that she won't tolerate any kitsch in her bordello since men come here to recover from the "false feelings" they live with in their homes every day. Even the judge Don Octavio protects Celestine from the authorities with the following words, "Leave this good madam alone. As long as we have fiction and poetry introducing so many false feelings to the world, we don't have a choice." Such a statement, then, claims that "fiction and poetry", "light literature" and perhaps, by extension, bad art are responsible for "false feelings" in this world, which could only be referred to as kitsch. But this possible interpretation of Frisch's play also indicates a reversal of values thanks to false feelings, or kitsch. For instance, the world outside of the bordello, which it refers to as a substitute world, appears to be less authentic than the bordello. Since the business of procuring doesn't pretend to be anything other than what it is, it has a higher degree of authenticity, meaning it's less kitschy than the reality that rejects kitsch.

To what extent is such an approach interesting within the context of the exhibition *Dear Painter, paint me ...*, to what extent is such a "reversal of values" worth mentioning? What does an exhibition on contemporary figurative painting that pays tribute to historic positions such as Picabia, Buffet, Polke, Kippenberger, and Katz have to do with a discourse on kitsch? Before responding to these questions, we first have to determine what art and kitsch have to do with each other. The problem is that they are sometimes too similar: they are hard to keep apart because they resort to the same means and both have aesthetic pleasure as their goal. And yet this proximity does not result from elective affinity, but from questionable relations: kitsch is always viewed negatively and art is (generally) viewed positively. Even though an accurate, precise definition of both is difficult to arrive at, the criterion of authenticity plays the decisive role in this opposition. Kitsch is denounced as something unreal, unoriginal, as a surrogate and pseudo-artistic product. These accusations are not leveled at a lack of skill—children's drawings, for instance, are never viewed as kitsch. Nor is the main point that kitsch doesn't have any qualities. What is frowned on above all is that kitsch fakes quality.

This is where the next absurdity comes in. Even though it has been disqualified, kitsch is still much more prevalent and popular than what is considered art. One of its characteristics is that it is generally mass-produced, which art works are not by their very nature—even in the "age of their mechanical reproduction." This doesn't mean that everything which is a copy rather than an original automatically becomes kitsch. But, as a 1971 Braunschweig dictionary on fine art terminology states, kitsch primarily concerns products that are mass produced (crafts and souvenir industry) and "speculate on the inferiority of emotionally needy buyers." Whether saccharin pop tunes, sentimental, tear-jerking films, or advertising that is focused on triggering consumer impulses or erotic instincts, all of these are commonly known appearances of kitsch that define our present understanding of the concept.

Critics agree that phenomena comparable to kitsch can be traced back as far as the late Renaissance, but that the word "kitsch", in its contemporary usage and corresponding meaning, is much more recent. First used as a negative term for artistic production, the term surfaced in art dealing circles in Munich around 1870 and later in Berlin in 1881. As an expression in art criticism, it was first used by Gustav Edmund Pazaurek in a guidebook to an exhibition called *Geschmacksverirrungen im Kunstgewerbe* ("Bad Taste in the Applied Arts") at the Landes-Gewerbe-Museum in Stuttgart. Since then the word has become increasingly common, finally evolving into the more common usage we are familiar with today, which has been around since the 1920s.[1] Critical writings on the topic of kitsch are so numerous that it is understandable that they can only be treated rudimentarily here. As for the status quo, however, reference should be made to a remark by Otto F. Best: "But a strange disparity can still be observed between kitsch as a phenomenon in a cultural and historic sphere of activity, the role it plays in modern mass society, and the extremely modest information that appears to be available on the semantic basis of the term" [2]

Etymologically, Ferdinand Avenarius, the editor of the magazine *Kunstwart,* traced the term back to the English word "sketch" and the German word "kitschen", which means "to scrape up mud off the road with a muck rake." This is not very significant for the interpretation of the phenomenon in our context. What seems much more important is the fact that the term–even if it serves to delineate aesthetic borderline cases–is by no means limited to that usage. We not only have kitsch as misguided art, we also have kitschy behavior and kitschy sentiments, and kitsch has ideological, moral, political, social and religious implications as well. But Hermann Broch formulated perhaps the best known and most concise examination of kitsch. In an essay, he classified kitsch as "the evil in the value system of art" and referred to it as a fatal confusion of the ethical and the aesthetical, of the finite and the infinite.[3] Historically speaking, Broch postulates that the occurrence of kitsch always coincided with times of deteriorating values. His judgment, which no critic after him has been able to get around, not only applies to the appearance of kitsch, which instead of "good" intentions only has "nice" intentions. It applies equally to "kitsch people", whom Broch doesn't view as harmless incompetents, but as "ethical degenerates and criminals" who "want what is radically evil"–not only in the artistic sense, but "evil in terms of every value system that is not an imitation system." Broch made an additional judgment here–entirely in the Modernist sense. In response to the question "Does art have to be beautiful?" he definitely would not have responded "yes" or "no", but "it has to be good." Viewed from an ethical perspective, the less Modernist question "Does kitsch have to be ugly?" probably would not have been of interest to Broch.

If we were to examine under what social and cultural conditions kitsch arises, there is one clear fact we would not be able to overlook: it is born of the spirit of Modernism, and this is something that most critical voices would agree to. With the onset of Modernism, the gap dividing progressive artists from mass taste has become increasingly larger. One could argue whether Hans-Dieter Gelfert is right when he considers modern artists to occupy "elitist heights" in this regard.[4] But one would have to agree that it is understandable that the "contemptuous lament over the kitschification of popular culture" started up at the same time. Carl Baumann's attempt to interpret kitsch as a "social neurosis of Modernism" outside of the pure art context goes so far as to define kitsch as a specific modern consciousness that expresses itself in a need for sentimentality and sentimentalization.

As early as 1939 the American art critic Clement Greenberg viewed kitsch as an antipode to avant-garde art. But he considered both phenomena to be closely connected. "If the avant-garde imitates the processes of art, kitsch, we can see, imitates its effects. The neatness of this antithesis is more than contrived; it corresponds to and defines the tremendous interval that separates from each other two such simultaneous cultural phenomena such as the avant-garde and kitsch." [5]

In his essay, Greenberg, a known defender of American Abstract Expressionism, is not only referring to abstraction. He juxtaposes Picasso and Repin–their figurative works–in order to elucidate kitsch among the social and political harbingers of Fascism and Stalinism, two phenomena that were emerging at the time and that targeted the manipulation of the masses. Where Picasso paints cause, Repin paints effect. Repin predigests art for the spectator and spares him effort, provides him with a short cut to the pleasure of art that detours what is necessarily difficult in genuine art. Repin, or kitsch, is synthetic art.

Interestingly enough, the discussion of kitsch coincides with positions that identify a fusion between the beginning of artistic abstraction and the avant-garde. At the same time as the rise of totalitarian regimes in Europe, figuration and realism, as the antithesis to Modernism, were devalued as reactionary. Production methods were considered academic and "stale", as Greenberg had already pointed out–if only in passing and without addressing in more detail the specific differences from non-realistic art. In terms of abstract art, however, there are several historical examples of how non-representationalism does not offer any security against artistic paralysis. Some recognition of this was useful during the Frankfurt School debates about realism versus Modernism from the mid-1930s. Whatever the case may be, in the art of the last century, figuration remained an important means of expression despite being frowned upon from a Modernist perspective. Although sporadic and by no means a dominant movement, figuration continued to exist but was given little consideration.

Just as the debates revolving around kitsch and realism were reaching their culmination, an unquestionable avant-gardist like Picabia seemed to have no inhibitions about basing his late works on pin-ups from magazines. Even though these works were long discredited as anti-Modernist, they could be viewed as useful examples of the critical and thus progressive reversal of values that occurs in kitsch, as discussed above. Picabia, it seems, was interested in a stubborn act of challenging contemporary art that was not reconcilable with the mainstream of his time. The results of his work were no less avant-garde than radical, non-figurative forms of representation. It seems unquestionable today that this artistic position should serve as an example for the unfinished debate of Modernism versus Realism.

If the goal of the exhibition today is to present young artists in succession to these historic connections, and to examine figurative painting on the basis of its conceptual strategies, then it is not only because–along with relativizing many other factors under the maxim "anything goes"–post-modernism has also relativized kitsch. This exhibition is not ahistoric, but on the contrary is based on a very historical approach. Kitsch has gained a historically conditioned relevance that is advanced by technological developments. Instead of denying this fact, or being satisfied with a discussion of "high and low culture", many contemporary artists take up strategies that use kitsch, regression, and projection in order to demonstrate a new definition of the artistic subject under changed conditions.[6] Looking at the many examples of painterly figuration, with different provenances, which provide a contrast to the media-saturated visual reality as well as use it for inspiration, it is clear that art today communicates the idea of kitsch as a conceptual tool that clears up a number of Modernist misconceptions.

(translated from the German by Susan Schwartz)

Endnotes

1 Cf. Hans-Dieter Gelfert, *Was ist Kitsch?*, Göttingen, 2000, p. 6, and the chronological bibliography on the historic treatment of the discussion of kitsch at the end of the book, which offers an insightful overview of the topic.

2 Otto F. Best, *Der weinende Leser. Kitsch als Tröstung, Droge und teuflische Verführung,* Frankfurt a.M., 1985, p. 9.

3 Hermann Broch, "Das Böse im Wertsystem der Kunst", first published in *Neue Rundschau,* 44.2, 1933, pp. 157-191. This quote is taken from *Geist und Zeitgeist,* Frankfurt a.M., 1997, pp. 7-42.

4 Hans-Dieter Gelfert, op. cit., p. 8.

5 Clement Greenberg, "Avant-Garde and Kitsch," first published in *Partisan Review,* vol. 6. no. 5, Fall 1939, pp. 34-49. This quote is taken from Karlheinz Lüdeking: "Clement Greenberg. Die Essenz der Moderne", Dresden, 1997, p. 29-55.

6 Hans-Dieter Gelfert, op. cit., pp. 65-80.

In the Studio

Painting, Photography, and Other Realities

Michael Glasmeier

Rembrandt's remarkably small painting *An Artist in His Studio* was produced around 1628. It is a self-portrait full of contradictions and allusions that to this day have not been properly clarified or considered. The 22-year-old painter's pose is restrained, but self-confident. He is dressed in the latest fashion (hat, ruff) and in a somewhat outdated, but magnificent overcoat in his pitifully poor Leiden home with its crumbling masonry and plaster. Across from the painter, on this miniature painted on wood which today hangs in Boston, is an easel with a panel that appears oversized. Both elements have merged to form a single object that is seen from the back, ominously jutting into the foreground. In this anamorphic distortion, the distance between the subject and object seems to be deliberately emphasized. The painter is holding a single brush in his right hand, and a bunch of brushes in the left along with a palette and mahlstick. Additional utensils of the craft, among them tools to produce paint, are behind him on the wall, on a tree stump and on a table.

So far so good. In terms of interpretation, the consensus is that this piece is an examination of theories about painting at the time. Ernst van de Wetering suggested that the painter is not depicting himself while working on a painting, but before starting to work. Painting, according to contemporary *concetti,* is based on *idea, fortuna* (chance), or *usus* (exercise). Rembrandt's studio painting refers to the first term, the "contemplative formation of an idea in the mind." (Simon Schama, *Rembrandt's Eyes*, 1999)

But such an interpretation can only work if you assume that the vague gaze of the painter is focused on the canvas. He could also be looking at the viewer. This frustrating staring phenomenon has to do with the way Rembrandt painted the eyes. While contemporary painters, as well as Rembrandt in most of his other works, can best demonstrate their skill by a precise rendering of eyes, the eyes in this studio painting appear like shadowy "black holes–hollow cavities behind which something is being created, not destroyed. Behind these holes, deep in the depths of the imagination, is where the real action is, the cogs and wheels; the mental machinery is whirling and turning, like the subtly interlocking parts of a chronometer. An idea is coming into being." (Simon Schama)

Now there are three versions of the gaze: one looking at the painting, one turned inward, one focused on the viewer. The first two, as we saw above, can be connected with the *idea;* the third, looking at the viewer, does not fit into the first interpretation. And yet it is worth our attention. It draws us into the painting and at the same time underscores the loneliness of the artist. Like the overcoat, there is something demonstrative, egomaniac, about him. Look, it's me! I stand before you as a prince in my miserable home. I am rich because I am the creator. This miniature you are standing before is the painting I created, and in this painting I am standing in front of a painting I have not yet painted, but it stands for all of the paintings I could paint. I am great in my smallness; my miniature proves my capacity to expand.

It is significant that this self-portrait in the studio is above all filled with emptiness, or void. Rembrandt demonstrates that he can master texture as well as an unmarked surface, the frills of clothing as well as the plaster in the wall, the soft as well as the hard and, of course, light in its subtly illuminating or broken effects.

The conspicuously white edge of the panel painting on the easel separates the painting diagonally into two halves. On the left is emptiness, light, and self-demonstration, on the right hard reality and shadows, with the door indicating a way out. It is the dilapidated door out to the world, and the artist will open it when the painting is finished. The door, oversized for this reason, leads to the sphere from which the idea comes. It is a symbol formed out of reality.

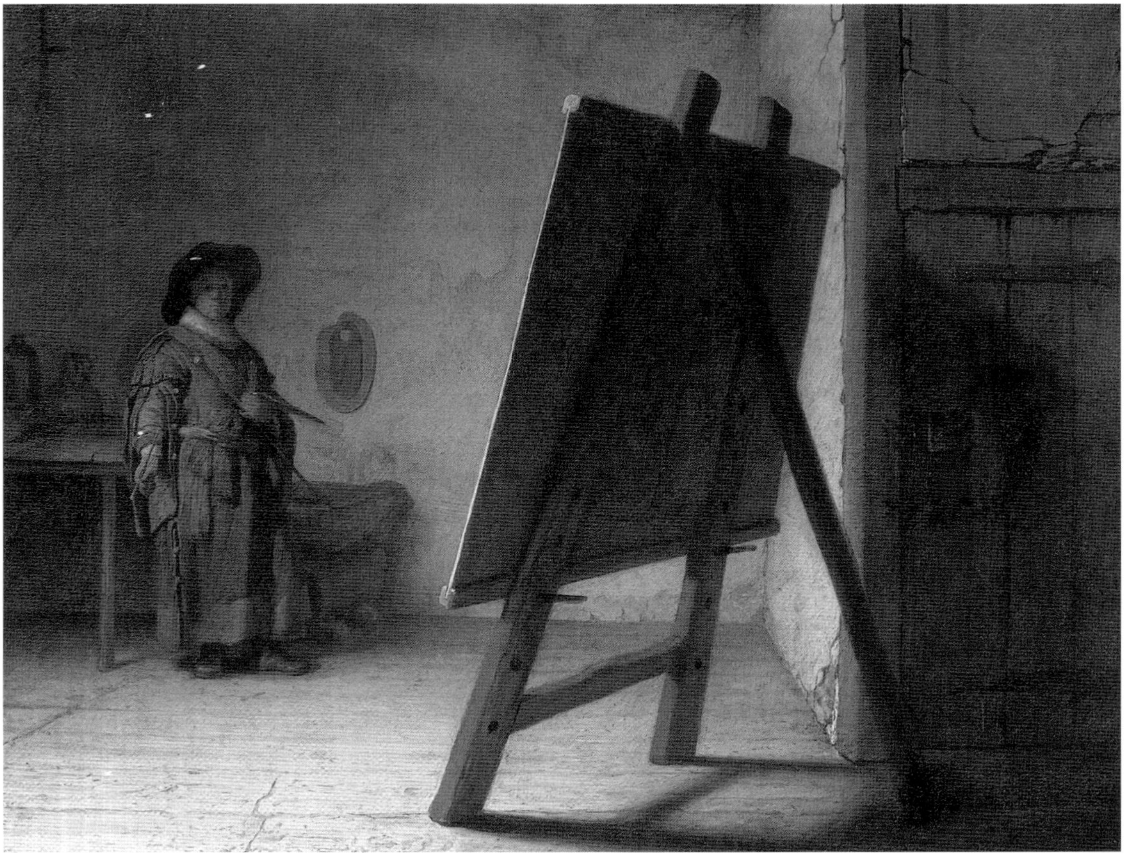

Rembrandt van Rijn
Schilder in zijn Atelier, c.1627–28
[" An Artist in His Studio "]
Oil on wood, 24,8 x 31,7 cm
Museum of Fine Arts, Boston

Our miniature is a fundamental work about the art of painting and is singular in the history of studio paintings. As art about art, the emptiness of the room and the back of the painting refer to the problems of Modernism. As a painting about painting, it unites technique and skill with idea in a mutually dependent condition. As a painting of eyes, it focuses attention on two points. As realism, it demonstrates the constructive ability of this art caught as it is between the objectivity of representation and the abstractions of surface and detail.

In Europe, this miniature was last shown at the exhibition *Der junge Rembrandt: Rätsel um seine Anfänge* ('The Young Rembrandt: Mysteries of His Early Years') in Kassel and Amsterdam. This fine exhibition demonstrated the impossibility of identifying the genesis of the painter's works. Instead it became clear that even at the beginning of his career Rembrandt mastered various styles and manners of painting which he experimented with simultaneously rather than consecutively. The painter's "rough style", for example, occurs in his early work alongside detailed painting, and in some instances both can be found in a single painting. The self-reflective quality which defines Rembrandt's entire oeuvre, expressed in the endless physiognomic explorations of his own face and the theatricalization of the self through personal loves, passions, and sufferings, is also characteristic of his religious work and public commissions. This quality finds its beginning in this miniature.

This is why this painting plays a key role in determining where painting is today. It proves that:

– it is necessary and sensible for painters to be aware of the concepts of their time, something we could refer to today as visual or media theory. This knowledge doesn't need to be spread too thickly in their work, but it must be present;
– realism has always been on the edge of abstraction (see, for example, the eyes or the delicate little area of unplastered wall near the floor in the right-hand of the room);
– conversely, a concept or an idea doesn't necessarily lead to abstraction, but can instead be expressed in elements of reality;
– the self-referential is not an invention of Modernism. It has been a condition of painting since the Renaissance, and in this painting it is passed on to Modernism as a conclusion;
– a painting is always an object, as demonstrated all too obviously in the miniature with the panel on the easel. Rembrandt's evocation of the edge of the painting is an astute contribution to this discussion of Modernism;
– a painting can contain several paintings, in this case a self-portrait, another painting, and an almost empty interior. These paintings do not have to correspond with each other, but can each lead an independent life. This triples the possibilities of interpretation;
– a painting need not show what we expect to see. It could, like the back of the painting seen here, be a negation. This also appears in the work, *Back of a Painting*, (ca. 1660-75) by Cornelis Norbertus Gijsbrecht, but this belongs to the baffling realm of *trompe l'oeil* rather than to direct artistic self-portrayal;
– painting as understood by Aby Warburg creates a "space for symbolic thinking" and thus results in a conscious distance between the painter and the painting and the viewer and the painting.

If, as recent Rembrandt research establishes, it poses a problem to constrict the oeuvre of an individual artist to the traditional categories of early and late works, it would be even less sufficient to adhere to an art history that consists of a sequence of styles. Since such an art history ultimately has to culminate in the abstraction of Modernism, art would become a banal accomplice of a Hegelian monumentalism, a notion that was rejected early on by Alois Riegl, Aby Warburg, Carl Einstein, and more recently Otto Stelzer, Werner Hofmann, Victor I. Stoichita and others. The essential moments of art history are always present in museums. It is necessary, therefore, to connect and combine individual histories in various innovative ways in order to reflect their distinct historic dimensions. Alongside archival research, one of the new tasks of aesthetics is to link material with a view to creating "space for symbolic thinking."

It becomes clear that, among other media, photography has tried since the beginning to imitate the pictorial presence of painting (tableaux vivants, pictorialism). However there is a common misconception that photography forced painting into abstraction because the camera was better equipped to represent reality. Such views need to be revised, especially since photography produced photograms which were an attempt to explore the cryptic language of abstraction at approximately the same time as painting.

In fact, as witnessed by the Rembrandt example, painting has always reflected its inherent challenge to be able to depict reality. Earlier artists such as Piero della Francesca, Michelangelo, Hieronymus Bosch, and Pontormo seem for example "less realistic" from today's perspective, while artists like El Greco, Diego Velázquez and Francisco Goya seem more powerful, simply because in their theoretical, ideological, and technical determination, they show that taking refuge in the unconditional abstraction inherent in their works was not an option.

From this perspective, a revision of the history of Modernism should rehabilitate painting's ability to examine these different realities. Just as Gustave Courbet and Adolph Menzel at the beginning of the photographic era reflected their path to reality by referencing this new medium in their paintings, our task today is to reevaluate the works of painters like Otto Dix, Max Beckmann, Salvador Dalí, Francis Picabia, Giorgio de Chirico, Charles Demuth, Karl Hofer, René Magritte, Richard Oelze, Edward Hopper, Anton Räderscheidt, Pierre Roy, Stuart Davis, and Christian Schad. Abstraction, then, no longer appears to be a compromise, but a path (an escape route?) which–among other things–has been taken in reaction to photography.

With the birth of abstraction, art history came to a standstill because abstract paintings required commentary–as proposed by Arnold Gehlen. To this day, art history is still confronted with the theories postulated by Clement Greenberg, whose historic interest lies only in his "modernist" terminology (kitsch, unity, identity, taste), since the world of images has long since changed. Compared to the current obsession with images, the abstractionists who used to be so revolutionary suddenly appear helplessly lost in their own colorful arbitrariness. They have mutated into the props of a poster culture for teenage girls' bedrooms, and museum shops do what they can to uphold this embarrassing status quo. The only reverence that can still be detected is in the academic world of art historians, where the number of masters or doctoral theses on artists like Paul Klee is in no way declining. Another alternative is for art history to turn its attention to photography and film and sell "new media" as a radical reorientation of the field. This trend has engendered an art that seems to be made for contemporary art historians–work by the likes of Cindy Sherman, Bill Viola, Peter Greenaway, James Turrell, Joseph Beuys, and Jenny Holzer. The only painter in this genre is Gerhard Richter, but he is perfectly suited for reflection on issues of new media since he once said that anyone who paints is on the wrong boat. But enough of this polemic digression. Let's get back to the topic.

The fact that the death of painting has been proclaimed every ten years since the beginning of photography is definitely a sign of tremendous uncertainty. After all, in the course of its existence, painting has experimented so much with its boundaries and with the transcendence of its possibilities that its failure has always been inherent. As suggested earlier, this has been the case at least since the Renaissance. We need only to think of the profound melancholy in the poems of Michelangelo and recurring in the letters of van Gogh or of the all-embracing love of experimentation espoused by artists like Leonardo and later Picabia. Samuel Beckett gets to the heart of the matter in his commentary *Peintres de l'empêchement* (1948): "What remains to be represented are the conditions of withdrawal ... The thing to paint is what prevents one from painting." But this prevention is also a liberty derived from the limitless possibilities of the medium. This is why the history of painting will not allow for naïveté anymore, unless you want to be a naïve painter. Painting, then, is connected with a philosophy that for good reason propagates its own continuation. The point is to constantly redefine oneself. And this brings us back to *idea*, *fortuna,* and *usus*.

In the same piece, Beckett writes: "What renews painting is first of all that there are always more things to paint ..." What remains unclear in this instance is whether the author was referring to the development of new media. Since Courbet, it's a fact that photography has expanded, strengthened its tasks, representational possibilities and subjects, in relation to the experience of reality. Painting has always been an artistic reflection on other works (Renaissance refers to Antiquity, Classicism to the Renaissance, Modernism to Mannerism, etc.), and since the inception of photography and film the kingdom of images has been enriched to no end. This was anticipated as early as 1907 by Alfred Lichtwark, for many years the director of the Hamburg Kunsthalle, who spoke of a revival of painting as a result of photography.

Painting has at its disposal not only the works of its past, but also the arsenal of all images and all realities. Abstraction negated these possibilities through romantic notions about elevating the inner life of the artist to an ersatz religion.

Painting dwells in an intermediary state of theory, craft, visual interpretation, and invention. Painting is an art of the external world and as such it is a political demonstration of the potential of realities and their images. It does not shy away from exposing silliness, banality, stupidity, sexism, and other repulsive qualities as part of these realities and images. As a practice of seeing bound to the body, it roughens the smoothness of the reality conveyed by the media and leads it back into the realm of the idea and hence the other reality of mental space.

(translated from the German by Susan Schwartz)

Bibliography

Hermann Ulrich Asemissen, Gunter Schweikhart, *Malerei als Thema der Malerei*, Berlin, 1994

Gottfried Boehm (ed.), *Was ist ein Bild?*, Munich, 1994

Ernst van de Wetering, Bernhard Schnackenburg, *Der junge Rembrandt. Rätsel um seine Anfänge*, exh. cat. Kassel: Staatliche Museen, Gemälde galerie Alte Meister (2001)

Georges Didi-Huberman, *Devant l'image: Question posée aux fins d'une histoire de l'art*, Paris, 1990

Philippe Dubois, *L'Acte photographique*, Paris, 1990

Carl Einstein, *Die Kunst des 20. Jahrhunderts*, Leipzig, 1988

Arnold Gehlen, *Zeit-Bilder. Zur Soziologie und Ästhetik der modernen Malerei*, Frankfurt/Bonn, 1960

Jean Genet, *Rembrandt*, Paris, 1995

Werner Hofmann, *Die Grundlagen der modernen Kunst*, Stuttgart, 1987

Werner Hofmann, *Die Moderne im Rückspiegel: Hauptwege der Kunstgeschichte*, Munich, 1998

Max Imdahl, *Gesammelte Schriften*, 3 vols., Frankfurt, 1996

Wolfgang Kemp, *Die Räume der Maler: Zur Bilderzählung seit Giotto*, Munich, 1996

Alfred Lichtwark, "Entwicklung und Einfluss der künstlerischen Photographie in Deutschland," in Fritz Matthies-Masuren (ed.), *Künstlerische Photographie*, Berlin, 1907

Sibylle Omlin, Beat Wismar (ed.), *Das Gedächtnis der Malerei: Ein Lesebuch zur Malerei im 20. Jahrhundert*, Aarau/Cologne, 2000

Alois Riegl, *Gesammelte Aufsätze*, Berlin, 1995

Simon Schama, *Rembrandt's Eyes*, New York, 1999

Otto Stelzer, *Die Vorgeschichte der abstrakten Kunst*, Munich, 1964

Victor I. Stoichita, *L'instauration du tableau*, Paris, 1993

Aby Warburg, *Gesammelte Schriften*, 2 vols., Berlin, 1998

Aby Warburg, *Der Bilderatlas Mnemosyne*, ed. Martin Warnke, Berlin, 2000

Catalogue

Francis Picabia

Delicious Monsters: Painting, Criticism, History

Carole Boulbès

"Here lies a critic! 'Cretin' I was going to say! Excuse me!"
Picabia was no lover of art critics. He often inveighed against those "animals with limp ideas" who bored the public stiff with their ravings about "luminosity", "harmony", "composition" and "the power of impasto".[1] But criticizing the critics was an activity both schizoid and paradoxical. It is a real cerebral sport—especially for Picabia, who published more than sixty polemical articles on the art of his day in newspapers and avant-garde journals between 1913 and 1953. The critic who criticizes the critic enters the kind of logical conundrum that Picabia clearly revelled in.

Iconoclast and iconophile
There are several different ways of approaching these contradictions. Some historians have taken them as an opportunity to give the nihilistic madman a dressing-down for his inconsistencies and tomfooleries. Others have made Picabia the apostle of a rather anachronistic brand of postmodern painting. The former have devalued the artist, the latter have praised him to the skies. But this dual vision is no doubt too limited to embrace Picabia's art, which is at once iconoclastic and iconophile, abstract and realistic, nihilistic and innovative, well done and badly done. Picabia thought that ugliness was simply the decadence of convention. He rejected the idea of avant-garde rupture, just as he did that of Modernism

Causes and effects
This penchant for contradiction comes as no surprise from a man who proclaimed that "every conviction is an illness"[2] Picabia yoked together "disparate words" for the pleasure of invention, and "transported every attempt at sequential wording into the realms of extravagance and paradox".[3] A virtuoso punsmith and aggravator of oppositions, he liked to say that he had "serious fun" and found "useless things essential". Behind all this, then, it is surprising that no one has detected an underpinning of profound philosophical scepticism. For classical philosophers such as Sextus Empiricus[4], tracking down the contradictions in phenomena and opinions was a necessary exercise, one that led to the suspension of judgement and then to ataraxia (oblivion). One thinks of Picabia's text on "immobile indifference"[5] or of the readymades that Duchamp said he chose in a state of "total anaesthesia", "with good or bad taste totally in abeyance".[6]

Painting and mimesis
In 1913 Picabia quoted Plato's *Philebus* to back up his first text on art. He hoped to convince the American public that form and colour have their own existence and "generate their own particular pleasures". Even in his first exhibition of watercolours inspired by New York, at Alfred Stieglitz's Photo Secession gallery at 291 Fifth Avenue, Picabia set out to warn his detractors about the ambiguities of photographic realism. Painting cannot be a copy of reality, and photography itself is only a subterfuge, a limited surrogate for the real.

Dialogues and paradoxes
From 1917, when the journal *391* was established, Picabia made frequent use of the dialogue form to criticise and defend painting. Sometimes he played the role of Socrates in Plato's dialogues, the figure who makes the other speaker express the ideas that he unknowingly has within him. But this is an unusual maieutic process conducted by a Socrates figure who is both eccentric and cynical.[7] Picabia always manages to ensnare his interlocutor's shortsighted artistic ideas in a web of paradoxes. One thinks of Martin Kippenberger in his *Lieber Maler, male mir ...* ("Dear Painter, paint me ...", 1981) series, or his sophist adages, founded on negatives, such as: "We have no problem with the Guggenheim, for we cannot say 'no' when we have not been invited" (1990).

Aphorisms, parables and self-contradiction
Picabia interwove his writings with numerous aphorisms about art, love, the family, glory and money. Conscious of this literary tradition, he even placed an aphorism by Oscar Wilde and another by Friedrich Nietzsche at the head of *Unique Eunuque* ("Unique Eunuch", 1920). Like the prophetic discourses that Zarathustra makes to his disciples in Nietzsche's *Thus Spoke Zarathustra* (1891), Picabia also tried writing parables about art. For example, he tells the story of a brilliant dog that does nothing but listen to his master's voice in *Le génie et le fox-terrier* ("The Genius and the Fox-terrier"), and that of a racing driver who teaches artists a lesson at dinner in *Classique et merveilleux* ("Classic and marvellous"). At the same time, Picabia's attitude towards himself is parodic and destructive. He is the "artist critic" who attacks himself by denying that his painting has any conceptual basis: "I like to paint so that I can stop thinking. Thinking in order to paint is just aping the great tide of the spirit." [8]

The critic and the transvaluation of values
When Picabia opts for scepticism and insists that there is nothing to understand; when he prefers the critique of values to superfluous commentary on the works, this is in fact the expression of a philosophy. Throughout his literary and visual work he calls into question the founding oppositions of western aesthetic categories (beautiful/ugly, pure/impure, good/evil). Like many other artists of his generation, from Breton to Bataille, via Ernst and de Chirico, the young Picabia was strongly influenced by his reading of Nietzsche. And this fascination was by no means limited to his Dada period. In fact, Picabia can be seen as a kind of prism diffracting and deforming Nietzschean concepts.

"The most learned and complete painting is grazing in my garden"
Like Nietzsche, Picabia uses animal figures to pour scorn on his colleagues' spiritual pretensions. As the aphorism quoted here suggests, it is not the philosopher but the performer-painter who chews on his past paintings as a cow chews the cud. For Picabia, painting exists only as a self-critical and necessarily ironic practice. Traditionalist painters must realise that "they are holding in their arms a legitimate old woman whom it is beyond the capacity of exotic makeup to rejuvenate." [9] Many years after Picabia's unhinged monsters, this cynicism towards ancient traditions might be illustrated by John Currin's oil painting of an aged *Minerva* (2000).

Self-portraits and confidences
The rejection of Socratic reason leads Picabia to praise "unvarnished" man and wild madness. This goes hand in hand with other Nietzschean figures with which he ironically identifies, all the better to deform and question them: the great man (who forces us to re-read History), the misunderstood genius, the heretic (who dares to think differently), the poet and, above all, the painter, the future philosopher whose mission is to care for painting (which he has made ill). Picabia's self-portraits and his personal correspondence with Suzanne Romain are particularly eloquent in this respect. There is something old-fashioned about them and, at the same time, they are intensely subversive. Like Glenn Brown's *The Rebel* (2001), Picabia's self-portrait *Papa Francis the loser* [10] is elusive: he is never where you expect him to be. Classical and fantastical, old fashioned and subversive, like painting and love letters.

Against profiteering
From 1945, for the series of paintings *Déclaration d'amour* ("illustrated" by an erect phallus) and *Hérésie et sorcellerie*, Picabia took their titles from poems and aphorisms in Nietzsche's *The Gay Science* (1882). But Picabia doesn't just play lucky dip with titles, he also writes in order to develop his aesthetic ideas *with* but also *against* Nietzsche. In 1932, in the first lines of *Monstres délicieux*, he writes: "Thinking differently from other people is not necessarily a sign of intelligence" [11], and then goes on to incriminate "speculators and profiteers". But if the beginning of the proposition simply plagiarises the aphorism "Heresy and witchcraft", what follows is radically different. Picabia is no longer talking about the witches they used to burn in the Middle Ages, but about the art dealers of his day. The rejection of profiteering and of the unimaginative trend-followers is a leitmotif of all his writings.

Pleasure, boredom and spectacle
On one hand, the myth: Picabia the dashing Don Juan, the perverse seducer and frivolous gambler, the man who runs away with the bride on her wedding day. On the other hand, his texts play a very different tune: "Boredom is vulgar, just as work is vulgar, if it does not give us pleasure for its own sake. I wonder what our true inner motives can be. The spectacle is secondary. The only difference between men is their degree of wretchedness, especially that of the body. The mind is best not mentioned." [12]

In writing this letter to Suzanne Romain, Picabia has synthesized five aphorisms from *The Gay Science* in only a few lines. Whether he is writing a love letter, a catalogue essay or a collection of poems addressed to one or several readers, his philosophical source remains the same. But quest for pleasure in all things in work as in boredom–has its foundations in a Cynical philosophy that Nietzsche may well have borrowed from Diogenes, "the philosopher dog" [13]. However, the idea of "spectacle" is a new concept not found in the source text. It implies a mistrust towards everything that is superficially visible, or on the surface of things, aware that the unconscious motivations of our actions remain obscure. By using the word "spectacle", Picabia creates a philosophical short-circuit.

Journalistic parody and the first attacks on the "Society of the Spectacle"
As early as 1917, in his journal *391*, Pharamousse (one of Picabia's pen names) concocts incendiary texts full of sarcasm and invective aimed at the art world. It was basically intended to plagiarise the journalistic style of

the "yellow press". Twenty-five years later, Picabia attacked another everyday myth: the star. Using photographs, he produced portraits of movie stars such as Greta Garbo, Marlene Dietrich and Madeleine Sologne. Uninterested in likeness, he deformed his models and caricatured the realist style of the period's posters and journals. Momentarily ignoring pictorial style, this grating painting which targets the idols of the 1930s "society of the spectacle", is not so far removed from Elizabeth Peyton's contemporary paintings of celebrities. Yet Picabia's most obvious heir is Kurt Kauper, whose vivid portraits of Cary Grant in the nude also oscillate between irony and fantasy.

The couple: art and love

I experience painting
As an object of passion
My pictures are acts of love
It's the way I work [14]

Like Sigmar Polke, whom he influenced, Picabia did many paintings of lovers, including himself, such as his 1940 self-portrait with two women. An obsession with love and physical possession shapes Picabia's painting, whether it is in the *Danse espagnole*, the *Monstres* series of the 1920s or the iconoclastic *Adam et Eve* (1930-1931). In *Portrait d'un couple* ("Portrait of a Couple", 1942-1943) he scales the heights of kitsch and spring-fresh sentimentalism. But so what! In these canvases the ageing Don Juan is mocking his own "porno kitsch". There is no ambiguity in all this. In the love letters written to Suzanne Romain between 1944 and 1948, Picabia clearly rejects the "will to power" and solitude of the Nietzschean superman. His own plans were indeed much more epicurean.

Paris-Nice

Picabis painted many nudes while he was living on the Côte d'Azur, particularly between 1940 and 1942. Suzanne Romain claimed to be the model. [15] In 1996, however, it was found that the source for these works was a selection of erotic magazines from the 1930s. [16] Picabia's *La femme blonde* ("Blonde Woman", 1942) was thus based on a photograph published in issue no. 5 (March 1936) of *Mon Paris, son visage, sa vie ardente* and the sitting woman in *La brune et la blonde* ("The Brunette and the Blonde", 1941) came from no. 3 (January 1936). Still, there was nothing to prevent Romain, who posed for *Modèle nu(e) debout* ("Standing Nude Model", 1941) from mimicking the postures in these photographs for Picabia's pictoral pleasure! It is also hard to believe that she would not have known about the magazines: Michel Georges-Michel, whom Suzanne met in Nice, had published texts in issues 3 and 4 of *Mon Paris* ("Mon bois" and "Ma Riviera"). And, above all, Paul Reboux, her brother-in-law, was a writer who had published three articles in another glamour magazine that Picabia also used, *Paris Sex Appeal*.

Copy, twist and parody

In spite of Picabia's apparent eclecticism, there are two things about his art that never change: the appropriation of photography, seen as a vehicle for pictorial pleasure [17] and the aesthetic appropriation of Nietzsche. Not that this can be pinned down to a method. It is more like a poetics, one with three basic principles: select, copy and deform. Picabia described this very clearly as early as 1921: "The painter makes a choice, then imitates his choice, the deformation of this then constitutes Art." [18]

Parody and irony need not exclude authenticity and purity. Nor are they something unique to post. They are simply vital modes of expression based in a critical and self-reflexive approach that has been around for centuries. When Picabia takes inspiration from Nietzsche's *The Gay Science* or *Thus Spoke Zarathustra*, he produces a new form of artistic thought. Insofar as it copies or subverts it, it is a parody of the earlier model. But it is also a self-parody that comes from knowing that one is part of History, just like Nietzsche, who never hesitated to plagiarize the Bible or Goethe's *Faust, Part II*. There can be no "immaculate conception", no "pure" writing or painting. Seek, and you will always find the umbilical cord.

(translated from the French by Charles Penwarden)

Endnotes

1. Francis Picabia, "Le Salon des indépendants", *La Vie moderne*, 11 February 1923, Id., "Encore un péché mortel", *Paris-Journal*, 20 December 1924.
2. Picabia used this maxim as an epigram for his book of poems, *Unique Eunuque*, (Paris: Au Sans Pareil, 1920).
3. Gabrielle Buffet-Picabia, [n.t.], *Francis Picabia* (exh. cat.), Paris: Grand Palais; Musée National d'Art Moderne (1976) p. 6 ; and Id., *Rencontres avec ...*, (Paris: P. Belfond,1977), p. 75-76.
4. A Greek physician and sceptic of the 2nd–3rd century AD, Sextus Empiricus was a proponent of Scepticism, the philosophical tradition which argued thatabsolute certainty or knowledge cannot be attained. [Editor's note]
5. F. Picabia, "Indifférence immobile", *Comœdia*, 31 March 1922.
6. Marcel Duchamp, talk given during the exhibition *The Art of Assemblage*, New York, The Museum of Modern Art, 1961, (reproduced in Michel Sanouillet, *Duchamp du signe*, [Paris: Flammarion, 1975], p. 191).
7. The "maieutic" process refers the Socratic mode of enquiry, a process dedicated to drawing out a person's latent ideas. [Editor's note]
8. F. Picabia, "L'humour poétique", *La Nef*, nos. 71-72, December 1950-January 1951, p. 116-123.
9. Id., "Sur les bords de la Seine", *Les Potins de Paris*, 3 February 1922.
10. In 1920, *Tableau rastadada* offered a montage of women's legs with a photographic portrait of Picabia, captioned: "Long live Papa Francis the loser!"
11. F. Picabia, "Monstres délicieux", *Orbes*, no. 3, spring 1932, p. 129-131.

12 Letter from Picabia to Suzanne Romain [not dated]. See the forthcoming Carole Boulbès, *Lettres d'amour de Francis Picabia à Suzanne Romain, 1944-1948*, Paris: Jean-Michel Place (late 2002).

13 Diogenes of Sinope (412-322 BC) was the founder of the philosophical sect of the Cynics. The word "cynicism" is derived from the Greek word for "dog", hence Diogenes' nickname as the "philosopher dog". [Editor's note]

14 Excerpt from [P.A. Benoît, ed.], F. Picabia, "Oui non, oui non, oui non", Alès: PAB (1953).

15 Francis Picabia met Suzanne Romain in 1940, at Juan-les-Pins.

16 Sara Cochran, "Les nus de Picabia, 1939-1944", *L'Image*, no. 3, December 1996, p. 193-202.

17 Carole Boulbès, "Picabia, the nudes, the photos, the life", catalogue of the exhibition *Francis Picabia, Fleurs de chair, fleurs d'âme, nus, transparences, tableaux abstraits*, Zurich, Galerie Hauser & Wirth; Cologne, Oktagon, May-June 1997. On Picabia's twisting of Nietzsche's ideas, see C. Boulbès, *Lettres d'amour de Francis Picabia à Suzanne Romain, 1944-1948, op. cit.*

18 F. Picabia, "L'œil cacodylate", *Comœdia*, 23 November 1921, p. 2.

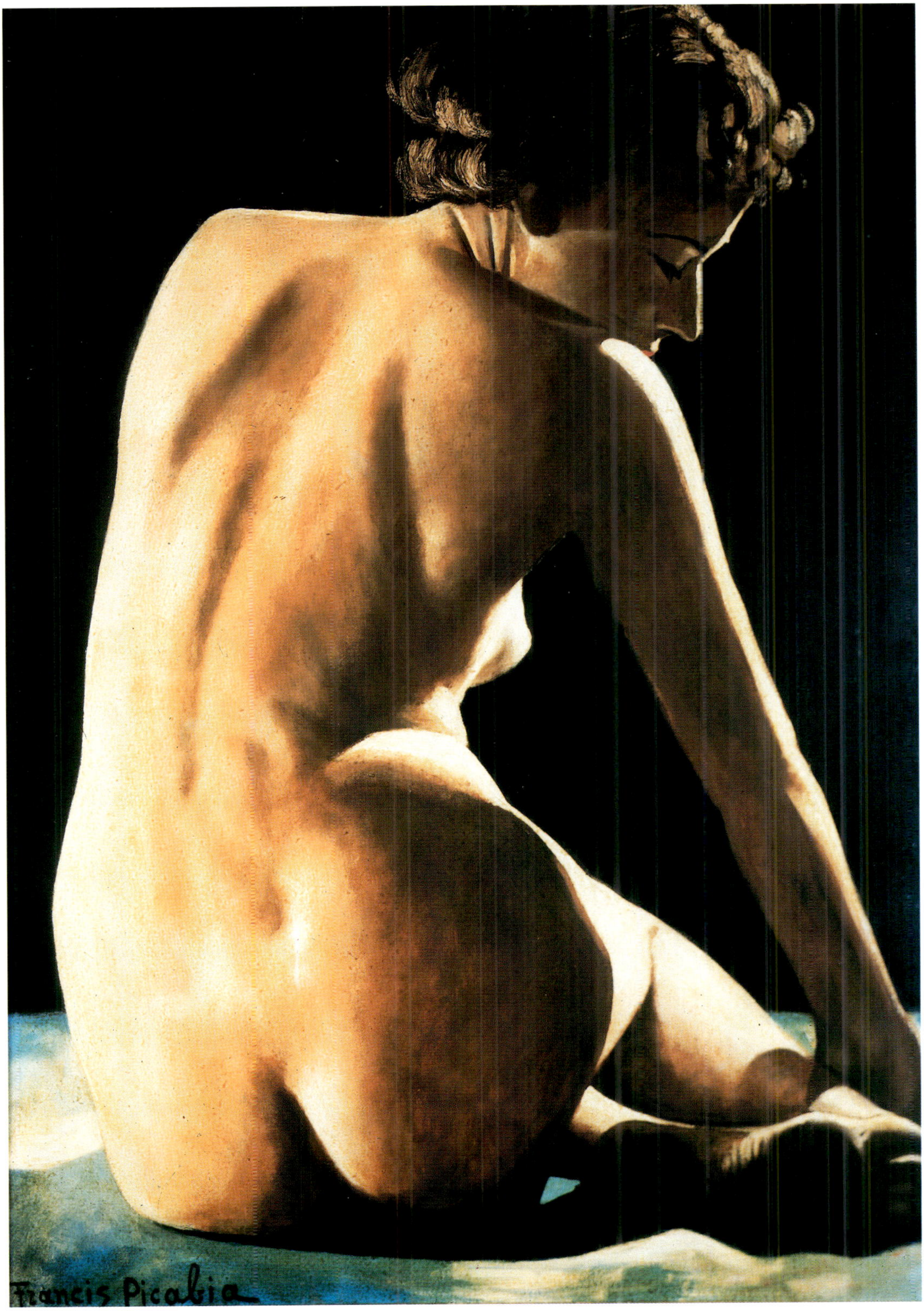

Francis Picabia
Nu de dos, 1940-1942
105 x 76 cm
The Dakis Joannou Collection, Athens

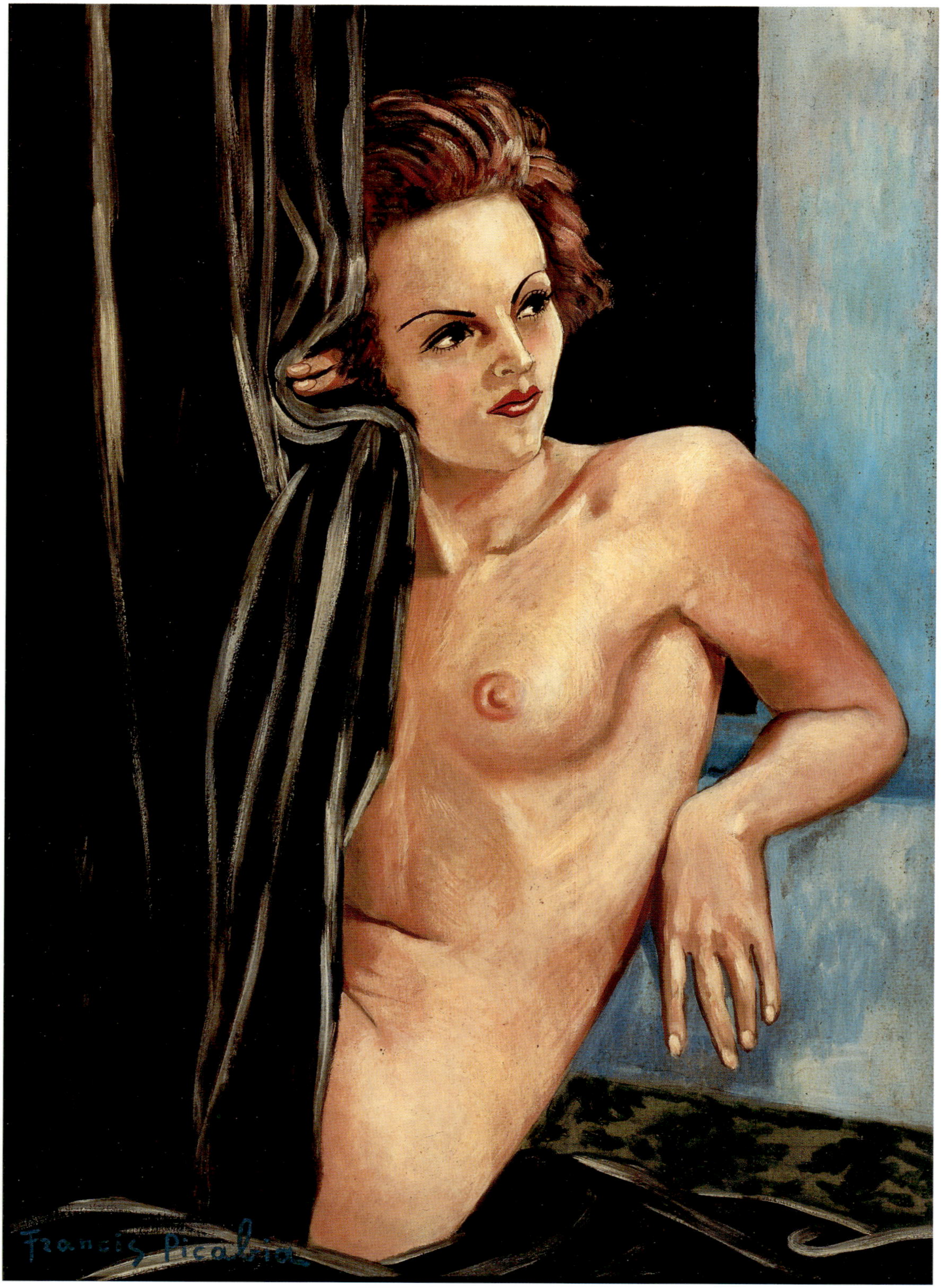

Francis Picabia
La Femme blonde / La Blonde, 1942
106 x 76 cm
Sammlung Hauser & Wirth, St. Gallen

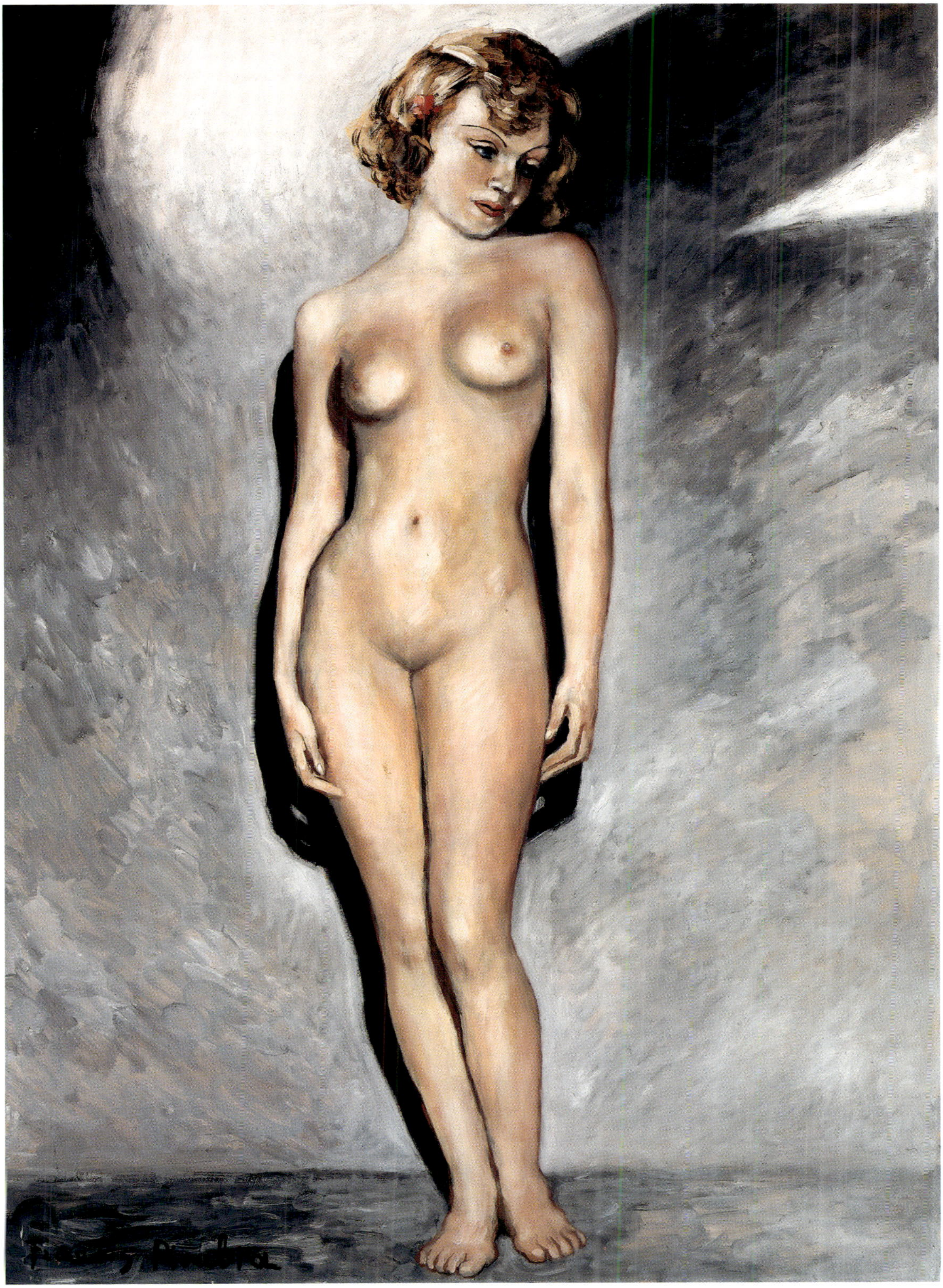

Francis Picabia
Modèle nu(e) debout, 1941
106,5 x 76,5 cm
Flick Collection

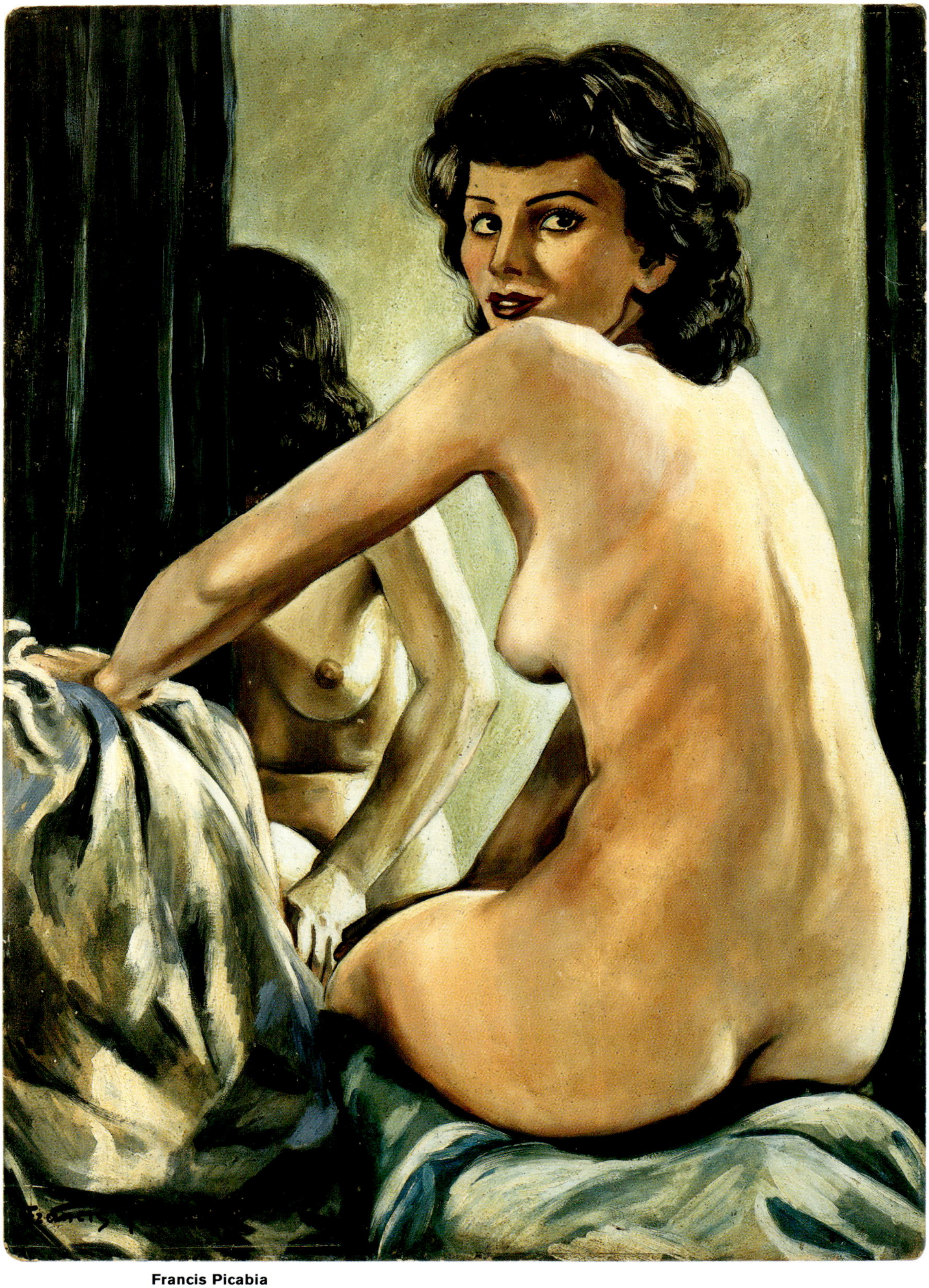

Francis Picabia
Femme nue devant la glace, 1941-1942
106 x 76,5 cm
Collection David & Monica Zwirner, New York

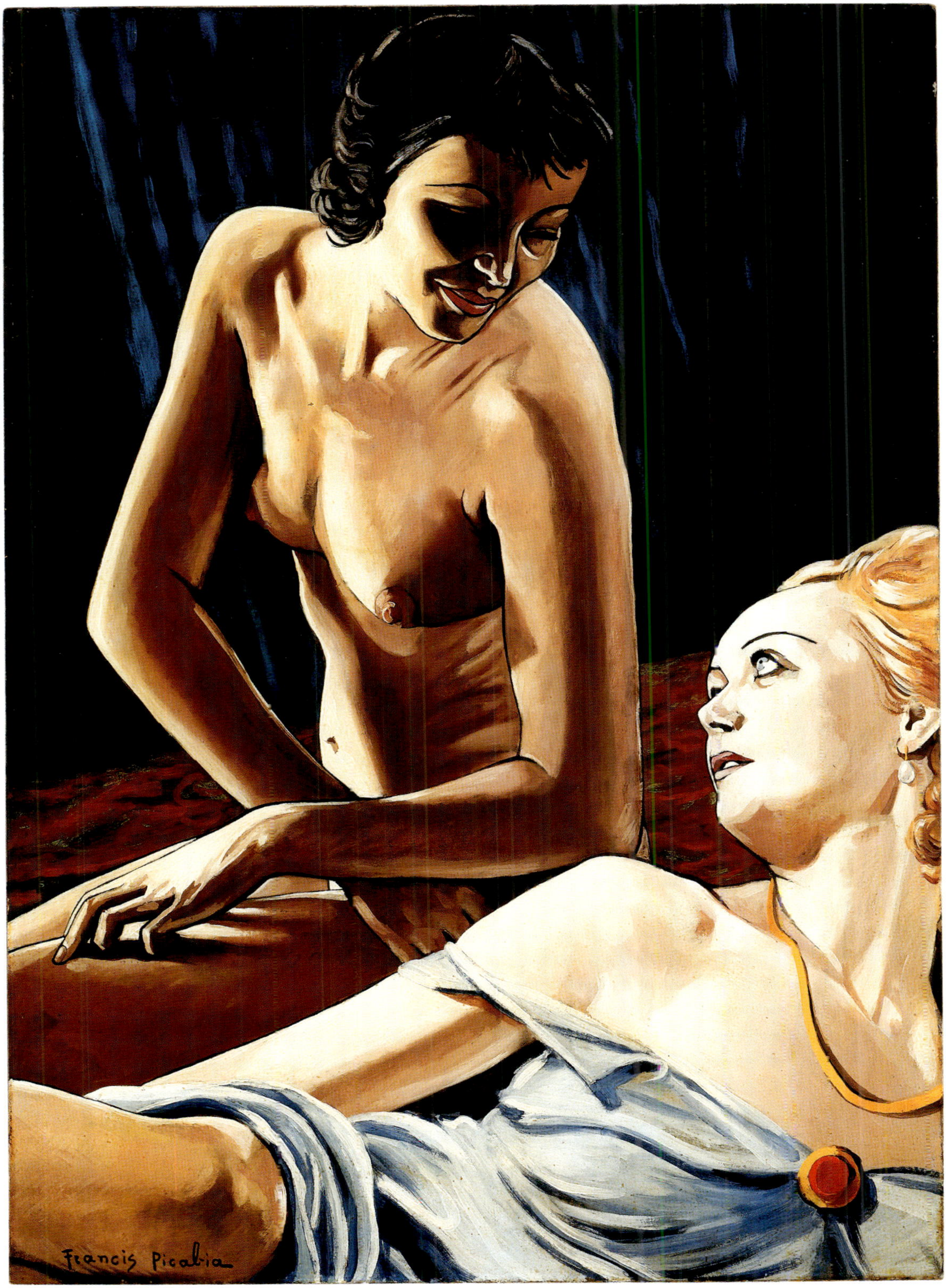

Francis Picabia
La Brune et la blonde, 1941
104 x 75 cm
Flick Collection

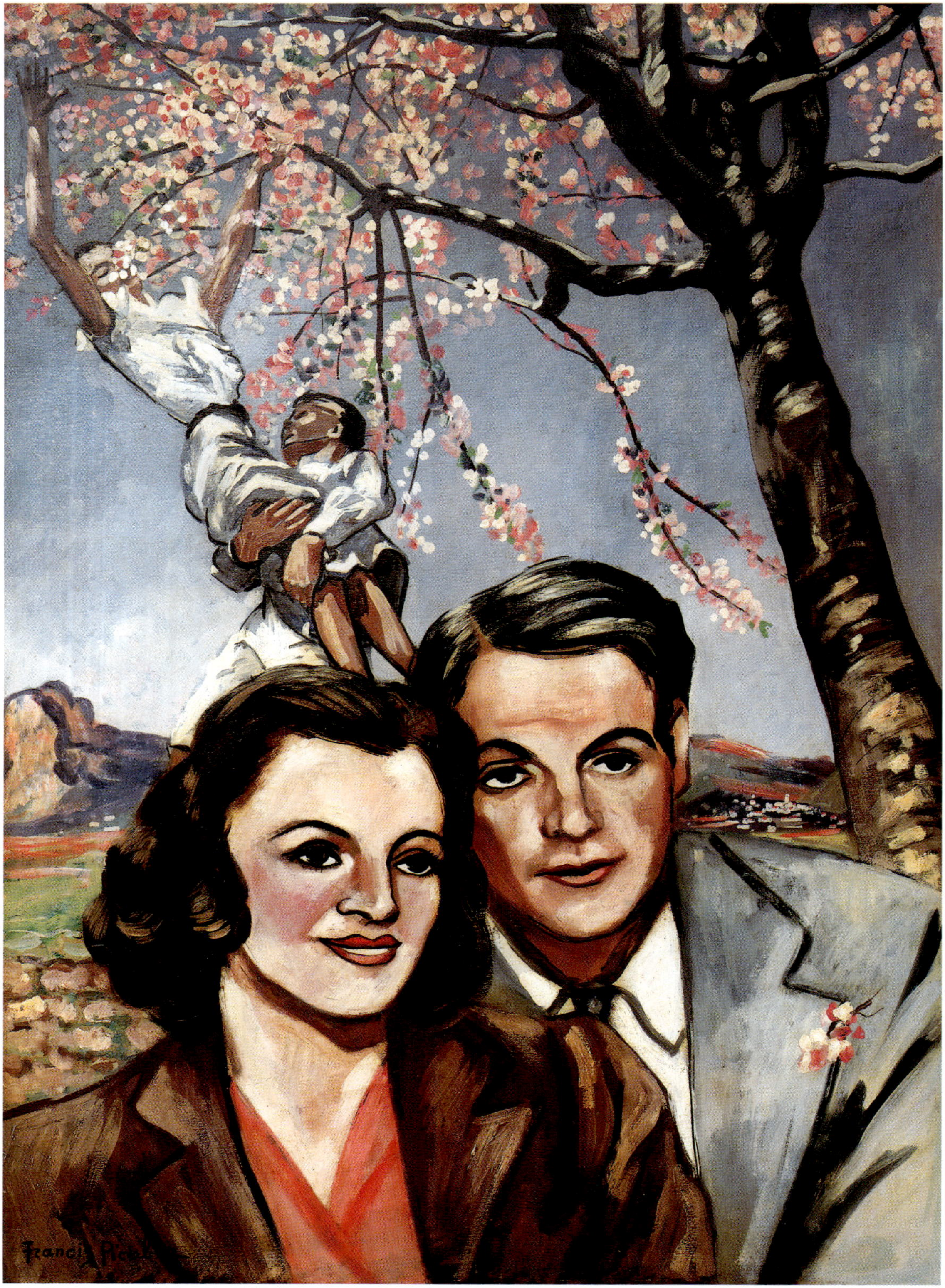

Francis Picabia
Portrait d'un couple, 1942 - 1943
105,7 x 77,4 cm
The Museum of Modern Art, New York, purchase, 2000

Bernard Buffet
Who's Afraid of Bernard Buffet?

Alexander Roob

> *The French do really have one good painter, I mean, my favorite artist would be the last big artist in Paris: Buffet.*
>
> Andy Warhol [1]

Buffet is the only Modernist fine arts practitioner who really was a pop star. In the Fifties there existed what amounted to a veritable Buffet-mania. The products of this one-man painting-manufacturer were omni-present, not just through countless exhibitions, but also through masses of reproductions as posters, postcards, postal stamps, magazine covers, and their use in advertising, souvenir items and fashion lines. Buffet was "cult" and the enthusiasm for his work cut through all strata of society.

An entire generation owes its initial encounter with art to his pictures, while another generation of artist-colleagues, critics and exhibitors was utterly traumatized by the comet-like rise to stardom of this young painter from the ashes of the post-war depression. And it was this generation that was seeking to forgo and forget him, with a relentlessness and persistence that is staggering.

In its utter uniqueness, the history of his fall from grace is equal to the history of his success. Within a few years, "the man with the golden arm", as *Der Spiegel* had called him in 1956, became the most reviled artist of the past century, a pariah who, even today, is shunned like the plague by curators, critics and publishers alike.

At a time when the art establishment was strictly set on canonization, delineation and the purity of its doctrine, Buffet's painting with all its indissoluble antagonisms must have seemed like an embarrassing provocation, a dog's mess of impurity. Simultaneously sentimentally dramatic, punkishly drastic and icily distant, it was related in the abstraction of its graphism to the École de Paris, while being unmistakably narrative and illustrative; a tense amalgamation of Grünewald and the jet set, comic books and Courbet, his work was a thing of the very liveliest impossibility.

In his early phase of Miserabilism, when he began to free himself from the influence of idols such as Francis Gruber, Buffet was developing a completely independent style within just a few, extremely work-intensive years. He succeeded in creating a series of stage-like representations and figurations that rank among the most incisive works of figurative painting the 20th century had to offer. Even decades later their pictorial reverberations would haunt the paintings of Georg Baselitz and make their ghost-like appearances in the productions of the "Mülheimer Freiheit". In these early pictures the mental state of a generation that enjoyed casting itself in the pretentious gestures of profundity and authenticity froze up into a game of terse poses.

At a time when art was bent on "cutting to the heart of the matter", in Picasso's very famous phrase about Giacometti, the world-weariness, the trauma of starvation and the *tristesse* of the post-war era coagulated within the spiderweb-like tension of Buffet's pictures into clichés of oppressive banality. Unlike, for instance, Beckmann, Hofer or Gruber, Buffet, in his stylistically-formative phase during the early 1950s no longer defined his scenery by a menacing depth of space; instead, it was wedged straight into the pale plane of the surface itself.

The reproach that he was a painter without substance has, as a consequence, been maintained to this day. Yet from the very beginning Buffet had never made a secret of the fact that his was a programme of the surface, Pop, as it were, before Pop. What else, after all, was to be expected, if not radical consistency, of a painter who had had himself quoted in his first exhibition catalogue of 1947, as saying: "I force myself not to think any longer."

Even more unforgivable than these acts of dragging existentialist theatralics into the shallow realms of banality, a veritable buffeting into the face of the generation that wrought the economic miracle, was the extension of his themes, which he brought about by employing the same footloose and fancyfree attitude and the same painterly approach he had used earlier for his images of poverty, only expending them now on the illustration of wealth.

The repulsive, consumptive characters of his starvation pictures now reappeared once more, dressed up as models in the fashionable world of the glitterati, Giacometti at the beach in St. Tropez, Manessier behind the grille-work of the Eiffel Tower, Rouault trapped in the bosom of a Rolls-Royce. In addition, there were de Gaulle, Mao, the Pope and Ludwig Erhard, all rendered as comic-book-like icons. A series of psychedaelic nightmare-pictures (*The Birds*), which far exceeded the limits of good taste acceptable at the time, brought him, in 1960, under the public prosecutor's suspicion of engaging in pornography. This accusation was a gift to the *Galerie Maurice Garnier*, presenting it with a crowd of curious connoisseurs that, for two months running, spilled a hundred meters across the Champs Elysées.

In the music business a figure such as Buffet would long since have been rehabilitated by the critics as an instigator and fore-runner of current trends, and showered by producers with tribute projects. Had Buffet, like Bacon and many other of his post-war contemporaries, clung timorously to the themes of his initial success and not pushed its boundaries, then surely he would have been saved an excommunication of such proportions. As it was, however, with his reputation in tatters, he was spurred on by a sense of complete liberation: "I need to spare nothing and no one. That is something very few people can claim." Almost unnoticed by the public he continued to create a boundless and bizarre complex of works, a baroque and Gargantuan panorama composed of both a crude day-to-day world and sparkling myths—a work that in its autistic resolution and over-the-top tomfoolery at best allows a comparison with the work of James Ensor.

This pantographic oeuvre, so abundantly rich in offensiveness against, and violation of, the rules and regulations of Modernism today reveals itself to be, contrary to all prejudices, which claim Buffet to have exhausted himself in empty bluster and tired mannerisms, as a seminal contribution to the cutting-edge art of today, as a body of work of quite uncommon freshness and explosive substance, Punk and Pop, obsessive and pithy, sentimentally touching and toughly dismissive all at once.

Painting is not to be confused with politeness.
Bernard Buffet [2]

(translated from the German by Tom Appleton)

Endnotes

The present text is a slightly modified version of a contribution to an exhibition, conceived by Stephan Berg and Alexander Roob, of a selection Bernard Buffet's works, which was shown 31 August to 21 December, 2001, at the Galerie Ursula Walbröl in Düsseldorf, Germany.

1 Andy Warhol in an interview with Benjamin Buchloh from 1985, in: *October*, no. 70, 1994.

2 Bernard Buffet in Maurice Druon, "Bernard Buffet", Paris 1964.

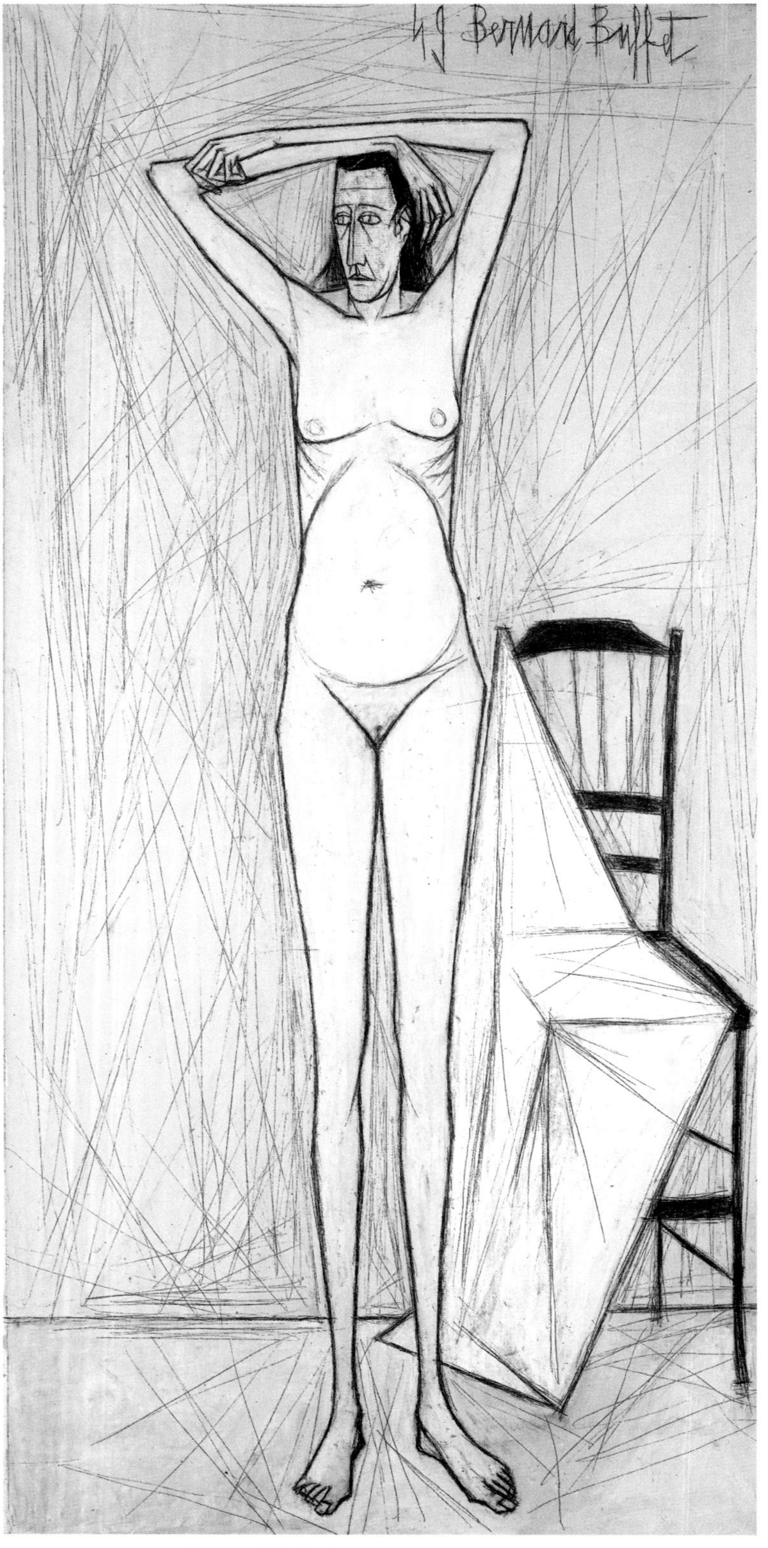

Bernard Buffet
Nu debout, 1949
193 x 95 cm
Musée d'Art moderne de la Ville de Paris

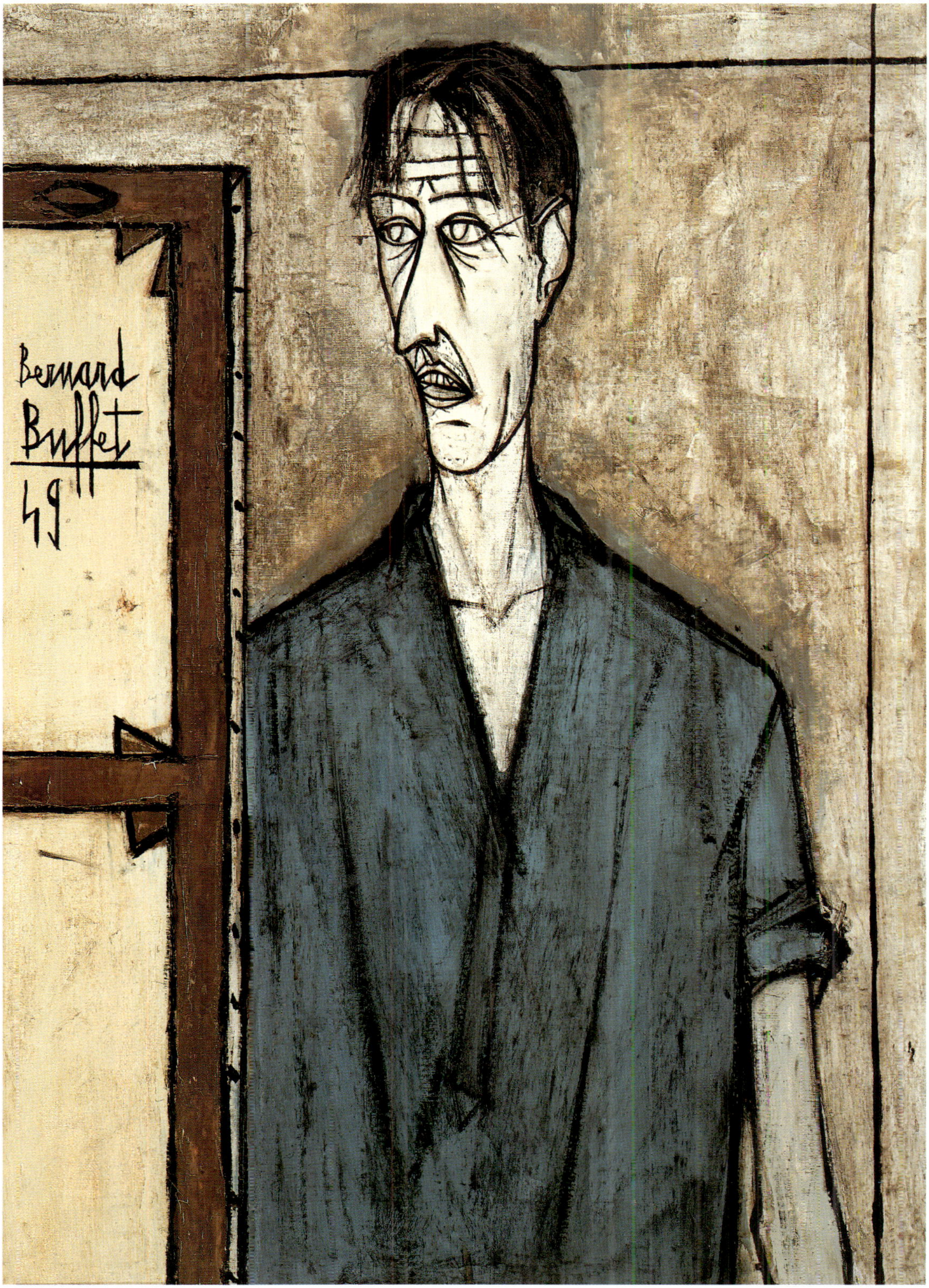

Bernard Buffet
Portrait de l'artiste, 1949
92 x 65 cm
Musée d'Art moderne de la Ville de Paris

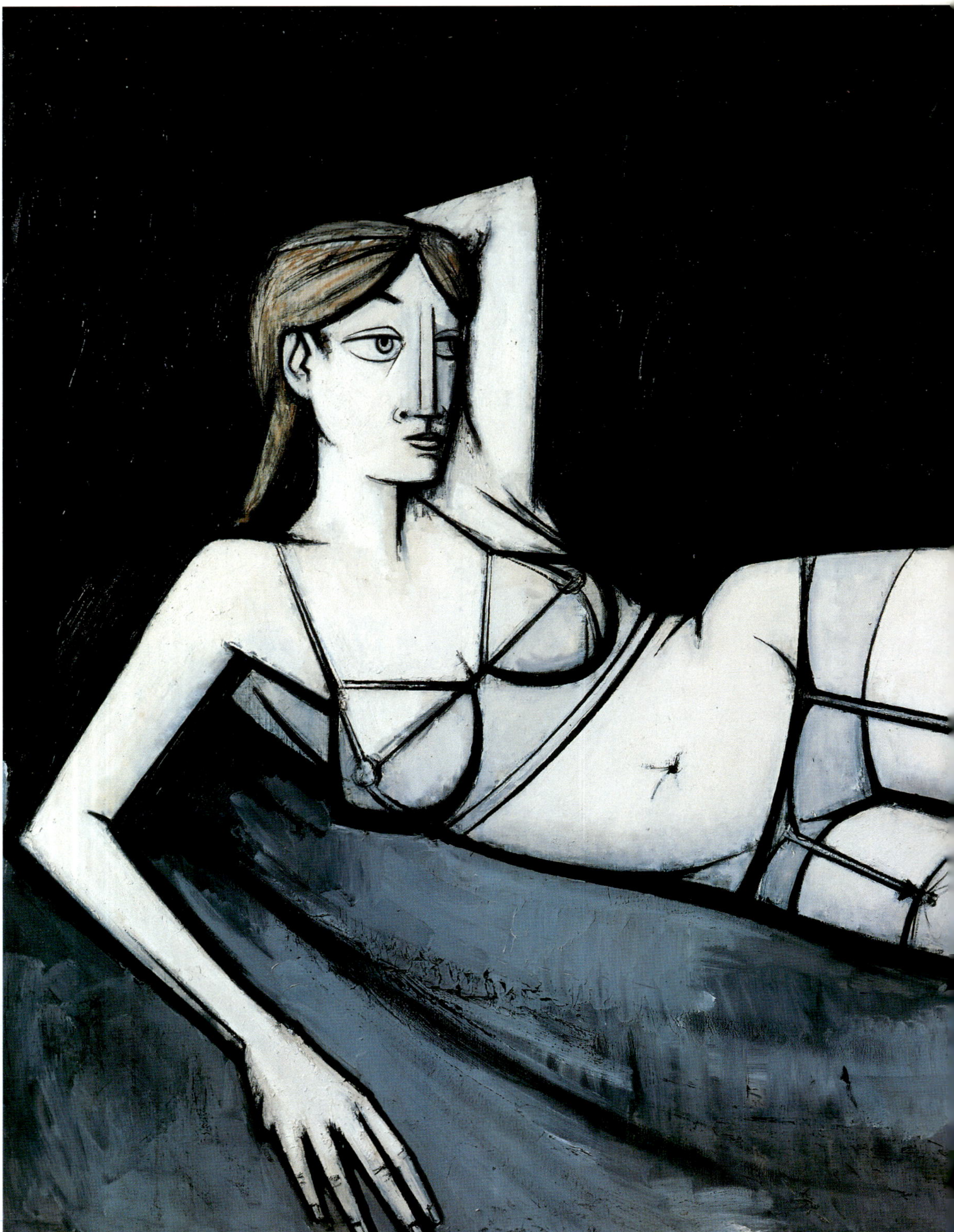

Bernard Buffet
Femme couchée (de la série *Femmes déshabillées*), 1965
200 x 300 cm
Collection Annabel Buffet, Paris

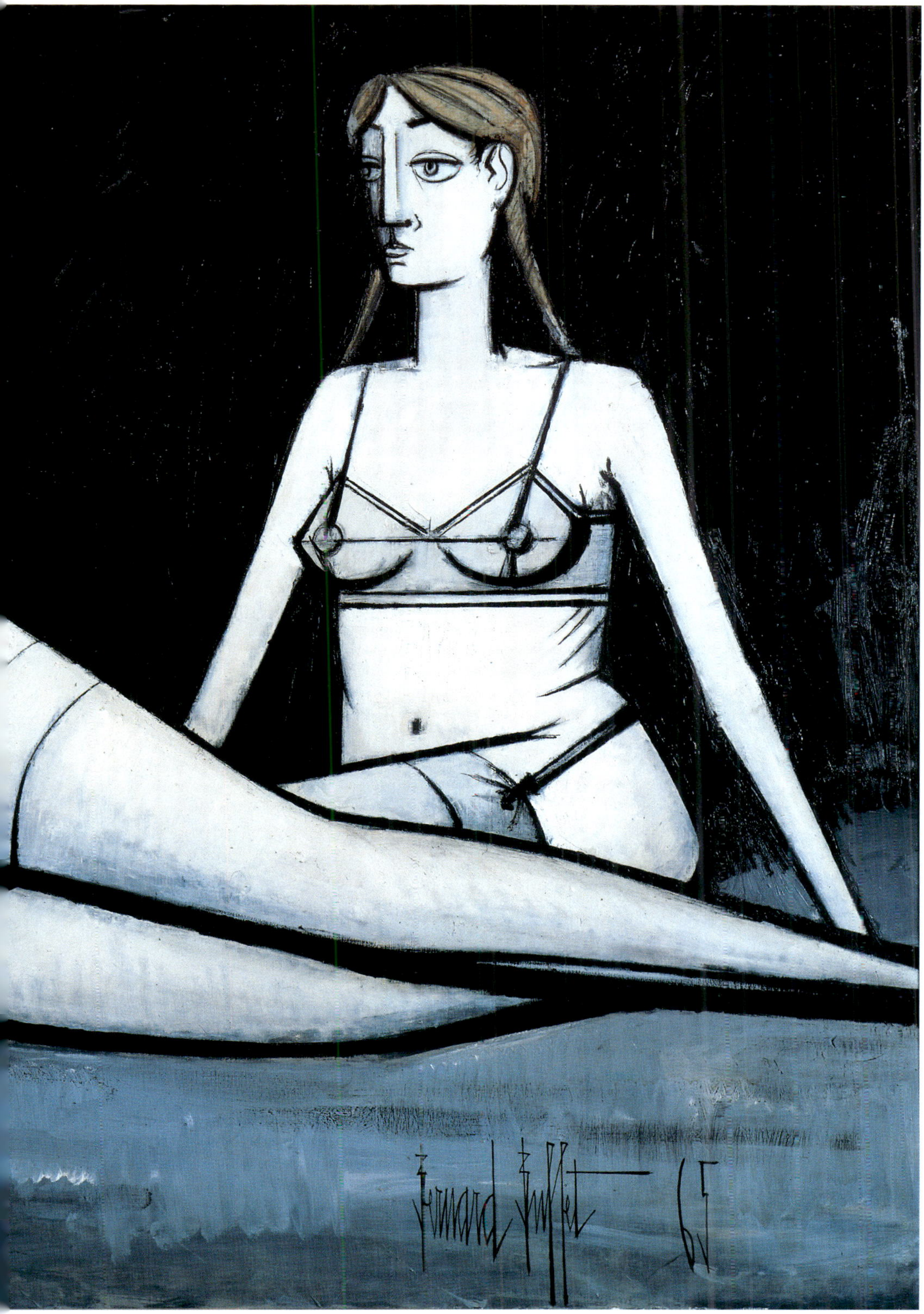

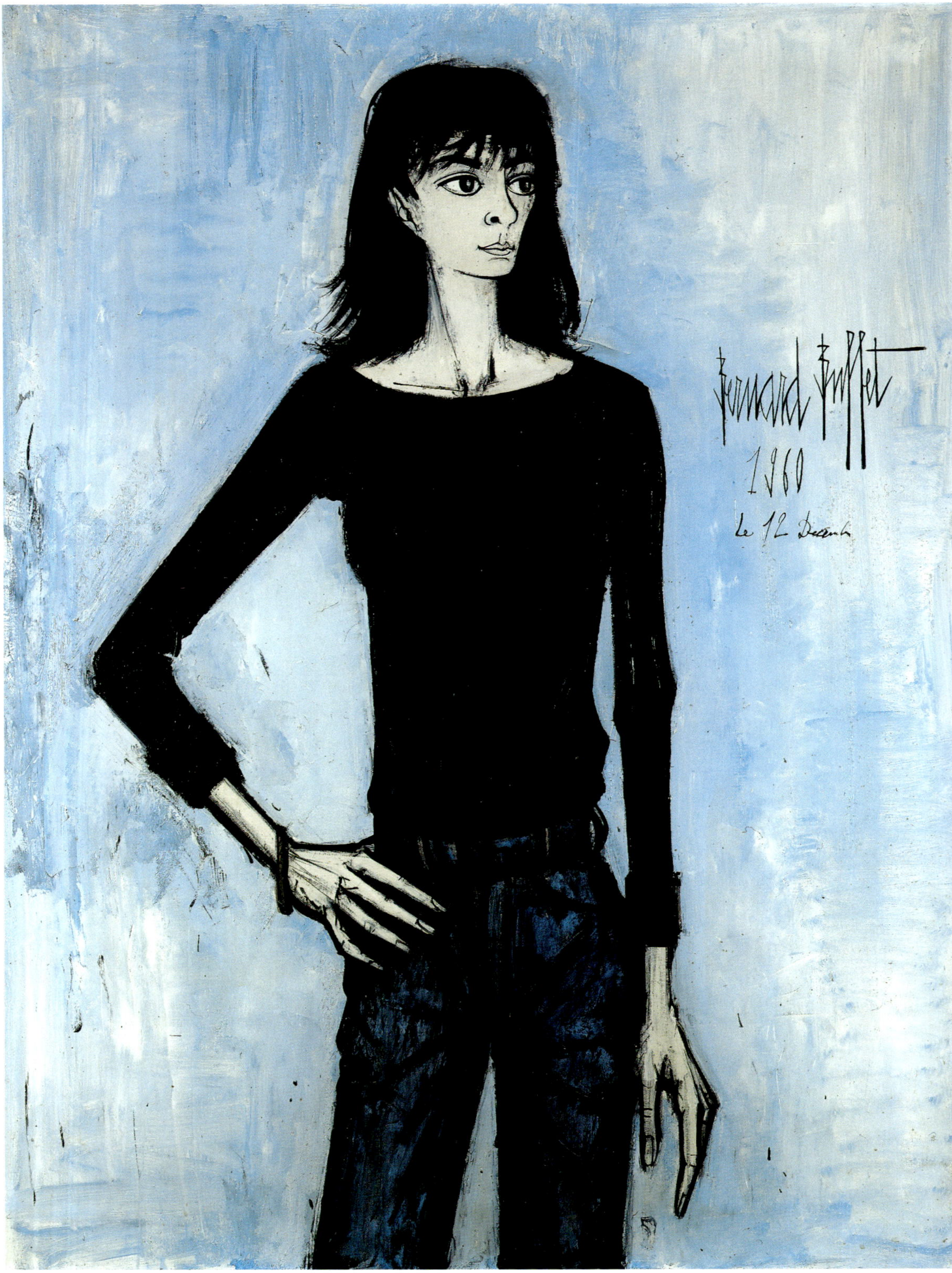

Bernard Buffet
Annabel en blue-jeans, 1960
130 x 97 cm
Collection Annabel Buffet, Paris

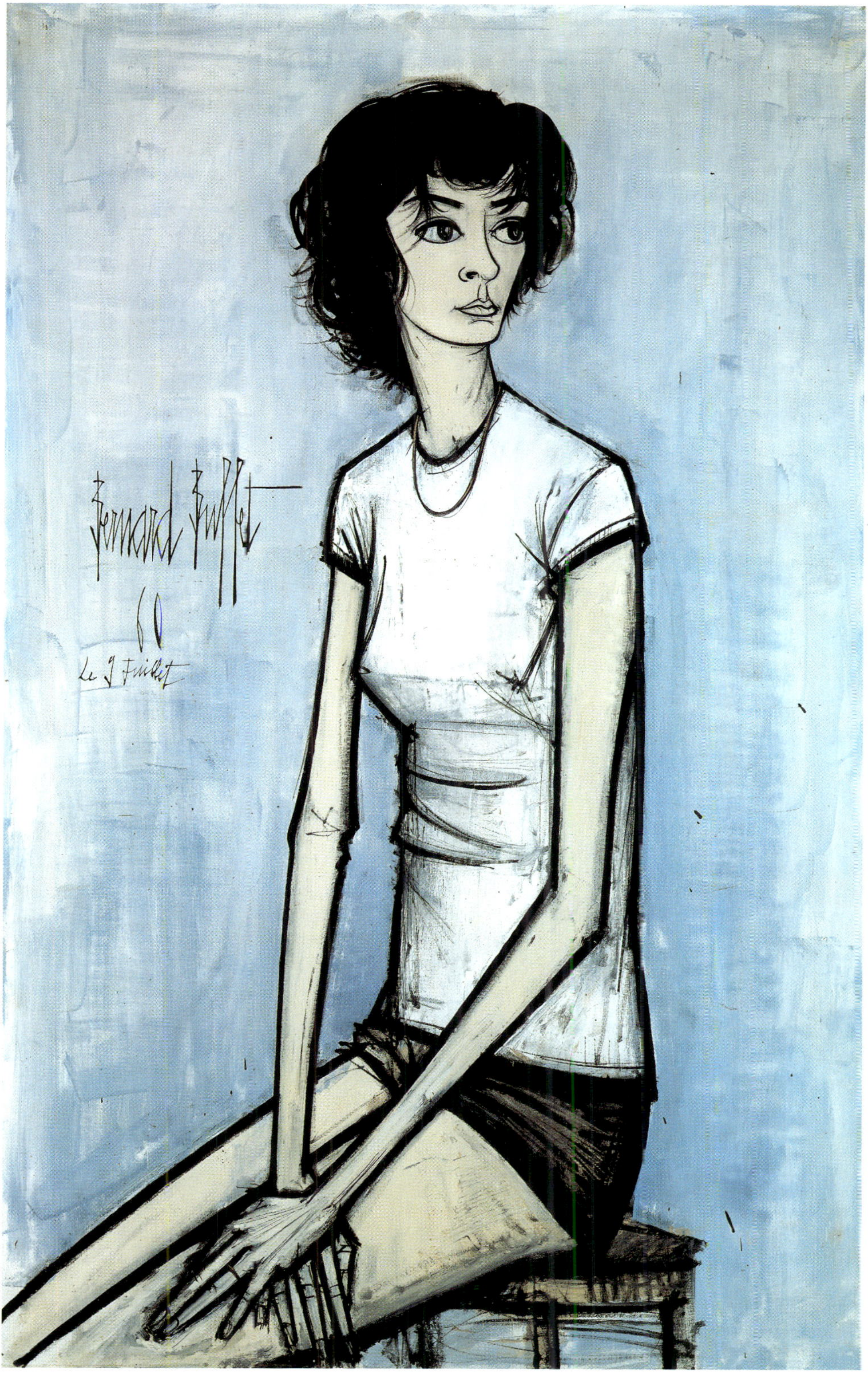

Bernard Buffet
Annabel en T-shirt, 1960
130 x 81 cm
Collection Annabel Buffet, Paris

Sigmar Polke

On the Difficulty of Approaching Sigmar Polke

Reiner Speck

Estragon — What exactly did we ask him for?
Vladimir — Were you not there?
Estragon — I can't have been listening.
Vladimir — Oh... Nothing very definite.
Estragon — A kind of prayer.
Vladimir — Precisely.
Estragon — A vague supplication.
Vladimir — Exactly.
Estragon — And what did he reply?
Vladimir — That he'd see.
Estragon — That he couldn't promise anything.
Vladimir — That he'd have to think it over.
Estragon — In the quiet of his home.
Vladimir — Consult his family.
Estragon — His friends.
Vladimir — His agents.
Estragon — His correspondents.
Vladimir — His books.
Estragon — His bank account.
Vladimir — Before making a decision.
Estragon — It's the normal thing.
Vladimir — Is it not?

Samuel Beckett
Waiting for Godot

In 1981 the gallery owner Erhard Klein exhibited a new work by Sigmar Polke at the Cologne Art Fair. It was an eye-catching work in more ways than one: its tremendous quality was at once apparent to many people who saw it, even though most of them found it unsettling; its price was exceptionally high, which, initially at least, discouraged a number of those who might have thought of buying it; and the curtain material that served as background was arranged in such a way that it hung down, monolithically, over the lower edge of the frame.

My decision to buy the painting was made in a matter of seconds, but all I could do at that time was reserve the work with a little green sticker until the artist himself had assessed my eligibility and signaled his approval. Until then, the dealers would go on wrangling, the critics would trade in rumors, and other collectors would whisper among themselves. A pitying smile was one trade journal's response to the price I had had to pay. In arriving at the asking price, the artist appeared to have doubled his age and added three noughts: I needed nearly as many 1000-mark notes as the century itself was old. Since then the painting–*Tischerücken* ("Moving Tables")–has been on the move, scarcely ever coming to rest in my own collection but appearing at exhibitions in countless public and private galleries on all five continents. This in itself was enough to inspire me to start saving up once again and to look for another of Polke's paintings, for the twenty or so of his other works that I already owned were clearly in need of company: comparisons had to be drawn and a critical confrontation made. The plan was as simple as it was naive, the difficulties great and insurmountable, as the following account of my seven year struggle will show.

After 1983 Polke's older and more recent work could be seen at a series of major exhibitions in Rotterdam, Bonn, Berlin, Zurich, Cologne, New York, Venice, Mönchengladbach, Paris, Düsseldorf, Amsterdam, and Baden-Baden ... On the evening before the official opening I would look at the works that were on display and generally note down some half-dozen titles still labeled “Collection of the Artist”, both signaling my interest and reminding Polke that I was still on his trail. In the course of the following day I would keep going back to the exhibition, but my earlier uncertainty about the significance of the works I had earmarked was certainly not diminished. Indeed, the labels that indicated their provenance often seemed to have been replaced by some invisible hand. Knowing that, for Polke, there could be no question of good or bad paintings but only of increasing understanding or else of continuing blindness, I finally sent him a list of my secret desires. “There is a kind of understanding that does not exclude the freedom of choice”, Jean Starobinski once said when discussing the subject of skepticism.

My stratagem seemed to me all the more sensible in that all the artist's gallery exhibitions were sold out weeks in advance (the hyenas are generally already present whenever I have to visit a patient) and it is, in any case, easier to make a rational choice in the calm, contextualized setting of a museum or municiple gallery than it is at a private showing. Agonized choice is a necessary part of collecting. I wrote to Polke, drawing my bow at a venture. I suspect that the letters wound up in Pandora's Box, since the cover address was a woman's ...

Motivated by desperation as much as by temerity, I assumed the artist knew the reason why he refused my requests. Impertinence and adoration spurred me on in my all too predictable actions: I went to Polke's exhibitions, drew up my list, and wrote him begging letters. A suitable moment seemed to present itself when, at a vernissage, I managed to draw him aside and question him on the subject, but he answered with a sardonic smile and said he had never been fully “conscious” of what it was that I wanted. The truth about an artist reveals itself in his works, but Polke hides his untruthfulness behind that camouflage which, recurring with leitmotivic regularity, gives his works their sense of style.

This raises the question to what extent the artist's life has left its mark on his art. Is Polke's life revealed in his works? In the case of Marcel Proust, this problem has been discussed in hundreds of learned papers and doctoral dissertations that involve their authors in snuffling under the bedclothes. In the case of Polke, by contrast, it needs no more than a glance at his pictures to see that, although he confronts us in person here, it is, for the most part, to disappear behind them once again. If we know the lines on the palms of his hands, it is through his images, not through the chiromancer's art. His name may be written in the stars, but all we can see of the artist himself is the head that is poked through *Die Schere*, a thoroughly tautological work. Does an artist have to emerge even *more* from his work before we can make head or tail of it?

The self-pitying way in which writer after writer of reviews and catalogue essays complains of Polke's invisibility seems to confirm the suspicion that the critics in question believe they have to shake the artist's hand before they can understand him. “Sigmar Polke is hard to catch”, “Polke likes going away on long journeys. He likes to be off and away.”, “Looking for Polke can be quite an adventure.”, “He is always running away from his follower and from his shadow.”

Only rarely does the critic demand that the artist keep his appointments and act as his own interpreter. His unattainability and the game of hide-and-seek that he plays then become part of a *nouvelle critique* approach to his works. Paul Groot has spoken of the way in which Polke, fleeing from his own past, has become a father figure for a whole generation–even if that generation is now decidedly elderly. And Katharina Hegewisch is altogether ambivalent in her assessment: “For, unlike many of his colleagues, this artist is not predictable.” How gratifying it is, then, to stumble upon a sentence that Werner Hofmann wrote some thirty years ago, when Polke first became a father, a sentence that defends those qualities that have always been the prerogative of the creative artist: the dignity of seclusion and the right to be unapproachable.

It was clear from what others had written on Polke that I was not alone in feeling frustrated. But it gave me little comfort to know that my reasons for trying to track him down were quite different from the army of hacks and reviewers that dogs his every step. Critics and collectors should, of course, be satisfied with the works themselves, but the collector needs to own them first. The true connoisseur must be able to choose, for otherwise collecting amounts to no more than hoarding things at random. On the other hand, the artist has a right to know where his works end up, for it is only outside the studio that the arbitrary nature of the context becomes at all significant. Sometimes the creative act lies in bypassing exegetical apparatus and placing the work in the peaceful setting of a private collection, a “launch” which guarantees the virginity of the work of art at least a little longer. After all, the fewer eyes to which it is exposed, the longer it remains verifiable.

Time passed, and I continued to visit Polke's major exhibitions, the unattainability of my ambitions adding to my depression but not yet inducing terminal resignation. For a while I took my cue from Franz Kafka and signed my letters with the letter *K*, but still failed to get through to the Other Side. It was both mystifying and unsettling to discover that the paintings to which I thought I had a claim were suddenly not in the artist's collection any longer. Instead they were labeled “Raschdorf Collection”, a collection which, completely unknown until then, had overnight acquired a series of paintings by Polke, but not by anybody else. What mysterious links might there be between the lists I'd drawn up of the works that I myself wanted and the greater portion of these marvelous paintings which seemed to have landed, as if by magic, in the hands of this apocryphal person who must have known my letters? The immensely high quality of these key works would often remind me of my *Tischerücken* and would make me suspect that some higher being must be involved, someone whose pseudonym had already struck me on reading some early catalogue essays which, among the best of their kind, were the work of a writer who never had to complain of not having met the artist ... Suspicions which I thought I would have to take to the grave with me were confirmed by the sight of a dedication that issued from the darkroom: the catalogue of a photography exhibition in Baden-Baden was dedicated to the photographer Else Raschdorf.

Still I refused to give up, though, given the artist's worldwide fame, I thought that I now stood little chance of succeeding. Rumors of were rife of lengthy waiting lists, shady deals, and even outright corruption. There were said to be seven prospective buyers for every painting that Polke had not even started. Attempts to make contact by means other than letter seemed to be ruled out, not least because, although my goal remained out of reach, I felt only sympathy for his wish, as an artist, to remain unattainable. A telephone call was out of the question for reasons of Proustian *politesse*, which demanded that calls be announced at least five days in advance by means of a *petit bleu*. After all it might disturb him while he was eating, sleeping, writing, painting, or talking to Raschdorf.

Instead, I made a habit of going past Polke's studio every couple of weeks, after I'd called on a patient who lived near the artist's atelier. Even when my patient died, it remained a favorite pastime of mine to cycle round the rectangular inner courtyard that was bounded on its left-hand side by a two-storey warehouse where (according to rumor) Polke sometimes worked and stayed. To the right were a number of rooms that were occupied by a Yugoslav family, but the rest of the building was given over to car mechanics, furniture restorers, scrap-metal dealers, and paint-spraying workshops. Since the stench of Polke's experiments with arsenic was mixed with the smell and the noise of this local light industry (the lethargy of the small community suggesting alchemical poisoning), it was never possible to say for certain whether the artist was working there. They came to tolerate me, growing used to me as an intruder who would cycle up and down only once, for no apparent reason, shouting out a friendly greeting but never knocking at any door. In the half-light some of these people looked like figures from Polke's paraphrases of Goya as they squatted on chairs or crates or old car seats. For me, they were well-known figures whom I came to like: I met shady second-hand car dealers, manual workers, my former cleaning lady, a man named Gohr who had lost his leg, a nursing sister, carpenters, patients, a man who was mentally ill, an unknown collector and Hermann Kreuz–but never a sign of Sigmar Polke.

Walter Benjamin was not the first to realize that everyone who is a collector leads a life between chance and systemization. Only posthumous research will reveal which of these was the dominant factor when I built up my own collection. I knew that Polke knew of my obsession. I knew he had not misunderstood what I meant when I let slip a saying of Beaumarchais's: "With goods of every kind, what matters is not to possess them but simply to enjoy them." And I also knew, of course, that Polke allows himself plenty of time for good paintings, just as every good butcher allows his beef to hang before putting it on sale. "Polke leaves his pictures sagging for months on end in a horizontal position, using them as containers for whole lakes of varnish," Harald Szeemann wrote at the time of Polke's Zurich retrospective.

To the freaks and monstrosities in that courtyard, my routine visits must have seemed like rounds of inspection made by someone planning to close down the building, though my aim was in fact to find a secret opening. And then, one day, in the course of one of those visits, I found the studio door ajar. I hesitated for a very long time before going up–not because I had already fallen down the steep steel steps on a previous occasion, one cold winter's evening, when they were covered in ice, sustaining extensive bruising (and nursing an injured foot for some time afterward), but because I felt inhibited, like Parsifal in the presence of the Grail. I remembered all of Gurnemanz's warnings–but even before I knew what I'd done, I was standing at the top of the stairs: *on frappe à la porte*. "Herr Polke!" Silence. "Pooolke!" Nothing. "Artist!" All was quiet as the grave.

I was turning to leave when I noticed him at the foot of the stairs. The artist himself, with Hermann, his Cerberus. He ignored the figure standing there, though I knew that he had seen me; such was my respect for art, he knew I would not have set foot in the room; and I knew that he was the only man who sees everything from behind his glasses but who does a good impression of someone who is blind. His camouflage achieved a high point here–no doubt he was hoping to see the collector flee empty-handed.

But then–he falls upon his works in progress, climbing over them, even destroying them, showing the nervous collector unfinished paintings, others that have been rejected, and yet others that are experimental. He destroys iconographic memorabilia in the collector's presence, his gestures and affected behavior evoking certain associations. He then proceeds to overturn them, disowning them and snubbing them, juggling with them and satirizing them, disillusioning the spectator; if he builds up one's hopes, it is only to dash them down again. (Hermann grins his approval, a knowing conspirator, helping to form and complete the little scene.) Politely but firmly Polke escorts his frustrated visitor to the doorway, which has all the time remained open. All at once we are back at the foot of the stairs, hurrying past the other occupants, who for years have observed my bizarre behavior and who suddenly all appear in the courtyard, as though on cue, to witness the scene. After running the gauntlet of their prying eyes, we come, as though by chance, to a warehouse. Fixed to the door–I can still remember it clearly–is a notice with the single word *Ruhrkohle*. The floor is unsafe and covered in clay, patches of oil, dirt, and a few dead mice; and *four paintings*, two of which have been arranged, as though by chance, to catch the light of a watery sun that filters through the grimy window: *entrons avec lui la cathédrale!* After this purgatory, stunned silence on my part, furtive observation on theirs, no one says another word. I look more closely. A seemingly insignificant movement to the four huge paintings (all of them similar in format) has the effect of an ordered rehanging: familiar fragments from Polke's work appear as part of their composition. Has the collector just been prevented from being the victim of a game of hide-and-seek that Polke plays with all who write about his works? No one could describe or catalogue these works in such a short space of time, no one could pass definitive judgement on them: at the very next encounter it would, I am sure be different. Polke never dips the same brush into the same pot twice. The pictures which are "simply found" and of which he speaks in connection with the creative process associated with his most recent works are–as I discovered on this occasion and as I shall never forget–the result of a brilliant act of calculation. Only now do I know when paintings are finished.

I go on secretly adding to my list of desiderata, though I know that these paintings will be packed up tomorrow and sent to San Francisco, after which they'll be seen in Washington and Chicago, and, after that, in New York. And on each occasion they'll be marked, "Collection of the Artist." Did anyone ever succeed in getting hold of Picasso's Picassos?

(translated from the German by Stewart Spencer)

First English published in exh. cat. San Francisco Museum of Modern Art (1990). First German published in Reiner Speck/ Martin Hentschel, "Polke! Polke!", Gesellschaft für moderne Kunst am Museum Ludwig, Cologne, 1992, pp.15-13.

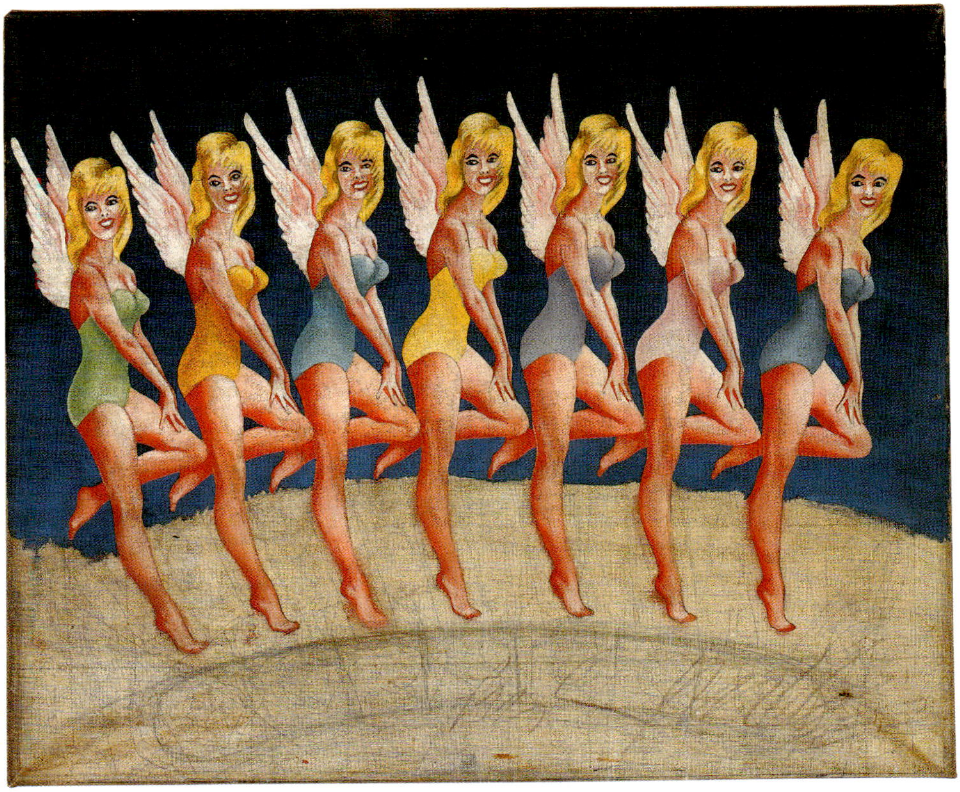

Sigmar Polke
Engel, 1962
49 x 60 cm
Collection Karin Polke, Berlin

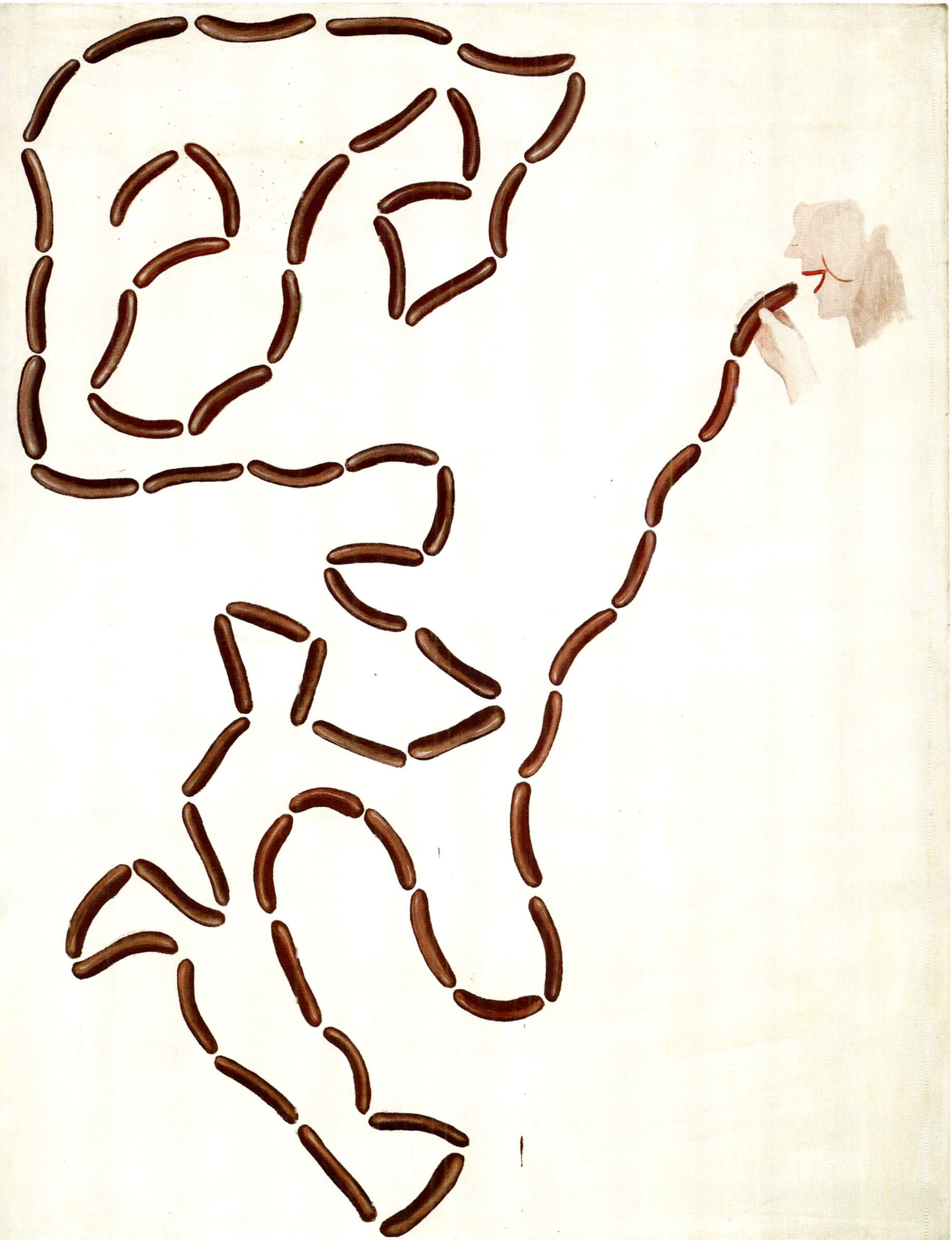

Sigmar Polke
Der Wurstesser, 1963
200 x 150 cm
Flick Collection

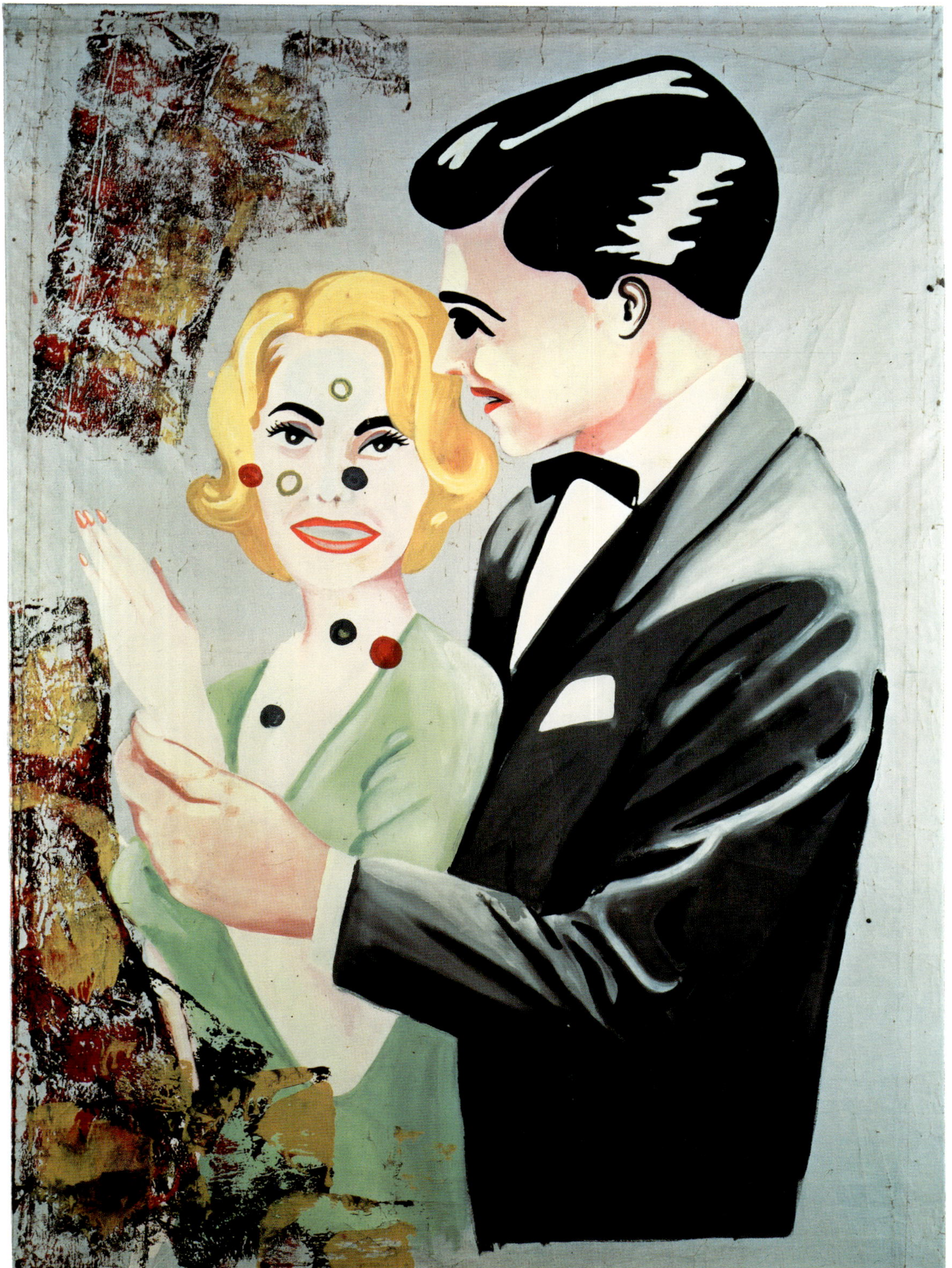

Sigmar Polke
Liebespaar II, 1965
190 x 142 cm
Collection particulière / Privatsammlung / Private Collection

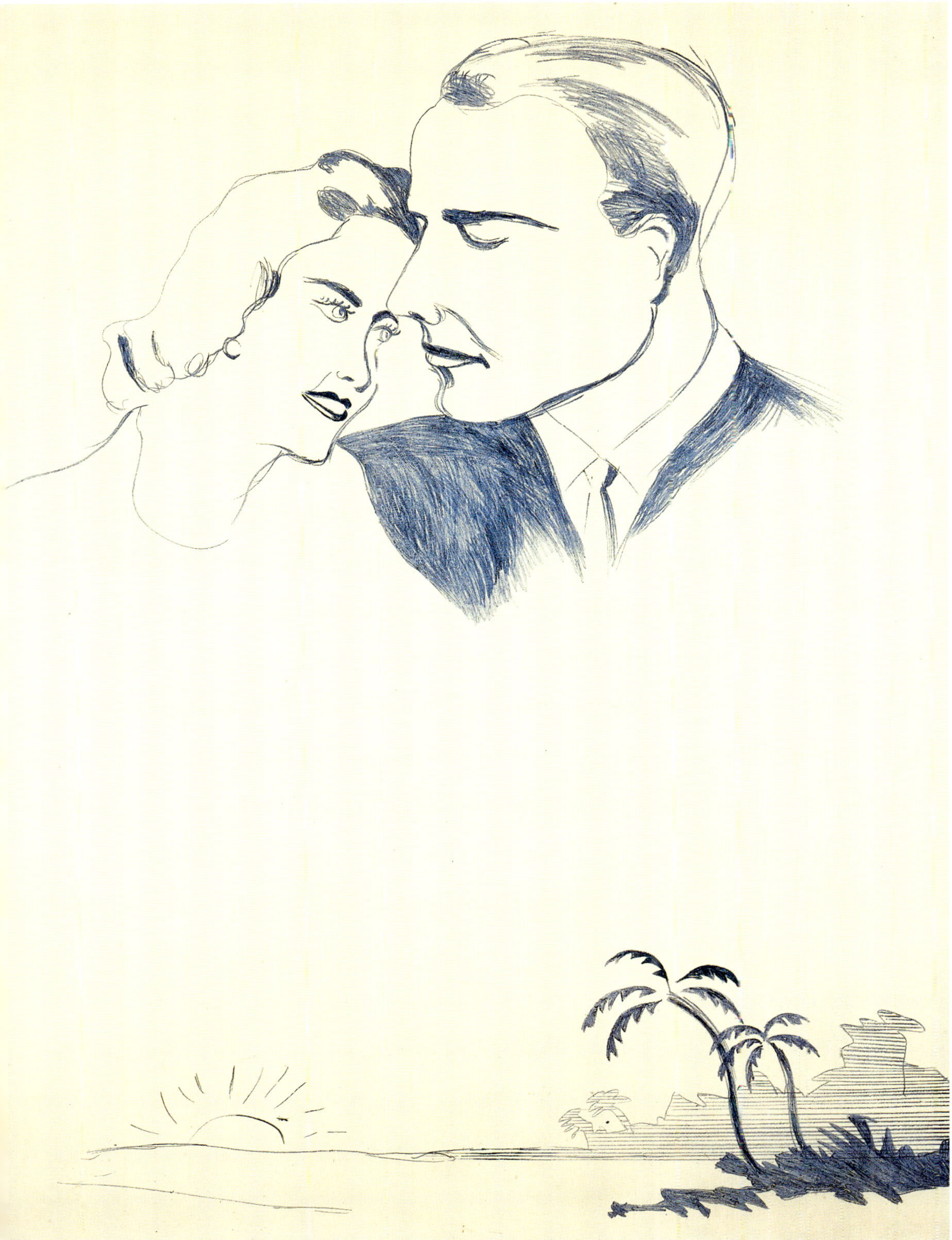

Sigmar Polke
Liebespaar, 1967
170 x 130 cm
Sammlung Speck, Köln

Alex Katz

The Big Chill

Massimiliano Gioni

> *... Meredith Monk's theater and music pieces. Godard's* À bout de souffle. *Andy Warhol's* Chelsea Girls. *Rainer Werner Fassbinder's* Die bitteren Trä nen der Petra von Kant. *Antonioni's* L'avventura. *Rudy Burckhardt's city and country films without acting. 1960s vinyl coats, white or black. Guillaume Apollinaire. John Ashbery's* Skaters. *Color TV. Ads. Football. Wide-angle Technicolor movies ...*
> Alex Katz interviewed by Richard Prince, 1991

An archeology of today filters through the blinds of Alex Katz's paintings: hidden between the creases of a dress, or lost in the waves of a hair cut, lies a contemporary history of poses and gestures, a philology of familiar expressions and in-jokes. But, just like family albums, Katz's paintings seem to say too little and yet too much: Katz's chronicles depict the cries and whispers of entire generations of Americans and New Yorkers, and yet his canvases are never anecdotal. Katz muffles the buzz of voices, the rustle of clothes, and the clinking of glasses, behind the thin surface of paint. And the sounds only reach us from afar.

Katz's conversation pieces–vast and hieratic as ancient frescoes–are always silent, his characters distant and enigmatic as sphinxes, for Katz is not simply interested in illustration or in description. He is neither a caricaturist nor an impressionist: instead his fascination with figures incorporates traces of both abstract expressionism and modernist painting, while also absorbing the pressure of popular culture, with its uncontrollable urge to transform images into empty icons. Thus, Katz's realism seems distilled through pure visibility: it has more to do with seeing than with representing.

Katz's paintings rely on a carefully posed contradiction: as he tries to approach his subjects, Katz preserves their unequivocal distance. He scrutinizes his friends and neighbors up close, while remaining almost impassible, strictly guarding his emotions. Immersed in a glacial, sharp, even light, borrowed from movies and television screens, Katz's choreography of figures attains metallic perfection, echoing the synthesis of form and color one finds in the work of Piero della Francesca.

Trying to do something that cuts across the span of art history while keeping basic and absolutely contemporary–the work of Alex Katz is as simple to describe as it is difficult to grasp. His gaze is after the dilated appearance of an infinite moment–a disciplined, almost frozen epiphany of the everyday, balanced between the frivolous variety of life and the terse solemnity of painting.

Absolute Beginners

MG: You started painting figures when everybody was mostly doing abstraction. How did it happen?

AK: It was primarily out of naïvety and instinct. I always thought abstract painting was very removed from the world you live in, and I wanted to make paintings for all people: I always hated the whole James Joyce thing, even though I was trained as a modernist painter. I studied Picasso, Braque and Matisse, but then I went to summer school and started working outdoors. The atmosphere and the teaching were very regional and traditional, but working outdoors also meant I started painting automatically, from the back of my head. That's how I found myself dealing directly with subject matter.

MG: So it wasn't in opposition to what you were seeing around you?

AK: No, I thought what I was doing was right, and I followed it. As I said, it was very instinctive: I didn't like regional painting at all, and I didn't like social painting either. And I wasn't into the American Modernist tradition. I could deal with French painting, but then there was Pollock, that made you forget about French art for a couple of minutes.

MG: Was there a friction between what you and others were doing in the 1950s?

AK: At the beginning my work was received in a totally patronizing way. People thought my paintings were okay, but they couldn't really take them seriously. And I was cut off from the older representational painters. The kids who were doing figurative paintings were mostly expressionists, and I wasn't interested in that. The other representational works were kind of retro, and I just wanted to make something that could look new. A lot had to do also with de Kooning I wanted to make a figurative painting that would knock one of those things off the wall.

MG: What was your problem with expressionism?

AK: It just didn't feel right: it was very excessive, and sort of macho. I wasn't comfortable with that.

A Little Bit of History Repeated

MG: History is a recurring theme in the writings about your work, which is quite unusual, especially in the 1950s and the 1960s, when everybody was trying to be radical.

AK: There was this ideal of modern art, as if it were something coming out of what had immediately proceeded it. "No carry no baggage", they said. I felt a different kind of pressure: I simply thought that the fifth guy who drips on the canvas is a conventional painter. The first guy who drips is a radical, the second is a follower, the third can be okay, but the forth and the fifth are just sticking to conventions. Any convention is the same, it doesn't matter when it starts. So I thought that an Egyptian sculpture or Matisse could be more interesting than dripping: to me history was an open field. You know, once in a while, a guy would come up and say: "Painting is dead?" And I would just say: "To whom? Certainly it's not dead to me".

MG: What did you look for in the past?

AK: You look at different people for different reasons. Like Manet, I think it's still very hard to unscramble your feelings about him. His imagery is outrageous and he still bothers people. At other times you look at the technique, like with Raphael or with Egyptian sculptures.

MG: How would you describe technique?

AK: Technique is what makes the image possible. In my work, I always want the image in front of the painting. My paintings are quite skilled stuff, all painted wet on wet: the technique is fancy, but the image goes first.

Interiors

MG: Why did you stick to images? Why did you stick to figures?

AK: I just paint what I see around me. So I started painting my friends, and looking for a gesture that was of my time. My time was people smoking and drinking, and I painted that.

MG: Is it important to know the people you are painting, to experience those moments directly?

AK: It's important to start from what you have right there, near you, simply because it's very hard to see something through your own eyes. We often see the world through some other visual form, but if you start from things that are around you, you have a better chance to experience them with your own eyes. Looking at the present makes it much easier: if you look too much at the past, you end up using the forms of the past.

MG: I often looked at your painting as if they were anthropological findings, a sociology of the everyday.

AK: A good painting is always beyond the artist's consciousness: different people see different paintings. When I'm working, my primary interest is to stick the paint on the canvas; I don't care about anything else. But all those other elements are there. Someone even wrote a book about the relationships between the people in my paintings: they studied the way they held each other, how they looked at each other, if they were happy or if the couples were just about to split up. That's not the kind of stuff I think about when I'm painting. I just paint the way they appear: if you get it right, everything follows. People stand there, and most of the time they look interesting. That's why you paint them.

In Cold Blood

MG: How would you describe the people in your paintings? Are they characters, motifs, human beings under scrutiny, or just friends?

AK: To me it's more like a movie: they are characters in a movie. When I started painting portraits in the 1950s, people called them cold, inhuman. Thirty years later, they started saying they were tender. Personally I always thought I was quite sympathetic to the people I paint, but my paintings don't carry those signs of excessive tenderness, simply because I'm not interested in that. My paintings are not trying to tell you a lot about themselves. I prefer a much more laid back attitude.

MG: Where do you think this attitude came from?

AK: I think it had to do with manners, social manners, and with the people around me. Art is always made by a group of people that you seem to represent. After all, I never thought I painted all my paintings by myself.

MG: Isn't that where the sense of detachment in your work comes from?

AK: That was the way I grew up. Back in high school we did something that was called cool dancing: we would move on every other beat, kind of stiff, almost still, dancing only on half times. And the whole style was about coolness: it was kind of conservative and cool. It was also part of the character of the country: there was something in the air, a restrained attitude that was taking the place of the overtly assertive macho types. That aesthetic stayed with me for my whole life, I think.

Time is on My Side

MG: There is always a precarious balance in your paintings, a strange tension between slowness and immediacy.

AK: Eternity is in the immediate moment. You just try to get an instant of consciousness, and that's it.

MG: Is that why your paintings have something photographic about them?

AK: I guess photography relies on the same assumption, that there is no other eternity beside the instant moment. But photography is past tense: painting, instead, is always present tense, even old painting.

MG: Do you think your work has influenced contemporary photography?

AK: I don't know. But I see a lot of it in advertising: they use my books. Once a guy even thanked me, he said he'd been stealing my paintings for his photos. Which is totally okay with me: I like the idea that my art can be useful sometimes. And I was influenced by all sorts of commercial media, so I guess now we are even.

MG: Is that how you got your cinematic angles?

AK: Actually those had more to do with the first color movies and with television. In America in the Sixties, TV was fantastic: they wanted to get the images right into your living room, so they really cropped them up close.

White Light, White Heat

MG: Where does the light in your paintings come from? There is a certain brightness, like an overexposure ...

AK: There was this guy who I met in the 1950s who said it was a light you could never see on earth. Maybe he had a point, but I thought I was painting the actual light. I've always been after the real light.

MG: Have you ever painted in different light, such as in Europe for example?

AK: Europe never really interested me, because even the light is very codified there. But I like the light in the South: I paint a lot in the Bahamas or in Mexico, mostly sketches and ocean paintings.

MG: Did the quality of light change as the scale of your paintings got larger?

AK: No, I think it's pretty much the same. It has to do more with color than with scale. I think my paintings got richer with time, but not very much brighter.

MG: It's still the same cold, dehumanized light, then.

AK: Humanism is just the way Europeans look at figuration, and it's something I don't really care about. To me painting is about the way things appear. When you start looking at things from that point of view, they always seem heartless and cold. I'm simply trying to get to the nature of appearance. We worry too much about what something means, and how it relates to humanity. And, every time you go that way, you weaken the whole idea of painting. Painting must try to get to the most mysterious thing, which is appearance.

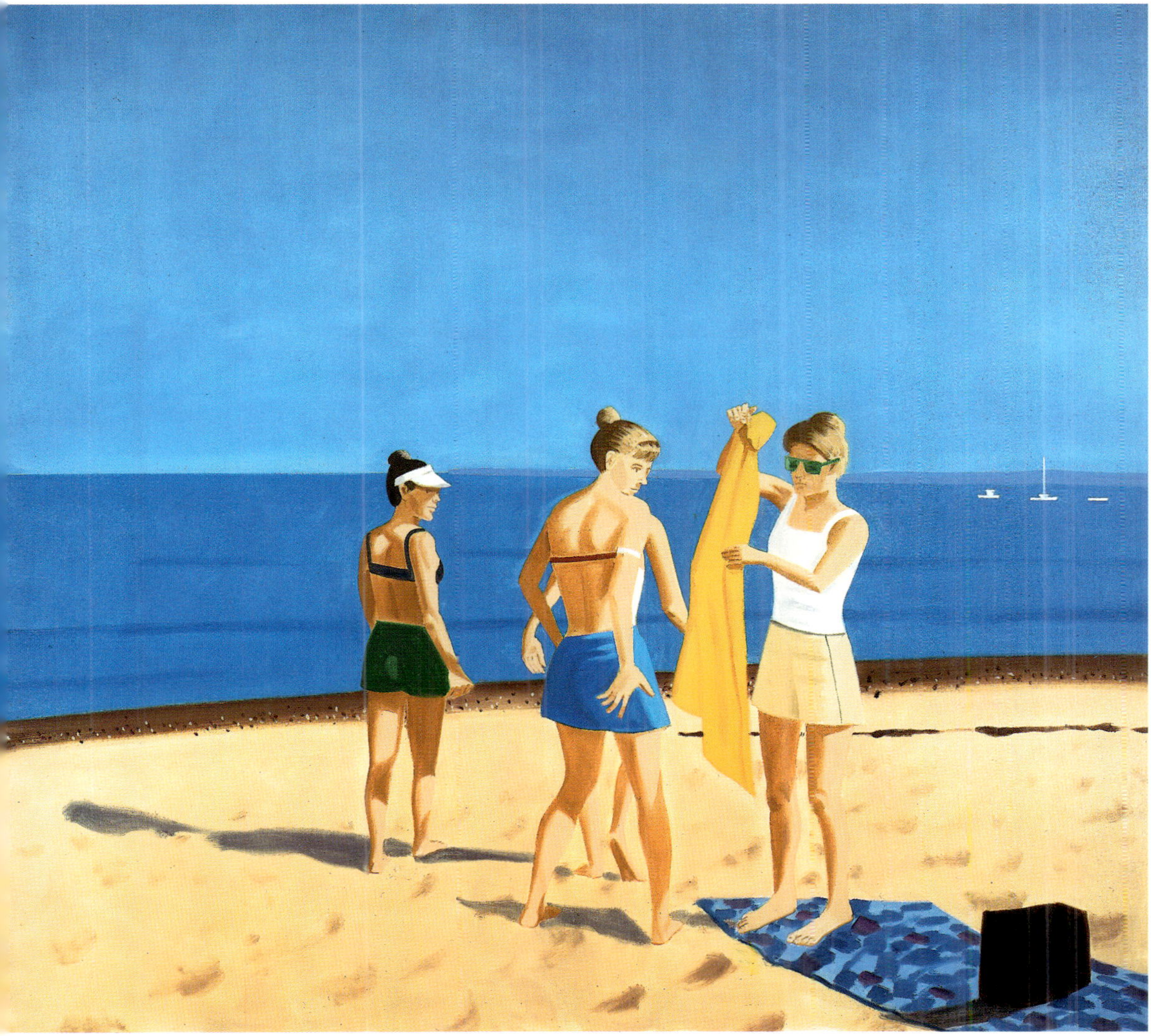

Alex Katz
Saturday, 2002
264,1 x 284,4 cm
Courtesy Pace Wildenste n, New Yo:k

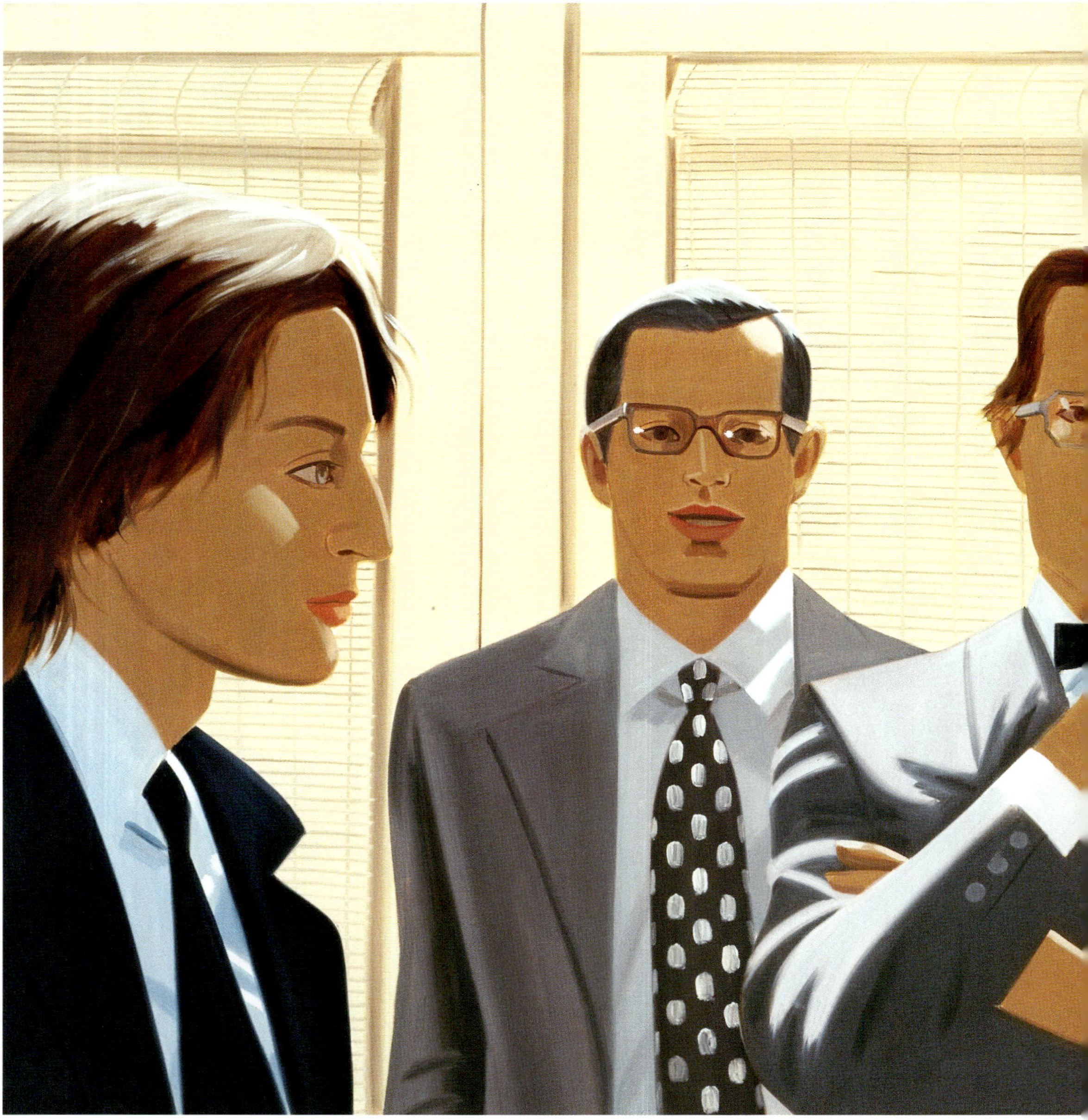

Alex Katz
Thursday Night # 2, 1974
183 x 366 cm
The Saatchi Gallery, London

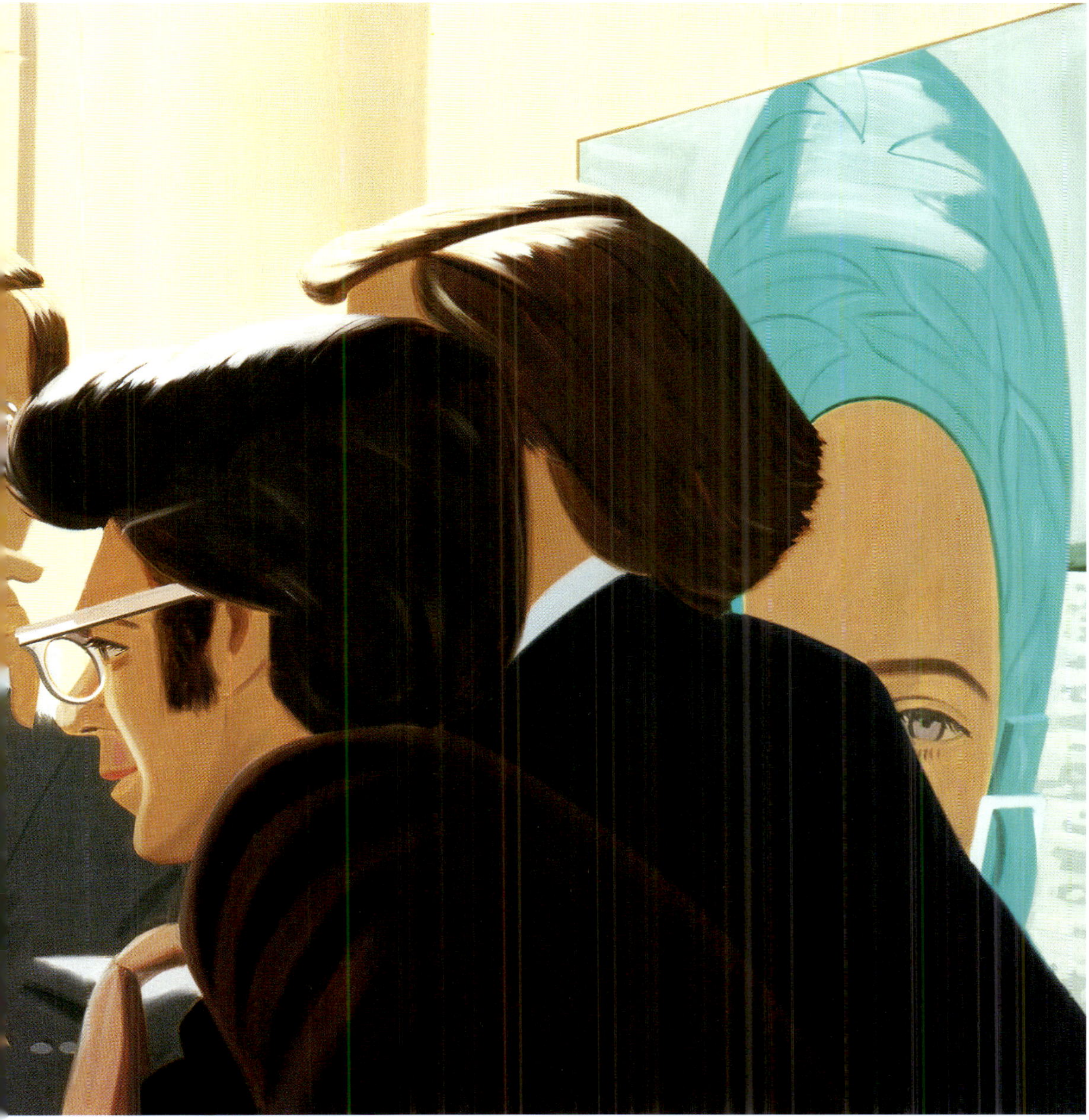

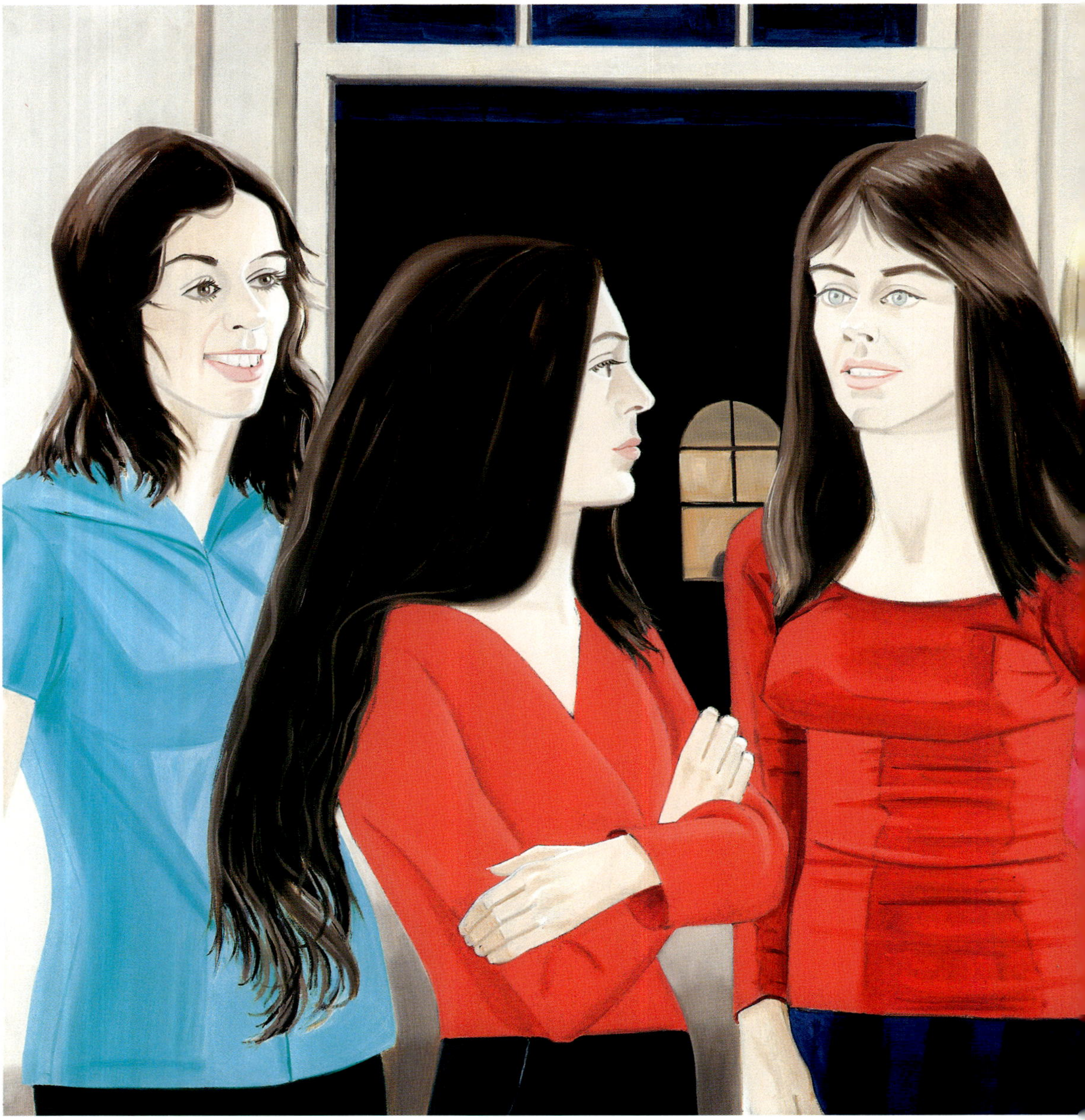

Alex Katz
February 5:30 P.M., 1972
183 x 366 cm
Collection de l'artiste / Besitz des Künstlers / Collection of the artist, New York

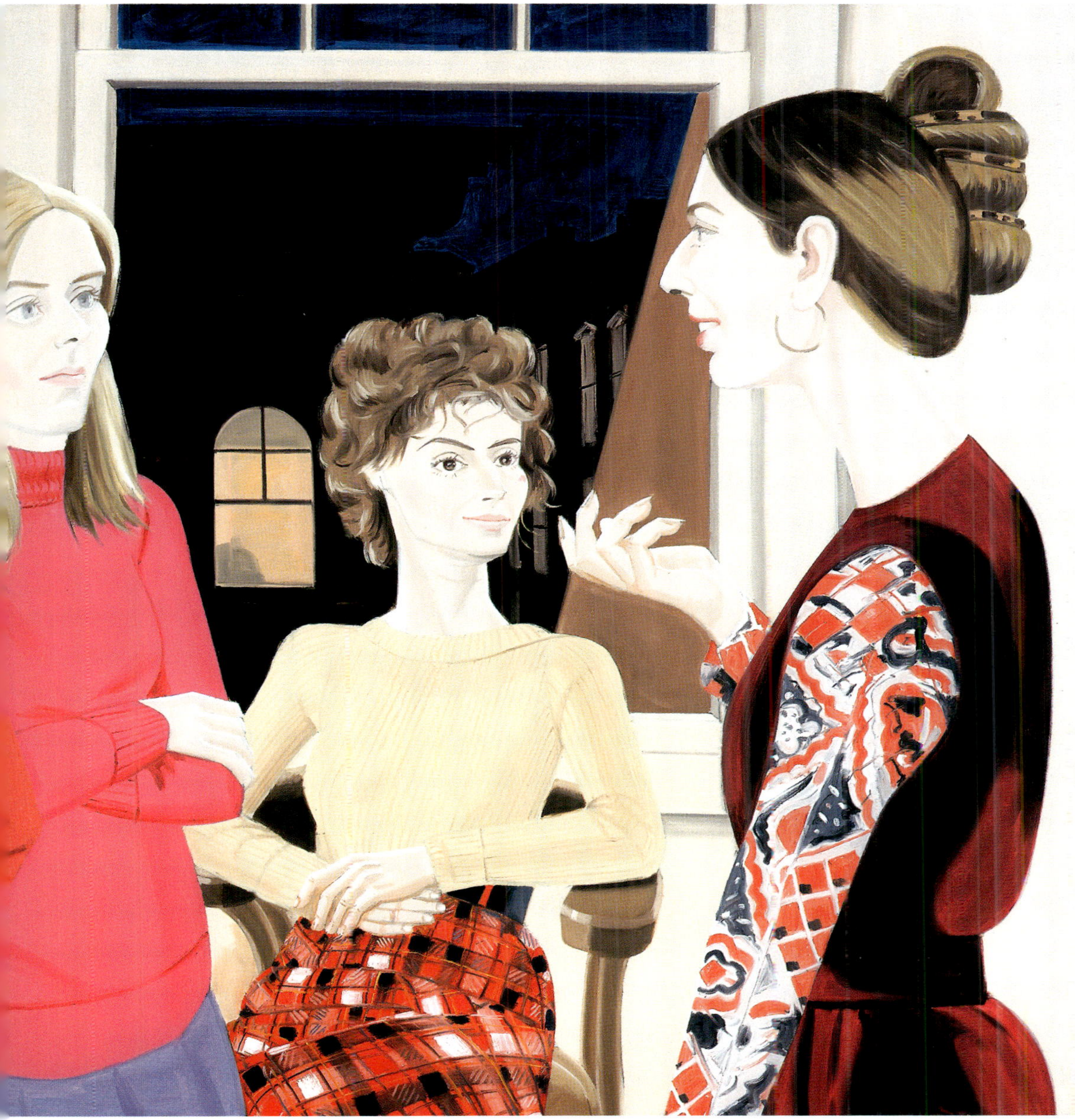

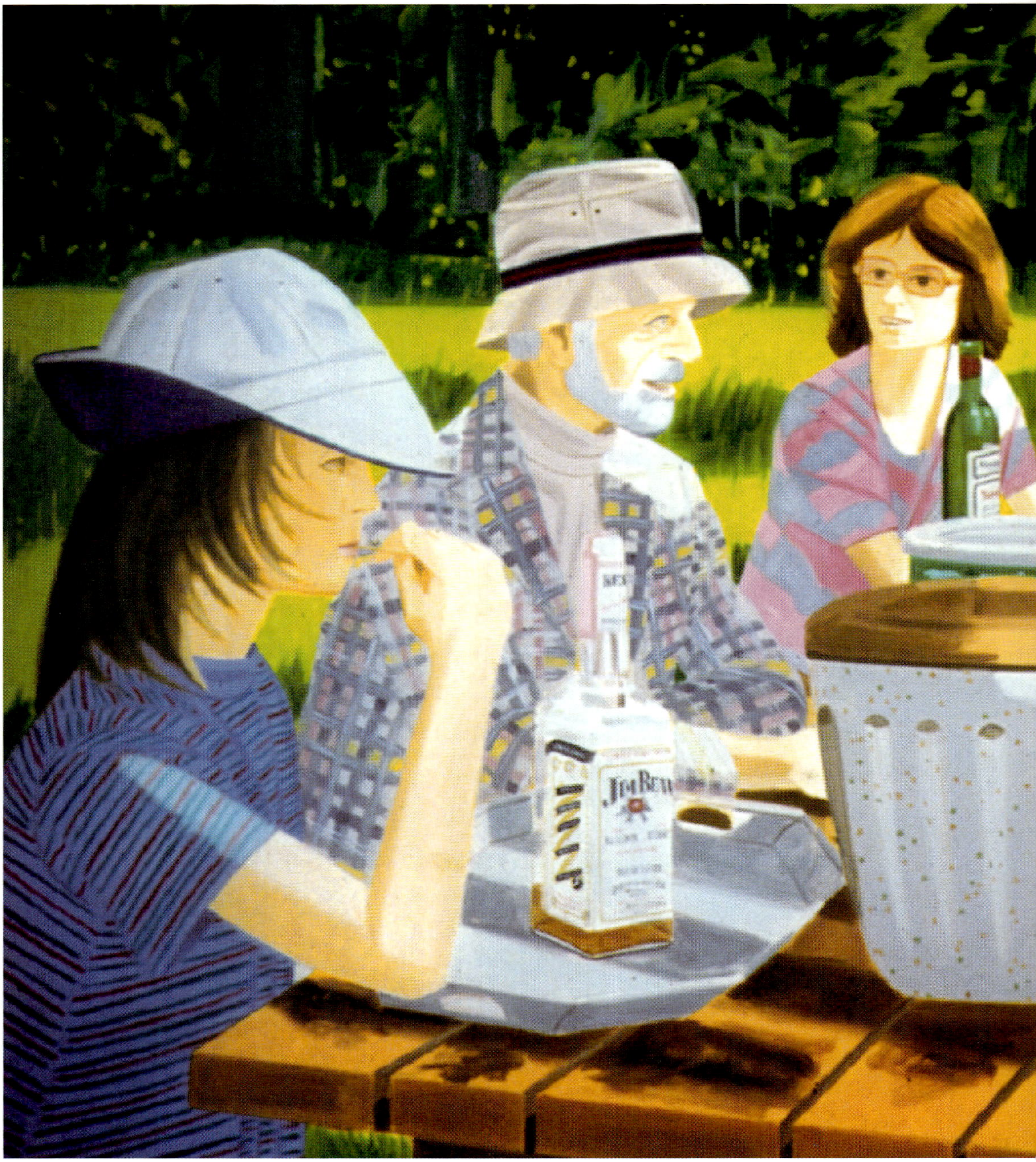

Alex Katz
Summer Picnic, 1975
198,1 x 365,8 cm
Courtesy Marlborough Gallery, New York

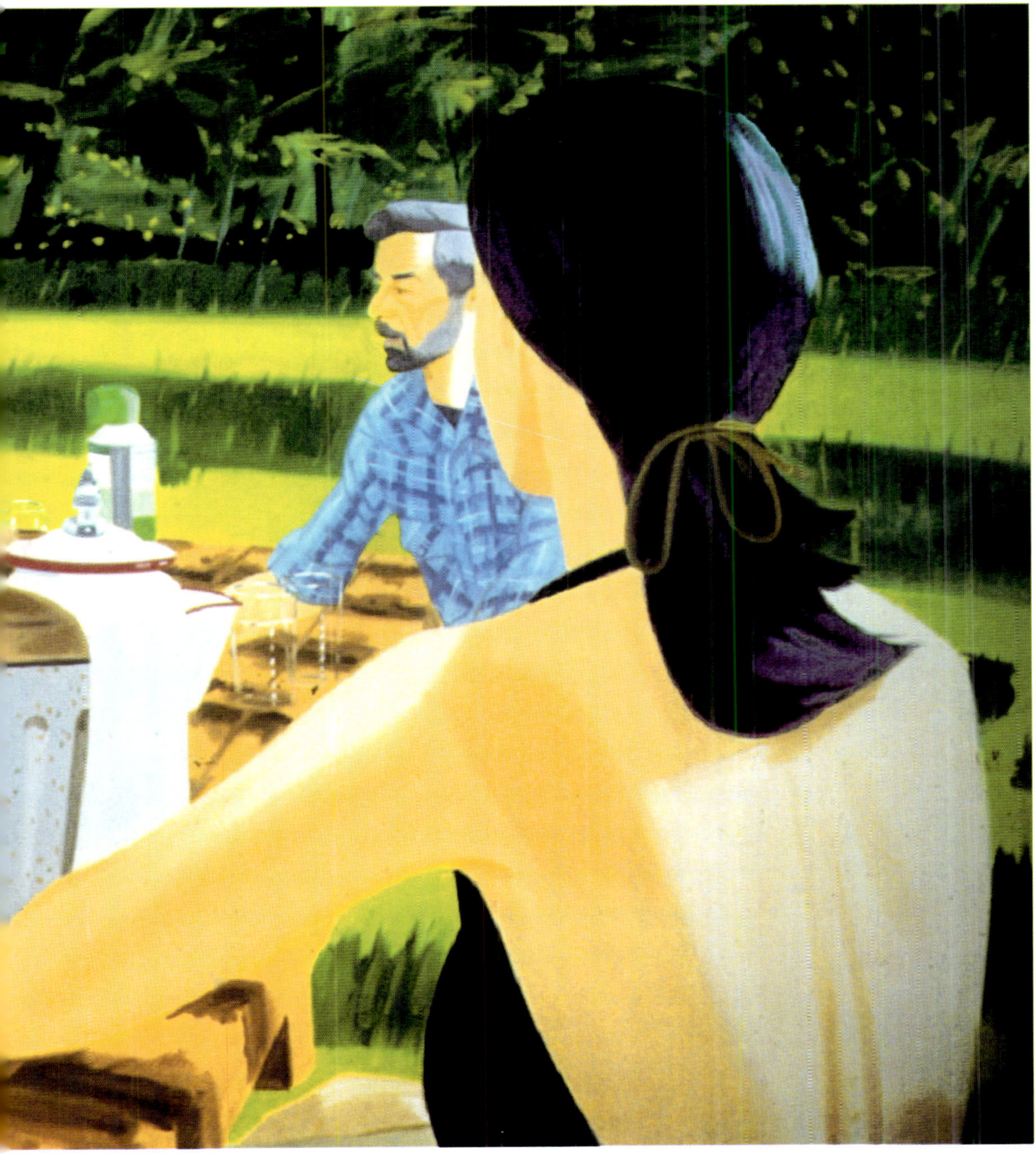

Martin Kippenberger

Of Painters and the Painted

Parisa Kind

We see a comical male couple from behind. The one on the left is walking arm-in-arm with his shorter, heavier friend. Both of them are walking or standing on a busy sidewalk and give the impression they've just been bar hopping and need each others' support because of the alcohol level they've reached. The taller of the two is the artist Martin Kippenberger. Knock-kneed, with ears that stick out, looking a little helpless, and wearing an ill-fitting suit: this is how he presents himself to the public. The motif described here is from a 12-part series of paintings by Martin Kippenberger from 1981 entitled *Lieber Maler, male mir ...* ("Dear Painter, paint me ..."). Kippenberger had these paintings executed according to his precise specifications by a professional cinema billboard painter, although the paintings are not signed by Kippenberger or the billboard painter. Painted in oil on canvas, these works either represent the artist himself or seemingly meaningless motifs, such as ballpoint pens in the breast pocket of a jacket, a still life with an Arabic jar of Nivea cream or an autograph card of the actor Hansjörg Felmy.

Another self-portrait also shows Kippenberger in an unfavorable light. He is wearing underpants that are reminiscent of diapers. His head is in profile and shadows darken his face. His stomach is protruding way out. His back is round and his hanging arm seems twisted. He's holding several rings of sausage or thick tubes in his hands, and their weight seems to be pulling him down. On the left is a parakeet perching lightly on a man's finger, and on the right is an oversized spring. "Gehobenes Statistenprogramm besser als Asmagruppe" it says in big letters above these motifs. Misspelled in the German, the English equivalent would roughly translate as "Refined extras porgram, better than as(th)ma group" [sic]. The entire picture is enveloped in a diffuse gray and magenta light, which lends the composition a surreal, nightmarish quality.

Kippenberger shows himself to the viewer from the front–and at the same time from an entirely different side in another painting from the series *Lieber Maler, male mir ...* Like a heroic film star from long-forgotten times, he poses with a cowboy hat and a coat with fur collar against a wall covered with posters celebrating the thirty-year existence of the German Democratic Republic. Whether as a cineaste hero or as someone deformed and pitiful, Kippenberger displays a perception of himself which oscillates between megalomania and self-destruction. To emphasize this, he slips into different characters which he stylizes until they almost become clichéd.

At the same time, this series explores the artist group called the *Neue Wilden*, or the "New Wild Ones". Since the eighties, this group was known for its "rediscovery" of traditional easel painting using oil and figurative motifs, which were until then considered unmodern. With this series of paintings, Kippenberger set himself apart from the emotionally charged neo-expressionism of the *Neue Wilde* by hiring other people to paint for him and consequently avoiding of the process of actively producing the paintings. He demonstrated his rejection of the *Neue Wilde* but at the same time used their media. In 1980 he announced, "I have forbidden myself to paint. I will now have others paint. (...) This is how I will contribute to full employment in the Expressionist city of Berlin."[1]

Even though the artist explored other media and themes in the same period, he repeatedly returned to portrait painting. Also in 1981, he produced a 21-part series entitled *Bekannt durch Film, Funk, Fernsehen und Polizeirufsäulen* ("A celebrity in film, radio, television and police stations") Kippenberger painted stylistically varied portraits of actors, politicians, and musicians such as Peter Maffay, Harald Juhnke, Ronald Reagan, Leonid Brezhnev, Yasser Arafat and Helmut Schmidt – people known from the mass media landscape. He modeled them after photos and caricatures from the everyday media that he reworked to a massive collection of known faces. In the Cold War era, Kippenberger not only indiscriminately placed politicians from the East and West side by side. He also put them next to stars from German popular culture and thus chose a theme in the eighties that today has become part of daily life: the medial construction of identity, which reduces people in the public eye to an image outside their various motivations

In 1976 Kippenberger worked on his first series of paintings, *Uno di voi, un tedesco in Firenze* ("One of You, a German in Florence"). He painted them during a one-year stay in Florence after leaving the art academy in Hamburg without graduating. This series consists of about seventy black-and-white portraits, each measuring 50 by 60 centimeters, of randomly selected people based on Italian newspaper clippings and photographs. It was Kippenberger's goal to paint as many paintings required to make the stacked stretchers measure 189 centimeters, his own body height. But he stopped at 179 centimeters. Even though these paintings do not include a self-portrait of Kippenberger, the artist made himself an integral part of the series by relating the production volume of his work to his own body, which in this case served as a unit of measurement. Additionally, the failure of the artist was stylized into being seen as a positive experience. In an exhibition catalogue, Kippenberger and his artist friends Albert Oehlen and Werner Büttner later propagated "expanding knowledge through failure."[2] Kippenberger thus ascribed a productive energy to the failure to reach a set goal and the resulting disappointment.

Not only does Martin Kippenberger depict personalities from public life in his work, he doesn't shy away from adopting art historic "classics" either. His last series was produced in 1996 and was entitled *Das Floß der Medusa* ("The Raft of the Medusa"). The work consists of 24 oil paintings, 14 lithographs, and a tapestry.[3] It is inspired by the famous painting by Théodore Géricault from 1818-19 by the same name (*Radeau de la Méduse*) that depicts a true story from the 19th century. When a ship called Medusa sank on the open sea, the rich people among the shipwrecked passengers first brought themselves into safety by climbing into the lifeboats. The others built a raft out of the remains of the sinking ship that could accommodate about 150 people. This raft was pulled by the lifeboats. But when the chance to reach dry land became slimmer, the rich people cut the lines to the raft in order to increase their own prospects of survival. When the raft was discovered by a ship almost two weeks later, only fifteen of the original 150 people had survived. In his painting, Géricault recorded this moment between tragedy and hope in the painting.

Taking his idea for the series from this story, Kippenberger had himself photographed by his wife, the photographer Elfie Semotan, while imitating the various gestures and facial expressions of the victims. These photographs, in which he identified with the tragic fate of the individuals, served as models for his oil paintings and lithographs. Working from many detail studies of Géricault's painting over the course of several years, Kippenberger created a single work of art which he then dissected into its individual parts again, making himself into the protagonist of a new body of work.

As an artist Martin Kippenberger always worked on various projects at the same time and used different styles concurrently. This means that contrary to conventional art historic concepts one cannot speak of a stylistic development within his oeuvre. He constantly alternated between the figurative and the abstract, and showed no preference in terms of media. A distinct characteristic of his art practice is his disregard for the difference between the abstract and figurative which should not, however, be mistaken for the modern tradition that uses the combination of this pair of opposites as a theme.[4] He was not interested in developing himself artistically in figurative painting. Rather, he used the possibilities of figurative painting in order to lend expression to his perspective of himself and his environment with exceptional clarity and lightness.

He also criticized the artistic concept of differentiating between the various disciplines by refusing to commit himself to any one genre of art. There is hardly an artistic discipline that Kippenberger did not explore. Among other things, he played and sang in bands, built sculptures and made objects, produced countless drawings (on hotel stationery, among other things), painted pictures or had them painted, photographed, curated exhibitions, produced (large-scale) installations, edited artists' books, and worked as an entertainer. Collecting art was another activity that he viewed as part of his artistic practice.[5] In his versatility he did not hesitate to make the work of other artists part of his own art, such as transforming a painting by Gerhard Richter that he had bought into a table by attaching table legs (*Modell Interconti,* 1986). His topics range from the banal to the sublime, but never give the impression of being haphazard. Martin Kippenberger's works express an attitude that cannot be categorized under the standard "zeitgeist" clichés. Many of today's generation of artists have found inspiration from Kippenberger's expanded understanding of art.

(translated from the German by Susan Schwartz)

Endnotes

1 No author : "Ich habe mir Malverbot erteilt, ich lasse jetzt malen," in *Berliner Morgenpost*, Berlin, August 7, 1980.

2 Werner Büttner, Albert Oehlen, Martin Kippenberger: *Wahrheit ist Arbeit,* exh. cat. Essen (1984), p. 29.

3 The reconstruction of the raft is incorporated in the tapestry.

4 Martin Prinzhorn, "Jenseits der Diskursanalyse: Der Kurator Kippenberger," in *T.K. (E.T.) Tiefes Kehlchen,* exh. cat. Vienna (1991), pp. 41-42.

5 Martin Kippenberger, *B – Gespräche mit Martin Kippenberger,* Ostfildern, 1994 p. 18.

Kippenberger: A Life in Images

Blaženka Perica

On the occasion of the fifth anniversary of her brother's death, Susanne Kippenberger wrote an article entitled "Who Was My Brother?"[1] and concluded "an anarchist and a gentleman, an *enfant terrible* and a child."

This description is surely more comprehensive and apt than if one attempted to define Martin Kippenberger in the conventional sense as a fine artist. "Every artist is a human being" he claimed, countering the myth of the Beuysian maxim that "Every human being an artist." The strategy of Kippenberger's art was to examine and ironically reversing the familiar.

Through the confrontation with other artistic models such as Polke and Richter, and even Géricault, he provoked a rearrangement of his environment and–as Zdenek Felix said–"liberated art from pure aestheticism." But through the self-productions that he stylized as a program for his life, he worked on the "Kippenberger legend," which has become a paradigm for younger artists today.

Art served him as a vehicle for identity just as his ego was not too good to constantly be examined as an art object. It was between these poles that he presented his self-portrayal of the question of the connection between art and life, and he made the transcendence of these poles his goal.

His self-portraits and portraits cannot therefore simply be categorized under the topics "realism versus modernism" or "figuration versus abstraction," even though they unquestionably represent an important position within the context of this exhibition, which is dedicated to such questions. His works are part of a more complex position in which narcissism and a special sense of self-irony occur side by side. In Kippenberger's work, self-mythologising becomes an effective attack on the mythology of the artist in general.

(translated from the German by Susan Schwartz)

Endnote

1 Susanne Kippenberger, "Wer war mein Bruder?," *Der Tagesspiegel,* March 3, 2002, p. 3.

Martin Kippenberger on Art

I renew my faith in people every day, and that takes a lot of effort. The disappointment is all the harder to take. They just don't get it. For example: art is not made anymore, it's just observed. [1]

I'm not a "real" painter, not a "real" sculptor; I just look at all that from the outside and sometimes intervene to add my own two cents. I'm not provoking, I'm constantly trying to appease. [2]

I just happen to be a living vehicle, and a very clear one at that. Others might be better styled and more focused on the project at hand. In my case, role-play wouldn't work because I don't have a style. Until I realized that my style happens where the person is, and this is conveyed through actions, individual things and deeds, and decisions, and this is what makes a story. Art is always viewed in retrospect anyway, from the outside, hardly ever in the moment when it is created. I would say the period is twenty years. After that you can see what kind of effect the work, or the artist, really had. The decisive thing is what people will SAY about me then. Did I inspire a good mood or not. That's what I'm working on, so people can say, Kippenberger was a good mood. [3]

As I said, today collection itself is part of my production. Unconsciously, I'm sure I'm still quoting others, but normally I now take a "fresh, pious, happy, and free" approach to my own production. Or it might be partly determined by what my assistants put together for "my production," according to Kippenberger's instructions, but with their tools and skills they are working on "my view." I realize that it's becoming increasingly important to become completely clear what context you are living in. To define this, to develop your own network, is a decisive task for an artist. This is what I'm working on now. It's not just about establishing this connection, it's also about making it visible and indelibly manifesting it. Creating a connection for posterity - and don't forget that posterity includes tomorrow. I want to influence the way people debate about this time in the future. [4]

Seeing the things you see on the road differently. And - very important! It can't be educational! That's the special art. It can't be too heavy-handed. To accomplish this, you have to use your own life as a base. But first you have to get to that point. It has nothing to do with the art market anymore. [5]

I am a traveling saleman. I deal in ideas. I do much more for the people than just paint them pictures. [6]

I am not an easel-kisser ... I actually have nothing to do with painted pictures. That's why one of my solutions for this problem has been to let others paint for me, but only in the way I need it, the way I see it. [7]

Endnotes

1 Martin Kippenberger, *B – Gespräche mit Martin Kippenberger*, Ostfildern 1994, p. 14 (translated from the German by Susan Schwartz).
2 op. cit., p. 15.
3 op. cit., p. 15 f.
4 op. cit., p. 18.
5 op. cit., p. 23.
6 Angelika Taschen, Burkhard Riemschneider (ed.), *Kippenberger*, Köln 1997, p. 49.
7 op. cit., p. 54.

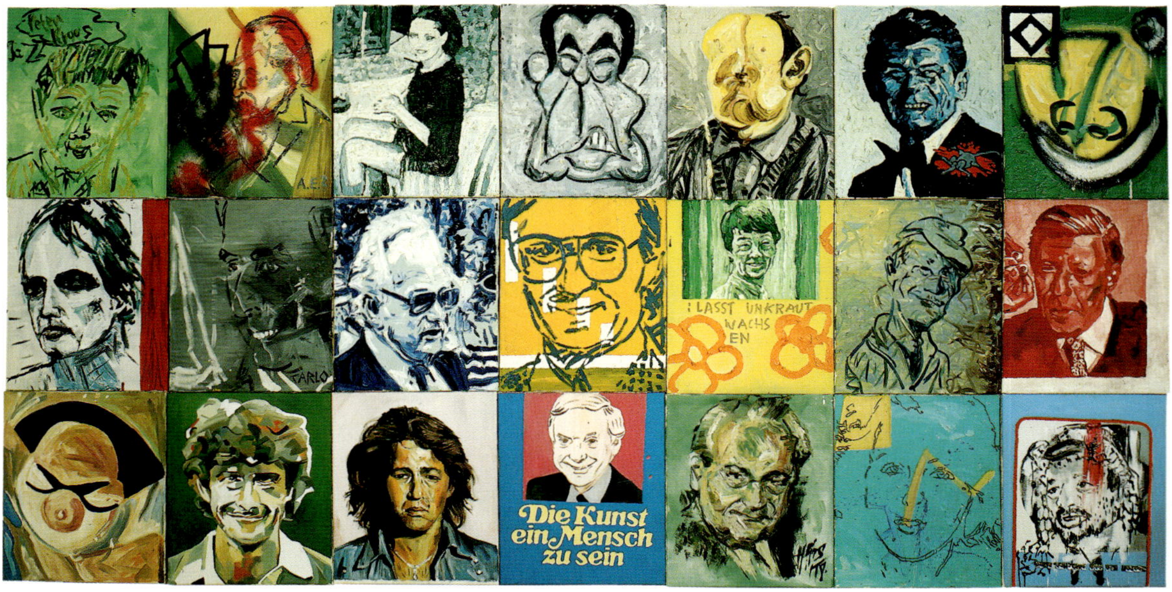

Martin Kippenberger
Bekannt durch Film, Funk, Fernsehen und Polizierufsäulen, 1981
21 parties / Teile / parts. Chacune / je / each 60 x 50 cm
Grässlin Collection, St-Georgen

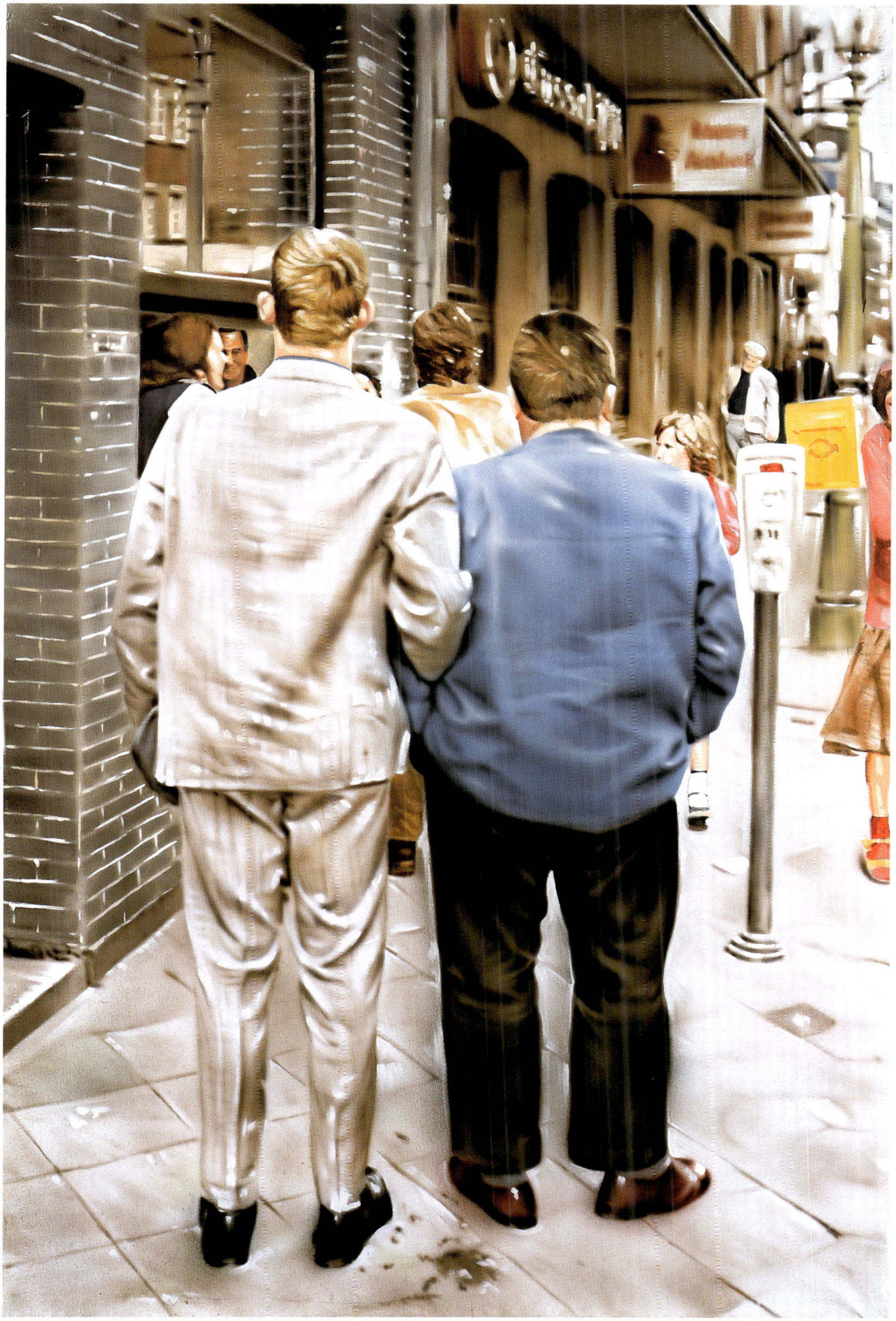

Martin Kippenberger
Ohne Titel (aus der Serie *Lieber Maler, male mir*), 1981
300 x 200 cm
Nachlass Martin Kippenberger, Köln
Courtesy Galerie Gisela Capitain, Köln

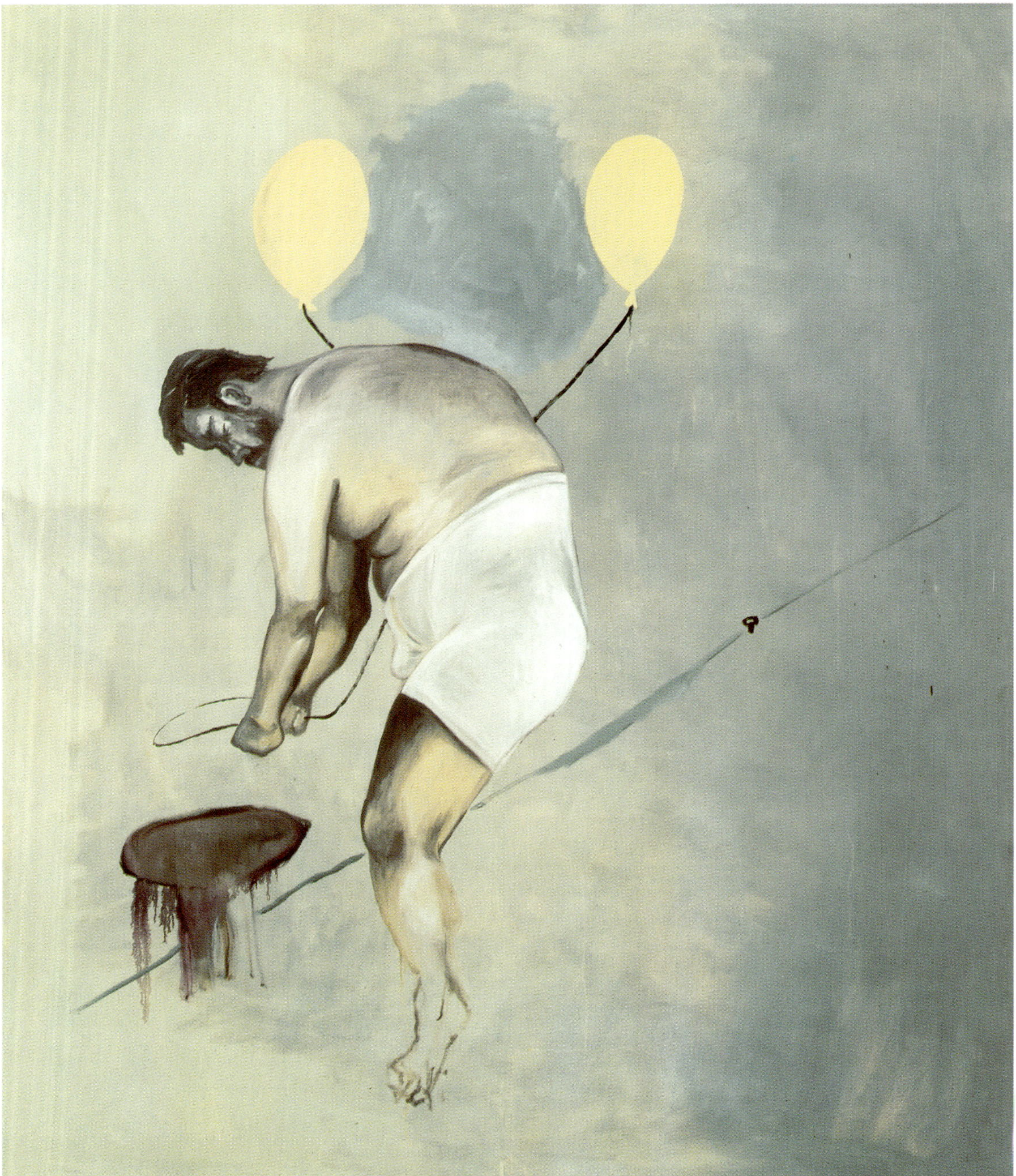

Martin Kippenberger
Ohne Titel (Selbstporträt), 1988
241 x 202 cm
The Dakis Joannou Collection, Athens

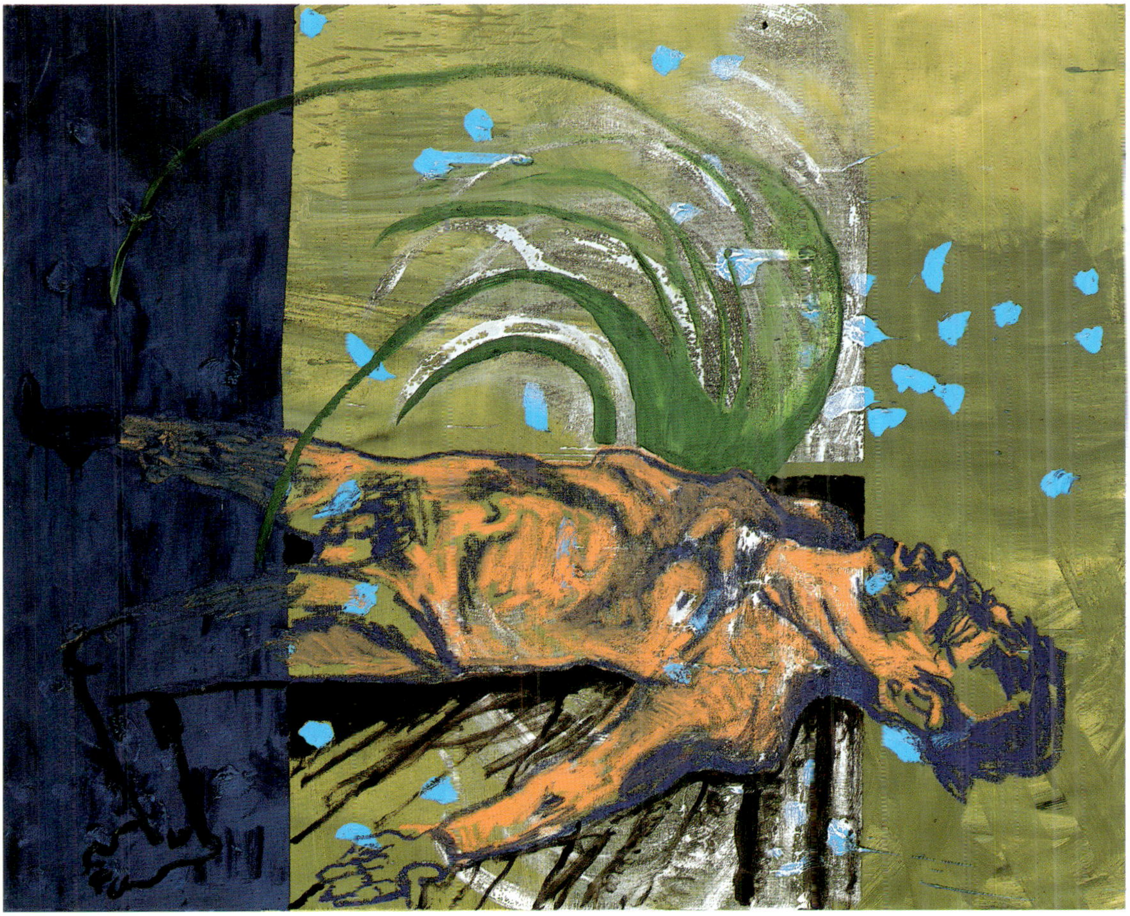

Martin Kippenberger
Ohne Titel (aus der Serie *Das Floss der Medusa*), 1996
150 x 180 cm
Collection particulière / Privatsammlung / Private Collection

John Currin

Alison M. Gingeras

Sticking out like a sore thumb from a loosely affiliated group of figurative painters that came to age in New York during the early 1990s, John Currin has always embraced his status as a polemical figure. His early work was read as a caustic, anti-Modernist transgression of the conventions of form and content in good painting. From his first series of portraits depicting fictional women "of a certain age", Currin's first reception garnered epithets of "kitsch" along with accusations of debasing his human (often female) subjects.

The term kitsch is rarely uttered let alone vindicated by Currin, though he confronts these negative readings by describing his work as an affirmative quest for an authentic cliché. "Clichés themselves are sort of a poor man's form of great art ...They're a recurring truth ... Ultimately, I think what I do is find a cliché and try to believe in it, try to get where I don't laugh at it." [1]

While drawing energy from the crudeness of the cliché, Currin's early portraits should not be interpreted as mocking a social class or as a misogynous exaggeration of female sexuality. Instead, Currin has constructed a complex, layered visual practice based in a sincere quest to, as Laura Hoptman has put it, "challenge set notions of radicalism and reaction, avant-garde and the academic," both in terms of painting's history and the contemporary subject matter that he depicts. [2]

Shifting away from this first reception, Currin seems to have made a long journey from "bad" to "good" painting. Never satisfied with a middle of the road stance, Currin has pushed his more recent engagement with the history of painting to virtuoso extremes over the course of the latter 1990s. While his early series were often rooted in low culture photographic sources, a string of canonical names–Fragonard, Cranach, Manet, Boucher, Tiepolo, Courbet–compose the extremely visible references in Currin's recent art historical vampirism.

Not to be confused with postmodernist pastiche, these recent works always contain a very contemporary element that acts as an anachronistic nudge. These paintings seem suspended in a constant state of imbalance in terms of the agglomeration of historical references and a range of subject matter rooted in the present tense. Referring not only to the uprooted, interchangeable nature of images in contemporary culture, Currin uses this seamless layering as a strategy to affirm the vitality of the practice of painting today, while simultaneously acknowledging the death of "the culture of painting" at large.

Endnotes

1 Keith Seward, "Boomerang," *John Currin: Œuvres/Works, 1989-1995*, exh. cat. Fonds regional d'art contemporain Limousin, Limoge (1995), p. 44.

2 Laura Hoptman. *Projects 60: John Currin, Elizabeth Peyton, Luc Tuymans.* Exhibition pamphlet, Museum of Modern Art, New York, (June 24–September 8, 1997).

AG: I thought we should start by talking about this group of paintings chosen for the exhibition, maybe beginning with the relation between older works and more recent paintings ...

JC: In the older works, I always think I am in this situation where they are seen as being about sex. Recently I have been trying to make paintings less about sex, and more about lust. I wanted to make the "sex" so up front that it would be neutralized.
I saw this movie where this guy is looking at his dead mother in her coffin in a funeral parlor, and he leans over to touch her face, and when he does the skin of her face starts to come off on his hand. He tries to put the make-up back on, but the more he touches it, the worse it gets. This scene is kind of like the palette knife paintings I made, where the bodies of the female subjects were rendered with a brush, but the faces were thickly painted with a palette knife. It was like a panic-ridden situation where the more you try to make it better, the more you damage the face.
I've also stopped making these

social class paintings like I was making in the early 1990s, thinking about different indicators of class, background …

AG: Works such as *Ms. Omni* … the middle aged, menopausal women paintings?

JC: Yes, the ones where there are obvious signs of plastic surgery and very specific social postures. There has been a rupture between these first paintings and more recent work because I want to think about more intimate situations that were less dependent on these social codes. This is why I was interested in these literally damaged faces made with a palette knife. These women always had fictional faces. What replaced the obvious social class markers were other kinds of signs, such as large breasts—like in *Dogwood*. Their faces weren't masks. Wherever you see palette knife paintings it either means "cheesy" landscapes in a thrift store paintings. Or it is like in Courbet, when he is using a palette knife to paint things that already look like "paint". It's like a doubling-up where the thing can become real …

AG: Where did you go after these palette knife paintings such as *Dogwood*?

JC: I started to paint this series of nudes on dark backgrounds.

AG: The ones that are often referred to as the "Cranach" paintings: the full body female nudes on a black background standing in classical, Venus-like poses?

JC: Yes, but they aren't Cranach. First, my technique is nowhere near Cranach, and second, they aren't really in that style.

AG: Is that important? The legibility of the art historical references and styles that are present in your work? Your work has so often been read as a sort of art historical vampirism …

JC: That may be the case, but that is not what it is about. There is no deeper meaning to be found by locating and naming my references. There may be references, but I am referring to them because I like them, I am not using them for content.
The way I am presenting the figure is coming from Cranach. The faces of these nudes, have a particular kind of liveliness that also comes from Cranach. But the black background is much more Italianate. But there is also a strong reference to Hans Baldung Grien (1484-1545) as well as other things going on in these paintings.

AG: Underlying my question is something that I have noticed about a shift in the reception of your work. In the beginning, most readings of your work focused on kitsch, bad painting, and the supposed debasement of your subject matter. Since your works have started to have a more promiscuous set of references to the history of painting, there is also much more virtuosity in your technique.

JC: When I was in art school, I remember seeing Kippenberger's paintings, and I thought they were really good. It seemed like the only place left to go. How to make painting look different.

AG: I think it is important to make a link here between your interest in bad painting and cliché, and more recent development towards "art history" your work …

JC: I've developed an ability or habit where I don't see how old something is. In fact sometimes 19th century paintings seem a lot older than 16th century paintings. You can almost still see the ideology present in those 19th century paintings, and that makes them seem old. Just like white patent leather boots and a miniskirt seem older than some of the old paintings I am looking at because we can measure the age of them against our own lifetime. In a funny way, my interest in Modernism when I was young is dated in the same way. modernism has lost its authority abstraction has lost its authority to me. It's like not feeling guilty about not going to church anymore. I just stopped worrying about what modernism thought of me … That was a big deal.

AG: Is this ability to create distance with modernism specific to painting today? Can the practice of painting provide a place to digest this baggage—whether in terms of ideology, formalism, or just in terms of images?

JC: Painting has become a sort of abject practice. It is not intellectually valued. The intellectual elite looks at painting as a gesture for right wing, rich people. Painting doesn't fit well within the leftist vision; I am not sure what they control, the university certainly, and in New York at least, they control to a certain extent what is artistically acceptable.

AG: Well, this Left position regulates intellectual capital …

JC: They are the clergy basically. They control who feels ashamed and who doesn't. They are the big shamers in our society. Painting has never been used to scold people, or to cast aspersions in the way that other forms of contemporary art making does. The way that museums have come to favor forms such as video art as being forms that are "good for the public", or as "educational". Painting is not a progressive form. It has too big a history to be used in this way.

AG: In a way, you seem to describe a paradoxical situation by acknowledging all this historical baggage in the history of painting while simultaneously purging or digesting this same history—without turning your own painting into a heavy ideological object. There is a fine negotiation between this historical weight and the kind of subtle complexity that resonates with contemporary culture in your work.

JC: Part of the problem is that painting is too complex. Even if you are a shitty painter any mark you make is going to have a lot of referential weight attached to it.

Part of the trick is to let that happen, and to let all the references happen without worrying about them.
I am not interested in manipulating the references. I don't intend them to make a trail that is supposed to lead you somewhere. I am conscious of them as they happen, but the trick is to try to put yourself back into some kind of ignorant state.

AG: I think this "ignorant state" you're speaking about echoes what you once brought up when you spoke about your desire to believe in clichés.

JC: Painting is like eating. I like this, I don't like that. It remains a mysterious activity to me and occasionally it becomes something bigger ... not every time.

AG: To bring up the classic form/-content issue, I think that the sexuality in the paintings seems to function in a similar way to this art historical vampirism. It is often "over read" ...

JC: The "sex" is partially a buffer against the art historical and ideological references. It annihilates all those concerns. Lust and desire offer some freedom from politically navigating what your art form means. Of course, these are regressive desires. I like double negatives. This sexuality is a metaphor for painting in a way.

AG: The works from your last exhibition at Andrea Rosen Gallery (Autumn 2001) seem to offer a synthesis between your older concern with the layering of charged socio-cultural codes and your more recent delving into painterly virtuosity.

JC: When I first started making these "synthetic" portraits, it started with the idea that the act of representation is an act of exploitation. I started these during the rise of a certain photographic practice, epitomized by the work of Cindy Sherman. At this time, the feeling was that painting was like lying. It was exploitative. The idea of a free-standing subject that sprays out meaning from a central source was under attack. The whole "French theory" attack on authorship was the accepted truth ... and I just couldn't disagree more. I was pissed off. My whole life I thought I wanted to be an author and when I got to school, I learned that this was a bad thing. It was like being a Nazi or a Fascist. So these fictional portraits I first made were like a first attempt to be really explicit.
I was trying to react against these accepted truths in the academy as well as a type of layered painting.

AG: The kind of "postmodern" painting that was okay to make at that time ...

JC: Yes, all these layering of images were supposed to neutralize the authorial charge. This kind of painting supposedly negated the author by using conflicting visual languages; they paid lip service to the idea that meaning is constructed by "interpretive communities". Culture is made by interpretive communities or consensus and not by individual geniuses.
I wanted to make work that came directly from the center. I wanted to make a situation that purged my guilt about this context. I started to make these paintings of middle aged, somewhat pathetic women put into situations that were sort of embarrassing. My idea was that they were divorced. There was a feeling of exploitation—not in a sexual way, like a gigolo—but that there was transference of blame on the victim. I thought of these women as harlequins, the way that Picasso looked at circus people as a corny way of talking about his own ruthlessness. In the same way, I thought of those women as irrelevant people. The way I was perceived of as a painter in our culture. These women had no more sexual value, they were only interested in culture, like museum patrons. That's why I gave them these short haircuts ...

AG: These paintings signal early on your artful manipulation of all kinds of visual and social codes ...

JC: These women mirrored my situation as a painter, the political problem of being a painter. When I was making these paintings, my validity as an artist was greatly challenged. People would say, why do you paint? Is painting possible? Michael Asher did institutional critique so didn't this negate the possibility of painting?

AG: It is a constant refrain that is sung in a cyclical fashion: "painting is dead"?

JC: On one hand painting is very much alive, but I definitely think that the *culture of painting* is dead.

AG: Is this necromancy, then?

JC: The culture is dead, but the practice is alive. I think that painting is still a very basic urge.

AG: When we started to talk about your early interest in "bad painting", it seemed that it was important to you to use that as a vehicle to stake a certain position – perhaps even a political one. Is there another position that you are announcing in your current engagement with this albeit dead painting culture?

JC: It gets me over the technical progression in my work. What I noticed as I got older, is that a lot of people tried to avoid the process of getting better. They try to "keep it real". You have to become middle aged. The rock and roll thing doesn't work in art, and it doesn't even work in the music industry. Eventually these old rockers want to have orchestras playing behind them, and they start to make songs about being faithful to their wives. It returns to this question of authenticity in our culture. It is the way that our culture continues to posit this authenticity on Black people, like in movies for example. In America, Black people are generally supposed to be imbued with qualities of honesty, simplicity, and authenticity—a connection to the street. Black people never get to stand for complexity, intelligence … it is something that is epidemic to Hollywood representation of Black people.

AG: I am looking at this painting here in the studio you are finishing, depicting a gay male couple brazenly looking out from the canvas. Do you think there is still a taboo about dealing with identity, especially if the identity of the depicted subject is not the same as the author?

JC: I am interested in this image of a male homosexual couple because it is about power, especially in our culture right now. It's an image of an elite, and I don't mean to say that in a derogatory way. It's not a neutral image culturally, but visually it's a very neutral image. It is an image of repose and comfort and of a confident culture. That's always under attack. The comfort of painting—painting as a culture, that is what pisses people off. What I am generally referring to is the *guilt* about painting, about pictures—this is part of the death of painting culture. There is still this feeling of shame in the late twentieth century about painting pictures, visual pleasure; these are still off limits.

AG: What about desire in all this? I am thinking about your intense relationship with this dead painting culture. Can you talk about love and desire in your work?

JC: Well, I am definitely not in love with the viewer. There is an assumption that the artist is supposed to put their arm around the viewer and both step back to admire this thing that you've made. I always thought it should be the opposite, it should be an *antagonistic* relationship. The painting should come between the viewer and myself.

AG: This conscious use of antagonism is a major thread that is shared by all the artists in this exhibition. Do you share this observation?

JC: Just making paintings today brings some of that antagonism with it. Painting has now been forced into an antagonistic position, despite what might be seen as a revival over the past six or seven years in the contemporary art scene.

AG: To explore this antagonism question further, there is a genealogical line that is being drawn—Picabia, Buffet, Polke, Katz, Kippenberger—that traces various types and strategies to provoke a sense of antagonism. For example, there is certain fluidity between good and very bad painting in your paintings in the exhibition …

JC: I keep wondering why painting is devalued so much. Part of the reason is that most of contemporary painting is terrible because the culture around it—apprenticeship, visual connoisseurship—is dead. It was easier for me ten years ago to see where painting stood as it was pretty much completely dead, but today it is a little more difficult. I am trying to think more about the connoisseur culture of painting. The overt political part of my work is no longer a primary motivation. It is getting really good at it that makes me more uncomfortable. That is where I am going. In a way, I guess that today it is a political act to get good at painting.
I don't have the guts to do it yet, but I would like to make a painting that had terrible drawing in it. In a way, it would be more offensive than sexual imagery or an overtly political image.
That is why I am interested in being in this exhibition with Bernard Buffet. He is a terrible painter that is not even interesting. Yet on another level, it is interesting! His painting is just awful; it makes me feel personally bad. But feeling that bad, *that* means something. It seems to me that Buffet offers a place to go today. After all this technically "good" painting I've been doing, I am getting newly interested in bad painting.

AG: It might be a back door …

JC: Exactly. The back door is the kind of Steely Danification of my painting. There is an analogy between starting out as a garage band—or as a bad painter. Underlying both is the sexual energy that is penned up in the garage band and in bad painting. But when you become a dusty, balding 40 year-old, you have to start thinking in different terms. It is about being honest. Turning to Buffet is like coming full circle. Ironies never exist for long. Given time, they wash away. Even if sappy music can be recuperated as being cool, in the end it is still sappy music. This analogy relates to what I am currently thinking about in terms of absolute quality, absolute ability and connoisseurship. The art establishment is against all kinds of absolute scale—in terms of aesthetics, morality, taste, etc.

AG: Our conversation has been referring to questions of representation, subject formation and identity politics. What is the difference in terms of *cultural impact* between taking a painted image and a photographic image as source material?

JC: If I make a photograph it brings up the whole problem of the subject having to really "exist" … It's always that this idea that the real version is out there, when it comes to the photographic image.
I wanted to make those "Cranach" nudes precisely because there was no real version out there in the world. This issue is like the prurient aspect of photographically based pornography—the great thing about porno is that when you look at the image, it is like sniffing the panties, because there are in fact real naked ladies out there. That is the tantalizing aspect of porno. It is a record of someone who was actually in a room with a flesh and blood naked lady and some light-sensitized film. It is this vicariousness that is tantalizing with photography.
In painting, this vicariousness doesn't exist. There is no recording of something that is real. With the deliberate sexual content of my

paintings, I was interested in there being no record, no other reality possible than this painted image.

AG: It sounds like this absence of an index of reality also gives you more freedom to push the envelope, so to speak, in terms of the subjects you were constructing, making up ... Isn't this is a more risky political position because you can't hide behind the "real"?

JC: Yes, there is this idea that I am controlling these images and their subjects completely.

AG: Is it too reductive to try to find something that underlies all of these different subjects you paint? Is there a recurring characteristic? A set of typologies?

JC: There are always burdened women in my work. Maybe that's the recurrent theme. And I am sure that there must be a specialized genre of pornography that has the burdened woman as its main fetish. Stressed out women—in one form or another. I am sure I am not the first painter to make metaphors about my art practice through the figure of the woman.

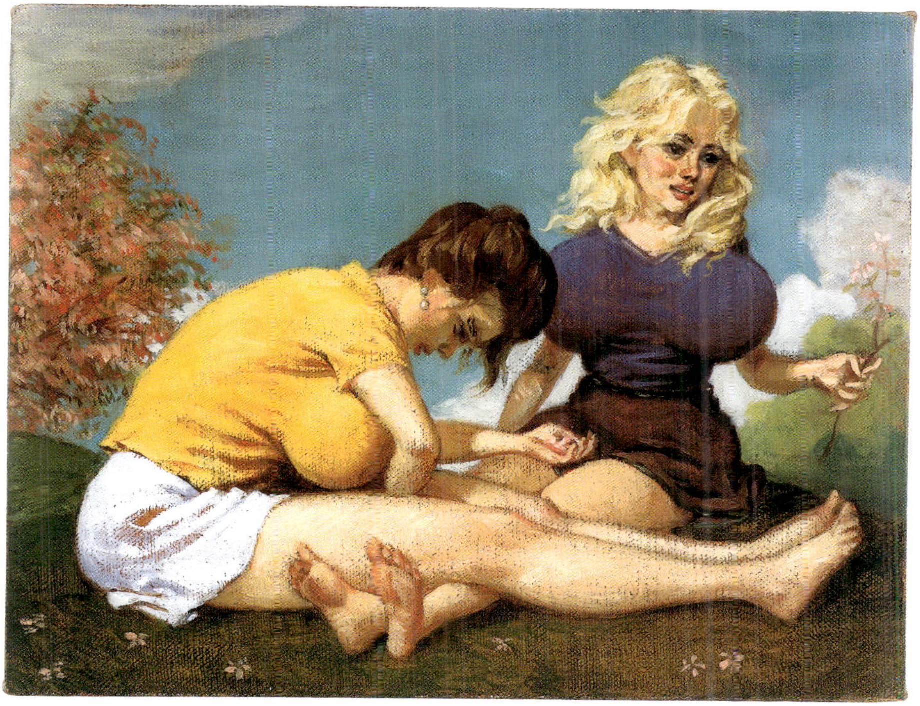

John Currin
Dogwood, 1997
27,9 x 35,5 cm
Collection particulière / Privatsammlung / Private Collection, New York

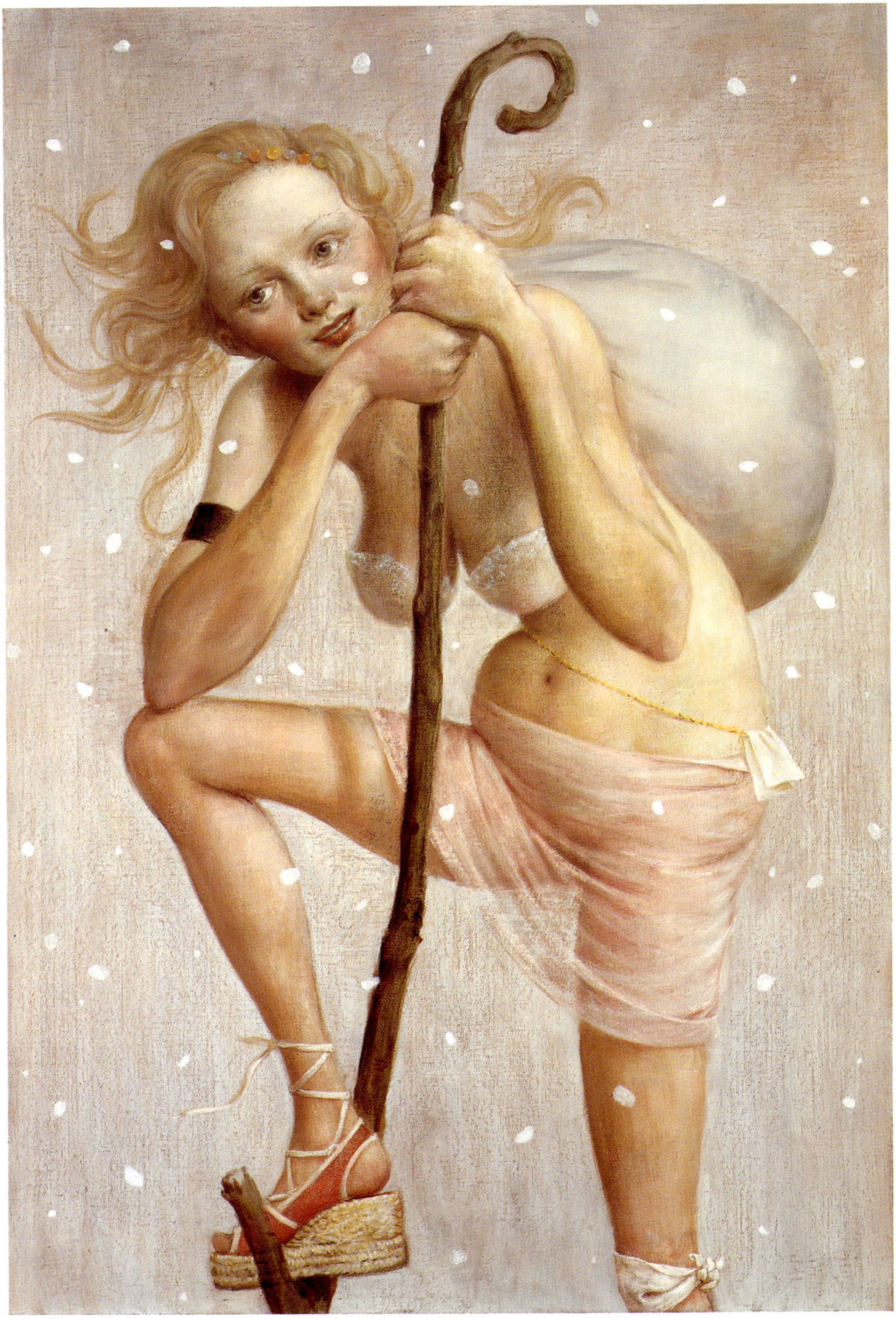

John Currin
Sno-bo, 1999
121,9 x 81,2 cm
Collection particulière / Privatsammlung / Private Collection, New York

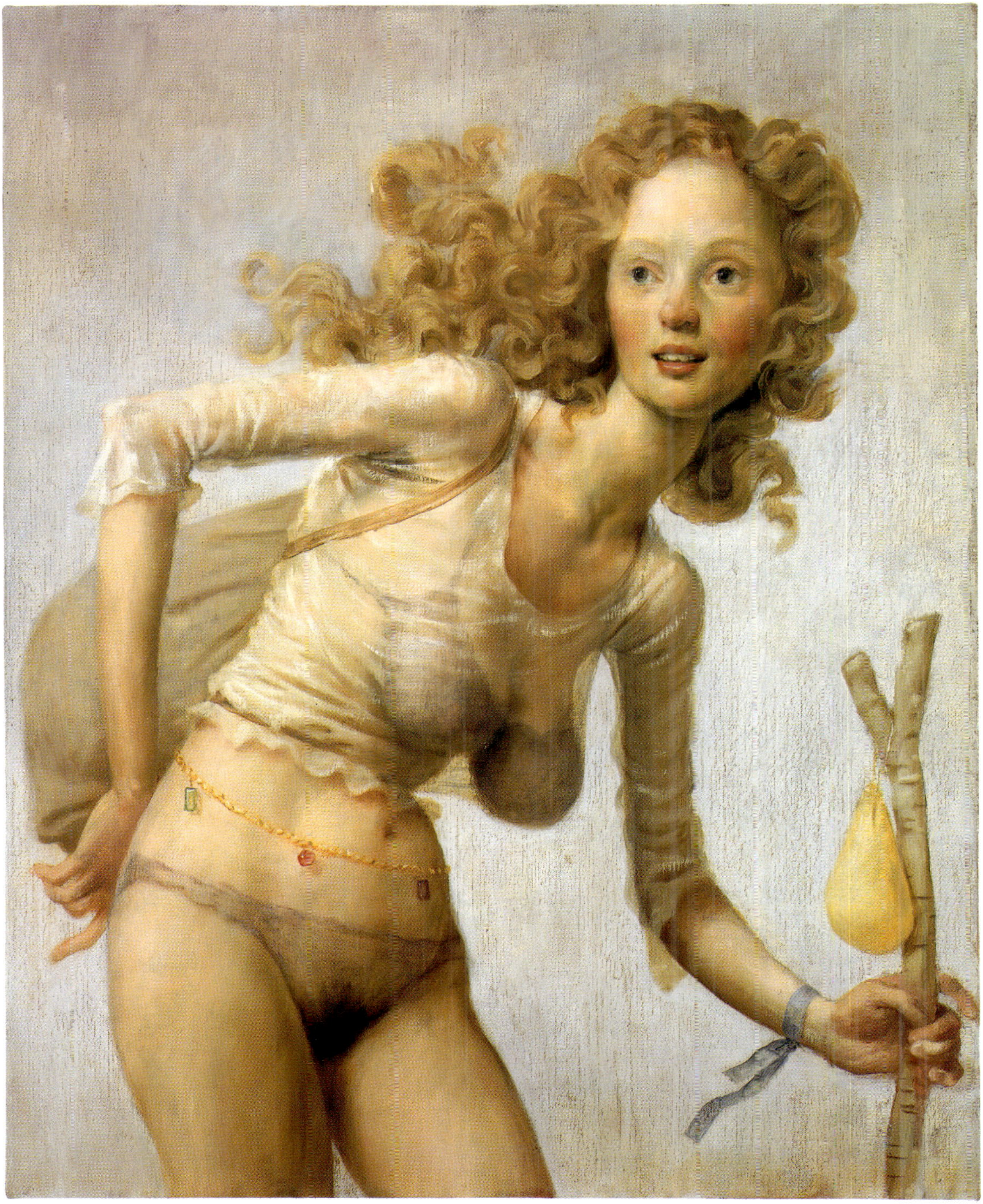

John Currin
The Hobo, 1999
101,6 x 81,2 cm
Museum of Contemporary Art, San Diego,
purchase, Contemporary Collectors' Fund

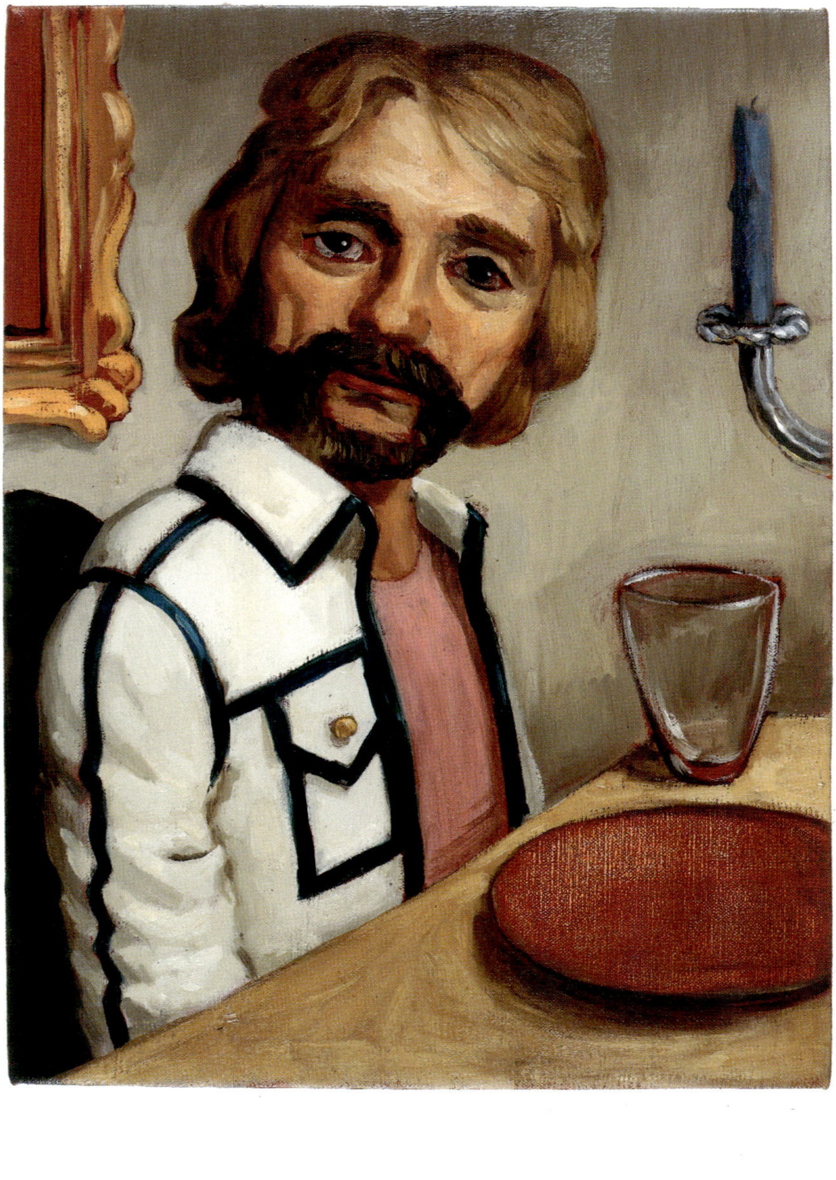

John Currin
The New Guy, 1994
40,5 x 30,5 cm
Collection particulière / Privatsammlung / Private Collection

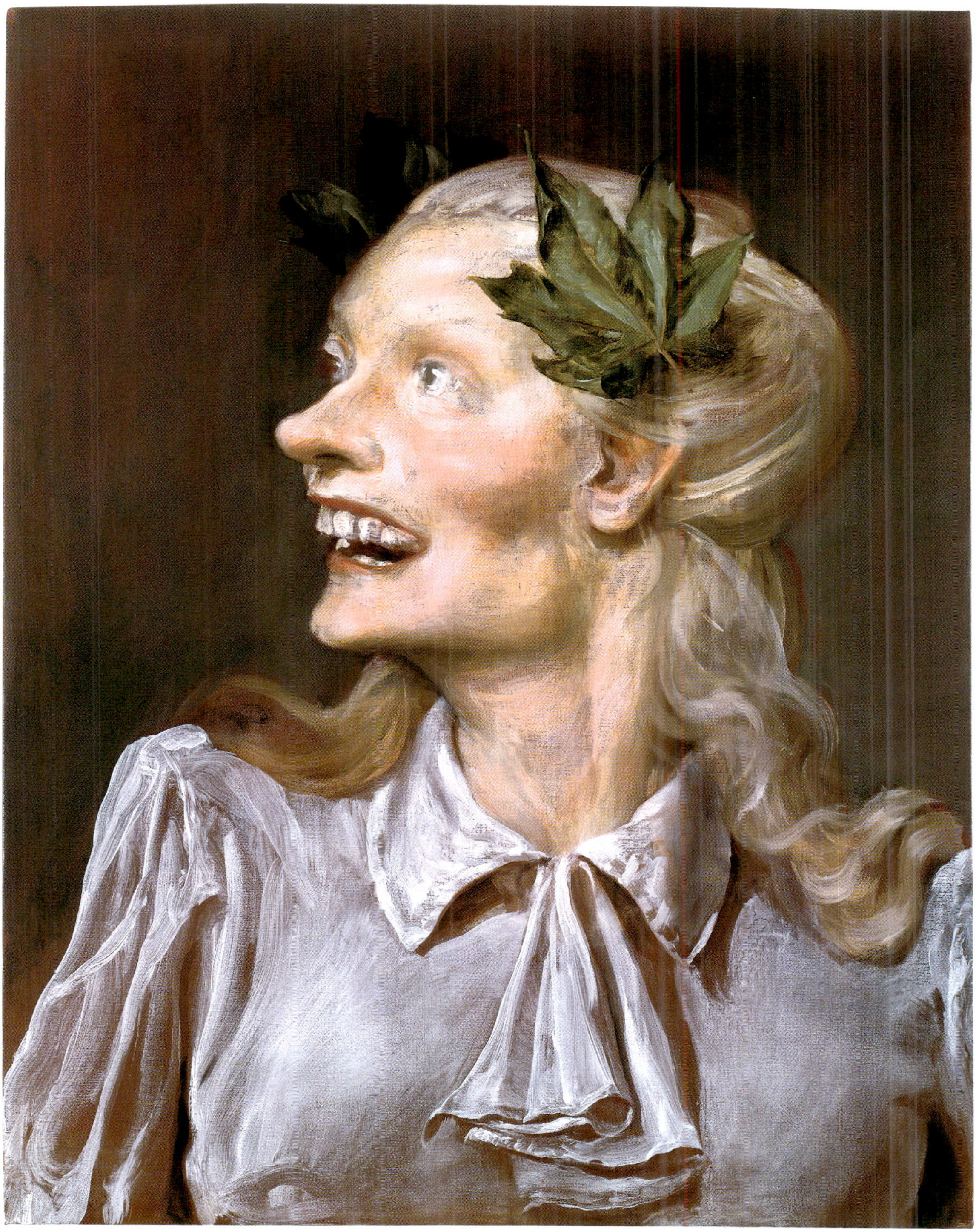

John Currin
Minerva, 2000
71,1 x 55,8 cm
Collection David Teiger

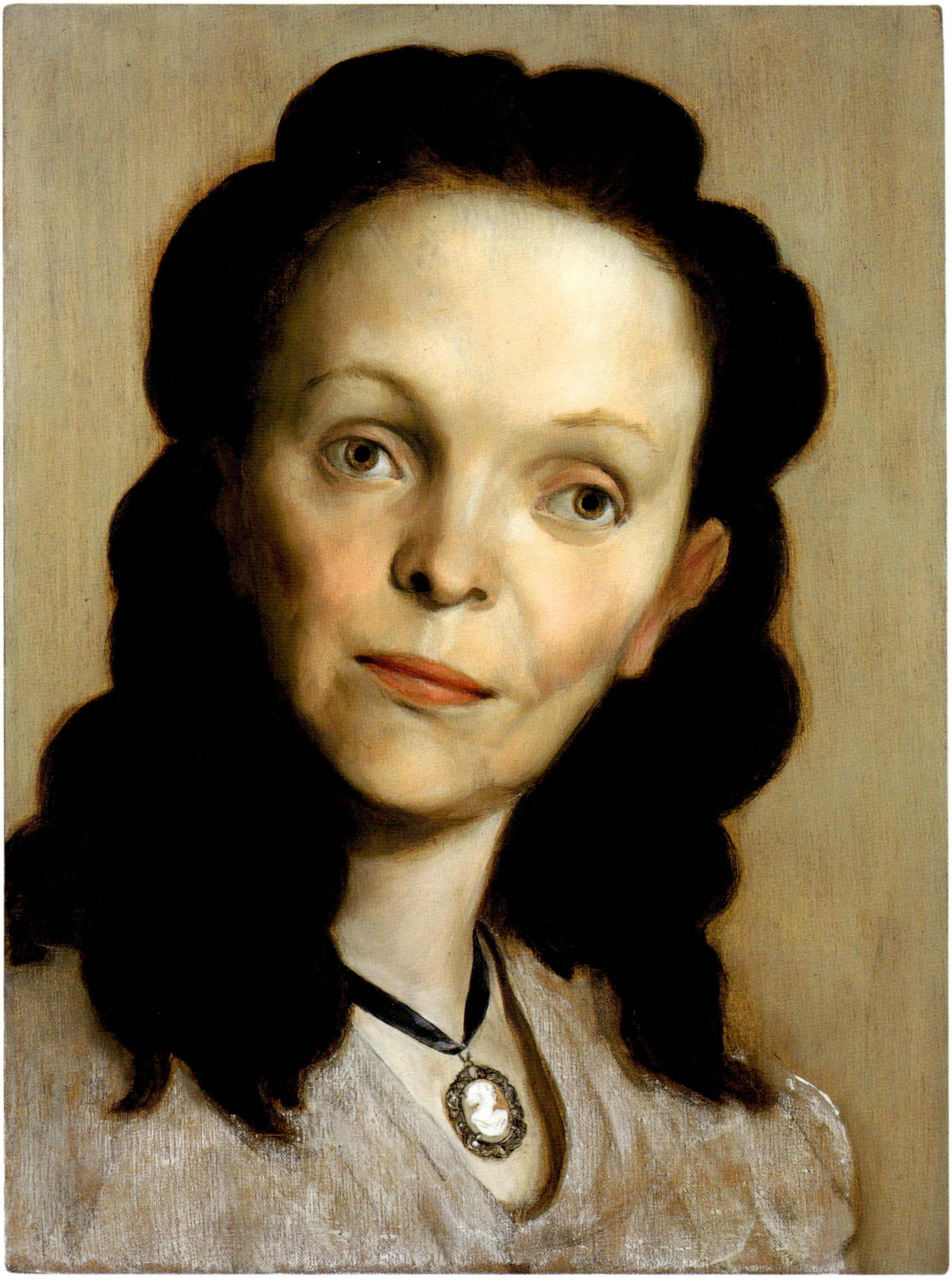

John Currin
Angela, 2001
55,8 x 40,6 cm
Collection Ninah & Michael Lynne, New York

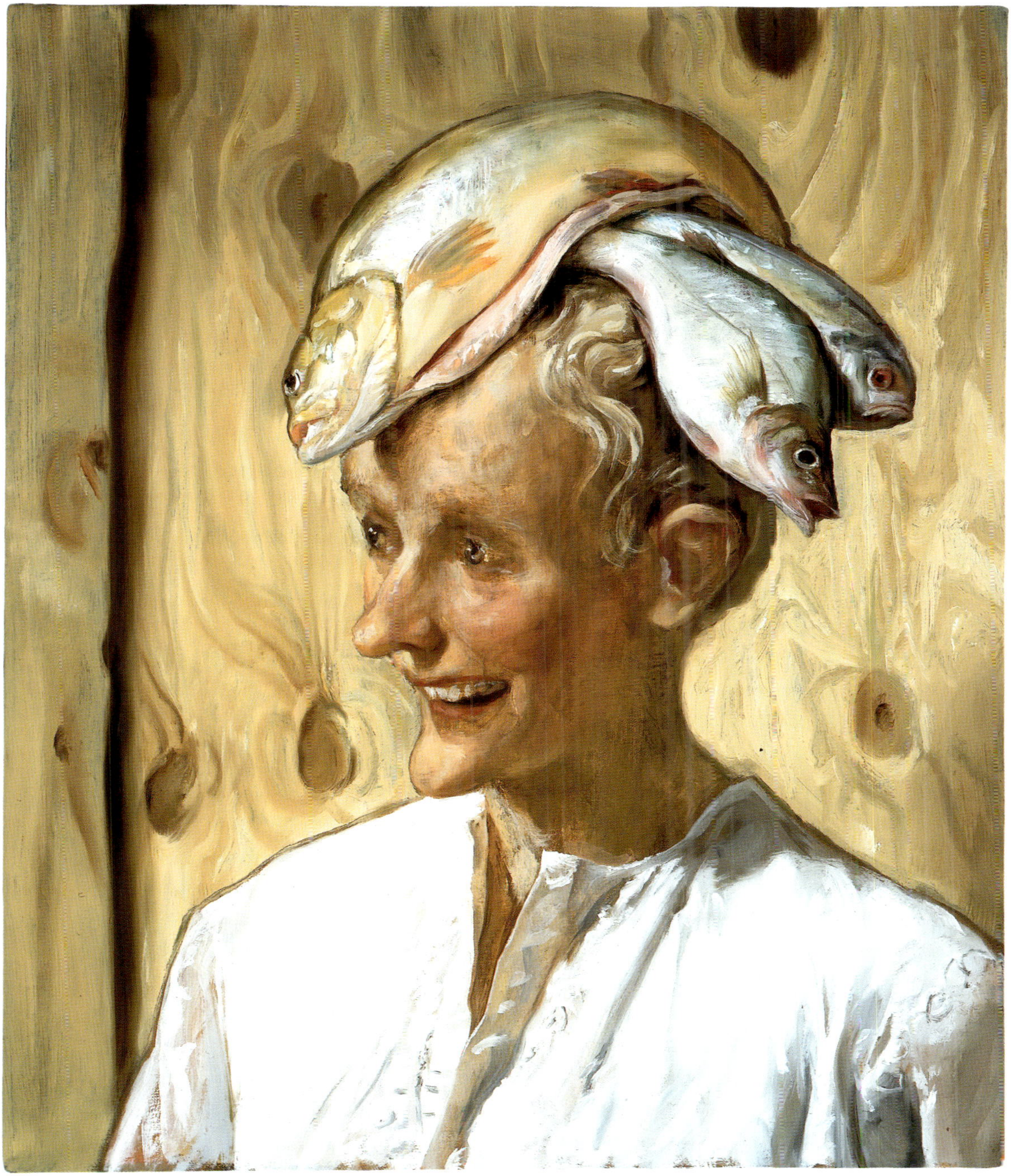

John Currin
The Moroccan, 2001
66 x 55,8 cm
Centre Pompidou, Musée national d'art moderne, Paris

Glenn Brown

Sabine Folie

Thus we do not live our own lives but rather those of the dead.

Oscar Wilde

The beautiful incorporates a feeling for what is holy. It surrounds an object with an aura of invul nerability, establishes the taboo of its injury. I am strongly attracted to this object whereas awe, as an equivalent countervailing force, holds me back from it. Interrupted in my movements, I stand there as if rooted to the ground. The beautiful is detachment.

Peter Schjeldahl

Since Glenn Brown first encountered the portrait *Head of JYM* (1973) in 1991, Frank Auerbach, the author of the work, has haunted Brown's reservoir of imagery. But not only Auerbach–Georg Baselitz, Philip Guston, Salvador Dalí, and even illustrators such as Chris Foss, have also been quoted in his work, blended and transformed until something entirely new has been created. The scope of the subject matter which is subjected to this process ranges from large-scale science-fiction paintings or portraits to sculptures, which are also portraits, translated, as it were, into two dimensions.

He starts with photocopied works of the great masters, first painting copies of them in *trompe-l'œil*, and then creates a metamorphosis by merging different subjects by several painters at once, as well as mass media products borrowed from film and literature. His science-fiction paintings of lunar landscapes, fantastic cities on meteorites whizzing about in outer space, dark expanses of nothingness executed in the trompe-l'œil technique are themselves translated into portraiture.

The distinction between "high" and "low" culture is immaterial. What counts is the result, which is intended to disturb viewers, keep them at an uncomfortable distance, astound them and alienate them. Black humor, the vile and obscene, cliché and ugliness, the sweet and the beautiful, rot and decay: these are all aspects of the artist's imaginary world. He seduces our senses in order to innoculate us against "sensory deprivation", and thus keeps our eyes moving.

His sources of inspiration are legion: the great masters and, more trivially, film and literature, or the hybrid sensualism and decadence of Blake, Böcklin or Füssli (Fuseli). His predilection for the sinister, the dark, for "nocturnal creatures", decay, the black side of human nature reveals a clear affinity with the aesthetic of the "gothic". Many of Brown's pictures are dedicated to Ian Curtis, the haunted hero of the gothic punk band Joy Division, who died young: dark, melancholy, delicate and immovable, floating alone in outer space.

Like a vampire Brown sucks blood from the myriad sources of inspiration feeding his imagination in order to transcend time as a "soulless" creature and to contemplate his work from a distant horizon: a reflective, cool, passionate and full-blooded painter.

(translated from the German by Joan Clough)

SF: When one looks at your paintings–in particular your "portraits" rather than your "science-fiction" paintings the first source of confusion comes from the kind of subject or person you are presenting to the viewer. A closer scrutinizing of the painting–its surface, the application of color–provides more insight into what is a rather disturbing mixture of visual information. There are many different elements pulling the viewer in various directions that might lead to totally opposite interpretations: title, subject, surface, pictorial attitude. Your paintings always seem to present a sort of puzzle or enigma. This is of course intrinsic to a "conceptual" or intellectual painterly behavior.
Let's begin to discuss your paintings first in terms of surface. Should one only encounter your paintings through photographic reproduction, it is likely that your allusions to impasto, color, corporeality, and texture would be missed. This is

especially striking in your "Auerbach" works since your paintings are not thick and daubed with earnest gesture like the originals. Your "Auerbachs" are flat, totally flat, though extremely elaborate. The viewer is shocked by this deception, betrayed by the *trompe l'oeil*.

If you know the original Auerbach paintings, you have the sensation of a reversed process regarding notions of proximity and distance: the original Auerbachs gain corporeality as you get physically closer to the painting, while your "Auerbach" paintings can only suggest texture and corporeality if one looks at them from a distance.

From these observations, I have a few questions: What is your conception of the bodily involvement of the painter in the process of painting? The notions of style (the personal, instinctive style of a painter) and manner (an acquired skill, dexterity) have a deep impact on your conception of painting. Can you speak about these notions?

GB: Why do I paint the way I do? I'm not a very good Modernist. I did try, I read my Clement Greenberg and Michael Fried, and I even enjoyed it. But life is too short to be guided by only one orthodoxy. Modernism still dominates visual thinking, so it is difficult to negate. I fell head over heels in love with painting, all of it, for better or for worse. 1000 years of art history stood before me, suggesting every mode of thinking possible, but which one to choose? The sad answer is that I chose to choose none of them, not fundamentally anyway.

I have different "bodies of work" - the sculptures, photographs, portraits and science fiction paintings–and each follows a different orthodoxy. In the "Auerbach" and other portraits you speak of, which is perhaps the dominant body within my work, my bodily involvement is as voyeur. It sounds dreadful, but I am perhaps only here in spirit. I could partake in the pleasures of the paint, but I prefer the invisible hand of the dematerialized artist, making dematerialized fake brush marks. I looked at the history of painting and couldn't see why expression should be aligned only with the brush mark. Though painters toy with it, the genuine is something that artists are too in awe of. High Modernism turned the hand of the artist into a cliché. However, I like clichés. I like portraits and flowers and still lifes and *trompe l'oeil* and the story of Van Gogh cutting off his ear. These things involve sentiment, and sentiment, like Steven Spielberg movies, makes me cry. For some strange reason along with the 80 % of the population these things make me feel real; genuine brush marks generally don't. Skill is another bad word, not even in the Modernist lexicon. To this day artists who show skill, craft or pride in their work hold themselves up to ridicule, or worse still, mediocrity; it's cool not to care. I have this vision of some collector holding up some piece of junk and announcing how many hundred thousand dollars he paid for it, all to rapturous applause. Don't get me wrong, a great deal of that junk would have me applauding too, its just that the more junky the junk, and exotically degenerate it looks, the more in control of his world the collector feels when he buys it. Degenerate art has become another dominant cliché. It may not sound like it but I adore the act of painting, it's so extraordinarily subtle, it is something you can never be too skilled at.

Color and its myriad of combinations always amazes me. To paint the expression of a face and to change that expression, from happy to sad by one miniscule change in the shadow of an eye, makes one never want to do anything else. Though it is difficult to see how the paintings are made, and what exactly one is looking at, it's not rocket science, it's just paint. The enigma is, why do I fall for clichés when I know how bad they are?

SF: It seems to me that you are a fairly good Modernist painter in respect to your self-referential method of investigation concerning the means of painting. At first glance, you are not referring to an immediate model or a subject, but to the sitter or subject of another painter who is part of another tradition, and who subsequently becomes your model or antagonist.

Frank Auerbach says: "As soon as I become consciously aware of what the paint is doing my involvement with the painting is weakened. Paint is at its most eloquent when it is a by-product of some corporeal, spatial, developing imaginative concept, a creative identification with the subject. I would no more fix my mind on the character of paint than if maybe an alchemist could fix his on mechanical chemistry."

Auerbach works with sitters with whom he imposes a sort of intimate, sometimes pragmatic, yet still intensive dialogue. If we take Auerbach at his word, this dialogue leads to a certain formal shape determined by many subconscious aspects. The dialogue is intended to last a long time; sometimes a painting takes years to finish.

This sensual and psychological approach seems to be the opposite of your starting point. In the Modernist tradition, a mature painter is not allowed to return to a bourgeois or even bohemian relationship between the painter and model. Instead, as you have already said about your work, you are a voyeur. This voyeurism is enacted by appropriating the subjects or sitters of other painters (such as Auerbach, Appel, Baselitz, Fragonard, Guston, de Kooning). Why those figures in particular? Why transform them into something new?

To use a cliché, this appropriation process seems to be a continuous oscillation between Dr. Jekyll and Mr. Hyde–your paintings seem to be the result of a painful, frivolous, comic and liberating process of transformation. This seems like a defiantly anti-Modernist gesture. Is there a relationship between you and the model even if it is mediated by this complicated process of appropriation? A kind of "love affair" between you and this mute object of desire? There is also a question of time it takes for you to make a painting, to "release" it into the world, for the eyes of other people. Can you speak about this "gestation" time? Can you describe further this logic of "transformation" in your paintings, perhaps by speaking about the almost blasphemous titles that is part of their transformation, such as *Seligsprechung* or *Ride with the Devil, Sympathy for the Poor* ...

GB: Sometimes we take the ones we love for granted. I think Frank is a bit guilty of that. Over the years you grow to love paint. The way each pigment and manufacturer have idiosyncrasies all of their own. Indian yellow, made from ox's urine, covers nothing, but glazes like a dream. Purple Lake goes from black to bright red, with a little help. I won't go on, but one grows to love the fights. The pigments become part of the way your brain works, and you get caught up in the language of brush marks and images. "Truth to materials"–you see, you can't get more Modernist than that and, ah, it's romantic too.
The self-abuser (I'm thinking of Salvador Dalí and his guilty hand) has a relationship with the model too! The naked flesh of the original model may be long dead but that just aids the imagination. I like painting wrinkles. Fragonard, Auerbach and Rembrandt painted the living. Their flesh has become paint, so I paint paint. The paint is the crusty residue left after the relationship between the artist and his model is over. It is all there is left of real love, so I paint that. Sad songs are the best. Oscar Wilde's *The Picture of Dorian Gray* has something to do with it.
I can see a progression in my work. Earlier paintings were softer, more akin to Gerhardt Richter's nostalgia. The paintings have now become harsher. The blur has all but gone, though the paintings in this exhibition still have traces. I seem to delight in making the white highlights of the distended brush marks sharp and less forgiving. When I paint I always imagine a delirious light source, literally Fragonard on acid, less "the cruel light of day", more the cruel artificial greens and ultraviolet of a dance-floor. I don't know if cadmium green is beautiful or just poisonous, but it lights the way for my "creatures of the night".
I usually have a number of paintings on the go, so I paint them for sometimes up to a year. A long gestation period often means that the painting bears little similarity to my original intention. Most works are made from two elements; an original painting, which acts as the skeleton, and a second painting, which acts as a color model or skin. I only have a rough idea what the skeleton will look like in its new skin, so by time I have had my little fight to get it to fit, the painting may be upside down, back to front, and I will have tried several other artists' work to help get it right. An atheist, in love with the history of painting and with a liking for the blackly frivolous, is forced to see through the eyes of the Catholic Church. Catholicism and the art it spawned had such a great effect on portraiture and representation that it has changed the language with which we read the world. Me, I'm just getting even.

SF: The dutch painter Cornelis Norbertus Gijsbrechts made a painting between 1670-75 called "Reversed Painting". It is a radical meditation about painting itself. The painting is a *trompe l'oeil* that represents the back of a painting (frame, stretcher, and canvas with an inventory number). When you try to turn round the painting you're supposed to discover the "real", painted representation, but there is "nothing" but the real back of a normal oil painting: the canvas, stretcher, and frame. Painting has come to its annihilation.
Like Gijsbrechts, your paintings also seem to be an effort to understand painting itself: it requires both the undermining and celebrating of painting. Stoichita speaks about painting as a way of investigating the inner and aesthetic limits of painting, the possibilities of communication, the absorption of the viewer and the traces of the painter. Your *trompe l'oeil* is, if I understand it properly, the appropriate method to evoke maximum polyfocality: a visceral, anamorphic, misty, romantic subversion.
You mesmerize the viewer by provoking paradoxical feelings through paradoxical means. Perhaps this derives from the overlapping of images from different historical eras. What does this compounding and cannibalization mean in your work? It seems that part of it stems from both a darkness and a vicious sense of humor. You have made simultaneous references to Blake, Füssli, and Böcklin all at once. What about literary sources: Edgar Allen Poe, Henry James or William Beckford? What about music? Cinema? Does literature, music or film have an influence on your imagination?

GB: There are certain painters, Fabian Marcaccio, or perhaps David Reed who talk about painting as some sort of "endgame" or "I can't go on I'll go on" strategy–very much in the spirit of Samuel Beckett. Whilst Beckett's very black comedy became a model for me I could not tolerate the sociological wasteland that is abstraction. If there is something that might attempt to emasculate painting and perhaps be the equivalent of Cornelis Norbertus Gijsbrecht's joke, I see it as abstraction. When asked "What do you do?", I reply, "I'm a painter". It feels like saying "Yes, I'm dull and irrelevant", so I try and explain my way out of it. The greatest danger lies in trying to look clever. Marcel Duchamp's phrase, "as stupid as a painter" describes how a painter's use of colour, form and line have an annoying habit of confounding our expectations of language. In other words "why do I find this oafish drivel so appealing?". I hope I celebrate some of painting's more clownish attributes, rather than just myopically mourn its problems.
I like the idea of "polyfocality", which in order to view multiple contradictions from a single perspective one must to adopt. A painting is such a still thing, in order to engender animation I want to move the viewer. It's a painting of flowers: no, it has a face. The figure is happy: no, it's sad. The painting looks new: no, perhaps it's quite old. I never saw a painting like it before: oh, but it's so derivative, etc, etc. I want an uneasy, chancy event to be taking place. I honestly don't see it as destroying painting: this is painting. If you take polyfocality away you have nothing but a blank canvas, and if you are still in the mood for contradiction there's Robert Ryman.

The titles of many of my paintings act as musical, literary or filmic references. Though these may initially seem like they confound meaning as in *The Rebel*, if one knows the film *The Rebel* (or *Call Me Genius*, 1960) the painting could easily be a stage prop. In the film, Tony Hancock manages to aggressively satirize the avant-garde painter whilst sincerely suggesting there to be no greater aspiration in life. The "dead soul", in the title of the painting, *Dead Souls (after Chris Foss)*, could simply refer to the inhabitants of the painting's deathly city. It also, however, recalls the song by the band Joy Division. Numerous other paintings have the prefix "painting for Ian Curtis", the band's dead singer. Joy Division's mournful yet euphoric, rock music, which can still be danced to like disco, encapsulates every painting I ever wanted to make. A more important reference is Nikoli Gogol's incredible book *Dead Souls*, in which the dead are more useful than the living–a sentiment close to my heart–and a more vicious humour would be difficult to find.

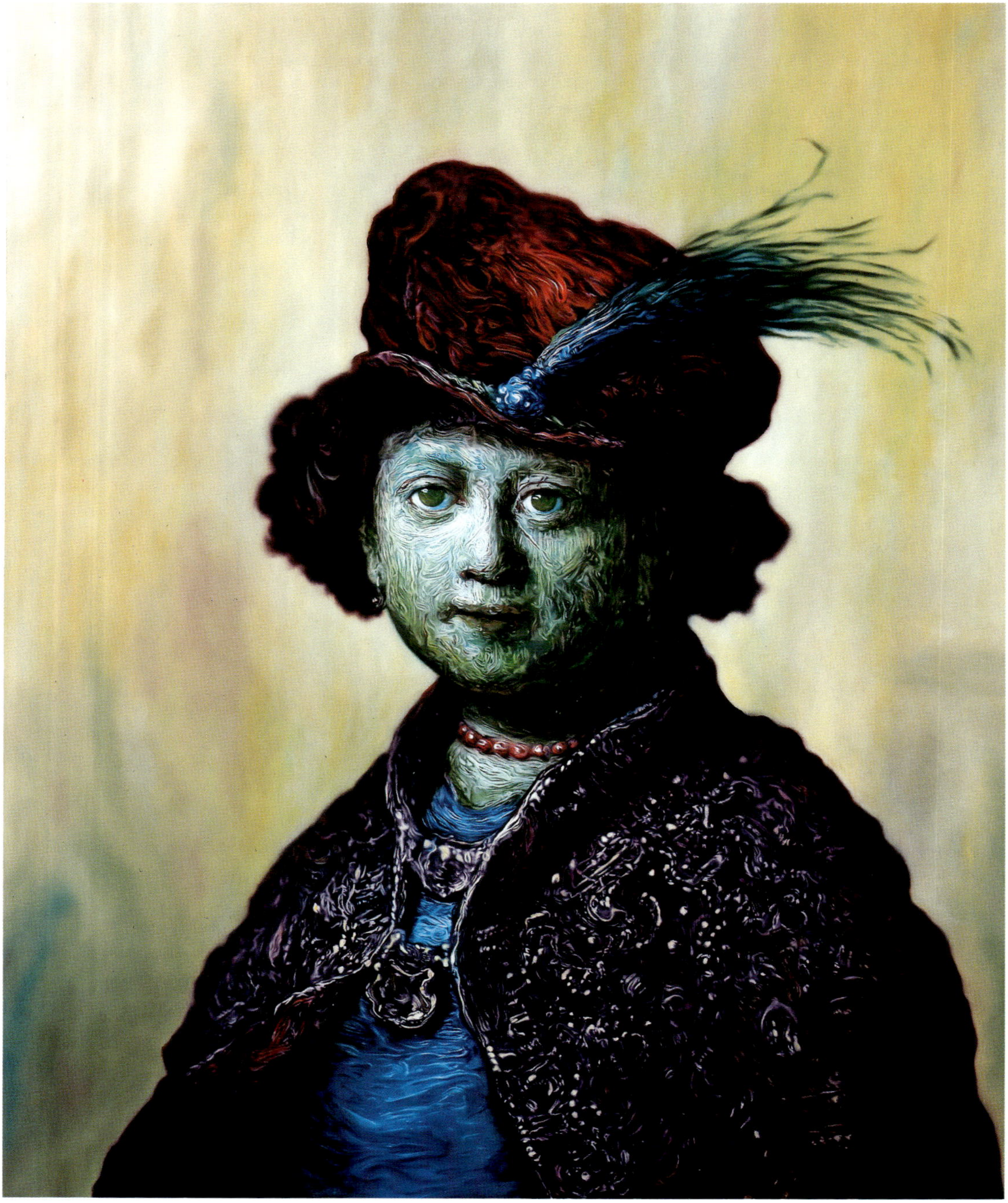

Glenn Brown
Joseph Beuys (after Rembrandt), 2001
97 x 79,5 cm
Collection Bobbi & Walter Zifkin, Los Angeles
Courtesy Patrick Painter, Inc., Santa Monica
& Galerie Max Hetzler, Berlin

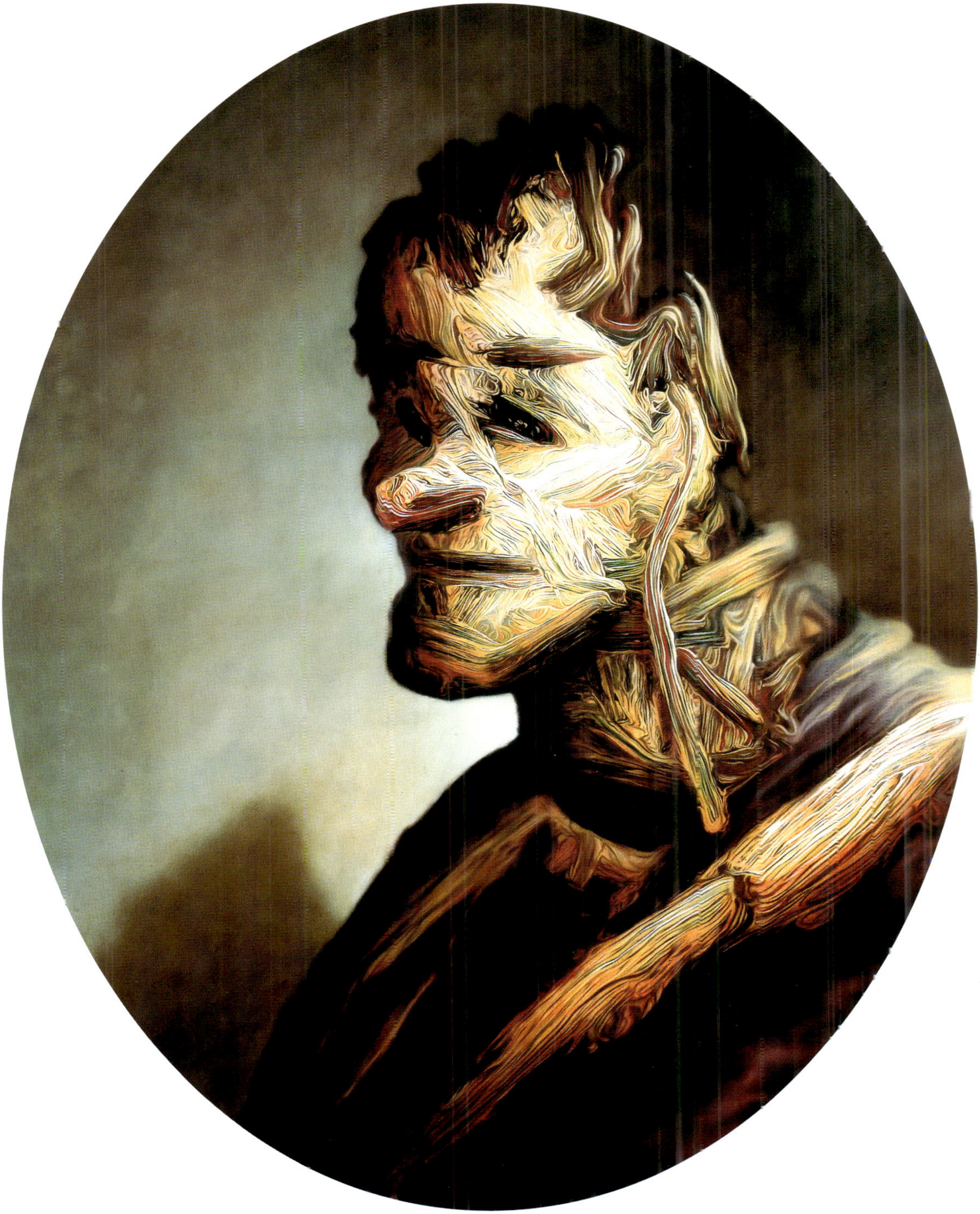

Glenn Brown
Seligsprechung, 2000
85 x 67,5 cm
Collection Bob Rennie, Vancouver
Courtesy Patrick Painter, Inc., Santa Monica
& Galerie Max Hetzler, Berlin

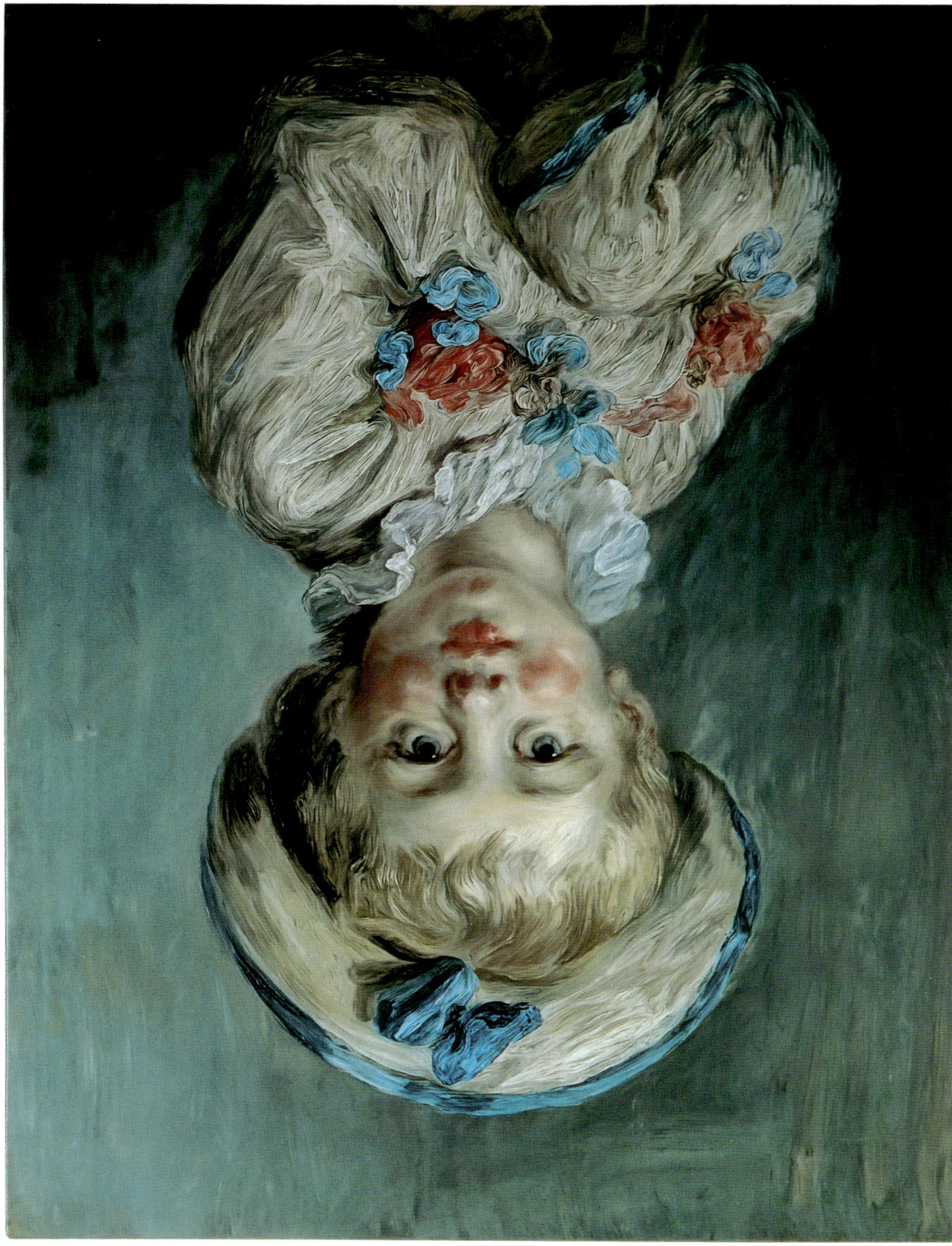

Glenn Brown
The End of the Twentieth Century (after Fragonard and Baselitz), 1996
79 x 57 cm
Collection Byron R. Meyer, San Francisco
Courtesy Patrick Painter, Inc., Santa Monica & Galerie Max Hetzler, Berlin

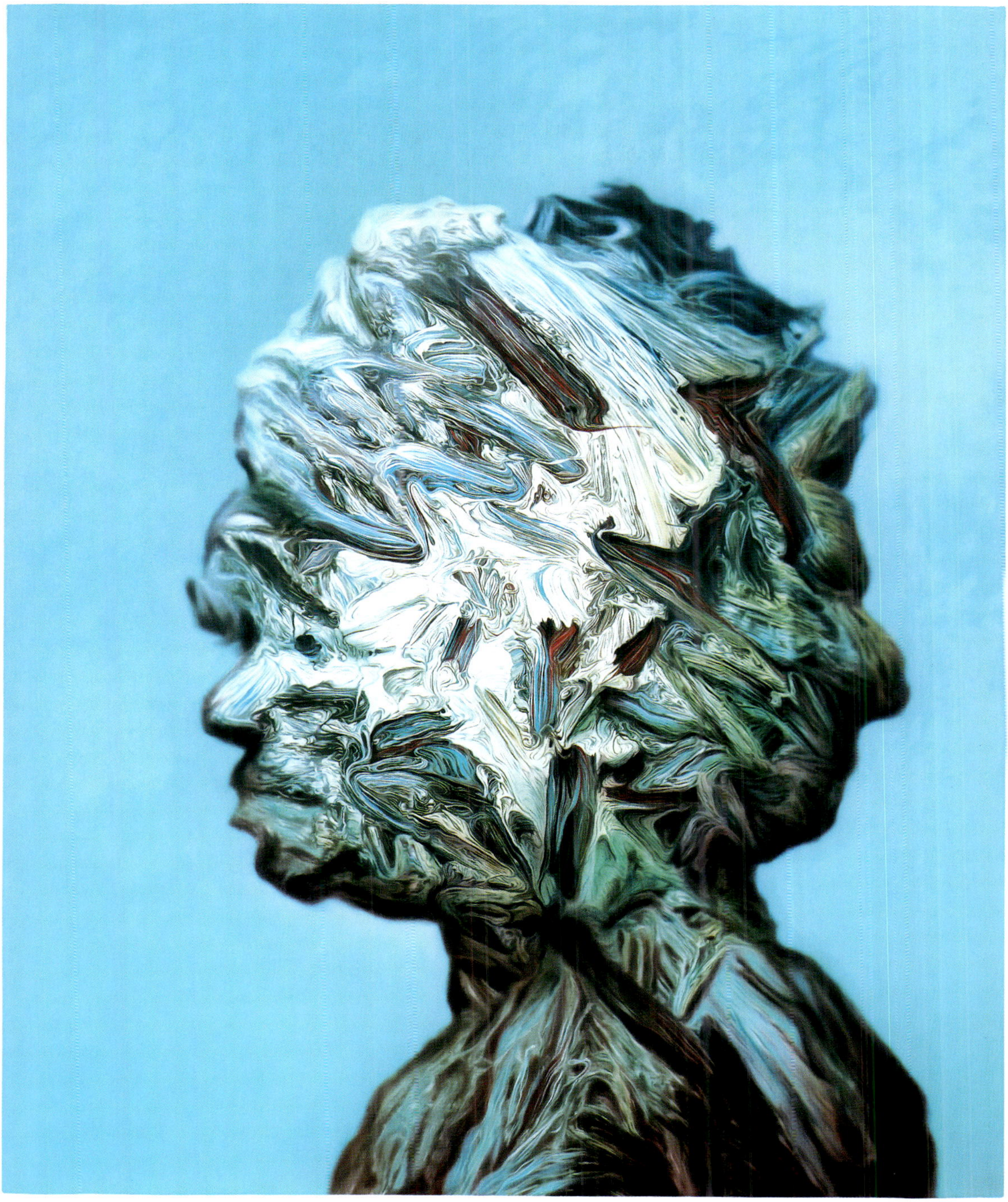

Glenn Brown
The Rebel, 2001
84,5 x 70 cm
Collection Leopoldo Villareal Fernandez, New York
Courtesy Patrick Painter, Inc., Santa Monica
& Galerie Max Hetzler, Berlin

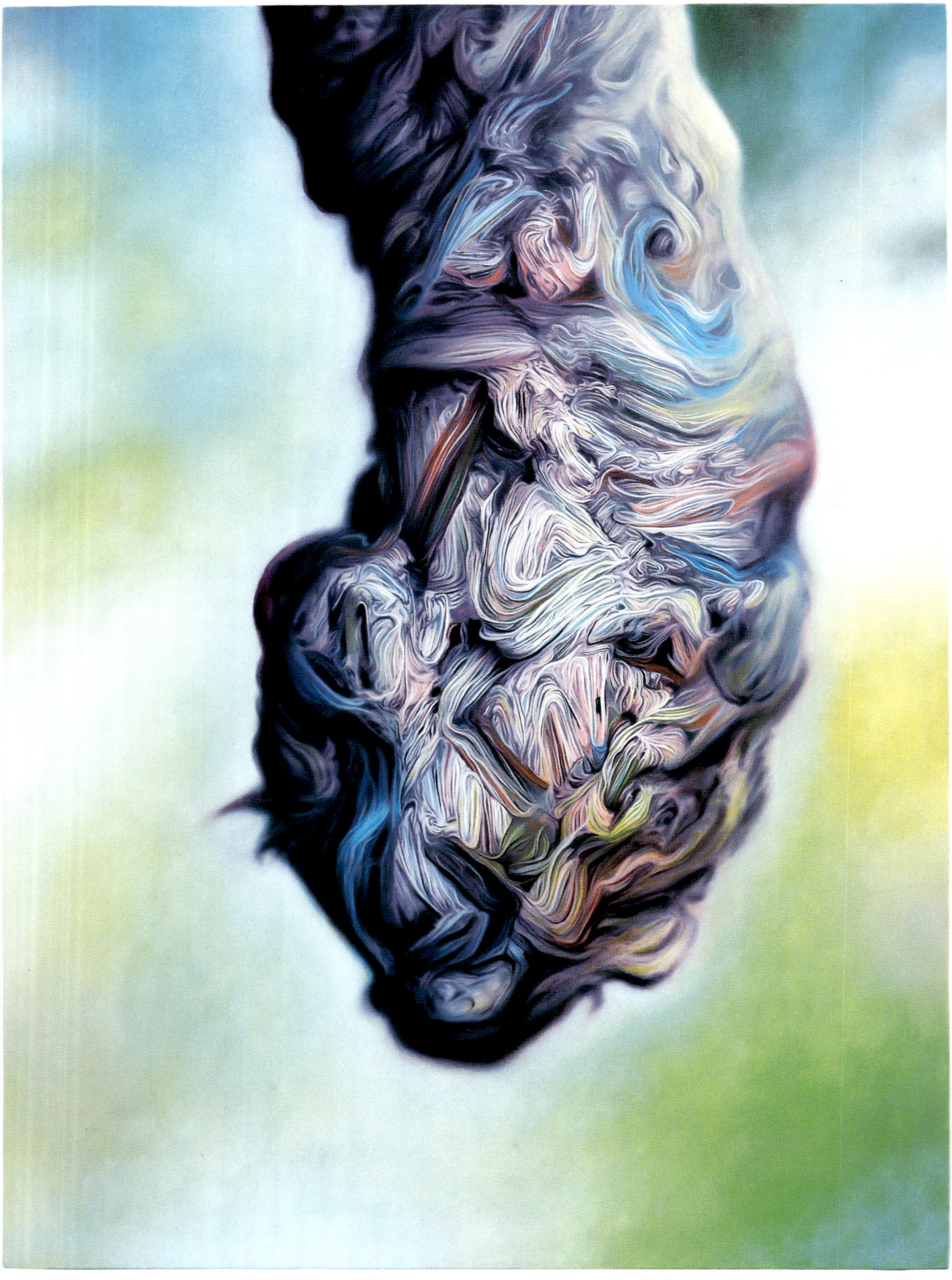

Glenn Brown
The Suicide of Guy Debord, 2001
58,5 x 46,7 cm
Courtesy de l'artiste & Patrick Painter, Inc., Santa Monica
& Galerie Max Hetzler, Berlin

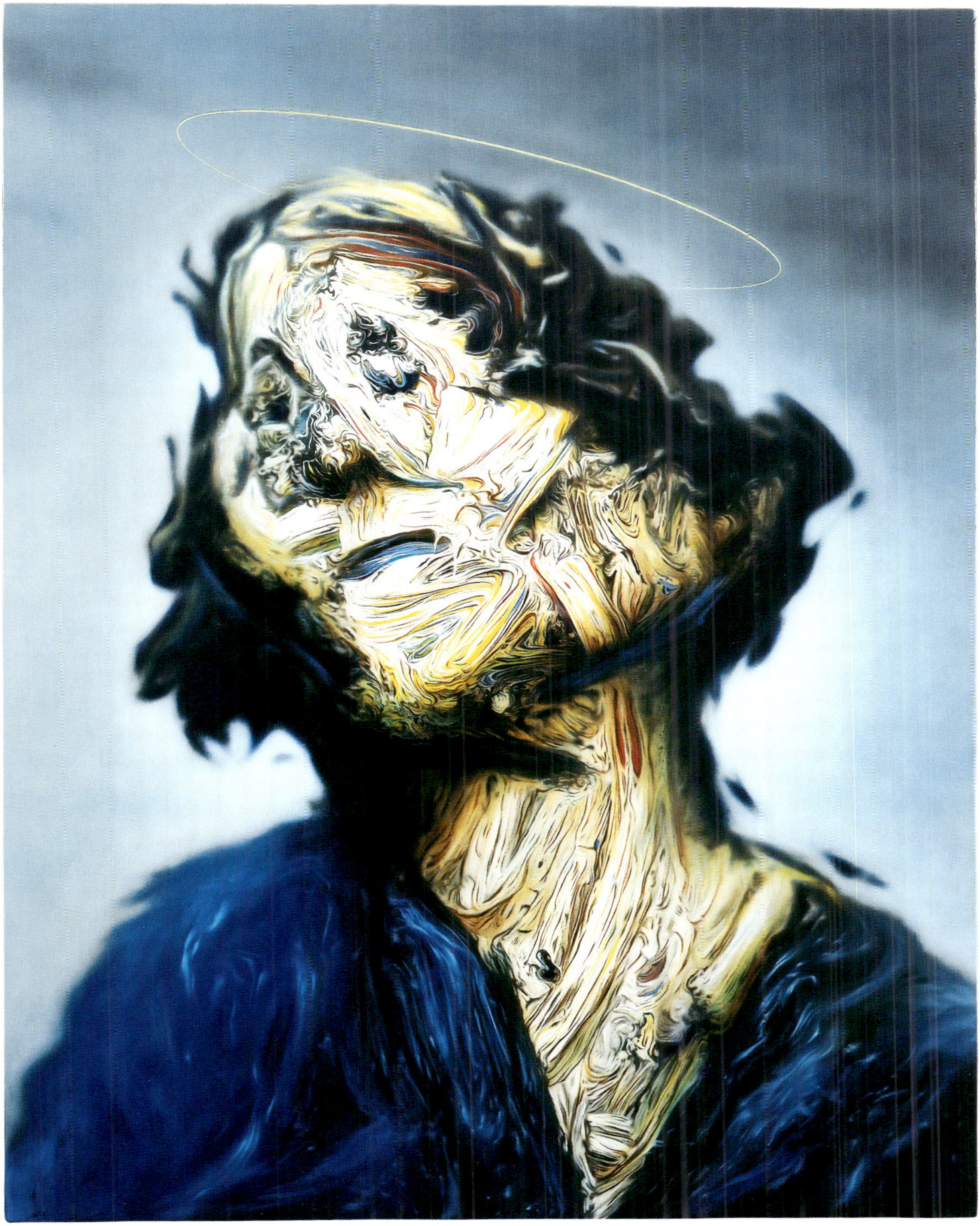

Glenn Brown
Ride with the Devil, Symbathy for the Poor, 2001
62,5 x 46 cm
Collection Rudolph & Ute Scharpff, Stuttgart

Neo Rauch

Correspondence with Alison M. Gingeras

Dear Neo,

Having been to visit you in Leipzig on two separate occasions in preparation for this exhibition, I would like to ask you a few questions that hopefully will help the viewer surpass some easy assumptions about your work in regards to your geopolitical context. Perhaps these questions are too invasive or explicit—of course, there is always a dangerous divide separating interpretation and intention. Here are a few questions that I hope do not trespass these interpretative boundaries.

I look forward to your answers,

Alison

Collective History, Strategic Fragmentation

There is a temptation to reduce a reading of your work to a socio-historical document: "Neo Rauch is the painter of the failed Utopia of the Eastern Bloc".

Yet it seems that the fragmented spaces of your paintings—their manipulation of naturalistic perspective; the impossible architectural ordering of the picture plane; the cinematic ruptures, jump-cuts, and close-ups contained within a single canvas—seem to refuse any notion of "wholeness" or easy conclusion about the time or place you that you are addressing.

Is this trope of spatial and temporal fragmentation a means of contesting the official discourse of a homogeneous German state? Or even by extension, a means of contesting the current negation of an Eastern and Western school of German art? Does this fragmentation reflect the condition of collective or historical memory—a conflicted, irreconcilable entity?

Buried Deep: Obliterating Nostalgia

Many of your contemporaries, including a number of artists included in this exhibition, engage in a lively dialogue with the history of painting. Often mistaken as a hermetic dialogue between painters (living and dead), it could also be an active strategy of resistance to the over-determined historical or social interpretation of an artist's work. These art historical engagements might take the form of "vampirism"—in the case of John Currin's obvious stylistic borrowings from Cranach to Boucher—or take the form of appropriation such as Glenn Brown's obsessive re-painting and manipulating of specific works by Rembrandt or Auerbach. Others take more subtle forms, borrowing gestures, tones, or palettes from artistic forbears in order to create trans-historical links that might be legible only to an extremely astute connoisseur of painting.

The early reception of your work has mostly focused on the aesthetic and political "residue" of the Soviet-bloc past—a strong resonance with East German illustration and graphic design spanning the 1930-50s, "official art" (Socialist Realist painting), an iconography derived from socialist architecture, the recurring theme of labor.

Having visited your studio recently, I suspect that there is a much broader historical and ideological dialogue imbedded in your work. There seems to be very subtle borrowings in the work, almost invisible to the naked eye—certain gestures that your recent figures have assumed, taken from Balthus or even Vermeer.

Do these "promiscuous" borrowings add another layer to the work that refutes the accusations of your work being "nostalgic" for the East? If so, is this a means of actively staking a claim or taking a position ("ORTER") against the passive connotations implicit in nostalgia about the immediate past and a reactive use of its artistic forms? Is it a means of refuting the current belief that "good" painting implies progress and embracing the "new" both in an artistic and ideological sense?

Giving Titles: Language and Anachronism

You have also answered this query about nostalgia in the very subtle word play in your titles. The palindrome you invented as the title of a recent work—RETRO.ORTER—is quite emblematic of your peculiar use of a rarefied strain of High German. Is it possible for you to speak about your very efficient yet troubling use of language and the way it is used for the titles that find themselves in your paintings? It seems that they add yet another layer of temporality, injecting a dose of anachronism, troubling the location of "time" in your work without slipping into nostalgia . . .

Figures of Violence, Allegory, and Forgetting

The figure of the "artist" that often appears in your works is almost always involved in some sort of violent struggle. This struggle can take the form of an "inward" conflict such as in the two headed figure of "painter and his double" in *Die Wahl* (1998). Artistic rivalry, competition and territoriality is suggested in such scenes as the fight between two street painters in your new work *Niederung* (2002). *Unerträglicher Naturalismus* (1998) which depicts the artist as marksman, shooting his rifle at a critic (?) in front of a crowd of spectators, in a cinematic space framed by the armature of an easel.

Beyond the narrative readings on the surface of these works—artmaking as inner-struggle, the violent competitiveness between artists, the clash between artist/critic and intentionality/-reception—can one also see this as an allegory for the lack of reconciliation between Modernism and Realism? Does this opposition between figuration and abstraction continue to persist?

Has "the painter" inherited these ideological debates (as discussed in the famous Frankfurt School correspondences of the 1940s), especially in the context of a recently reunited Germany? Is there still an ideological struggle to assert the primacy of a figurative mode of painting, especially when addressing certain subject matter? Or is this allegory of violent struggle reflecting another type of historical violence, an "active forgetting" of this ideological burden?

I suspect that on another (allegorical) level, there is an overarching project in your work to create an (impossible) portrait of a collective "Eastern German" subject. These figures seem to be caught in a real temporal as well as socio-political split:

On one hand there is pressure to "integrate" with the West, to embrace the 'Modern' (your "quotation" of abstraction that often float in the paintings) and the contemporary;

On the other hand, your work reflects a daily confrontation with the vestiges of the past (abandoned factories, socialist architecture, high unemployment) without slipping into nostalgia.

Is this a possible or valid reading?

Do you feel the mood of your work reflects the world around you, that of Leipzig in 2002? It seems important to say something about this given that the Western European and American reception of your work does not have the first hand experience of the social and physical landscape around you and can easily over-emphasize the "retro" look of the work.

Dear Alison,

I'll try to respond to all of these questions even though I'd actually have to take half a year off to do so with the necessary thoroughness.

First of all, I think I should establish the location ["Ortung" in the German] of my workshop landscape in its lack of a reference to time. I hope that by setting the stage in this manner will cause some of the questions to dissolve. In my case, things are probably much simpler than people seem to tend to assume, and yet, or perhaps precisely for this reason, they are infinitely complicated.

I view the process of painting as an extraordinarily natural form of discovering the world, almost as natural as breathing. Outwardly it is almost entirely without intention. It is predominantly limited to the process of a concentrated flow. I am deliberately neglecting to contemplate all of the catalytic influences that would have the power to undermine the innocence of this approach because I would like to express a degree of clarity in these lines by way of example. If I view myself as a kind of peristaltic filtration system in the river of time, then it seems appropriate to examine the composition and hence perhaps also the quality of this filtration system.

Let me make it clear at this point that I always attempt to respond to the question of the artistic quality of painting in general by excluding the contextual to the greatest extent possible. If a painting reveals itself to me as a memorable and unsettling expression of an irritatingly weird painter personality, then as a rule the threshold from being just a painting to being a picture has been transcended and I accept this constructive disruption of my habits with gratitude. If the impression is strong, my interest in the time of origin, social background, and deeper intentions of the artist wane; the painting becomes an autonomous, auratic aggregate.

I am entirely aware of the fact that from the perspective of common positions my artistic understanding can only be interpreted as deeply anachronistic. This self-referential and amorphous existence, which is accompanied by a cyclical ejection of filtered out material, simply does not work within the context of this discourse. So, since I can't give up this form of existence at the risk of my own downfall, the point is to expand on the category of being an anachronism with relish and energy (it has already become meaningless as it is), and thus act as a pioneer in developing the normative power of the factual.

The constitution of my collection system certainly corresponds to my mental and morphological idiosyncrasies; it has been influenced by animosities and affinities adopted very early on and is therefore modifiable to a limited extent only. To draw a creative benefit from this sobering recognition and declare it as the basis of a far-reaching process of development whose goal is to unravel the peculiar also means to get used to the role of the author. I don't consider my workshop to be part of the flow of time, but rather a passenger terminal connected with a dam of time. Its bulky contours cause whirlpools to form and special deposits to collect. What is important is the confidence in the reliability of this sorting system so that the condition of amorphousness can be retained.

These half-awake moments in which the flotsam accumulates in my catch basin and rearranges itself to a new organization are the essence of my painting. Perhaps it is understandable that for instance a conscious and deliberate discussion of issues of domestic German cultural policy would have to take place far outside the borders of my workshop. As a private person I would have something to contribute, but other worlds are reflected on my canvases.

What is deeper, though, is the question of the circumstances of our collective memory. I expect that the special characteristics of the apparatus I so elaborately described greatly facilitate the identification of archetypical ciphers, and that the measured influx of memory and perception particles can lead to visual condensate of surprising and unpredictable intensity of expression. This is why I believe that I can view painting as the continuation of the dream with other media.

Some apparently unavoidable side effects of this perspective on painting are certain indifferences with respect to the chronological sortability; because my practice does not include trimming what is washed up in the direction of current modes of seeing. I also refrain both from any hierarchization and from a conscious evaluation of my pictorial inventory. This means that elements like Balthus, Vermeer, Tintin, Donald Judd, Donald Duck, agitprop, and cheap advertising garbage with headline character can flow together in a furrow of my childhood landscape and there generate an intermingled conglomerate of surprising plausibility.

Since in the meantime I paint in a fairly conventional figurative style, which roughly condensed can mean that allegorically ambitioned staffage is introduced to landscape or interior settings, the landscape itself can become a flood zone and germination zone for the confusion of foreign material that accumulates. It seems quite reasonable to make use of this landscape of my own development, which in this case serves as reliable and fertile ground for my labors. I am a careful person who even when making the riskiest of advances needs some semblance of the familiar. In this way, then, amalgamations of the most wondrous kind arise in my central German fields, and I dare to claim that the eternal accusation of having nostalgia for the East can only be made to someone whose origins one knows exactly.

I was once told that if you wouldn't know you could hardly guess in what place and time my paintings were created, and I have no intention of hiding the fact that I liked this idea. Some people even detect Americanisms in my work, others in turn even think its Far Eastern, and only the spiteful fellow painter who lives in the next village recognizes my paintings to be nothing other than the same provincial manure he has in front of his own nose. And somewhere of course they're all right; my arsenal is so robustly constructed that it can withstand being burdened with loads of any type and consistency.

Paintings the way I would have them are in a position to lead viewers off the path at a right angle. They captivate them in their rational behavior and give them an opportunity to diverge from the course of reason. It is one of this author's obligations to design this intersection with a sense of responsibility, and I believe that a reduction of these devices to novelties and pure progressiveness would be of little use. The characteristics of quality that I consider important are originality, suggestiveness, and timelessness; the predicate "one hundred percent zeitgeist" to me has the ring of an execution cry. Zeitgeist painting scrapes at spots that are already sore, while timeless art elevates us from the commonplace and at most incites a delicate phantom pain that indicates the presence of archetypical wounds.

When I stand in front of a blank canvas, it's as if I'm standing in front of a wall of fog. Before taking a brave step into this uncharted territory, the question arises what I will encounter there and what equipment I will need to successfully undertake the excursion. As a rule, a relatively high risk should be guaranteed, and this is where the degree of your ability becomes apparent.

I realized to my surprise that younger artists are attempting to uncover the trenches from the fifties by claiming that only those who operate with abstract instruments demonstrate true courage in the wall of fog. The war between figuration and abstraction seemed to have ended up as Sunday painter skirmishes and from there has now regrettably leaked over into some painting groups in Eastern Germany. For me, the question of risky behavior certainly arises in a manner that is unintelligible for late abstract hegemonists.

With a shudder I open the various contamination chambers and remove a variety of material from them to temporarily store it in the territories of my paintings. I lead frightened staffage out of quarantine barracks and offer them an opportunity to move into my chambers of fog. I make sure that it's comfortable there by instilling a bit of culture there, and in all these actions I am blissfully aware of the narrow ridge from which I could plunge headlong into absurdity, harmlessness, and embarrassment. And so in my own way I work in border territories, and it is worth noting here that an artist's workshop should always be installed on the fringe. I am also aware of the fact that the abysses into which I could potentially fall are already inherent in my oeuvre and by all means should be there. But anyone who is still fooling around with secure positions of postmodernism should show me where their risks lie.

The subliminal character of painting was once defined by Otto Dix when he said something to the effect that he was capable of committing a murder out of sexual passion but not capable of painting it. The various confrontational subjects to be found in my work have a similar character–more subtle recipients even believe they detect a general undercurrent of latent aggression. I'm only mentioning this because it is in confusing contrast with the much more frequent accusation of harmlessness. In any event, I definitely deal with states of tension in my canvases; sometimes they can only be conveyed through compositional elements. They are only negotiated directly in exceptional instances, and I assume that they have to do on the one hand with tension in deeper sediments of my personality structure and on the other with the sublimination of defensive aggressions.

After all, in the last decade, my painting contemporaries were literally pushed into the underground and they had to fit into the role of cultural pariah according to the will of a clique of curators addicted to progress. This phenomenon no doubt not only led to muscular tension among the more self-confident representatives of this banished caste. Aside from this objective source of tension, I still have the ongoing confrontation with the opponent in me who in some paintings emerges like an allegory. I constantly have to suppress the hesitant one, the pubescent one, the conservative one, and the virtuoso in me, or at least to attempt to balance out the antagonists appropriately. The allegorical qualities of these circumstances automatically head straight for the canvas. In all of these productions, I sometimes blend in blocks of words that, like awkward Band-Aids, occasionally indicate critical areas or introduce a cheap form of commercial art elegance.

The words are usually identical to the titles of my works. Coming up with titles is often an arduous process because my interest in the etymological roots of even the most banal terms leads me to sediments of meaning that sometimes introduce unexpected impulses to the intentions of the painting. But occasionally a word can trigger a painting. It can happen that a word develops an incredible atmospheric undertow in the direction of a painting that produces itself, where my only duty is to assist. Such moments are precious, and they bring me even closer to my mother tongue, for it is only here that such experiences can occur.

I have attempted to respond to at least some of your questions here, but in a very unorganized manner. Finally, there is the question of the mood of the year 2002 in Leipzig and whether I believe that I reflect it in my paintings. I'm afraid I cannot answer this question, because I am not aware of any objective moods. Rather, I experience everything through my individual filtration systems. This leads us back to the beginning again. But if anyone should think the work of Neo Rauch could be viewed as flotsam of the atmosphere in Leipzig in the year 2002, I wouldn't mind.

Neo Rauch

(responses translated from the German by Susan Schwartz)

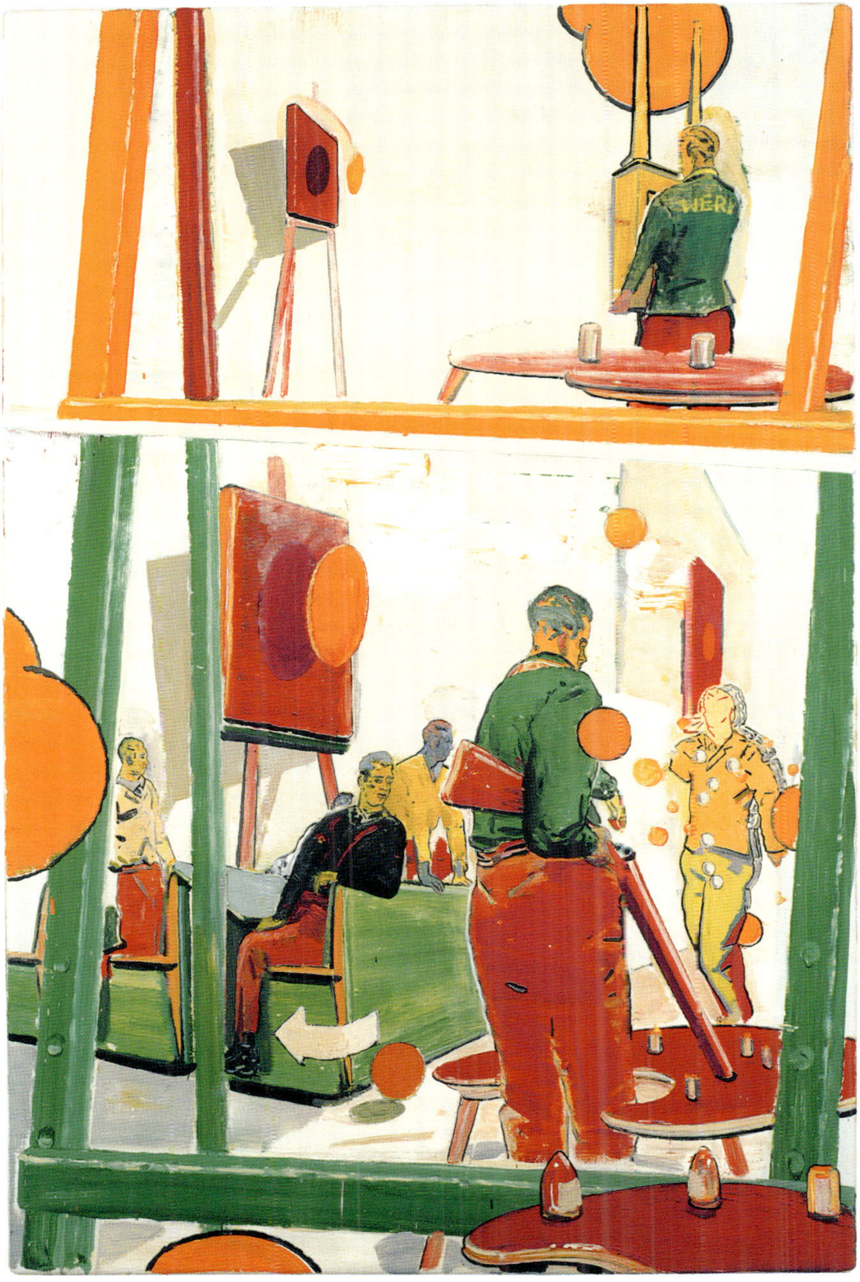

Neo Rauch
Unerträglicher Naturalismus, 1998
160 x 105 cm
Sammlung Ruth
Courtesy Galerie EIGEN+ART, Berlin • Leipzig
Courtesy David Zwirner Gallery, New York

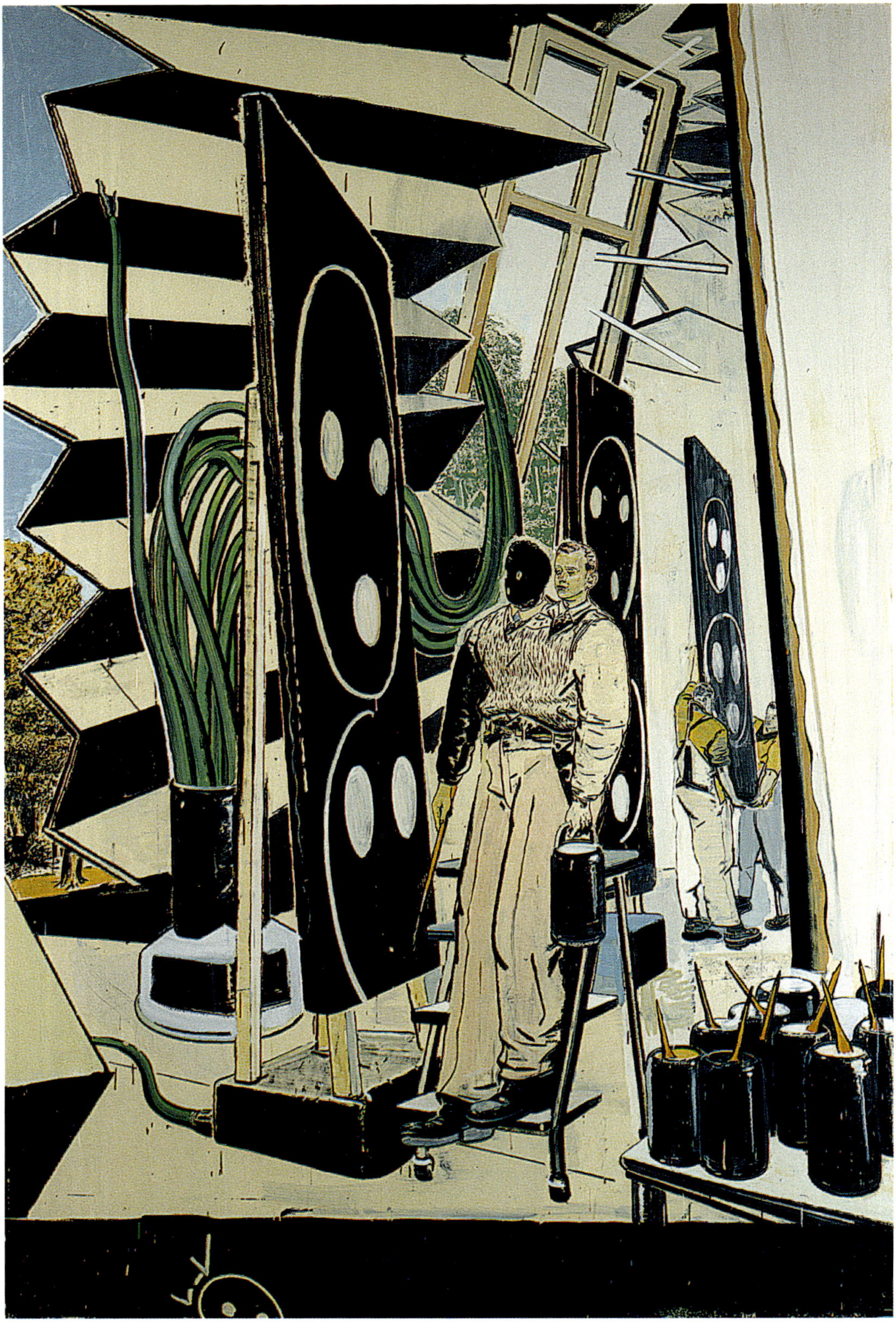

Neo Rauch
Die Wahl, 1998
300 x 200 cm
Sammlung Ruth
Courtesy Galerie EIGEN+ART, Berlin / Leipzig
Courtesy David Zwirner Gallery, New York

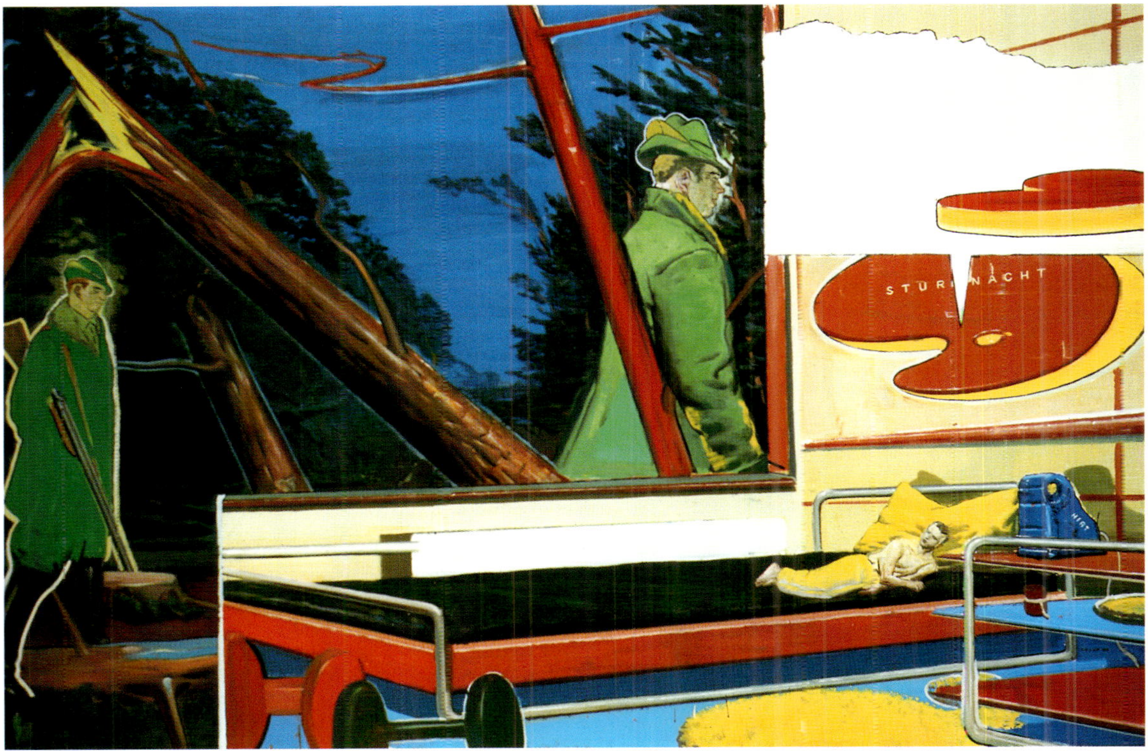

Neo Rauch
Sturmnacht, 2000
200 x 300 cm
Sammlung Goetz, München

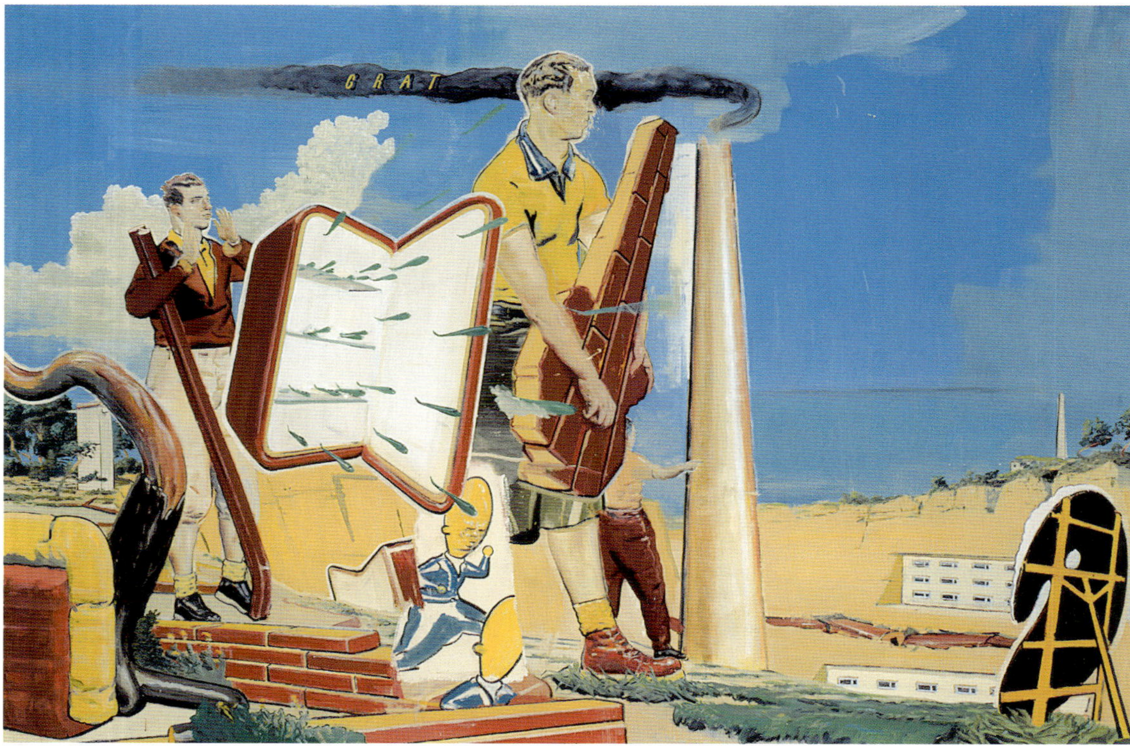

Neo Rauch
Grat, 2000
200 x 300 cm
Collection particulière / Privatsammlung / Private Collection
Courtesy Galerie EIGEN+ART, Berlin / Leipzig

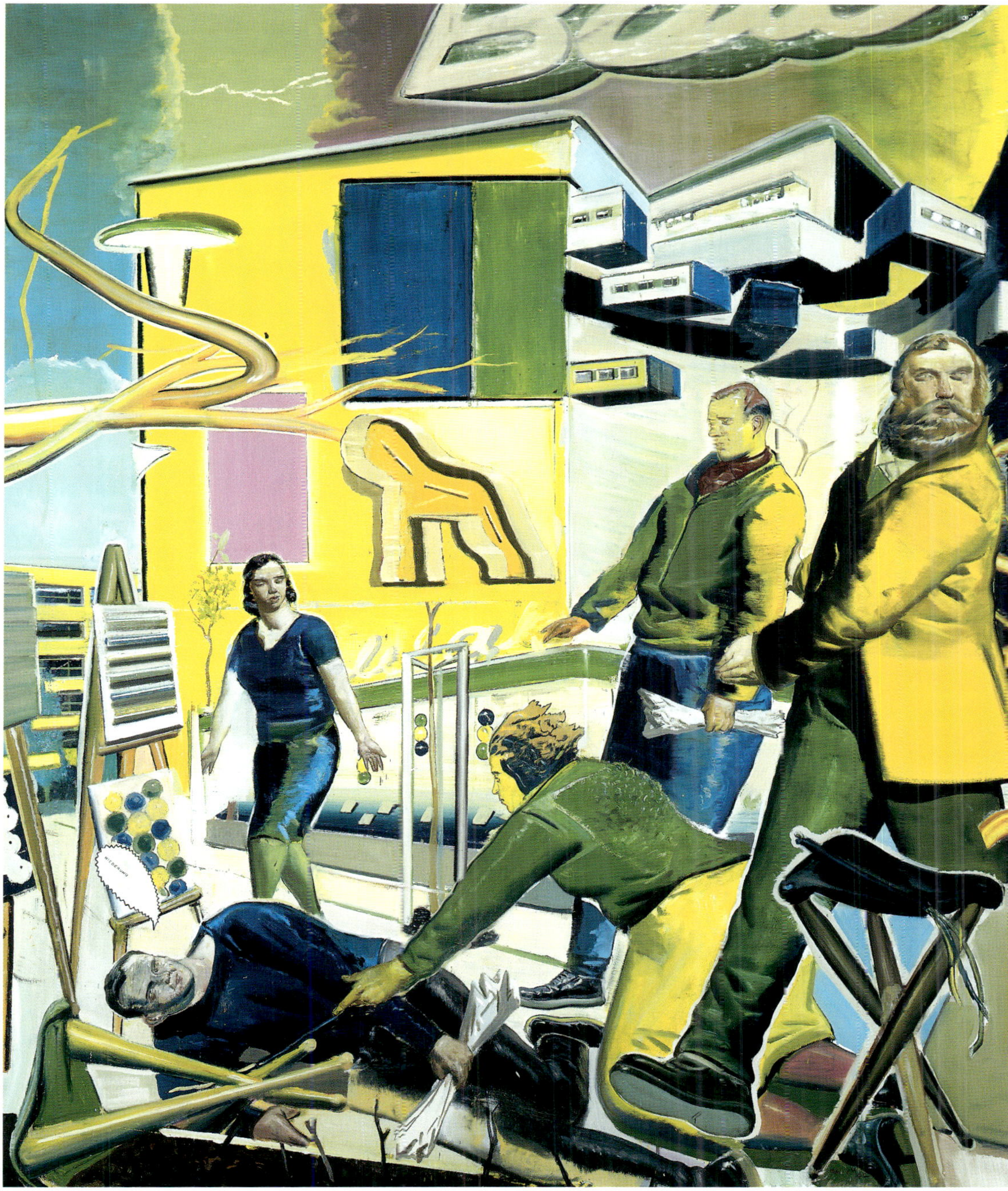

Neo Rauch
Niederung, 2001-2002
250 x 210 cm
Collection particulière / Privatsammlung / Private Collection
Courtesy Galerie EIGEN+ART, Berlin / Leipzig

Kai Althoff

Gabriele Mackert

Kai Althoff draws pictures and creates sculptures, he engages in performance work and unites various other elements to create space-filling ensembles. His hybrid installations are almost always accompanied by textual utterances–he also writes the scripts for his own performances, videos, and films. Far from being a painter in the narrow sense of the word, he does not want to be identified solely with painting nor any other single medium. Instead, Althoff sees painting as just one opportunity of focusing his attention on things, while drawing offers another, faster and more efficient means. His practice is characterized by a sense of fascination with his ability to create a new world and at the same time take on the role of a discoverer in that world; to experience the moment of a first sighting and to view one's own creation full of amazement. Althoff expresses this dual, distanced, vision in his amazement at "who it was inside you that is now standing before you." It seems like a wondrous state of schizophrenia, one without the side effects: resulting from a desire for an autopoetic system that connects production and reception in an eternal circular closure.

Althoff's most conspicuous artistic modes are his strong sense of ambivalence and a celebration of styles. His work is a multi-layered conglomeration of private worlds, various pop universes, and seemingly unremarkable, everyday moments. His attitude perfectly reflects the contemporary climate where a variety of alternatives and perspectives are concurrently available–whether in the fields of fashion, music, or art. This heterogeneous pattern of possibilities extends to current models of identity and gender. Althoff embraces a thematic and stylistic plurality that defies any definitive classification–his panorama is without direction. Althoff repeatedly introduces historic references that he transforms into timeless elements of his work by the manner in which they are integrated into an endless system of references: the past, as a harbinger of what is to come, potentially holds the future. This attitude crystallizes a sense of the utopian while also giving Althoff's œuvre a strange, un-contemporary appearance. This hermetic agglomeration of historical layers and references makes it difficult for the viewer to access Althoff's work.

Points of orientation are formal codes and narrative structures. To take a specific example, Althoff is fascinated by the exceptionally succinct and graphic art that emerged in the wake of World War II in the 1950s; its reductive effects express an impressive simplification. A second important artistic reservoir for Althoff is the 1970s with its radically different mood rooted in a utopian spirit, youthful immaturity, and latent desire. Althoff combined this fascination in the founding of a fictitious band called *Ashley's*. He produced an edition of an elaborate booklet in the shape of a record sleeve that was designed like an homage to the [Beatles'] *Yellow Submarine* stylistic period. On the record cover, the band members are posing under the slogan *A Coming Out*. Inside the sleeve, song titles such as *Liberated*, *Supergroup*, and *Thinking People* are listed, functioning as a commentary on the 13 felt-tip-pen-drawings that illustrate the communal life of the group of musicians. Althoff's depiction of this extravagant community reveals a frightening uniformity and an eerie sameness of the individuals. This transformation from utopia to conformity results in part from the androgyny of the members of the band and partly from the fact that the images focus primarily on an expression of the fashion of the day.

Other works of his, again, in their colorful and comic strip-like, blatant style come close to Pop Art. In more recent pieces, Althoff seems to be drawing on an Expressive Realism that could be related to Grosz as much as to Barlach and Kollwitz. His palette of muted greens, reds, and browns seems to convey a somewhat stale atmosphere. All of these references are not found citations but Althoff's own experiences, concrete memories, and socialization. He re-visualizes this cosmos.

Quite often formal conventions are confronted with subject matter that initially seems to be unrelated. In an early series of drawings, he drew a scene of a young man's coming out as a homosexual in the style of illustrations found in Enid Blyton books. In this example, form functions as a conservative, handed-down experience, while content functions as a revolutionary principle that can update this relationship or subject it to a test of greater elasticity. This dialectic creates a distancing effect and provokes a disconcerting appeal. In Althoff's cryptic world of references, viewers will have to come up with their own images and their own conclusions. Unlike the realm of politics, where an ambivalent relationship to reality can potentially be a disaster, that very sort of relationship can be productive in art—especially with regard to either the wealth of reciprocal social, formal, and aesthetic or the individual sensory dispositions it can produce. Beyond concrete political partisanship or aggressive positioning there is a merely critical potential in the figure of the (artist) subject who becomes a filter that can transmit social imagery from various periods and contexts to the individual viewer.

In his mixing-together of existential desires, subversion, and extravagance, Althoff's subject matter refuses to have a theoretical or distanced analysis of our preoccupation with the everyday and the trivial. He is not interested in a juxtaposition of high and low. Without prejudice, Althoff experiments with languages of form that for various reasons have been shunned or have negative connotations. He often borrows motifs and patterns from applied art or popular art that is usually dismissed as decorative kitsch of the bourgeoisie. In the same manner, without any reservation or prejudice, he can also introduce elements of abstract forms into otherwise concretely figurative works.

This art practice is characterized by an incredible sense of seriousness, precision, and calculation and exudes an atmosphere of organized craft courses or is imbued with a sense of melancholy, failure, and incompleteness. In his rendering of human figures, for example, faces are treated in great detail, while other areas of the figure are drawn in simple outline or as volumes, filled, almost in a manner of conscientious slogging, with lines or cross-hatchings. His tendency to employ fairy-tale-like subjects as well as spiritual, esoteric, and socially utopian themes is evocative of Althoff's own memories or interpretations of Romanticism. This recollection of an important part of the German artistic past acts as a protest movement against the alienating effects of the emergence of ubiquitous Capitalist functionalism. In the same manner, Althoff's evocation of Dandyism can be seen as a response to industrialization or Neo-Liberalism. His confrontation of past and present recalls the humanist concerns of the Enlightenment as well as the continual crisis of the Self.

Indeed, this reference to Romanticism in Althoff's œuvre garners results on many levels. The desires of that historical era are characterised by terms such as infinite, elementary, and universal—while at the same time,—lead to a break away from these concepts. The heroes of Novalis and similar writers of the time had to endure whole series of incredible adventures and extreme tests until they would reach a state of catharsis. The romantic notion of "all-in-one" implied that text, image, and music production should be unified and that such artistic activity should be carried out communally, in pairs, or in groups. In her examination of this romantic notion and its connection to contemporary reference points in Althoff's work, art critic Anja Dorn speaks not only about sampling or hyperlink methods, but as well about production partnerships that Althoff repeatedly enters into with Cosima von Bonin and others. These elements make up a Romantic superstructure in this œuvre. "Moreover, though, Althoff's proximity to Romanticism lies precisely in his critical questioning of what art wants to or is able to do."[1]

The stories that Althoff creates for his installations as well as his texts stand somewhat encrypted on one side of his practice. They describe in great detail a relationship or establish a narrative context for a work through titles alone. Even if these stories are partially reminiscent of instruction manuals or situation reports, they are never explanatory (my work deals with ...) or didactic (the purpose of my work is ...). Instead, they actually function as a set of guidelines for Althoff's own artistic production—in the manner of dramatic scripts or the voice-over of a narrator-guide in an epic theater. This narrative strategy defines Althoff's work and positions the viewers as protagonists in his scenario.

In 1994 Althoff exhibited three drawings that formally recalled children's picture books. One work depicts a teenager on a train, his left hand on a flag, his gaze focused out the window on a rural village backdrop with timber-framed houses. In the second work, a youth is standing in front of a medieval house making a threatening gesture. In the third, a baker is greeting passers-by with a (politically) misleading gesture. All of the drawings were presented in a overtly dignified style: black mats and conservative wooden frames. The title of this trio of drawings, *Uwe: Auf guten Rat folgt Missetat* (Uwe: Misdeeds Follow Good Advice) suggests the formulaic quality of proverbs or standardized epigrams. The relationship between the titles of these works and the content of the drawings is similar to the illustration of a parable. Yet the drawings do not exactly fulfill this task as the viewer is left to imagine what the moral of the parable, or the misdeed of the title, might actually be.

In a gallery exhibition entitled *In Search of Eulenkippstadt* in London in 1997, Althoff created a similar, complex arrangement. The exhibition also began with an accompanying text that recounts a (fictitious) background story: When researching the history of her hometown—a place called Eulenkippstadt in Southwestern Germany—a young bookseller named Karin comes across references to an occult society that used to live there. In the forest, she encounters the spirits of the dead who try to convince her to overthrow the existing society and reinstate an old, more socially responsible state. Through this introductory narrative, the individual elements that make up the gallery installation are endowed with more specific meanings. papier-mâché balloons illuminated from the inside become a conspiratorial society. Empty wine bottles characterize these secret nocturnal meetings. Nature is introduced by way of animal drawings, and Eulenkipp-stadt itself is represented by corresponding depictions of village architecture. Karin's forest hut also contains various allusions to the philosophical tradition of German forest imagery further contextualizing the scenery.

Althoff designed the installation *Aus Dir* (From Within You) as a space for experiences that provoked narration through its textual quality. This space gave the impression that it was a room for reflection; it was to be a "Christian place of encounter," as Althoff put it. Green light came from above, there was a pervasive scent of perfumed candles, partitions that were half the height of the ceiling divided the room into individual observation boxes. The walls were decorated with images of typically German scenes such as photographs of the Nuremberg Christmas market. Photocopied flyers were pinned to the walls showing found objects from the Christian aesthetic sphere or photographs of monastic brotherhoods. Althoff's own drawings were also affixed to the wall like posters. The drawings used Christian mythology as their source material, showing for example well known episodes from the life of Francis of Assisi, or monks whose torsos were depicted as color compositions with cross-hatched surfaces. Only the strangely helpless and bashful faces of these figures were drawn with more plasticity. The shrouded, sack-like figures turned away from naked physicality with horror. They cast a forbidden glance at such physical temptation from the corner of their eyes as in the last image of the series. It was in this way that the cryptic series of works, *Aus Dir,* examined the question of happiness achieved through renunciation.

Althoff's protagonists do not exist, nor are they individual characters. Despite their names (Uwe or Karin, for example), their function is circumstantial–they serve to incarnate abstract beings and ideas. Althoff emphasizes constellations, interactions and socio-emotional expressions that he finds remarkable not merely in paintings or drawings, but equally so, for example, in accumulations of garbage. Because of his implicit references to social concerns, his work can be easily linked to the context-oriented art of the 1980s and 1990s. His criticism of visual culture draws on props from the past, leads us through realms of the mythical, and consequently distances itself from an analytic-minimalist tradition. Althoff's time machine is equally permeated by the negation of the present, nostalgia, a sense of non-simultaneousness, as well as a strong sentiment of optimism.

Perhaps his most recent exhibition in New York can be read as a cross-section of his idiosyncratic body of work. Abstract pictorial works were presented alongside figurative paintings. Thirty small-scale paintings, drawings, and photographs were hung in a loose configuration. The various materials Althoff used–marine lacquer, varnish, and resin–seemed to continue the habit of packaging art works in plastic covers. The surfaces of his paintings are simultaneously shiny and greasy; they are both voluminous and fragile. Althoff seemed to assemble a little gallery of his ancestors: withered, elongated figures that flirt with androgyny; coarse, aggressive creatures; soldiers; monks. The resulting pantheon is an eerie, foreboding collection of figures, a melange of mentalities. Seen in an American context, it was immediately read as a commentary on German history. "From canvas to canvas, a flawed but exquisite family tree arises, real and illusory ghosts of the fatherland emerge, and the frightful Nazi motto "Blut und Boden" (Blood and Soil) is given new meaning."[2] Althoff himself has found this reception to be exaggerated. After all, he attempts to use his ambivalence–manifested in the almost indifferent arrangement of the works in terms of appearance and content–to motivate the viewer to search for underlying meaning. Althoff's re-installation strategy is designed to provoke an examination of each work's emotional value.

(translated from the German by Tom Appleton)

Endnotes

1 Anja Dorn, "Kai Althoff: Unendliche Differenz," first published in Dutch language: "Eindeloze differentie", in *Metropolis M*, no. 5, October/November 2001, pp. 38-42.

2 Jerry Saltz, "History Painting," *The Village Voice,* New York, December 4, 2001.

Excerpts from an Interview with Kai Althoff by Angela Rosenberg

AR: How important is language for your work?

KA: I am using language in both music and art. Thus it is very important to me. I spend a lot of time to find the right words who'd exactly tell me what I want to know, that in themselves carry the preconceived contents that ease all misunderstanding. Or I build sentences that demand slow reading. I try to use easy, good words. I don't use technical terms, unless unavoidable, or foreign words. Often the more educated people are, the more hideous their talking becomes. You can tell something complex in straight words, if you're a good person. I love German dialects of various kinds, they influenced me a lot.

AR: Is there anything specifically "German" in your work and the subjects you choose? Are you a storyteller?

KA: There must be, as I consider it truly "Heimat" to me. I wouldn't want to be anywhere else. I am telling stories on it sometimes. I tell them rather to myself in the first place. It happens almost automatically that these stories arise within, and I guess I use them to find out why I feel about something the way I do. Or where this feeling derives from, furthermore why feelings of the same kind may be apparent in other, maybe fictional people's lives too. Maybe I'm trying to keep something apart from myself, that will already be me, or is me forever. Watching myself from afar and seeing all the others, thank God, amongst whom I live.

AR: In your installations, paintings and drawings you refer to imagery of the middle ages, as well as to icons of popular culture, primarily from the 1970s. Would you compare your artistic strategy to the method of "sampling"?

KA: Yeah, maybe sampling. I collect things, but I don't go and hunt for them. I see things, and some stir my heart so much, like some photograph in a magazine that tells everything I ever wanted to utter in that moment – or the way somebody has decorated the room he lives in, that kills me and I watch in awe, stunned and keep quiet, and feel there's no more I'd want to see in life. Once I saw three young police officers on a sunny day, one female in the middle and two males to her left and right, slightly proud of their freshly gained powerful position. Yet still a little awkward in their walking and wish and eagerness to be helpful when asked by the public. It said: how beautiful a start in life can be. I keep things like that like an icon in my head.

AR: Do you consider specific historical paintings or icons as relevant or influential for you? What about found material or news clippings?

KA: As I said before, all of it may be of importance, also a historical painting that I like so much. It is also influential for me in the sense of "what it stands for to collect old Bavarian peasant furniture or gothic church-sculpture" by a maybe wealthy household. But then I look closely into the face of the saint's sculpture and it tells: you do wrong, you make me suffer even more.

AR: Your installations and drawings refer to historical sources, but switch between times and styles. How important is timelessness for you?

KA: All really important things in life are timeless. One is often unintentionally timeless, let's say when you love somebody, or when you are in such rage that you beat somebody up really badly. Very good art and music is timeless, but is also limited to only exist some time.

AR: What social and political relevance does "style" have for you? I read you consider 'style as resistance'?

KA: Style to me is what you can do to let outsiders know: I am not like you. I want to be like all of you. I am militant. I know exactly how I look. I am a member of a society which has very strong concepts about how to live and so on. It is what people do to where they live. Everything and everyone has got style, and therefore is visible in all the things I do too. Is attitude and composure, what I mean? Yes.

AR: You treat your sources from the 1970s not simply as archive material, but as perceptual memories that go right back into your own childhood. What are the reasons for using these sources now?

KA: That childhood is really a revelation to me. Everything is there already. It is ever so mysterious and all-over powerful to me.

Things that happened have become archetypal in my mind, they loom large. The way things were perceived by myself then is something that I try to get back to again and again even I don't realize it happily. I seem to have absorbed something there badly, in the late 1960s and 1970s. Probably it could have been any other time. I also gladly feel that it loosens its grip on me. In general I like the past, and how it could have been and become a perfect future.

Endnote

First published: *Kai Althoff, Interview by Angela Rosenberg*, in Flash Art International, May-June 2002, No. 224. It was written by the artist in English and has not been altered from its original version.

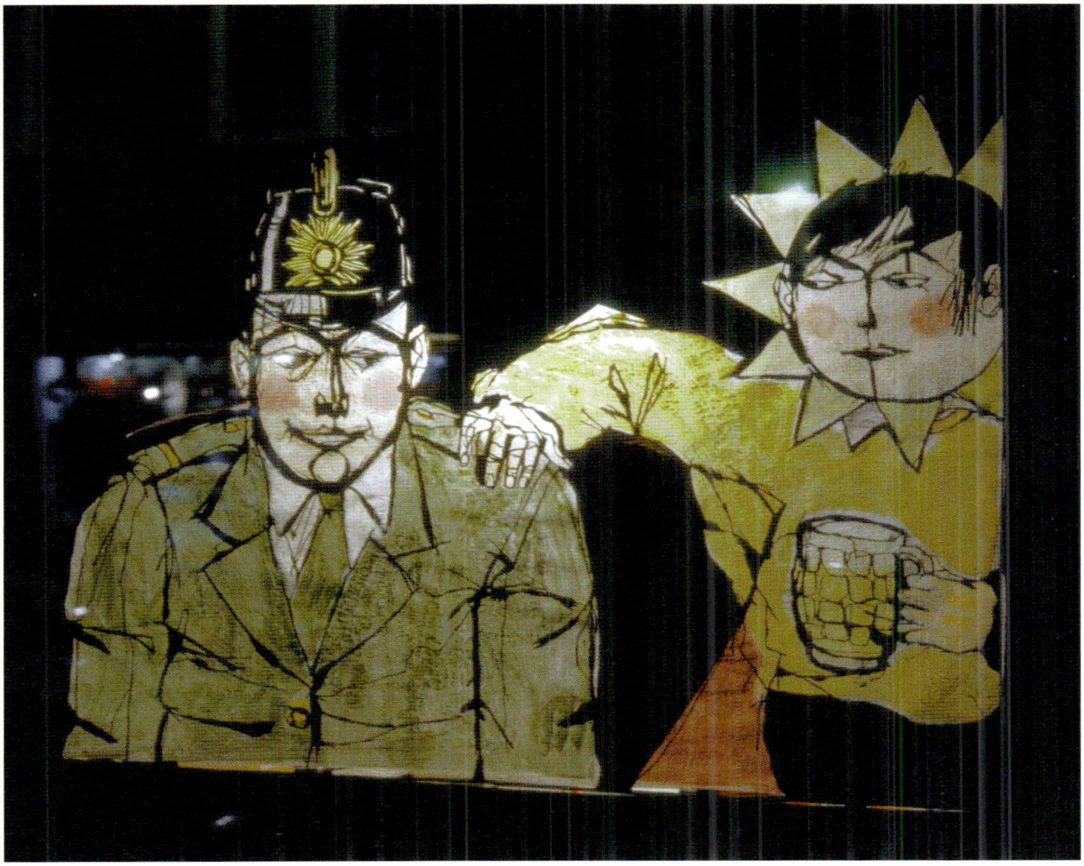

Kai Althoff
Ohne Titel, 1993
100 x 135 cm
Collection de l'artiste / Besitz des Künstlers / Collection of the artist, Köln
Courtesy Galerie Christian Nagel, Köln

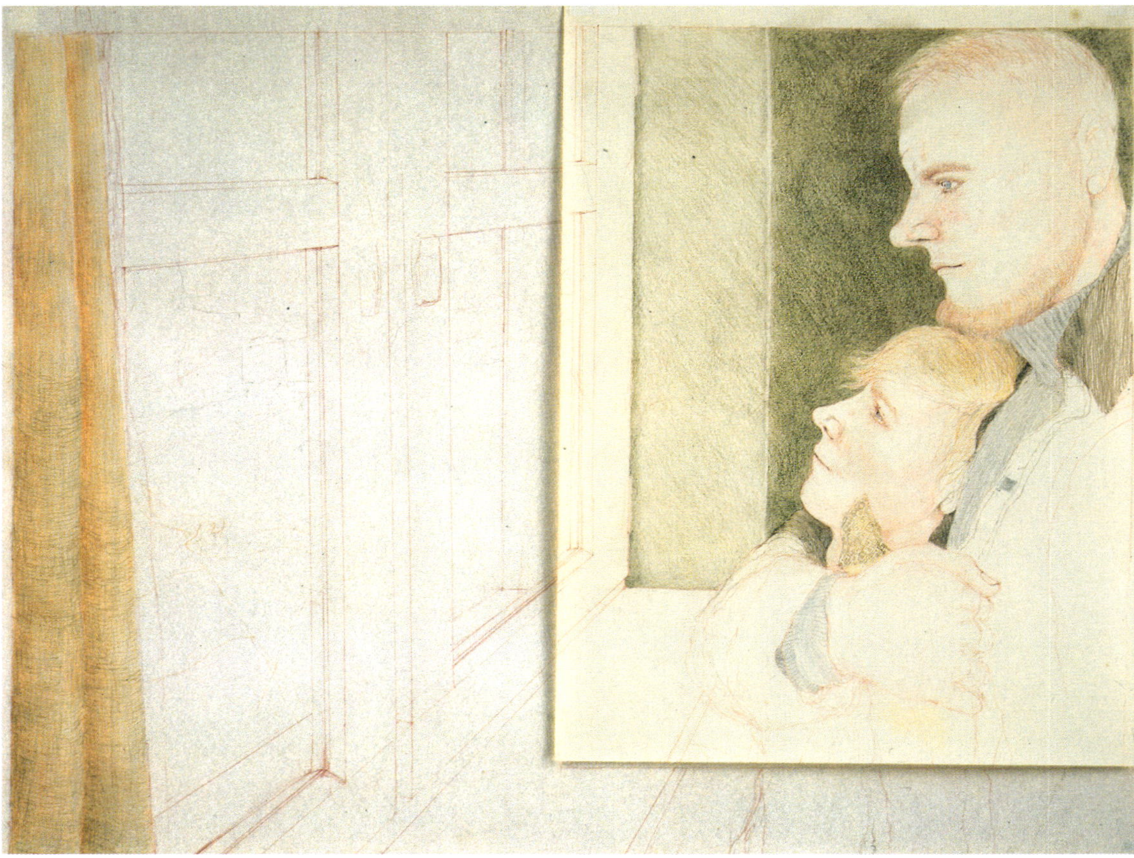

Kai Althoff
Ohne Titel, 1998
35,2 x 47,2 cm
Collection Alexander Schröder, Berlin

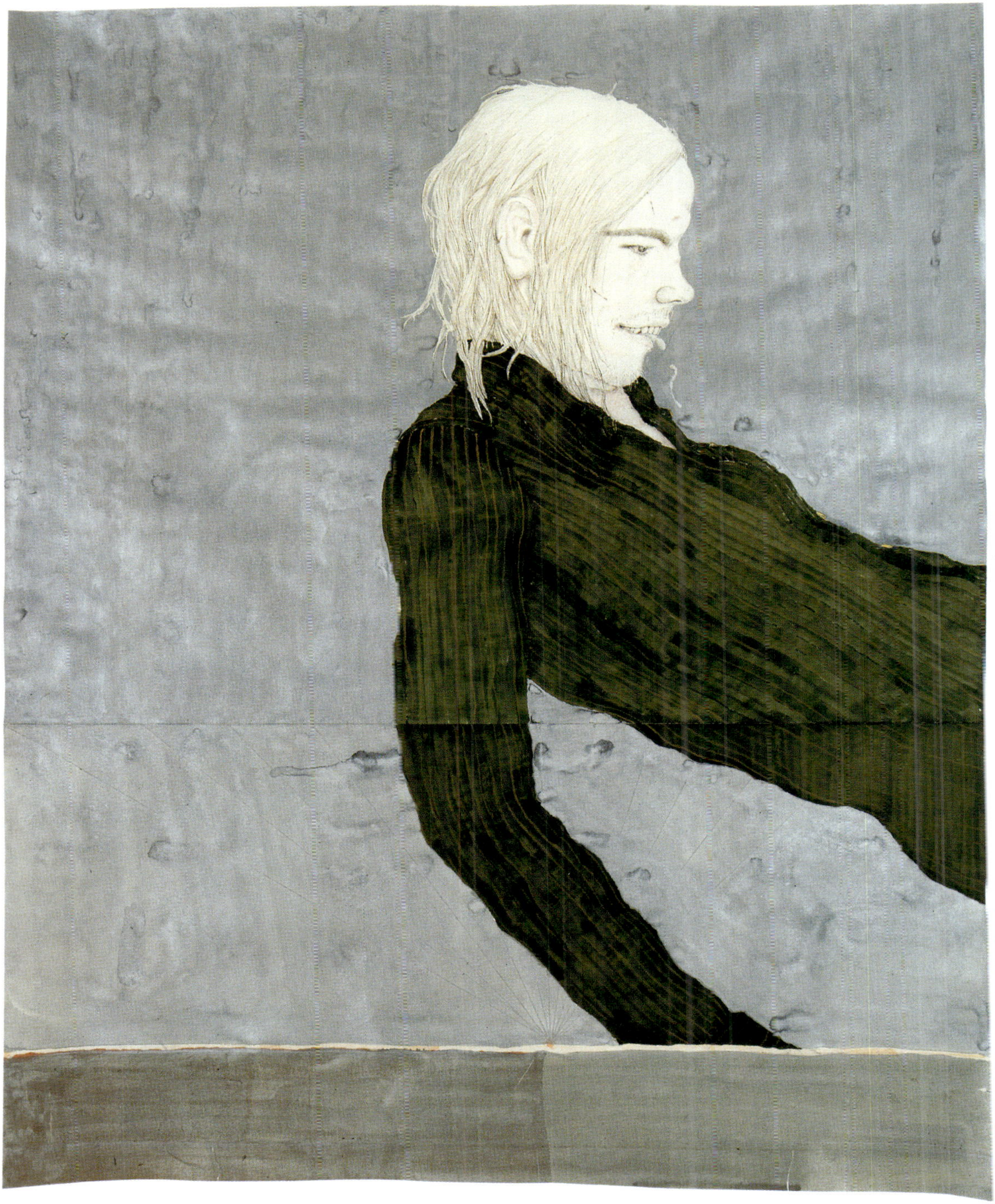

Kai Althoff
Aleph, 2000
68,5 x 55,8 cm
Collection Dean Valentine & Amy Adelson, Los Angeles
Courtesy Galerie Daniel Buchholz, Köln

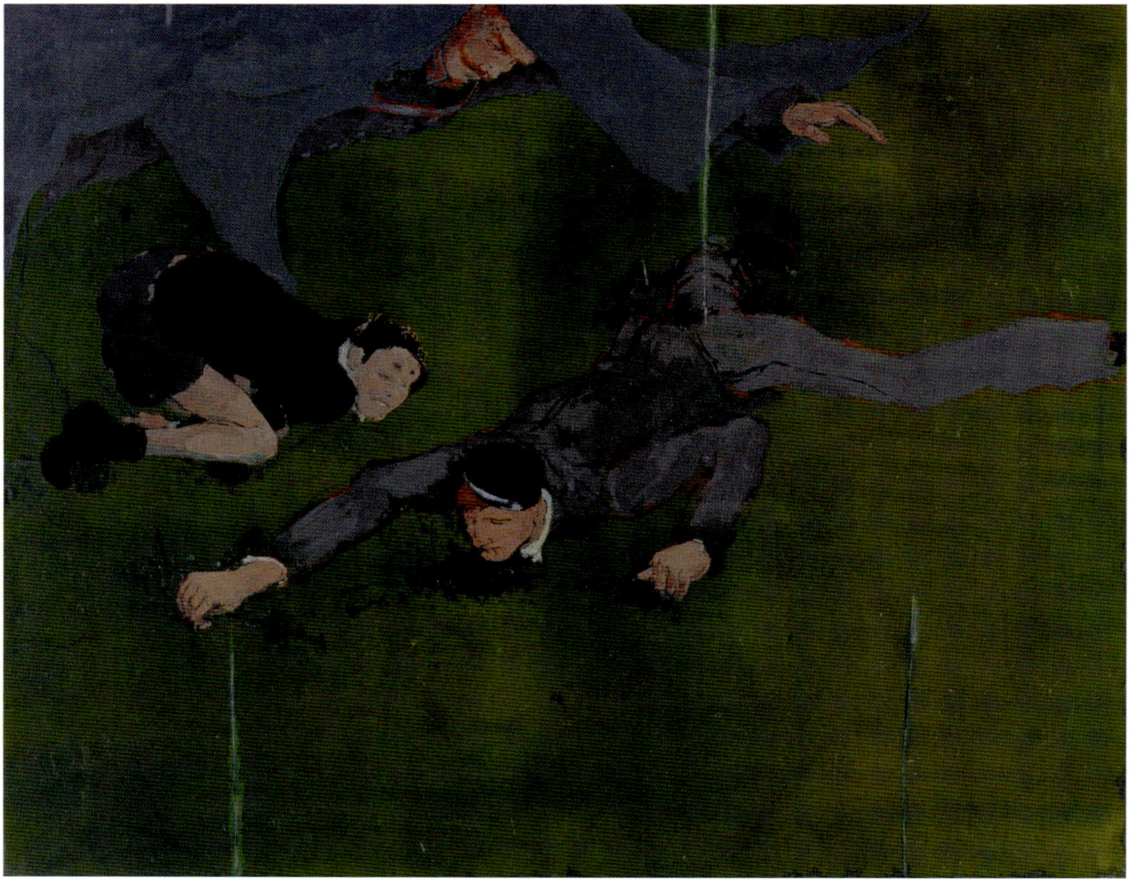

Kai Althoff
Ohne Titel, (aus der Serie *Impulse)*, 2001
40 x 50 x 4,2 cm
Collection Ivelin & Craig Robins, Miami Beach
Courtesy Anton Kern Gallery, New York

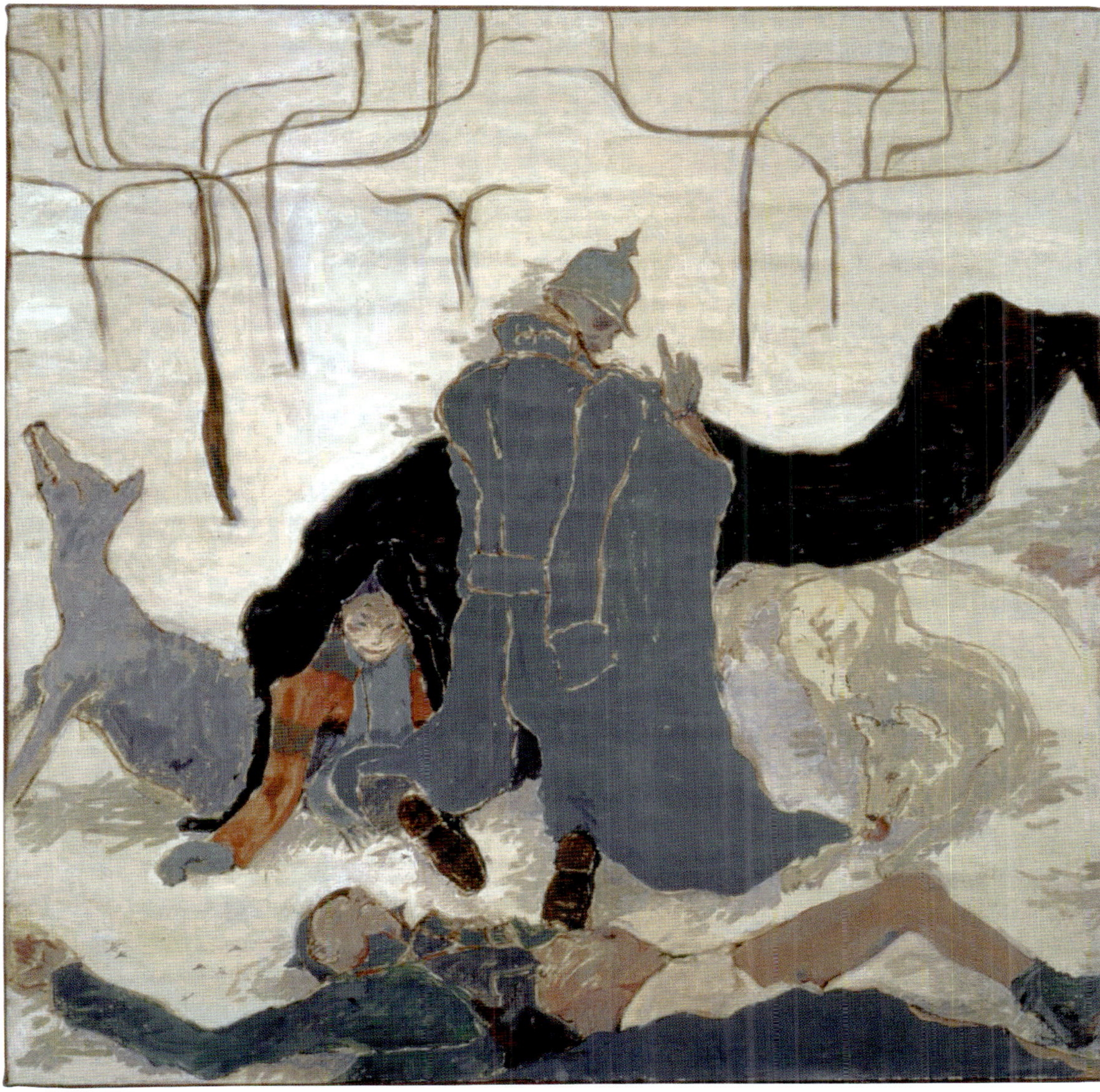

Kai Althoff
Ohne Titel, (aus der Serie *Impulse)*, 200[illegible]
40 x 40 x 4,5 cm
Collection Karola Grässlin, Köln
Courtesy Galerie Christian Nagel, Köln

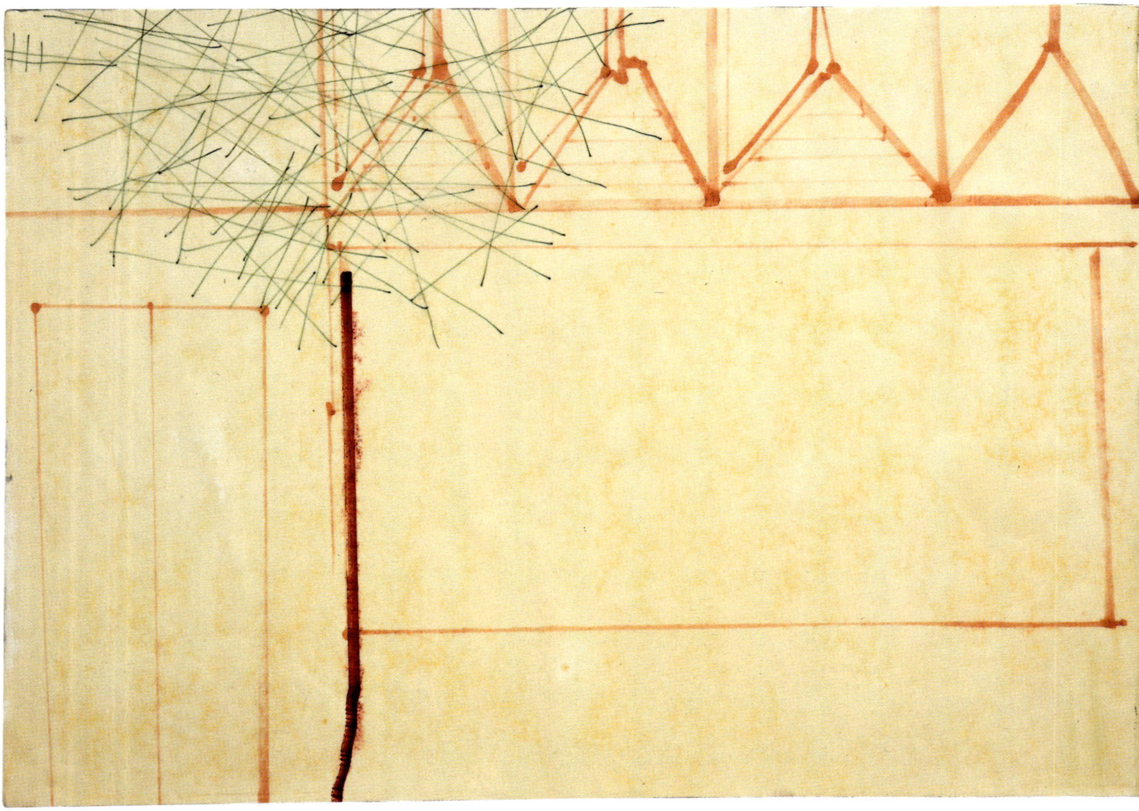

Kai Althoff
Ohne Titel, (aus der Serie *Impulse),* 2001
50 x 70 x 8 cm
Collection particulière / Privatsammlung / Private Collection, Chicago
Courtesy Anton Kern Gallery, New York

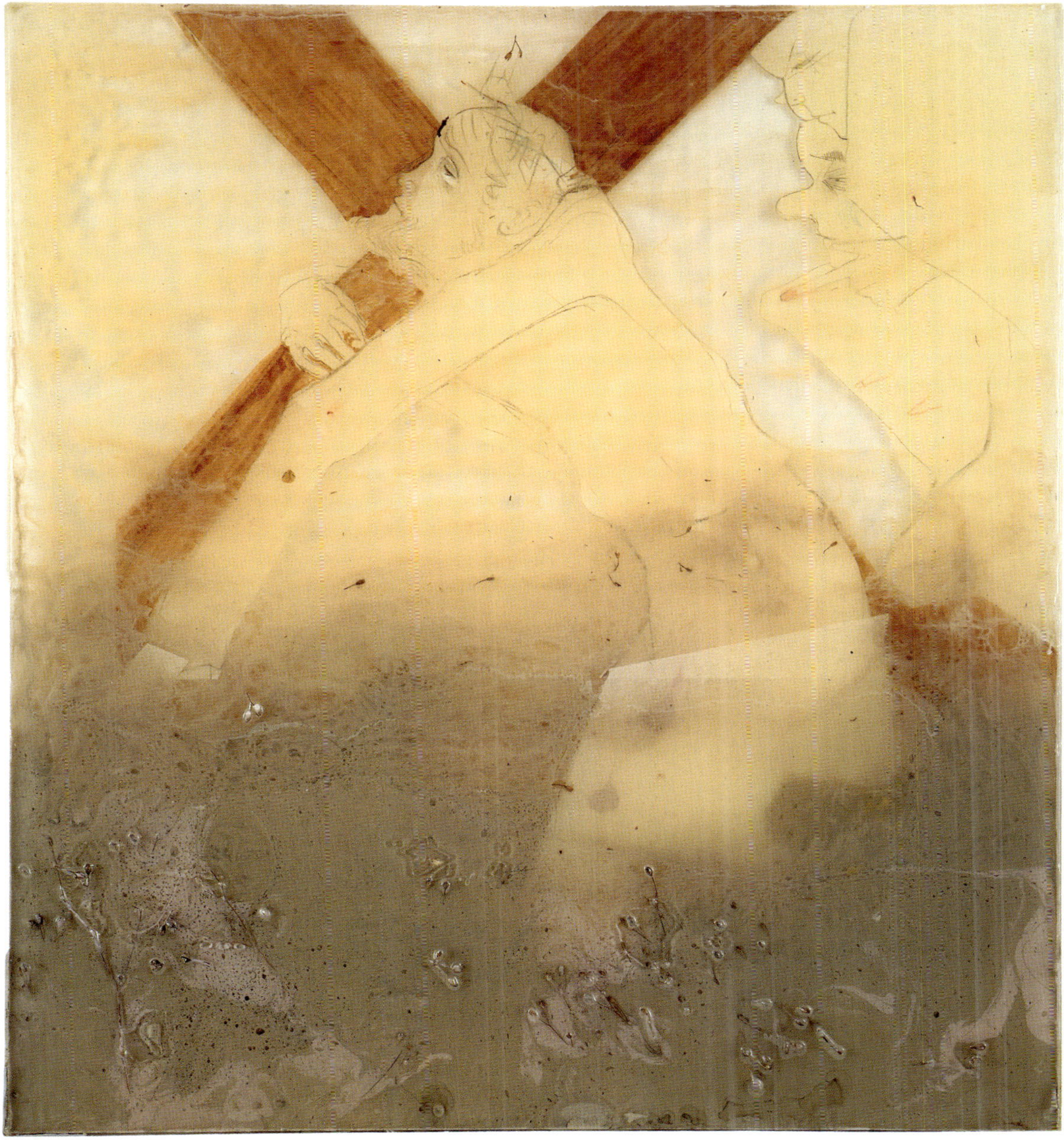

Kai Althoff
Ohne Titel, (aus der Serie *Impulse)*, 2001
70 x 64 x 4 cm
Collection Susan & Michael Hort, New York
Courtesy Anton Kern Gallery, New York

Luc Tuymans

Sabine Folie

SF: In his essay on modern art, *Peintres de l'empêchement* (1948), Samuel Beckett pointed out that it is dangerous to elevate the appearance of failure in art—an absence of "expression"—to the status of an end in itself. The lack of reference points would itself become the absolute expression and, therefore, the impossibility of action would become expressive action. Artists find themselves in this double bind which involves paradoxes which even Beckett couldn't escape. One might think of his films such as *Comédie* (1966) or *Ghost Trio* (1976), which exemplify his abstract, "voided" conception of space. Figures surface in these spaces and, as Expressionist characters, they stand for something and convey meaning. What importance, conversely, do you place in the confrontation between abstract space and the trace, or recollection, of human action in your painting?

LT: Beckett was, of course, entirely right in pointing out in his notes on Modernism that the totality of meanings entails a danger of loss of meaning and might subvert both the subjective and the objective sides. This approach is, however, in a certain sense, also a non-sustainable hypothesis, because it simply prolongs the dilemma and this is of great existential significance. Modern painters such as Mondrian or Malevich always stuck to their goals or to masterminding them, which was considered the only historical justification of contemporary painting without the need for conjuring up the spectre of the end of painting. Viewed in this light, the stance adopted by Beckett in the 1940s was already an anachronistic one and, from the standpoint of artistic praxis, obsolete. Nonetheless, his ideas about theatre and representation, which have been or are represented by the three types of sign—*icon, index* and *symbol*—are still relevant today. His redefinition of the role of the "document" in art, which gave artists the possibility of placing their work in a context, has also proved applicable to contemporary art.
Most of my works are concerned with pre-existing or "third-order" representations. My pictures usually focus on a particular meaning which cannot be inferred solely from the picture. The content of pictures is sometimes an interpretation of historical circumstances—but always in a processed form so as to divert attention from the aspect of reproduction. It should be emphasized in this context that all representation fundamentally implies the absence of the object represented and can never allay uncertainty about whether what is represented ever did in fact exist at all. Consequently, all my pictures might be called questionable or ambivalent; it really isn't all that easy to classify where they stand as art. What is at stake is the point at which the sublime becomes the antithesis of discourse, thus removing painting from the sphere of "the exoticism of self". This idea of self-referentiality is linked to the way painting has already been sublimated in Western culture so that paintings become something peculiar. The subject of painting has become self-aware. Bertrand Russell was right when he wrote as long ago as 1964 that we have become democratic, not only in externals but also in our innermost convictions.

SF: I don't think that Beckett's stance was obsolete by any means; after all, he did raise the issue, which was sparked by the Suprematism of a Malevich or the teleology of a Mondrian–only to be exacerbated by Abstract Expressionism. What was at stake was questioning the validity of truth, which crept in by the back door in the absolutism of the Abstract Expressionists. Picabia's assault on public taste directly targeted this artistic expressiveness.
The problem of representing the unrepresentable after the collosal catastrophe of the Second World War brought about abstraction. In turn abstraction, at least in Beckett's theater, produced a realism, which then turned into a peculiarly "Existential" reductionism because of its high degree of aesthetic sophistication. This, as you say, naturally raised the question of representing representation—a question which became crucial with the invention of photography and even more so in early cinema.
The theory of the *icon*, the *symbol* and the *index*, which C. S. Peirce (1839-1914) formulated in the latter half of the 19th century, seems to me to be relevant in this context. If, as you have said, painting is a "delayed" medium, then we must consider Peirce's formula in the following manner: painting is the *icon*, a mediated form of representation which seeks to imitate or approach reality; the *symbol* is linguistic expression; and, finally, the *index* is the trace left by reality

on the photographic plate, the imprint or chemical residue of reality. In what way does your painting that draws on photographic and filmic models constitute an "authentic forgery", as you have called it?
Roland Barthes famously wrote that photography attests to "that has been", arguing that something of reality emanates from a photo, like the shining of a distant star.[1] In what way does painting function as a document in your work? What transformation does the indexical trace undergo in your pictures? Perhaps you could discuss your series *Der diagnostische Blick* ("Diagnostic View", 1992), which is being shown in this exhibition?

LT: Apart from my very early, realistic works, the pictures from *Der diagnostische Blick* have been most strongly influenced by the realism of photography and are the most naturalistic of all my work to date. They are based on illustrations in a handbook of the same title. As far as this series is concerned, one might call the subjects of the pictures *indices* since the illustrations were used to show the symptoms which enable a physician to diagnose particular diseases. For a long time I was unable to paint any portraits and needed illness as a pretext for doing so. I didn't want to paint portraits in the literal sense of the word, either to express a personality or to illustrate a recollection, which might merely have induced yet another failure of representation. My turning to the medical function of representation, which presupposes a direct relationship between the signifier and the signified as a given, has allowed the picture to become once again an uncoded image. The various expressions of indifference and the complete passivity shown by the subjects indicate that these portraits are concerned with the illnesses they have and not with them as people. In referring explicitly to an iconic index—a symptom—a work seems to be seeking reality yet, in *Der diagnostische Blick*, the very quality which might make representation an encounter of this kind with reality is also a means of over-looking it because it focuses solely on the symptoms. I haven't painted any signs indicating a particular illness or suggesting how these signs might change the organism; instead I've represented what the diagnostic glance achieves: empty shells are all that are left of the people affected by the diagnoses. In this respect, the diagnostic glance makes faces congeal into masks, into impersonal façades, and it's hardly surprising that these close-up shots of pathological changes on the skin recall landscapes.
In this sense I've done my best to make the attempt at a confrontation with reality fail. In these pictures I've also worked for the first time with brush strokes which run across the picture surface in the horizontal without really bothering about the contours of the figures—a closure strategy which entails ignoring both the subject and the represention of it, consequently increasing the autonomy of the painterly in order to underscore that pictures themselves are symptomatic of illness. In *Der diagnostische Blick* the representation of indexical signs becomes the indicator of a disease in the picture, which, by ignoring reality, configures its own trauma.

SF: In *Der diagnostische Blick* the appearance of reality is almost brutally experienced more as a disguise than a revelation. The subject of these paintings is the act of looking from an instrumental, scientific and hypostasizing perspective. Your usual strategies of omission, allusion and empty space are absent in these paintings. What is also absent is what could be described as an auratic or atmospheric quality—despite the fact that the faces and bodies are made melancholic and enigmatic by being displayed and objectified. Proust speaks of the "the latent image" in reference to photography. He views photography as the equivalent of reality. To him it doesn't represent a loss of meaning or reality, but rather a gain in knowledge, an experience of something that remains invisible, of something "more" than would normally be perceived by the unfocused, mundane glance. The eye of the camera is non-human, as Brassaï stated. In other words, it has a gaze which penetrates. In this sense Proust overestimated the objectivizing eye of the camera. After all, the photo is a product of both the photographer's and the spectator's subjective viewpoints, which results in a polyfocal world of meaning. It is the polyfocality of photography that also surfaces in Proust's narrative technique. In this sense one could think of painting as a medium which can only speak indirectly about reality and the latent truth it contains—especially when it derives from photographs, as it does in your work.
Although one can identify a distinct tendency towards abstraction in your pictures, there is also the will to document, to reconstruct memory through the pictoral process, albeit fragmentarily, just as details from photos and film clips are always denotative yet still generate meaning.
Your abstract painting works with realism, or under the guise of realism. Subversion takes place both in terms of form and content or as Eisenstein put it: "Color begins where it no longer corresponds to natural coloring." Eisenstein is calling here for a process of alienation, a detachment from factual reality, e.g. the significance of history. Roland Barthes speaks about this in terms of numbness, where "touching", "sensitive" or fetishist emotions no longer generate meaning but in fact invalidate meaning. This numbness is disturbing in the same way as the apparently decontextualized objects features or people in your pictures. This raises quite a number of questions. What constitutes recollection or memory in your pictures? How does detail relate to totality in your painting, compared, say, with film? What roles do the fetish, veiling and metonymy play?

LT: I've already pointed out that I deal primarily with existing images

in my work in order to demonstrate the inadequacy of memory. I still remember that, in the context of a symposium on recollecting and forgetting held several years ago at Amsterdam University, I happened to speak about whether we shouldn't ask ourselves, since the contemporary world is so imbued with its contemporaneity, whether there is still a need for recollection at all. When we go to the seaside nowadays, we are also visiting the image of the sea and, as a result, some images are obviously more archaic than others. I believe that painting is primarily concerned with archaic or iconic types of images. As to whether filmic aspects or details in close-up play a role in my work, you should know that I stopped painting between 1982 and 1985 in order to make films.
When I returned to painting, the way I approached pictures clearly showed the effect of this experience. A lot more was at stake than simply painting a still. My approach to the picture was different; it was as if painting and film were superimposed on one another—unlike photography, in which one has to give oneself entirely up to the moment. Of course there's a difference even when painting and film parallel each other: a film is written by movement into a context and brings forth a story whereas, in my pictures, the stillness decontextualizes the image so that a different narrative evolves through the process of reduction. Images which make an impact on me are mute: they don't evoke any sensations of sound in me; I can't recall objects in terms of scale, they're very colorful and radiate the color temperature of the colors. I'm very much in awe of painters like Manet, who were the first to mute images deliberately so that they can mutate - who gave their subject matter scope for abstraction and thus initiated a metonymical rather than metaphorical precept.

SF: As Foucault wrote about Manet: "Manet did certainly not invent non-representational painting since everything in his work is representational. However, he incorporated the basic material elements of painting into representation. He was on the brink of inventing the picture as object, the painting as object. This was basically the prerequisite for being able to liberate oneself entirely from representation and to allow the surface to play exclusively with its properties, the physical or material properties."[2]
After a detour through modernist painting, we have come full circle to Manet and "other" possible forms of realism. In between there has been quite a violent backlash in the form of strategies of rupture, distortion, quotation and wit, exemplifed by Picabia, who is the point of departure for this exhibition. What effect has Picabia's shameless eclecticism had on you? What, on the other hand, do you think of the realism of stillness found in the work of a van Eyck, van Hoogstraten, Saenredam or Vermeer? This stillness is also present in your pictures, created by your characteristic empty spaces (W. Iser) and indeterminacies (R. Ingarden). In 19th century debates about realism, the question of comprehensibility was particularly significant: Hegel, Lessing, Diderot all grappled with it. Diderot asked: "In painting, is it necessary to paint everything? Be merciful and leave a gap which my imagination can fill in." Gaps, then, need not necessarily be incomprehensible: they are themselves a sort of content and, paradoxically, can be referential. They broaden the picture. There are several examples of this in your work.
Your pictures make us particularly aware that what is involved is, according to the Italian philosopher Benedetto Croce (1866-1952), an "intuizione espressa" or "expressed intuition", that is, a rather "Neo-Classical-Idealistic" approach, if you will, to a metonymical painting of ideas. In your work an idea reaches maturity at the moment of being captured, hence the speed with which your pictures are executed. The sense of the fragmentary, ephemeral and instantaneous is thereby emphasised more strongly. What bearing does time have on your "metaphysical-realist" painting?

LT: I do appreciate Picabia's unabashed eclecticism although I consider him extremely amateurish and I think that his approach stemmed from whimsy and the luxury of belonging to the upper class. In the course of time his work became too much a sort of commentary on art history and its innumerable forms of interpretation. Viewed in this light, it developed into an idiosyncratic variety of self-indulgent outsider art that emerged from a very comfortable niche within the 1920s avant-garde. There is a certain similarity between this stance and the rather more fiendish posturing expressed in Kippenberger's pictures. Both were playing at being *enfants terribles* so as not to be pigeon-holed and, in this sense, Picabia was really a post-modernist.
As far as Jan van Eyck's realism is concerned, I can only answer with his motto: "als ic can" ("I do the best I can"), that means: modesty linked with vaulting ambition. As a Belgian painter, I am only all too aware of the importance of these pictures. Van Eyck (c.1390-1441) developed one of the most, if not the most, uncompromising forms of realism. On the whole, he viewed the spiritual with detachment but, by meticulously detailed rendering of fabric, clothing, the fall of folds of drapery and even figures, succeeded in making them present for all time. This is the aspect of eternity that was cultivated in those days by religion as the sole justification for science and that is why it's so difficult to draw comparisons with the amateurish painting that followed van Eyck.
And, in answer to your question on the role of time in my so-called meta-realist pictures, I can only say: time stands still.

(Sabine Folie's questions translated from the German by Joan Clough)

Endnotes

1 Roland Barthes. *Camera Lucida: Reflections on Photography*, Harper Collins, London 1984 [orig. 1980].

2 This is taken from Foucault's unpublished notes on Manet, *Le Noir et la couleur* ("Black and color"), delivered as a lecture at a conference on Manet at the Club Tahar Haddad in Tunisia in 1971. [Editor's note]

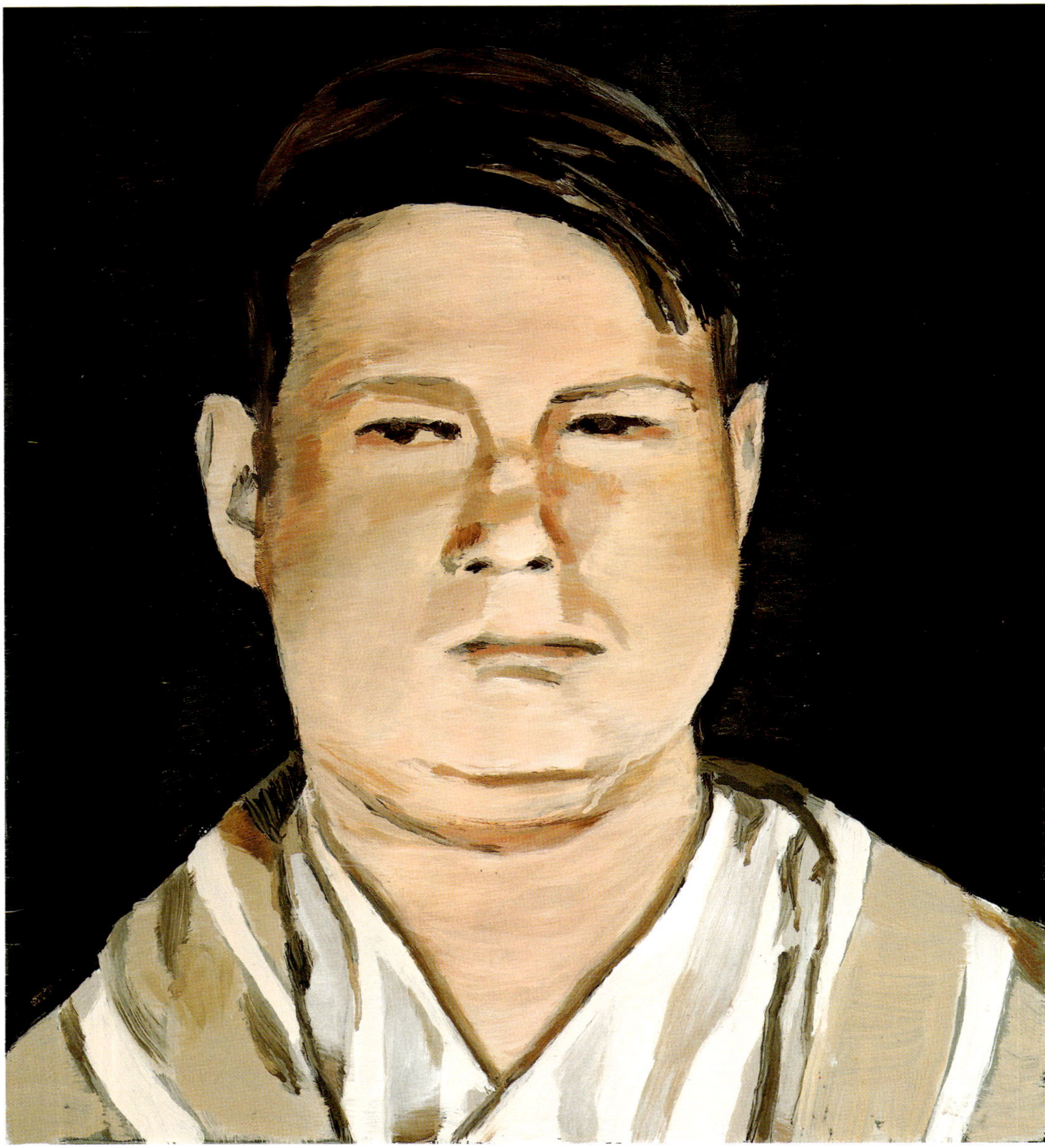

Luc Tuymans
Der Diagnostische Blick I, 1992
53 x 48 cm
Collection particulière / Privatsammlung / Private Collection, Suisse
Courtesy David Zwirner Gallery, New York

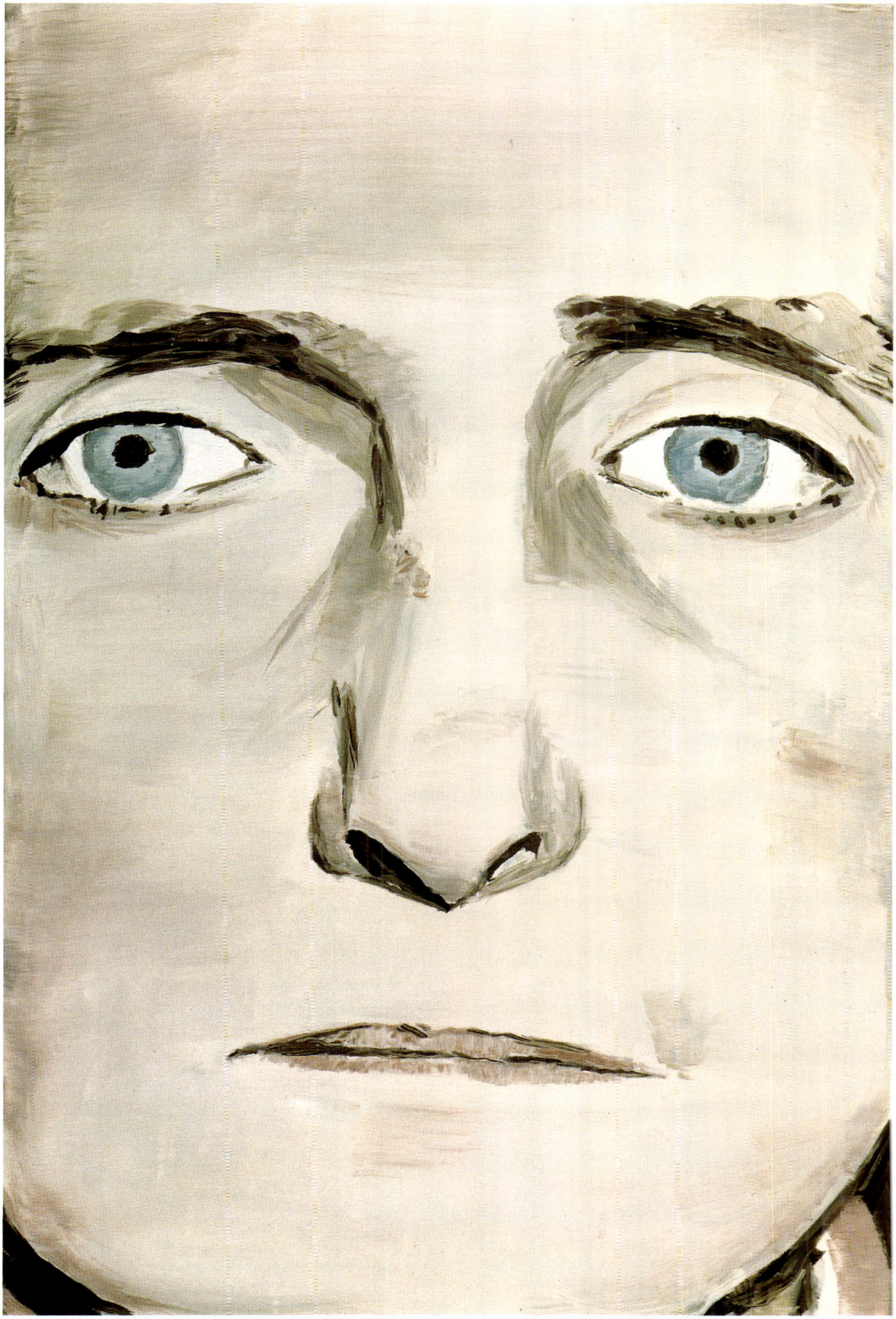

Luc Tuymans
Der Diagnostische Blick IV, 1992
57 x 38 cm
Courtesy Zeno X Gallery, Antwerpen
Prêt à long terme auprès de la De Pont Stichting
voor hedendaagse Kunst, Tilburg

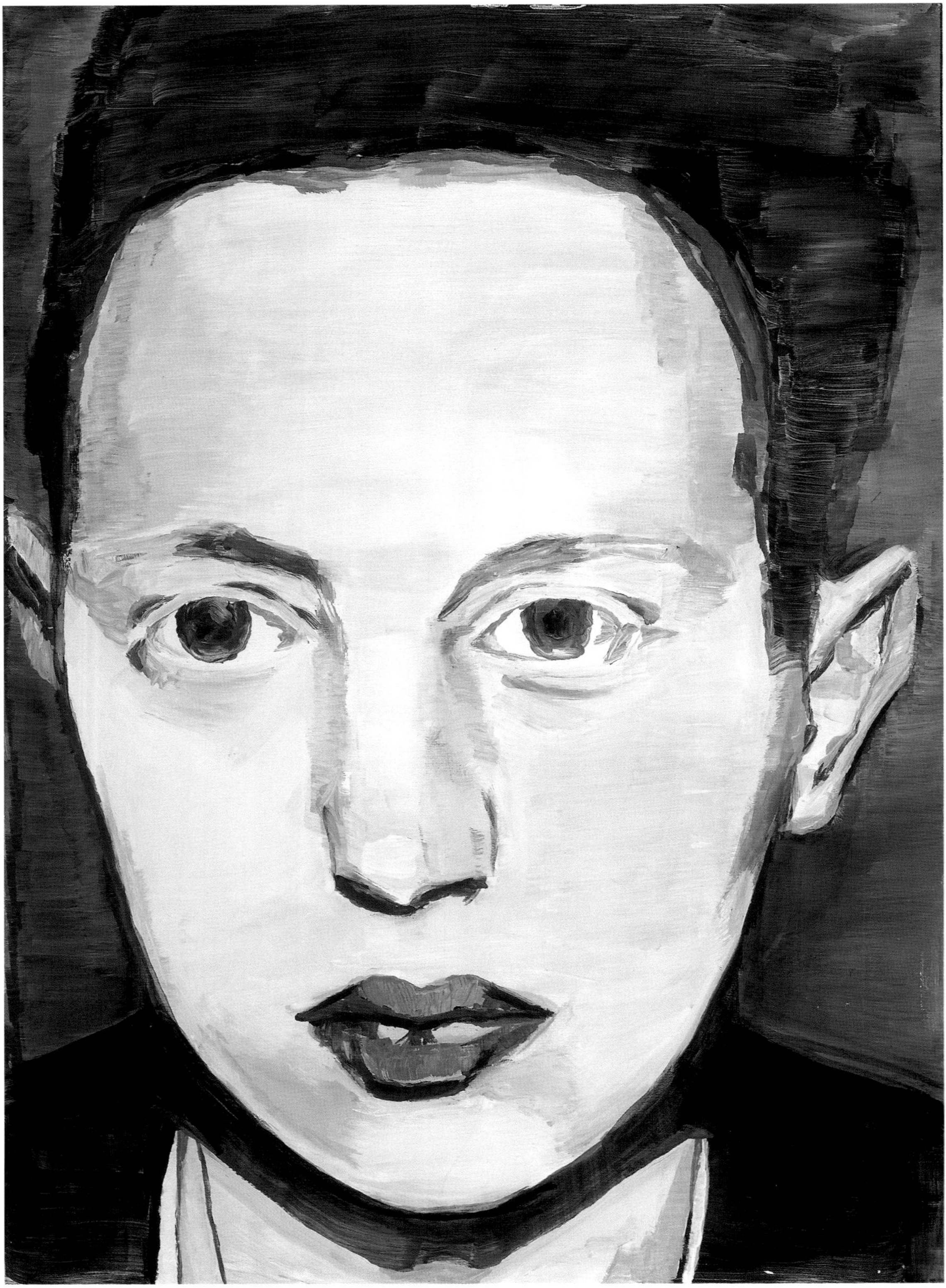

Luc Tuymans
Der Diagnostische Blick V, 1992
58 x 42 cm
Collection F. Vranckx, Ostende

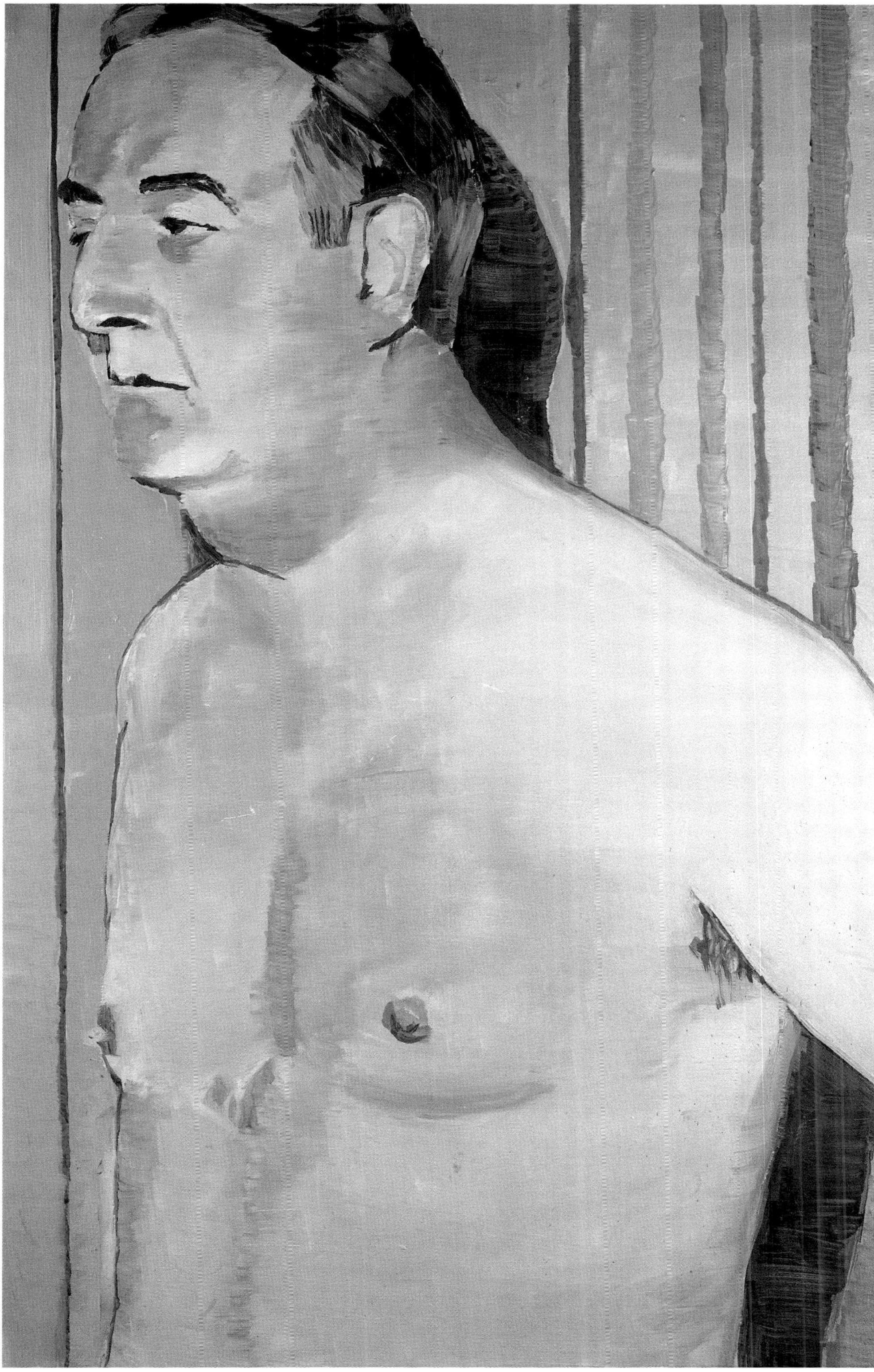

Luc Tuymans
Der Diagnostische Blick VI, 1992
75 x 48 cm
Collection Debra-Houtsaeger, De Panne

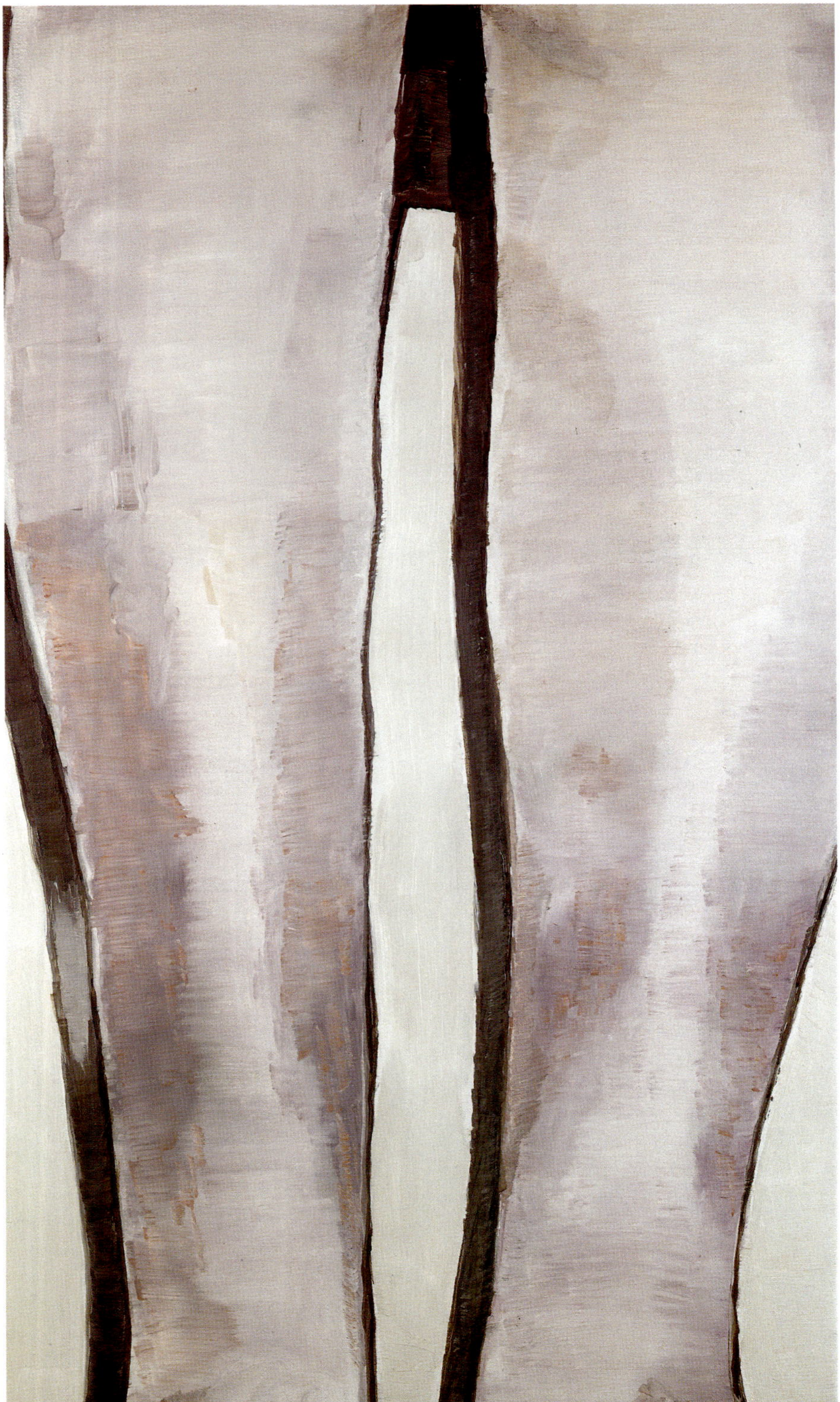

Luc Tuymans
Der Diagnostische Blick VIII, 1992
68,8 x 39,5 cm
Collection Peter & Heidi Aaen, Neustadt

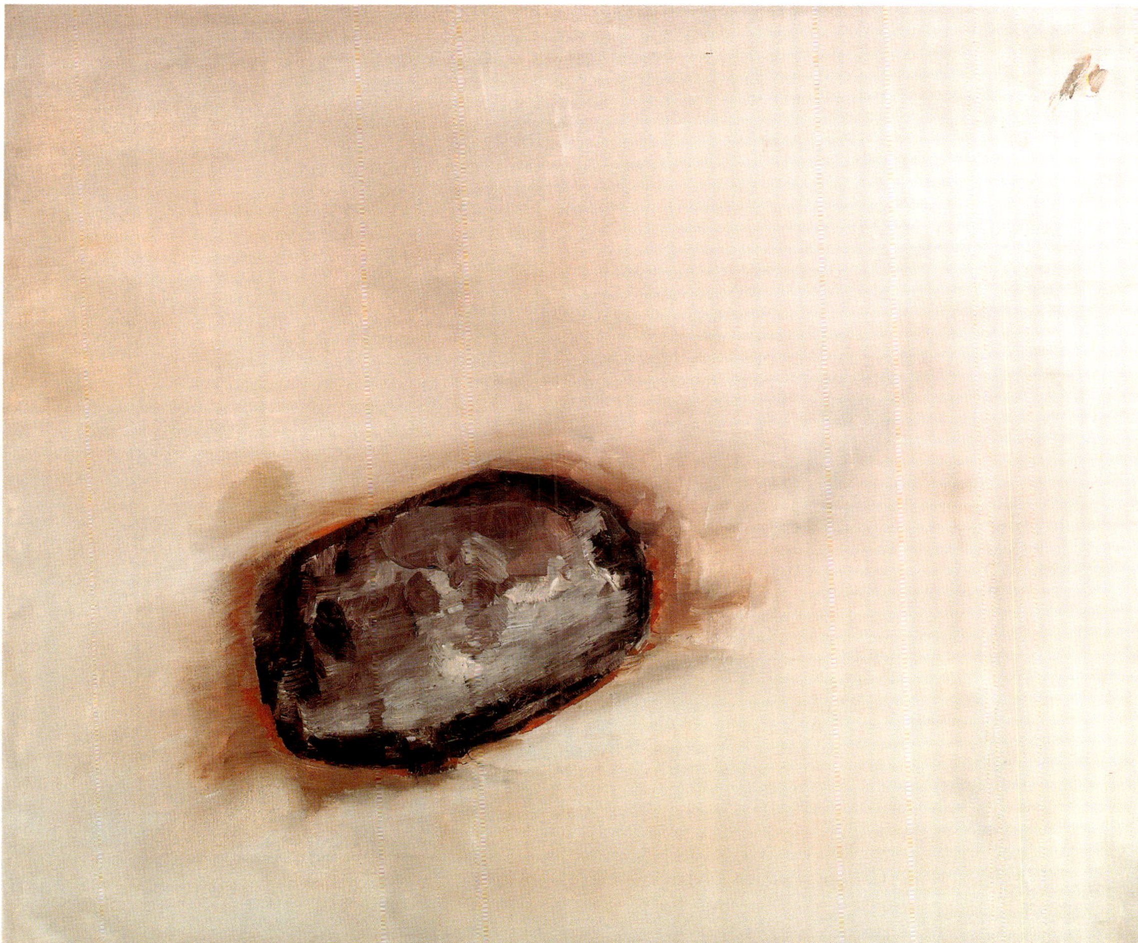

Luc Tuymans
Der Diagnostische Blick X 1992
48,5 x 55,5 cm
Collection Jean-Paul Jungo, Genève

Bruno Perramant

Text Jemima Montagu
Interview Jemima Montagu and Alison M. Gingeras

Painting's troubled relationship to representation is given a new spin by Bruno Perramant. In his practice as a painter, he does not simply question the apparatus and history of painting itself, but questions the concept of "reality" that painting is supposed to represent. For Perramant, the idea of "reality" has been devalorised, coded by socio-political or philosophical discourse to the point of meaninglessness. Instead he suggests that the "real" only exists as an "apparition", and it is these ghosts which haunt his mysterious and compelling canvases.

Using a muted palette dominated by dreamy pastel hues of grey, green, violet or ochre, Perramant's subject matter is diverse and hard to summarise. Glimpses of figures or objects–the cool gaze of a disembodied female head, figures cropped mid-action or strangely abstracted body parts–mix with ambiguous abstract imagery, objects shown at such close range that the form hovers at the point of disintegration. Symbols, as banal as advertising logos and yet simultaneously loaded with occult potency, and blurred fragments of text also populate his paintings. His works are often conceived as polyptichs, although Perramant regularly reconfigures the arrangements. Certain paintings can also stand alone. The groups of works, like a fragmented selection of found film stills, obliquely hint at hidden narratives but remain indecipherable. These "apparitions" of the real deliberately evade any sense of wholeness or fixedness, and instead function as loose signs, which create meaning through a patchwork hints and allusions.

The five-part work *Dessous dessous maintenant/toujours plus* (1997) shows a sequence of interiors infused with luminous golden light. Lights, lamps, light-bulbs, which are a recurrent theme in Perramant's work, are a central focus of this group. In one painting a table lamp stands in an elegant modern lounge, a red hotel-lobby chandelier dominates another canvas and in another light streams through a stained glass window in the form of a six-pointed star. The crux of the group are the two central works: in the first a man examines photographs through a light box, but behind him on the wall are images of the two other paintings in the group (the red chandelier and the lounge interior); in the second a chequer-patterned skull, a work by Gabriel Orozco, has been flattened, like the famous anamorphic skull in Hans Holbein's painting *The Ambassadors*, into a geometric abstract. The examination of the "image", or the meaning of the image, is (literally) the subject of this work. Perramant's use of self-quotation implies the uprootedness of the image in contemporary visual culture. He therefore uses images freely–distorted, disguised, referential, blurred or simply as they are–and through this freedom he creates new resonances, or to use his own musical metaphor, a "multi-layered chord".

In his large body of work, *Matrice* (1999), Perramant plays with the double-meaning of the word "matrice" in French, which means literally a mathematical matrix or a womb. The nine canvases are reinterpretations of a documentary film in which a woman's body is being given an autopsy. At the same time a dialogue takes place between the doctor performing the autopsy and the son of the woman. Images of a dissection of a dead woman's heart merge with this bizarre medico-legal conversation. Fascinated by this film, Perramant re-staged and filmed the scene himself (using props and a pig's heart) and used it as the basis for this group of paintings. In a surprising inversion, the descriptive, figurative imagery of these paintings is transformed by the highly emotive subject-matter. Any dissection of a heart is gory, but in conjunction with a dialogue between the doctor and the dead woman's son, a detachment takes place between recognisable imagery and emotional content. The heart becomes abstract in the viewer's mind, stripped of its usual meaning. Perramant heightens this abstraction through techniques of cropping and distortion, and by doing so he evokes something beyond the physical. The theme of light recurs again, and in this case implies another, other-worldly space.

The works contrast the recognizable and the abstract, the precise language of medical dissection and the evocation of a dream space. This contrast is extended by the title, which draws out the impossible conjunction of a mathematical matrix (reflected in the neat arrangement of the canvases) and the highly symbolic and resonant image of the womb. Perramant's work deliberately maneouvres between conventional or instinctive readings of imagery. He creates clashes, ambiguity and, above all, a dense, multi-layered visual experience.

The temporarlity of painting

Don't forget that in spite ot the so-called antiquarian aspect of painting it is a highly mobile medium ... The speed of the medium is underestimated.
Luc Tuymans as quoted by
Bruno Perramant

JM/AG: Your citation of this quote by Luc Tuymans in a previous text seems connected to the "time-based" strategies you have borrowed from the cinema: jump-cut, close up, cropping, framing, etc. But far from a simple "imitation" of cinema, you have also expressed an interest in the "dilated" or "infinite" moment expressed in painting. Is there a tension between the "speed" of painting and its "eternal" qualities (its ability to transform banal images—photographic, cinematic—into "iconic" images)? It seems that these two notions obliquely touch upon one of the central "questions" of the exhibition. Do you find figurative painting a privileged medium for the digestion of the images that saturate contemporary culture?

BP: If there is the creation of a space-time—and it is sometimes an excessive ambition which one should be aware of—it is inseparable from an essential or structural complexity which is able to contradict the immediacy of the perception of painting. You speak of temporal strategies, borrowed from cinema, but it's greater than that. Film-maker or painter, we see the same world, we find ourselves in the same time, in the same light. If one speaks of strategy, it is based on the fragmented perception of the everyday world. Evidently the relationship between painting and other image-based mediums is incontestable and yet has barely been analysed—as if there were production secrets to hide, as if the method itself should be shrouded in mystery. Painters have always swallowed up, experimented without inhibition, all techniques related to perception and representation of the real.
A work is the place where the present exists and the present of a work is like a musical chord. A musical chord is composed of many notes of equal duration. Perhaps this example can be applied to my polyptichs : several compatible presents. The present, perceived as a point, not a point which is displaced on the scale of the duration, but a point where different strata cross each other, different temporary layers.
Briefly, for the work *Matrice*, I can describe some of the sources. A medico-legal dialogue concerning a post-mortem on a mother's body was happening in the background; filming took place; a pig's heart was purchased; and there was a pseudo-autopsy set to the music of Haydn, as I recall. The lights: high up, a lamp lighting a lamp, the reflection in the mirror, and below an infinite whirlwind, the effect of feedback obtained by placing the camera in front of an empty screen. *In girum imus nocte et consumimur igni* ("We turn round in the night and are consumed by fire"), the last film of Guy Debord (Simar Films, 1978); I have never thought about it: that's cinema about cinema. And the word "matrice" in French has two meanings—and that's why I don't want to translate it—on the one hand, it's a mathematical matrix : nine paintings, three by three, calculations and connections, horizontals, verticals, obliques ... On the other hand, it's like a "Chinese square", that game where you try to make a line of noughts or crosses in a square ; here the game is played between the hearts and lights, and if the heart dominates by strength or number, the winning line is the light.

Painting and poetics

JM/AG: You keep returning to the structures of writing and poetry as ways to get outside the socio-cultural determinism of our habitual engagement with images (the analytical and critical deconstruction of images). Does your painting aspire to the condition of poetry, in the way that poetry creates slippage of meaning, plays with arbitrary or fluid signs, and evokes a non-linear and multi-layered structure? Your methods of cropping, framing, layering seem to resist the idea of a singular, unitary image—the concept of "wholeness"—traditionally attributed to painting.

BP: The single eye, that of the Cyclops, that of technique. Of course I resist this monocular vision of the world which is bound up with the idea of representation in the western tradition. It is untenable today. Perspective is no longer linked to humanism in the tradition of representation. At the same time I use everything at my disposal with complete freedom. Techniques (this time in the plural), are not the only motors which allow you to keep going forward, that's to say, overtaking them. The speed of the medium is also the speed obtained by the draught made by overtaking one's own technique. Pilots are aware of this phenomenon.
This concept of "wholeness" attributed to painting is attached to the idea of permanence—in a vase by Morandi or a painting by Poussin. And yet it's not so simple. There are many examples of works which evade this idea of the unitary image : the polyptichs showing the story of the Passion or even the *Four Seasons* works by Nicholas Poussin. Four completely separate pictures which at the same time respond to each other, complete each other and illuminate each other. This vision of the classical unitary image is no longer as dominant as one would like to believe. Poussin's ability to stop time and to offer the present or the real is indisputable in the history of art. Regarding poetry, I leave to poets what concerns poets. I do not aspire to this "condition". Of all the words which I have painted, none are taken from poetry, none at all, except perhaps the exception which proves the rule. Words are treated like images, equalled, and both enter into the formalisation of the work. Of course, I am not the first to work in this manner.
What interests me most about poetry is the rapport between language and its efficiency. Poetry,

like thought, is something that is linked to an "apparition" and not to an appearance of reality. Returning to the theme of the earlier question: time, space, language, poetry and thought are connected and each ensures the existence of a subject. I recently read some scientific reports on research into capturing sonic echoes from the creation of the universe and this idea, so rich in the ripples of time, demonstrates well that space and time are inconceivable without each other. There is no time before space and no space outside time. It is difficult to avoid this level of paradox. If I say that it's in the time of the apparition that space is created, then I must also add that it is space which gives the time frame of the apparition.

Poetics and the human subject

JM/AG: While there are often figures, your paintings don't function as traditional portraiture. Inanimate objects are often placed on the same pictorial and conceptual plane as images of people, who can be cropped, objectified, fragmented, or simply suggested via metonymic association (as in *Matrice*—the loaded figured of the Mother is implied through a dissected heart). Can one draw any conclusion about a certain kind of alienated or fragmented human "subjectivity" in your work? Or is it instead something more poetic—a luminous, dreamy layering where the self is not whole but resists the negative aspect of fragmentation?

BP: I don't really know how to speak of subjectivity—it is about me or a collective subjectivity ? I have the feeling that I am always in retreat, slipping away, discrete. I love to see and to hear. To take charge of an alienated subjectivity one must, without doubt, feel concerned, or worse, feel culpable. But if this appears amoral, it is not the case. Adorno's statement that all poetry is impossible after the death camps still seems strange to me. I do not feel culpable for others or for history. The greater culpability would be, I believe, to allow language to fail—and there is a long list of those who are damned for it.

So a schema begins to be drawn. A circle which brings together time, space, language, and constitutes that which one might call a place for a subject. If one were to describe this circle as "poetic", I would not see this as unsuitable, because it becomes a political resistance to negation.

The mediation of reality

JM/AG: How, within the context of the fixed nature of painting (in terms of fixing a single image in time), do you feel able to respond to this fluid notion of reality in your work? Is it possible to get outside these socio-cultural systems or filters, attached to experience, and in what way does your work achieve this?

BP: I think it is possible, yes. Now, can I succeed ? I don't know, but in any case, the fluid relationships of the real have become genuine causes for celebration. One can't look for it—let it come, let it go—one must only be there when necessary, without effort. It is, beyond all theory, an experience of life. A painting doesn't succeed in fixing anything, not even an image. "That which is not seen before" (in the sense of the word *imprévu* meaning "foreseen" in French) concerning the real, is, I believe, imperative for figurative work, that which concerns the figure. There is another phrase in my previous text which can also shed some light on this: "One doesn't change the world, one changes the figures in the world"—a quote from the poet Francis Ponge.

(responses translated from the French by Jemima Montagu & Dominique Moyen)

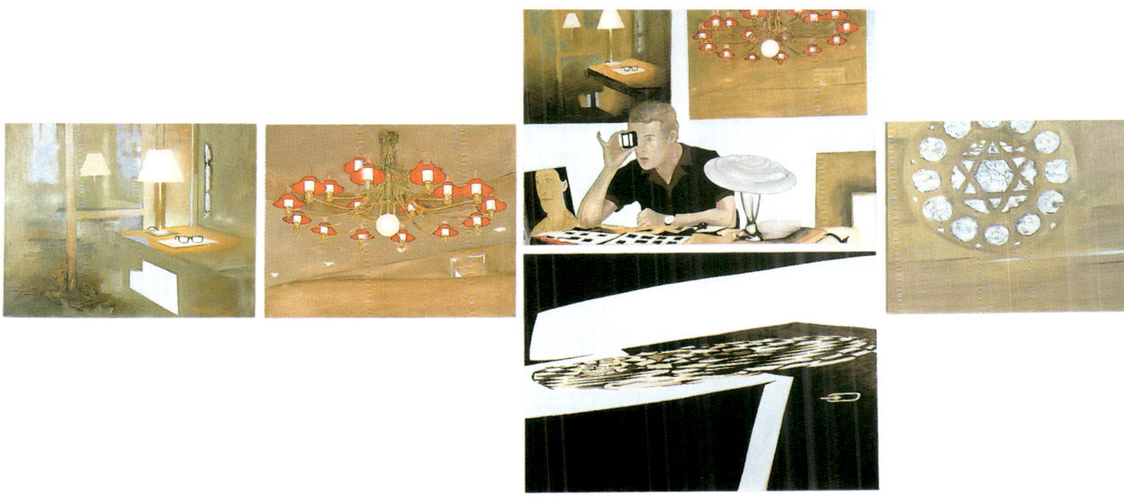

Bruno Perramant
Dessous dessous maintenant toujours plus, 1997
Dimension totale / Maß / Overall dimensions 182 x 415 cm
Collection Fabienne Leclerc, Paris

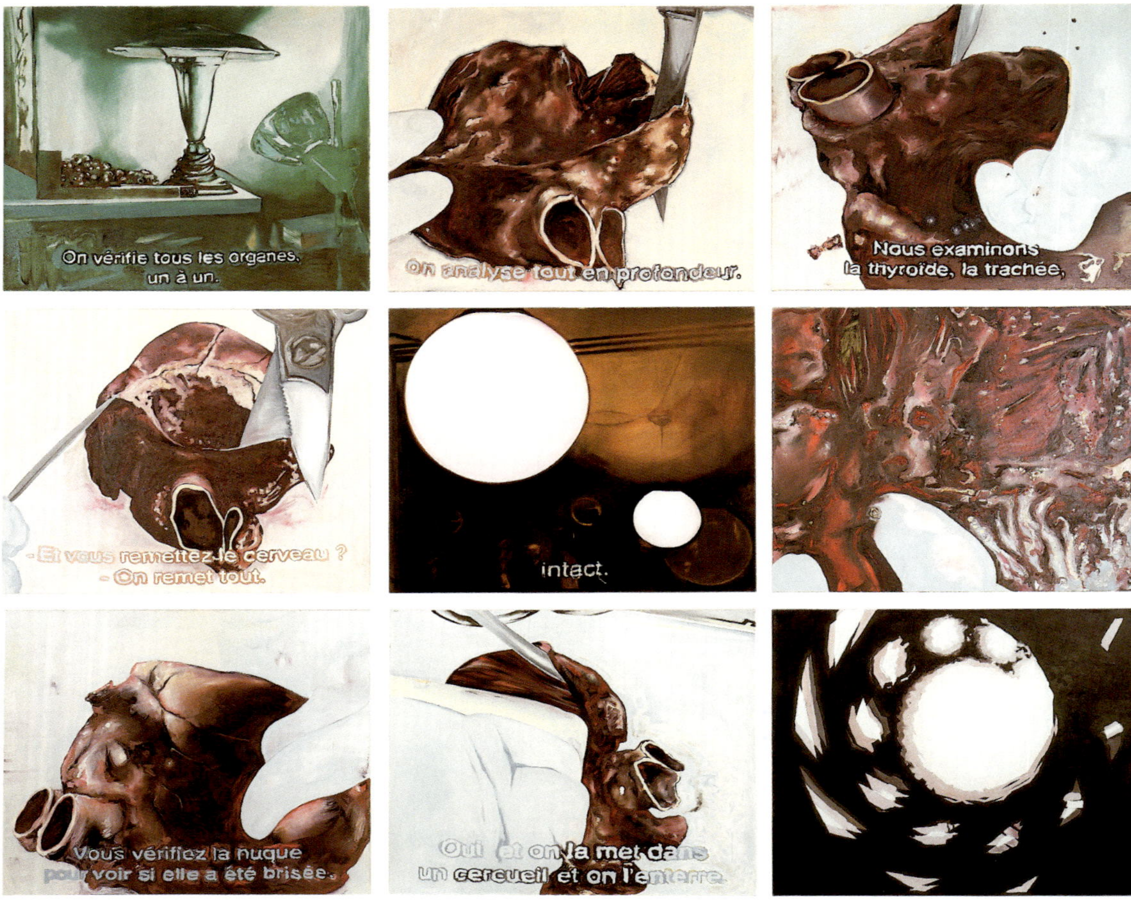

Bruno Perramant
Matrice, 1997–1998
Dimension totale / Maß / Overall dimensions 276 x 219 cm
Courtesy galerie In Situ, Paris

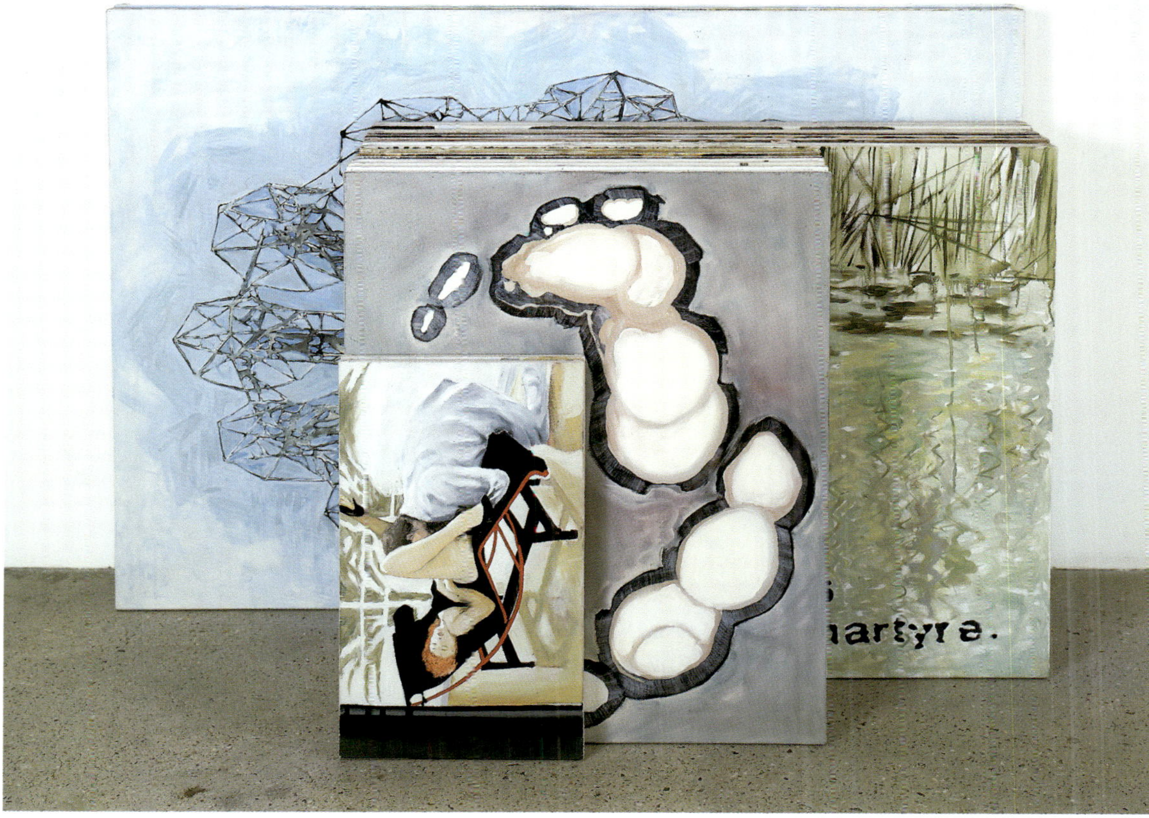

Bruno Perramant
Stacks of Time, 2002
(Sélection Alison Gingeras ; arrangement Bruno Perramant)
Dimensions variables / Maße variabel / Dimensions variable
Monsieur et Madame Agostini, Paris ; Joanna Chevalier-Sèvres, Paris ;
Gilles Fuchs, Paris & galerie In Situ, Paris

Enoc Perez

Blaženka Perica

Perception is a form of attention.
Novalis

When I first saw the portraits of Enoc Perez they exuded a strangely attractive mood that I tried in vain to explain. The more I thought about the reasons for this mood, the more they eluded me and refused to subject themselves to any "analysis." It seemed to me as if I was standing directly in front of the "appearance of distance" in which, according to Walter Benjamin, the aura dwells.

At first sight everything about these portraits seems so simple. The women and girls that Perez paints are beautiful. They are young, friendly, and situated in a relaxed environment. Whether "Sarah" or "Charlotte" or "Ashley"–they're usually party girls–the communication of their names unmistakably informs us that the artist was in personal contact with them. "Love and beauty are my themes," [1] Perez has said, speaking with surprising openness and unmistakable conviction about "desire" and art as "references between images and one's own life." He claims that his objective is not the unapproachable and distant, but to create a kind of intimate catalogue of these women, all of whom he has either personally loved or were "someone else's girlfriend." However Perez does not always express his admiration for these women directly and when we look at the paintings, mysteriousness is the first impression. Why? This sense of mystery is largely the result of the complicated and drawn-out process Perez uses to produce his paintings. Perez, a Puerto Rican living in New York, belongs to a younger generation of artists who should be seen within the context of the revival of figuration in the 1990s and who base their paintings on photographs. This has been a common technique since the invention of photography, despite the fact that photography is often cited as a reason to declare painting dead. In fact, it was during the 1960s and 1970s–the era of Minimalism and Conceptual Art–when photography's predominance over painting became noticeable. But the end of the century has brought about radical changes. Alongside the explosive technological development of the media, including the presence of photographic iconography in everyday life, a number of younger artists, including Enoc Perez, developed a new interest in painting, deciding to examine the ever-present world of images through painterly means.

The catalogue published for the exhibition *At Century's End* in 1998 in the Museum of Contemporary Art in Lake Worth, Florida, examined the phenomenon of figurative painting in the art of the 1990s. Three primary currents were identified. The paintings of Enoc Perez shown in Florida were not allocated to the category of "art of identity and representation" or the interest in "popular culture as a source of inspiration", but to the "rise of the pathetic aesthetic" in which the "images of failure" played the leading role. But this is only partially valid. What characterizes Perez's art in the context described above is precisely that it fits into all three categories. Even though his subject matter is predominantly parties, which can be viewed as a central aspect of pop culture, Perez presents his figures as an extremely important part of his own life. They are part of his personal history in which his (sometimes unfulfilled) desires are portrayed as a source of creativity and identity. The process he uses in creating his paintings is decisive. It also informs us about the difference between photography and painting in general.

The transitory moment of the snapshot, with which Perez starts his portraits, is emphasized by the hidden poses of the oversized faces and figures. Similarly Perez retains the atmosphere of nostalgia which emanates from photography's ability to record a private moment. But it is not Kairos alone, the god of the opportune moment, who rules Perez's creative process. Perez translates a photograph into several drawings, which are used as surfaces for the individual colors which are applied separately to the canvas by hand "using a kind of frottage technique."[2] The creation of such paintings, sometimes consisting of as many as thirty different layers of paint, demands a lot of time and obsessive patience.

If photography represents the evidence of reality at a certain moment, its translation to painting has been, since the early days of Modernism, a conscious confrontation with time as the decisive difference between the two media. The multiple layers of Perez's pictorial surfaces and the way he transfers photography to painting are also a literal demonstration of the fact that painting is created in time, or, as Joseph R. Wollin put it, "As a photograph is an actual impression of the real as visual phenomenon, so Perez's paintings are truly imprinted, their images physical traces of process."[3]

Due to this technique, pictorial space remains undefined. The blurry and predominantly dark palette adds to the mysterious, undramatic appearance of the figures but offers no conclusive explanations. You see what you want to see, but this is not limited to "What you see is what you see", the maxim that is supposed to apply to Andy Warhol's portraits. Perez's works have often been compared to Warhol's portraits, and not unjustifiably so. Perez gives the women he paints an atmosphere which is at the same time melancholic and auratic; the familiar alternates with the withdrawn. Without being shocking or dramatic, Perez shares Baudelaire's desires for the women of Paris who passed him by forever as strangers in a transient crowd. In Perez's paintings there are no crowds. His figures partake of a trusting attentiveness that exists somewhere between photography and painting, between love at first and last sight.

(translated from the German by Susan Schwartz)

Endnotes

1 From a conversation between the author and the artist on March 5, 2002. Unless otherwise stated, quotes from the artist come from this conversation.

2 Press release of Galerie Michael Janssen, Cologne, for the exhibition The Secret by Enoc Perez, November 2 to December 22, 2001.

3 Joseph R. Wolin, "Painting Photography: Migratory Images and the Space of Time," a lecture given at the conference La Graphica Migratoria, Casa Blanca, Instituto de Cultura Puertorriquena, San Juan, Puerto Rico, March 30, 2001.

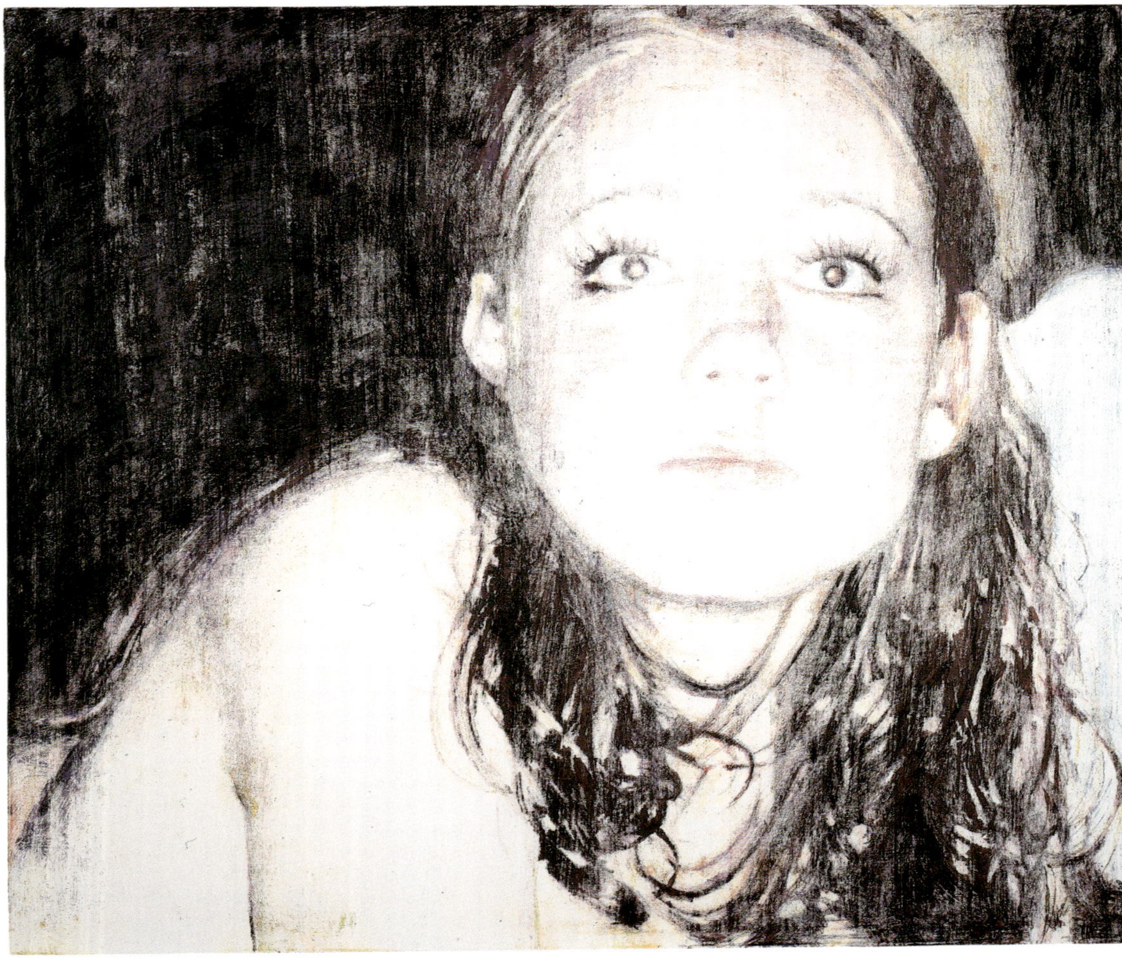

Enoc Perez
Someone else's girlfriend, 2000
106,5 x 152,5 cm
Courtesy Galerie Michael Janssen, Köln

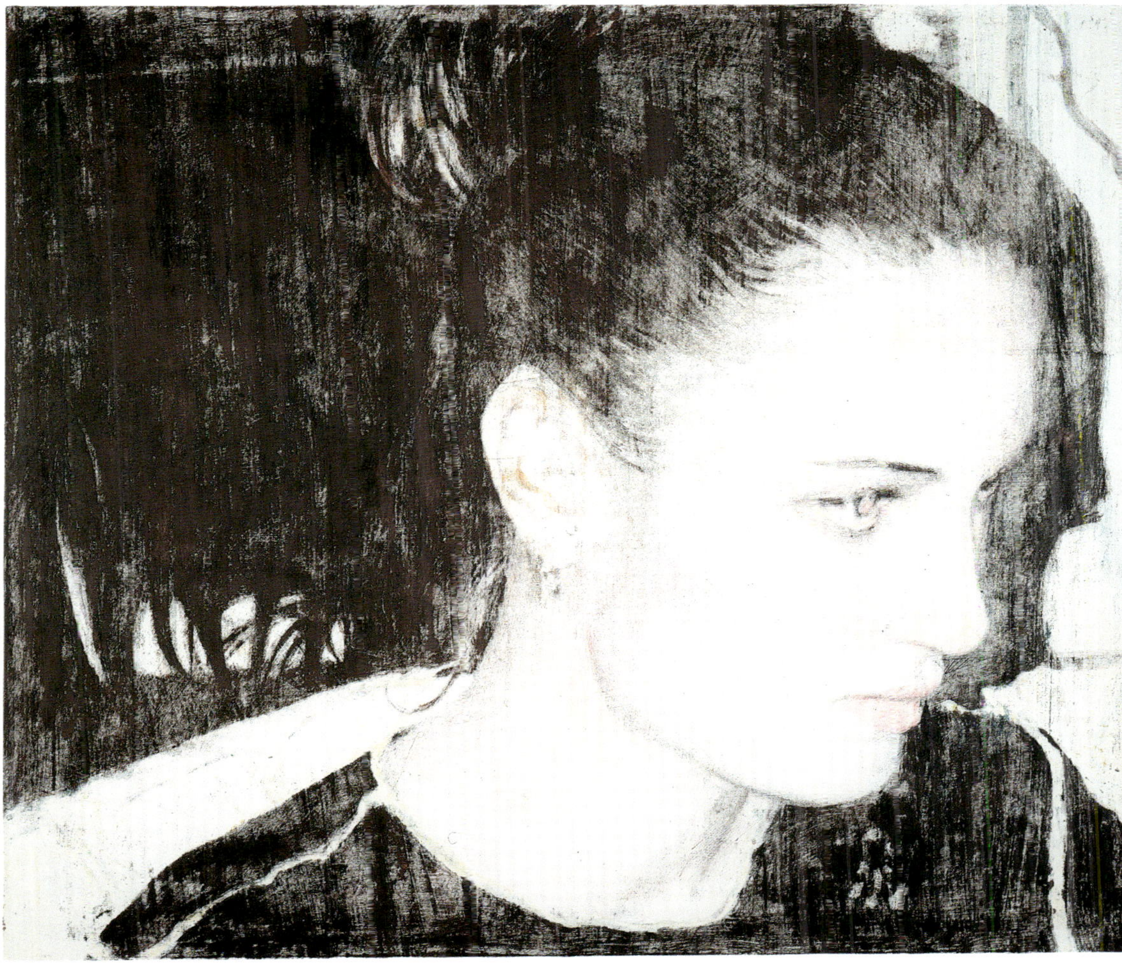

Enoc Perez
Catherine, 1999
124,5 x 144,5 cm
Courtesy Galerie Michael Janssen, Köln

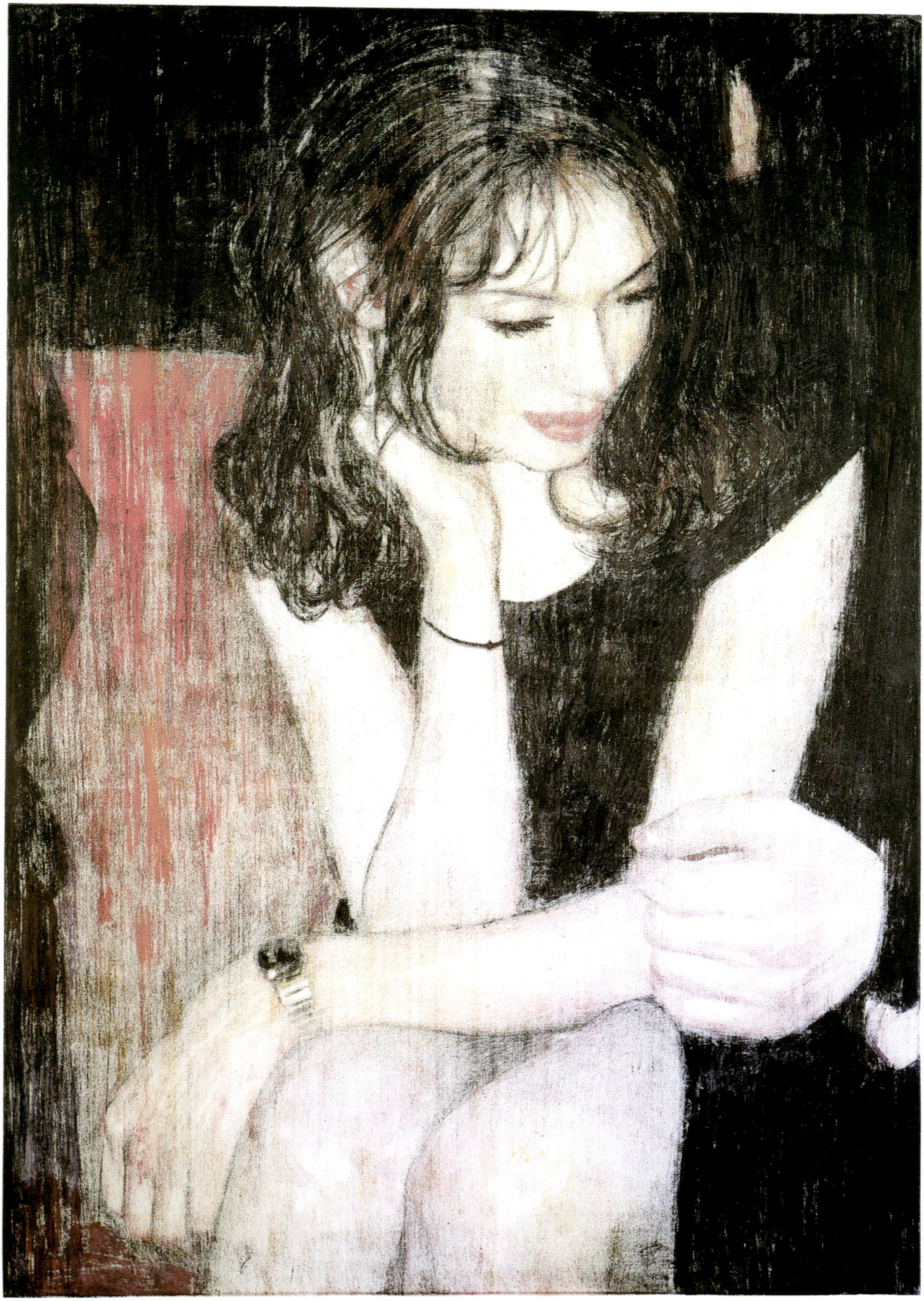

Enoc Perez
Sarah, 1998
144,5 x 124,5 cm
Courtesy Galerie Michael Janssen, Köln

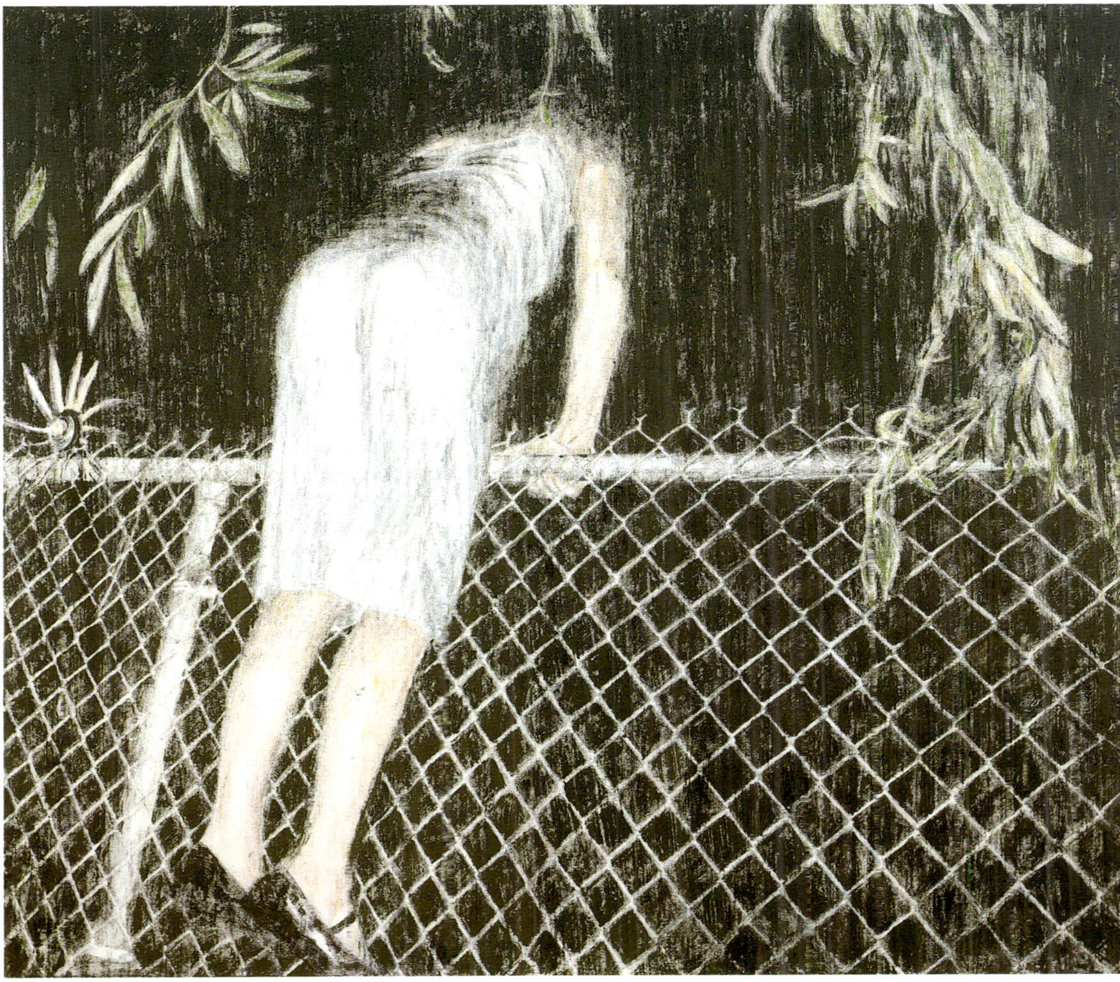

Enoc Perez
The Love that got away, 2001
152,5 x 172,5 cm
Courtesy Galerie Michael Janssen, Köln

Carole Benzaken

Jemima Montagu

Carole Benzaken approaches figurative painting through the fragmented and fast-moving lens of the camera. Even in her early still life series, *Tulips*, the image was abstracted into a fleeting impression. These paintings showed an engagement with the tradition of abstraction, but more recent works are preoccupied almost entirely with the tools of the mass media–magazine and newspaper imagery, photography, film and video footage. In her major body of work, *Diana's Funeral* (2000), Benzaken uses a technique of fragmentation and distortion which recalls Raymond Hains' "hypnogogic" works. She depicted the entourage of the Princess's funeral procession through a painted montage of images taken from the vast number of international television cameras which beamed the event across the world. Despite her obvious love of rich color and loose brushwork, Benzaken's real interest lay in recreating a sense of the mass media spectacle: black and white clips of the crowd of mourners or color snapshots of red-coated soldiers were placed together in haphazard layers, reminiscent of the visual effects of channel surfing or flipping through the daily newspaper. These works draw attention to the apparatus of image consumption, and by creating this flattening effect, she demonstrates the non-judgmental and non-hierarchical nature of mass media.

In 1989 Benzaken began to translate her personal archive of images–the images which she selects daily from snapshots, found photographs, newspapers and magazines–into a painted roll, or *rouleau*, of images. Constructed in the physical form of a cinematic "reel", one image follows another in a sequence of small-format works which are painted directly onto a roll of paper. Each image has been painted with the intimacy and care of a traditional miniature painting. Her *Rouleau à peintures* ("Roll of Paintings") has become a kind of personal diary, showing her changing interests and styles over the years. She mixes personal photographs with images from the mass media, creating an archive which places events of both individual and collective importance on the same plane. The iconic image of the demonstration in Tianamen Square sits alongside an unidentifiable photograph of swimmers, while other images seem familiar but are not–such as a photograph of Afghan horsemen that could easily be mistaken for the cowboys of Marlboro cigarette advertising. The images tease our desire to recognize, to find icons, and demonstrate that as a result of the global media industry a personal stream-of-consciousness has also become a collective stream-of-consciousness. Despite the emphasis Benzaken places on her instinctive choice of images, the subjective process of selecting, editing and painting her *rouleau*, the completed works have a generic or universal quality that robs them of her subjective lens. Benzaken's *Rouleau à peintures* is a physical manifestation of collective memory, a reel of images which are already frozen in the minds of visually-sensitized media consumers.

Although Benzaken's *Rouleau à peintures* has not been exhibited before, she has already used many of these images for subsequent works, repainting and modifying the small individual paintings into large canvases or groups of works. This laborious practice of imitation and translation reveals Benzaken's interest in the physical process of painting itself, a process she deliberately contrasts with the transitory and immediate nature of her source imagery. Benzaken's luxuriant handling of paint, intense use of color and elaborate working practice all work against the deliberate photographic references inherent in the images themselves–the camera's bird's eye view, cropped images, unusual angles, the grainy texture of the close-up or the blurred edges of the video still. Benzaken's attachment to the history of the painted image has developed into groups of works which mix together abstract–plain color-field canvases–with figurative painting. She has recently translated these images into ceramics, carefully learning the subtleties of producing line and color through this traditional craft technique. Both of these methods engage with the problems posed by mixing together images from so-called high and low culture: mass media or personal photographic imagery mixes with references to high Modernism, and craft techniques are mixed with traditional painting.

This confusion of different frames of reference relates back to Benzaken's interest in flattening out the hierarchies inherent to different media styles and subjects. By doing this she creates imagery which does not belong to one single history. Benzaken currently lives in Los Angeles where she has found that her daily integration with the African-American community in Inglewood led to a reluctance to use the traditional medium of painting. She preferred to use video as a more immediate and open means of engaging with a culture so different from her own, particularly when loaded with the socio-cultural issues of being a European woman making "art" about African-American culture. These videos have subsequently acted as source material for paintings, but Benzaken needed the distance and detachment of the translation between media, from video and photography to painting, to offer her the space to work freely. Decontextualized, these source images become just like any of the other in her archive. They become free-floating signs belonging not to Benzaken's own personal experience, but to a collective consciousness.

JM: Can you describe the process of making your *Rouleau à peintures*?

CB: My *rouleau* is very personal and non-rational. I use both an individual and universal way of telling stories. But it's not something that I can decide to do everyday. It's really a whim. It has to be done at a specific moment. It's very privileged personal time.

JM: You have been accumulating these images everyday, over time. There is already an archive, or rather two archives; one is an archive of information and imagery, and the other is this filtered presentation, in paint, of a personal collection of images and ideas. But it seems that although you emphasize this whim, this personal choice of images, nevertheless, these images resonate for all of us. Are you trying to take out the detail from the images so that you transform what might be a specific image into something more generic?

CB: Yes, I am conscious of making my imagery generic. And I like to create a style that is on the edge, between the personal and generic. I also like the way an image can be used as what it is, as a surface made of colors and shapes and also in a metaphoric way. It is open. You can use your own personal imagery and you can still touch the world. And the opposite is true too. You can use political or local-political images, such as a story in the States about a child that killed his teacher, but this can take on very personal meanings. That's what I like, all these ramifications. Nobody knows exactly what the images are or mean. I don't care about my own particular story, it's about me as part of a bigger history.

JM: You have been living in Inglewood, California since 1998. After finishing an earlier series, you bought a camera and started to make films about your local environment. You didn't make paintings immediately, apart from your *rouleau*. Does this suggest that some images are still too weighted culturally? Although you and I have just been talking about how images can take on personal as well as collective dimension—it means something to me and something to you—in fact some images are so problematic that we cannot approach them immediately.

CB: That's both true and untrue in my experience. I know that some things are forbidden. When you know America and these communities, the issues in these neighborhoods, it feels weird to deal with such subjects. You can—and I do—because I ask people if I can film and paint them. It's not about whether it is politically correct or not. The question was how to deal with this subject. I needed time and distance. It's not an appropriation of the culture. There is this danger, but I want to engage with this. There are traps of projection, of looking at my neighborhood in a touristic way. But there is an exoticism in painting that I like. Exoticism is a genre in painting, for example the Orientalist desert paintings of the nineteenth century. Delacroix went to Morocco, and Matisse after him. My exoticism is to be in LA today, in a very poor urban environment, a culture that I do not belong to but to which I feel deeply connected.

JM: You work simultaneously on two levels–you collect images, paint them onto the *rouleau* and then later paint larger works based on these small images. It seems to me that these large works are very different. It is not this continuous portrait of your perception, as the *rouleau* is, it's a much more deliberate, constructed image. And a more conventional format. The image is changed and manipulated, it becomes more exaggerated.

CB: At first the tininess of the *rouleau* helped me to tame this huge issue of scale. LA to me is a city that makes you understand the whole world's problems and contradictions. In the *rouleau* I was able to deal with these issues via a bunch of images and to locate myself as part of them. The story in this work is a bit like Homer's *Iliad* and *Odyssey*. It's a transcription of "orality" (images) into "textuality" (the roll of painting). The paintings are about me in the city, in a part of town that nobody wants to see. The emphasis, if there is one, is on scale. Big and non-linear. The paintings are more about broadcasting the city itself, using clichés, billboards, portraits of people I've met and filmed, self-portraits. The street scenes are not in the *rouleau*.

JM: In the big paintings you are evoking the simultaneity of cinema, video–through a montage of recognizable but random images. The images are very disparate, but at the same time, there is that script you speak of.

CB: In the *rouleau* the images are placed in succession, like a film, a cinematic reel. But the way you see them is horizontal, the opposite of cinema, because the band of a film and the way it is projected on the screen is vertical. In cinema, when these images are projected, you don't see the editing but a succession of scenes fused together. I want to make the montage of film, the editing process, which we don't usually see, come to the surface of my paintings.

JM: You are trying to expose the montage–of life, of cinema.

CB: When I first came to LA I imagined that I was going to deal with the reality of images, I thought I was going to be more "Pop" on the surface. Then with my last series I went behind the image; under the screen; inside the TV. Now, I'm living it. In Inglewood, where I live, I can hear gunshots or see helicopters everyday from the roof, and hear people screaming. Or I can go into the street and the landscape looks like TV. You feel like you are on TV. But you realize that these images are in fact telling a terrible truth. What I knew about LA before going to LA was nowhere near the reality. I had idealized the images and believed that they were stronger than reality. But now the opposite is true.

JM: So how did this affect your work as a painter?

CB: At first it paralyzed me. I couldn't paint at all for a year. Now I feel freer to paint, and think deeply about the subject, to meditate on my personal use of cliché through the reality I explore. I realized that the so-called ghetto was a part of me too. It is no longer a problem because nobody owns the imagery. Plus, I'm here everyday, I'm a part of it, and I really need to paint my environment.

JM: I like the idea that you discovered that real images, or real experiences, in LA were better than the images or clichés, and so somehow you realized that figurative painting doesn't own reality. You realized that you can use painting because it doesn't equal reality but is just another tool.

CB: Yes and no. I feel that real experience is constantly toppled over by cliché, and vice-versa. I use painting to deal with this—this is the power of painting in my opinion. You don't just have the pressure of time, as the "now" time, you have a digestion of time. You can feel different times operating, and cliché can also be used as the spatialization of time. It can be as real as paint is real.

JM: Do you think there is a tension between the way you evoke many different times in one painting, the layers of time, and the sense of "now" that you also create. You evoke a fractured "now-ness" of everything happening all at once but in different places. On another level the history of painting suggests a kind of eternality, that the work will last forever. So you have these three ideas of time going on in a single work. Can you comment on your relationship to time, and the way time functions in your recent ceramic "painting"?

CB: The unlimited ceramic floor painting brings in another set of issues. I want to put the viewer physically into this visual question of time and space. The painting has been made on ceramic tiles where, like in the *rouleau*, all kinds of images are represented and added in succession. So when you walk on it you wont be able to see the whole as a painting because it is huge. In this way the question of scale giving space to time will be emphasized all the more, and it continues the proposition of the *rouleau*. The floor is unlimited, like the *rouleau*, and I can continue to add as many tiles as I want. Painting is decoration, just like photographic or video imagery today. All images have been flattened. How can you bring back meaning? If not the original one, then at least a structural or symbolic one? I am very interested in the "now" culture which is impossible to pin down in one time or place. LA is a very interesting place for these issues—to understand the impossibility of understanding, to see the impossibility of seeing—of seeing the whole.

JM: You could say this is the condition of painting. Why have you chosen to use the decorative arts?

CB: LA is great because of the decorative tradition. The decorative is high art as well as low art. Everything is accepted, there are no boundaries. This gave me the idea of making this ornamental piece. Any imagery can be decorative—dramatic or violent images can be as decorative as an image of a flower. On one level, I want to be a decorator, dealing with this contradiction. Sometimes a flower can, in fact, be more violent or can affect you more than dramatic news imagery because this has become so banal.

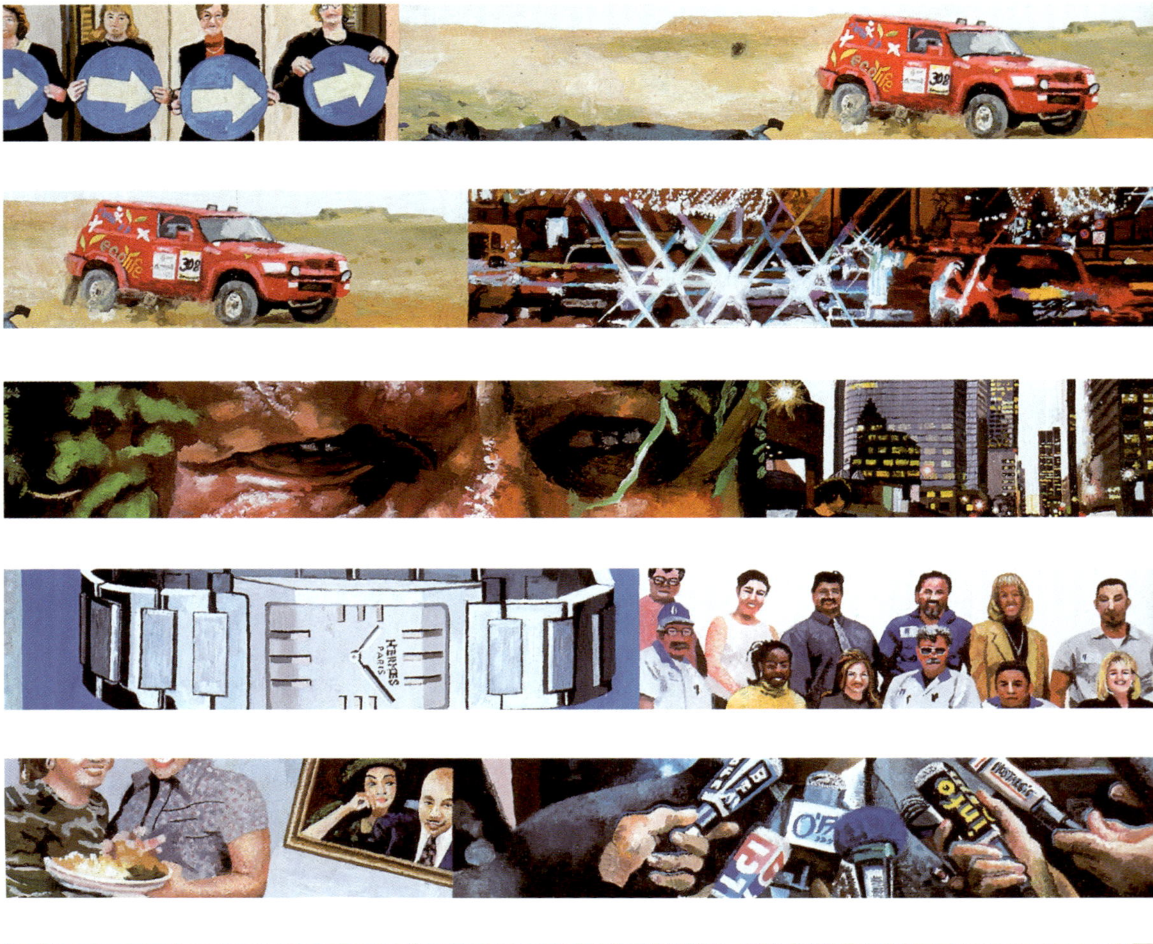

Carole Benzaken
Rouleau à peintures, débuté en 1989
5 x 4500 cm
Collection de l'artiste / Besitz der Künstlerin / Collection of the artist, Paris
Courtesyggalerie Nathalie Obadia, Paris

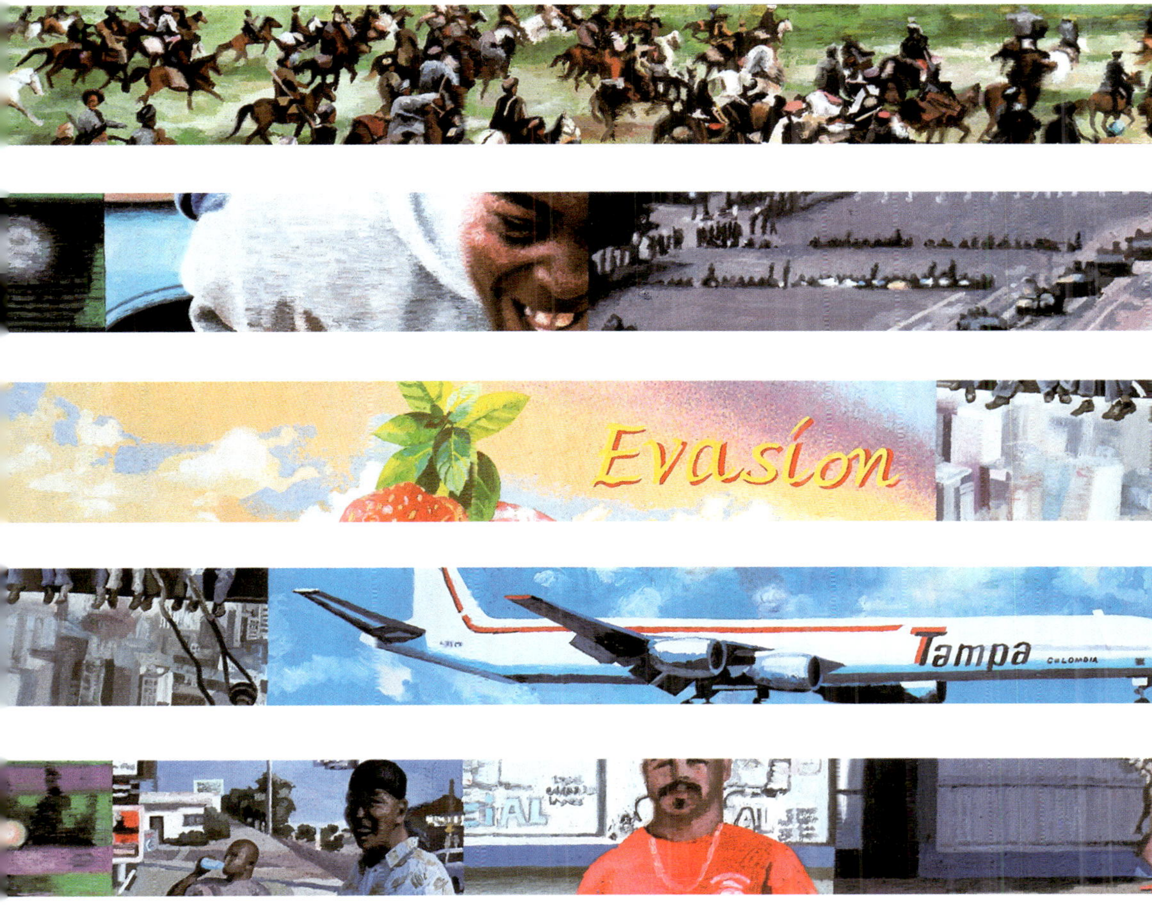
Evasion
Tampa
COLOMBIA
5725 WY 63
100
AMERICA
100

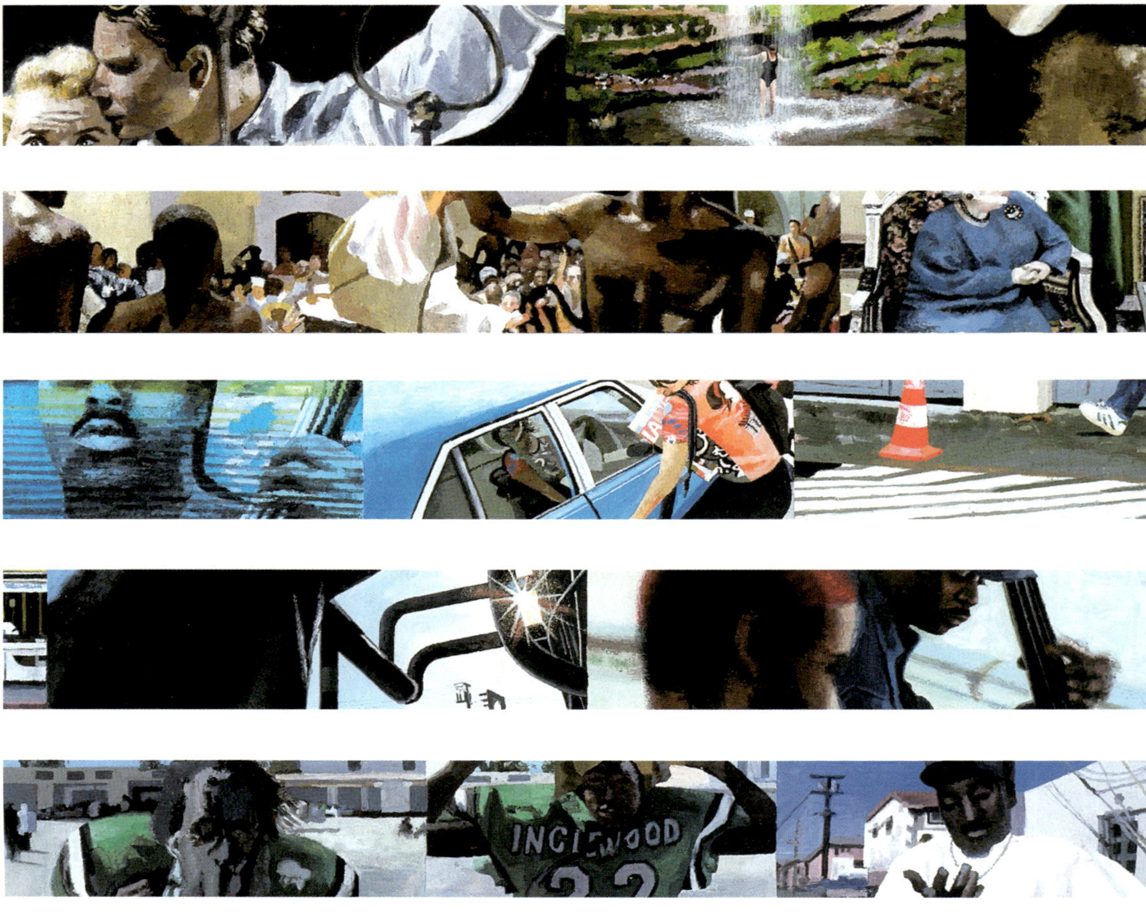
INGLEWOOD
NK'S MINI MAR
ENS' TRANSMIS ION

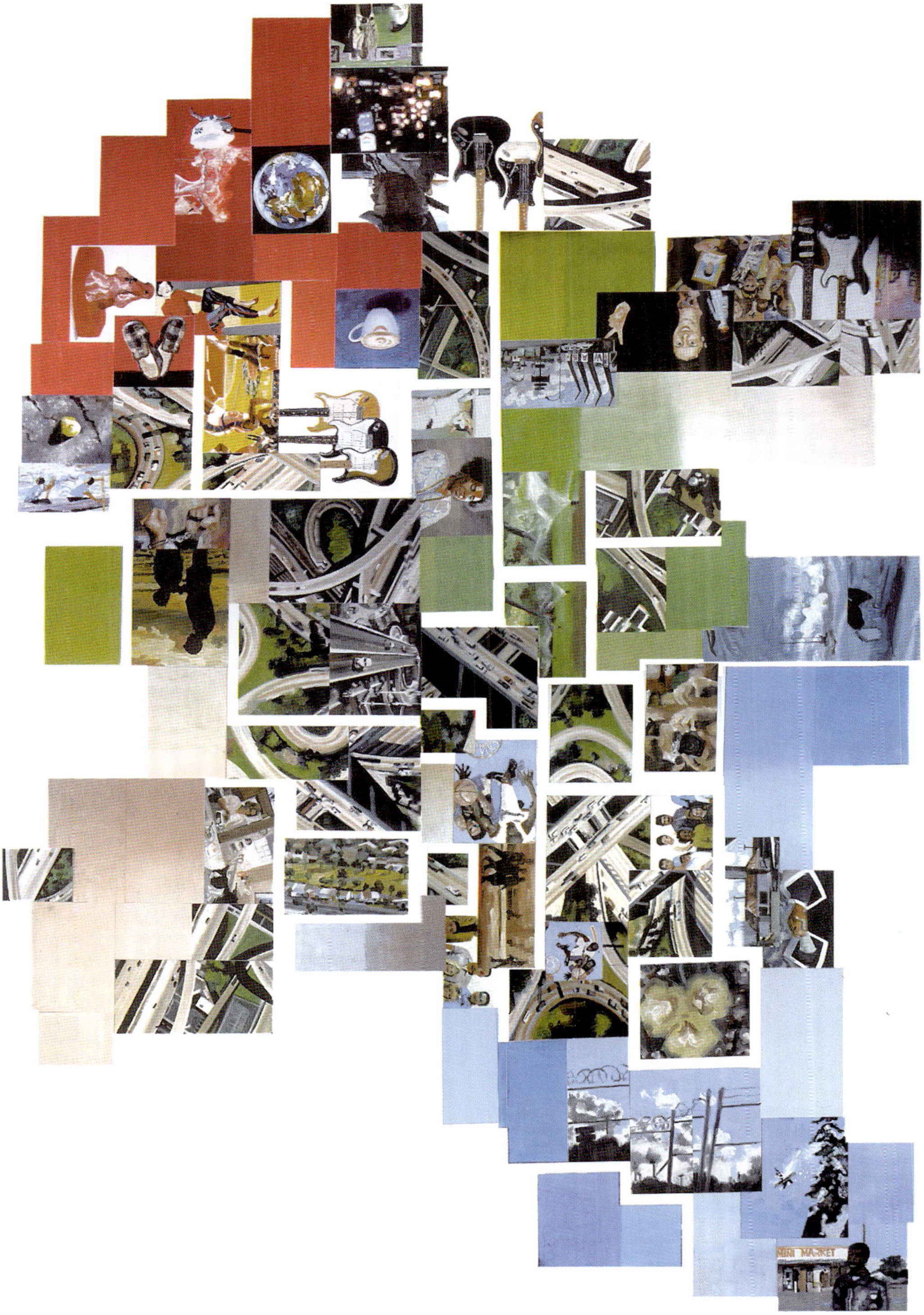

Carole Benzaken
Projet pour un sol en faïence, 2001-2002
Maquette / Model / maquette
c. 700 x 600 cm
Courtesy galerie Nathalie Obadia, Paris

Kurt Kauper

Martina Weinhart

"Face off" was the watchword in the last few years. Painting sometimes seemed to have died the same death as figuration and along with it the conventional portrait, which only with difficulty finds its place in the gap between the "death of the author" and the difficulty of comprehending the subject since the late sixties. Deconstructions and questions of representation and representability have replaced traditional patterns. But in the center of it all—particularly in the United States—is the gender debate which sits alongside the more general examination of identity.

It is against this backdrop that we encounter Kurt Kauper's powerful manifestations from the world of the opera. He presents his monumental, almost statuesque, *Diva Fictions* (1996-2000) as larger-than-life primadonnas in a "hyperspace without atmosphere." They appear self-conscious, one after the other in grand evening gowns, the work clothing of these celebrated artistes. Almost without time or place, they are equipped only with a certain nostalgia that recalls the elegance of the thirties. Their effect is sculptural, rigid. As if carved out of stone, they offer a view of the entire figure in restrained physicality. Their gender is established more by their clothing than pronounced bodily features. The figures therefore exude a certain androgynous quality despite—or perhaps because of—their dramatic attire. They are representational and official, and yet they betray a touch of individuality and private taste. Formally similar, but always different in type and dress, they could be lined up in a hall of fame of opera. None is like the other. There's the somewhat awkward looking African American in a pink satin dress posing as if for the prom (she could easily appear alongside Diana Ross); the severe type, wearing hardly any makeup and definitely good for Wagner; the aging diva, seated and wearing a turban; the capricious one, the cool one, the silly one, the energetic one, the hysterical one. They could have just as easily come out of a Hollywood movie as off the stage of the Metropolitan Opera, or from a mixture of star photos and government portraits from the 18th century.

If it weren't for the warning word "fiction" in the title, we would probably try to recognize the face of a favorite singer or the young talent we read about yesterday in a magazine. But Kauper is a step ahead of the portrait. In many respects larger than life, his paintings are traps that have been carefully laid for the viewer. In a style almost reminiscent of the Old Masters for their painterly meticulousness and obsession for detail, his divas are imaginary people that never existed and yet still seem to have a personal story. His realism makes do without the real—or at least what we usually understand the word to mean. Almost tangible individuals turn out to be shells without a core, pure color. Absolute, subjectless emptiness. In the midst of figuration, this has an almost iconoclastic quality. And yet Kauper's paintings do not live so much from negation as Appropriation Art, for example, with which he shares both a criticism of subject matter and a dialog with art history. His work lives on the invention of a separate cosmos. He devises his paintings as an intervention in everyday culture, falling back into the arms of tradition by way of the thoroughly classical concept of *inventio*.

In his paintings, Kauper brings together two systems that are anachronistic or at least have highly traditional connotations: the worlds of the opera and painting. His objective is to revive them through rediscovery and imbue them with an artistic or social presence that is vital by virtue of having been modified.[1] Using props that consist of both real and imaginary references, he creates new identities from memories, photographs and portrait drawings of real people, even recombining the voice and disposition of historic opera singers to make his own versions. For instance, the pose of *Diva # 3* (1997) is based on a photograph of Maria Callas, the *Assoluta,* with which the series started. Two little *grisailles* that show her at a performance at London's Covent Garden mark the prelude. It is important to note, however, that this event was broadcast on television and hence documents the medial transition to which both this art form and its protagonists are subjected.

These fictions are real down to the last detail. Kauper is shaking the foundations of representation. What is real? What is true? What is genuine? What is original? These are all core questions which post-modernism has long refrained from responding to in a simple manner. Kauper, too, knows the filtered medial realities. His painting clearly speaks of the relationship to photography, not only through his painterly approximations of the precision of the hyperreal, which already introduces strong arguments for approximation as such. On the whole, beyond associations of stage lighting, the paintings evoke a well-lit studio photography with diffused light and shadows. The entire production indicates such a context: the neutral, monochrome backgrounds that merge walls and floors to a homogenous surface that is color-coordinated with the clothing, the sparing and succinctly placed accessories, the concentration on the figure—indicating a central focus on representation. In the use of the medium, Kurt Kauper also understands how to relate elements that appear to be in contrast with each other and thus introduce a dialog between various systems. It does not seem contradictory that he achieves photographic effects with classic panel painting—he often chooses the traditional wooden panel and in doing so he interlinks the two media with each other.

In his most recent works, Kauper still remains true to this strategy, albeit with a slight twist. You could say that he is introducing a third layer to painting and photography, which is film. As in the *Diva Fictions,* the object is once again the representation of heroes and myth. This time he has chosen to depict Cary Grant, one of the great figures of Hollywood and thus, in contrast to the earlier series, he has selected a real person as his subject. He has produced two paintings so far, both showing Grant in familiar poses. A tondo presents him sitting cross-legged on a bed, facing the viewer with a clever smile, open appearance, and a well-trained body—in other words, he is the glowing, youthful hero par excellence, but more of a beach boy than a brilliant entertainer.

In the second painting, larger than life-size and in portrait format, he is the quintessence of cultivation, as befits his public image. In a classical *contrapposto*, he is leaning against an open fireplace in a country house or perhaps a villa. The ambience seems upper-class or at least privileged. Tasteful furnishings in English cottage style, a painting, no crafts on the mantelpiece. A cozy evening atmosphere. The fire is lit. A wall light provides additional light. The ambiance is warm in every respect, which makes the break in the narrative all the more emphatic. The man whom we have seen so many times in movies as a well-dressed gentleman in a tailored suit with perfect manners, elegance, and charming appeal, is exactly the way he always is—except for the fact that in both paintings he is naked.

Of course this factor changes everything in one fell swoop. In this setting, the dandy doesn't become a classic Greek nude; instead he acquires a kind of shady quality. The cliché is broken. The athletic body we saw so often in movies loses its innocence, if it ever existed at all. In this case, above all his posture and the tan line from his bathing suit create the transition from the representation of an actor to the private sphere. The person behind the myth, in particular his ambivalence, is what interested Kauper in this motif.[2] The paintings were not based on film stills from one of the seventy-plus films that Grant made during his career. Kauper is playing with the dynamic tension that arises from the image of the completely constructed artificial figure of a film star the myth of a public person, the representation, and the private sphere. He researched the interiors using photographs showing Grant's homes in order to show him in his *private* environment. In this setting, he presents the clever hero not as a film figure, but as an almost fragile object of desire. It becomes clear what the figure truly is: a projection of the imagination charged with meaning. A myth as a transformation of reality, unreal by nature and yet formative. Grant is especially well suited for this operation. Like all great Hollywood figures—people like Marilyn Monroe and Charlie Chaplin—he served as a special projection surface for the private storyline of the individual viewers. And Grant never allowed himself to be pinpointed to a specific role. Sometimes he was the playboy, then the professor. In seconds he could transform into an anarchistic hysteric. Then there were always rumors about his sexual preferences. He was surrounded by an aura of sexual ambiguity that was repeatedly underscored in his movies. Who wouldn't remember the enthusiastic travesty in *Bringing Up Baby* (USA, 1938), where with great dignity he wore Katherine Hepburn's fluffy negligee with its feather trimming[3] or the clearly female quality of his hysteric gestures as the theater critic Mortimer Brewster in *Arsenic and Old Lace* (USA, 1944), or the feminine uniform and wig made of horse hair in *I Was a Male War Bride* (USA, 1949), and finally the iconic power of a submarine painted pink in *Operation Petticoat* (USA, 1959). In his visual embellishment, Kauper reveals voyeuristic structures and allows the erotic subtext in light living-room comedies to become clearly legible. He lends it an explicitness in his painting that the other genre more obviously represses and leaves up to the imagination. Like Cindy Sherman in her *Untitled Film Stills,* he takes over the narration of the script in order to formulate it anew. Here is where is divas come in again. Full of innuendo, Kauper declines his universe of popular aesthetics that not infrequently can be referred to with terms like "camp." Kauper is not afraid of clichés. He is undeterred by the danger of slipping into the absolute banality of the commonplace. Theatrics, trash, and travesty are the cornerstones that our pop culture offers him for the task.

(translated from the German by Susan Schwartz)

Endnotes

1 Based on an unpublished text by the artist.

2 From a conversation between the author and the artist, March 2002.

3 It is interesting that the *Random House Historical Dictionary of American Slang,* vol. 1, 1994, says under the term "gay" that it was first used in a homosexual con text in a 1938 scene. Responding to the question of an older woman who surprises him in this disguise ("But why are you wearing these clothes?"), Grant's character answers, "Because I just went gay all of a sudden!".

Notes on the *Diva Fictions* paintings

Kurt Kauper

Diva Fictions are paintings of imaginary Opera Divas. I don't call them portraits because the word portrait implies a psychological or physical likeness of someone who actually exists. The word painting, on the other hand, immediately signals artificiality. I'm interested in using the vernacular of painterly realism to create an entirely invented, or artificial, person; a person who has never existed, but appears to have a personal history as real and verifiable as that of the viewer looking at the painting.

The Divas in my paintings are constructed from a variety of sources and use a wide range of both real and imaginary references. The references and sources include photographs and drawings of actual people (always highly altered), drawings done from memory and imagination, the voice and comportment of historical Divas (experienced in person or through publicity photographs and recordings), as well as personal aspirations.

I love the Operatic Diva who constructs a prominent and celebrated persona within a traditional world in which she would, if it weren't for the existence of her voice, be a marginalized outsider: both as a woman within the patriarchal repertoire of opera and as an individual from a social strata different from those of season ticket holders at the world's opera houses. I love the Diva's bearing, glamorous condescension, studied postures, and cultivation of brilliant fashion. I love that these postures are evidence of her success in conquering an elite world.
I love that in a world where persona is presented as given and natural, the Opera Diva celebrates persona as a highly artificial construct. I hope that my imaginary Divas' embodiment of these traits suggests to the viewer themes of reinvention–the construction of a new and vital artistic and social identity–out of tradition: a process I am constantly aware of both as a painter and a social being. I paint imaginary Divas instead of historical ones because I love constructing a new Diva's persona; I'm not interested in merely reporting on one that already exists: the paintings are, therefore, as much about the construction of my own persona as they are about the persona of the Diva represented. I would like the paintings facture to parallel the construction and celebration of this highly artificial persona, and I hope the execution of the images suggests the care and deliberation with which the Diva constructs and maintains her physical and psychological exterior.

Notes on the *Cary Grant* paintings

Kurt Kauper

These paintings started first, because I love Cary Grant (his elegant and atypical masculinity and his simultaneous embodiment of multiple cultural origins), and second, because I wanted to see if I could make the heroic male nude convincing in the twenty first century. I wanted to erase the distinction between the heroic and the erotic. I wanted a tension between my intent to immortalize the subject through nude representation and the perceived irreverence of painting Cary Grant without his clothes. I'm interested in desire represented as complex, nuanced, and polymorphous; I'm suspicious of the resuscitation of traditionally defined desire and the renewed belief in authentic expression. I have always been interested in how representations of sexuality via cultural iconography are perceived and understood by viewers. Cary Grant seemed the perfect subject through which to continue that investigation. I want viewers to wonder whose desire is being represented and to be uncertain as to the identity of the artist. I want the paintings to be funny.

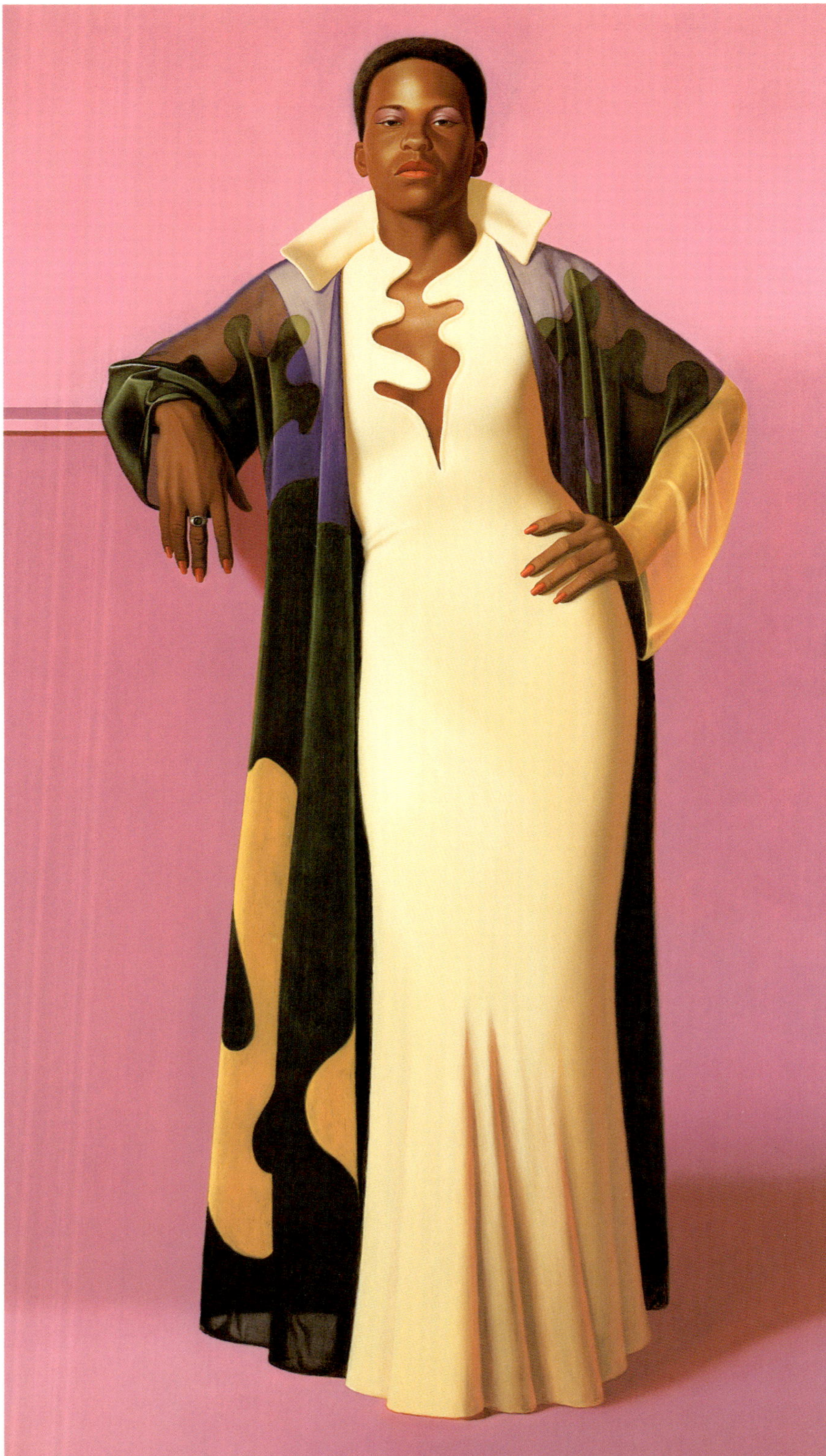

Kurt Kauper
Diva Fiction # 11, 1999
216 x 121,9 cm
The Dakis Joannou Collection, Athens

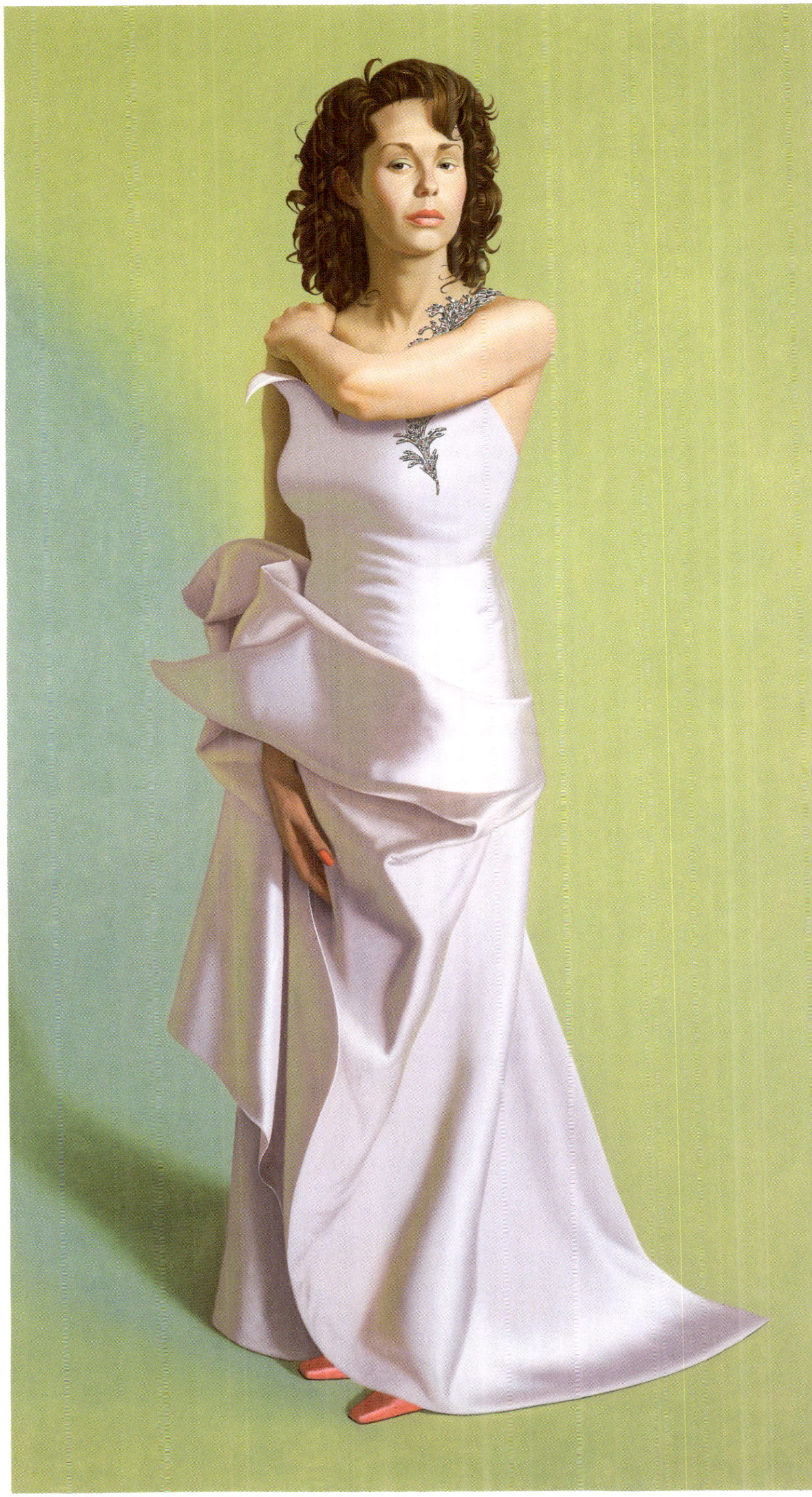

Kurt Kauper
Diva Fiction # 12, 1999
223,5 x 120,7 cm
Collection Jeffrey Deitch, New York

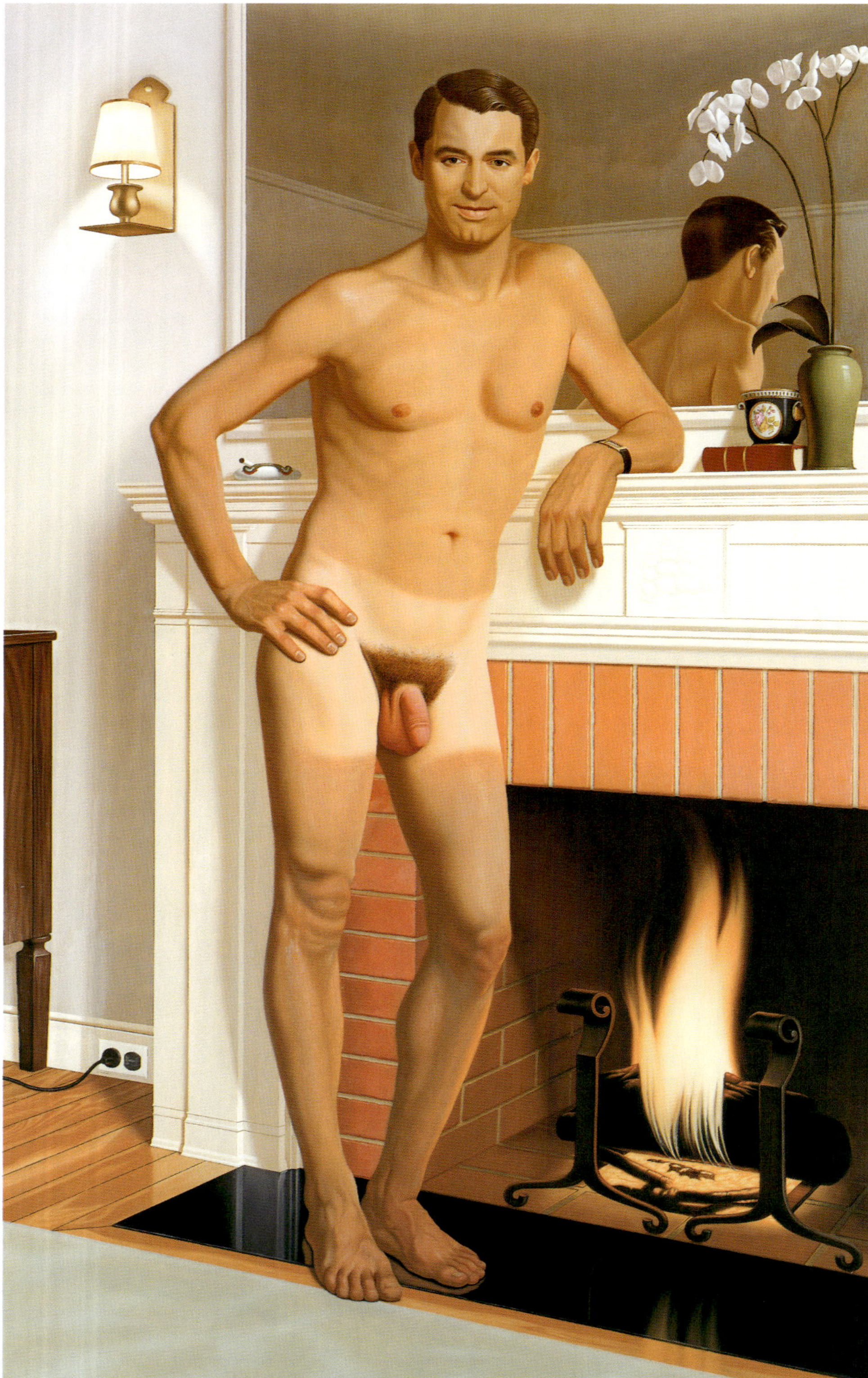

Kurt Kauper
Cary Grant # 1, 2001
228,6 x 142,2 cm
Collection Dean Valentine & Amy Adelson, Los Angeles

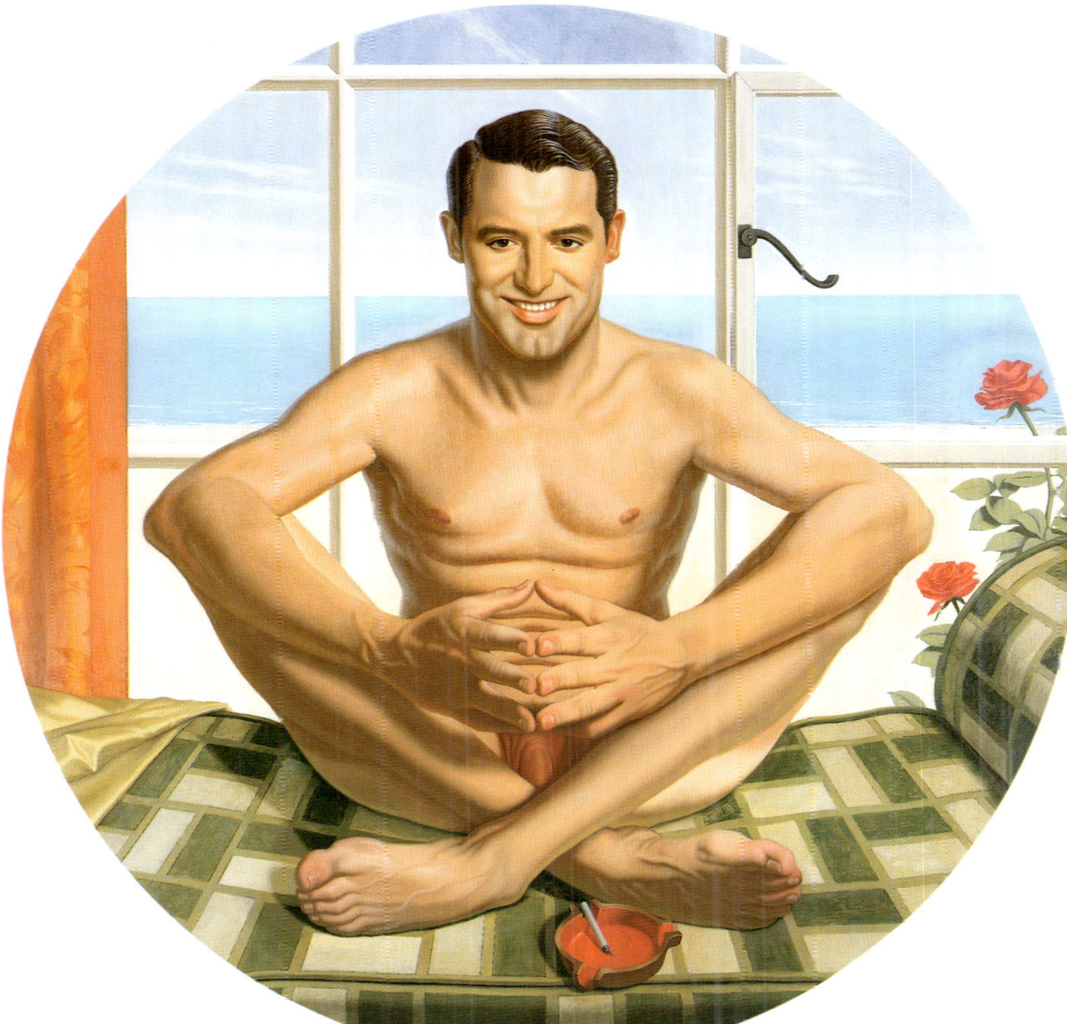

Kurt Kauper
Cary Grant # 2, 2001–2002
Diamètre / Durchmesser / Diameter 119,3 cm
Courtesy ACME, Los Angeles

Elizabeth Peyton

Alison M. Gingeras

Just as New York was recovering from its hangover from a spectacular brand of figuration born in the 1980s, Elizabeth Peyton began to make a quiet stir with her precious, jewel-like paintings. Beginning the mid-1990s, Peyton was resuscitating what was considered an out-moded art historical genre–portraiture. Though with a highly subjective twist. Almost never painting from "life", her early subjects were almost all celebrities, culled from photographic images taken from popular cultural sources such as *People* magazine or MTV. Diminutive in scale, Peyton's canvases transform the larger-than-life status of her famous subjects into intimately familiar individuals through her loose brushstrokes, lush palette, and light-capturing glazes.

In this first period, Peyton's celebrity fixations could be split into two camps. On one side, androgynous, romantic, and dangerous-living rock stars selected from the pantheon of posters on a teenager's bedroom wall: Sid Vicious, Kurt Cobain, Liam Gallagher, Jarvis Cocker. On the other, a courtly gathering of dandies, discriminatingly chosen from the annals of history: Napoleon, Ludwig II of Bavaria, Lord Alfred Douglas, Prince Harry and even David Hockney. While Peyton makes a sincere declaration of "love" for each member of her celebrity menagerie, it is key to note that each painting "is not so much a portrait of a particular individual as it is a wildly idealistic celebration of an individual image."[1]

Systematically mediated through carefully chosen photographs, Peyton never paints or falls in love with (the two acts are impossible to unravel) a whole individual. Instead she falls for a fleeting instant–the intimate detail, transitory posture, and ephemeral expression–captured and immortalized by the camera's lens. The delicate angle of Pulp's lead man Jarvis Cocker's (*Jarvis*, 1996) head leaning on the delicate folds his purple blazer with his insouciant gaze; the crystalline strands of straw blonde hair that delicately frame Kurt Cobain's angelic, not yet martyred face (*Blur Kurt*, 1995); the momentarily vulnerable shrug of David Hockney's shoulders as he sits in a mustard-yellow boudoir, reminiscent of a setting for a seedy Victorian novel (*David Hockney, Powis Terrace Bedroom*, 1998). Peyton renders the subjects of her paintings more "human" by honing in on these details and by exploiting the same means employed by mass media photographers in order to seduce the public. Unlike the calculated marketing techniques of promotional photography, Peyton capitalizes on devices such as blurry close ups and dramatic cropping to create a sort of emotional realism. The manner in which her highly effective sentimentality functions parallels the genre of cinematic melodrama. Peyton's most successful portraits could be compared to Douglas Sirk's melodramatic masterpiece *Imitation of Life* (1959): both director and artist effectively pull on the viewer's heartstrings, provoking "real" tears and genuine empathy, while simultaneously calling the viewer's attention to the tools (camera tricks; drippy paint; Technicolor palettes) used to create these sentimental manipulations.

While Peyton's more recent work has shifted inwards to a more personal realm, painting and drawing close friends and lovers, she still mediates her subjects through the same universalizing lens of emotional realism. Her boyfriend Tony Just is her current muse. As the primary focus of her recent body of work Tony has been transformed into a timeless icon. Her attraction for Tony was sparked by his uncanny likeness to one of her favorite historical subjects, Napoleon, although Peyton's brushstrokes have propelled his physical beauty and inner charm beyond being a mere *Doppelgänger* for someone famous (epitomized in a painting such as *Luing*, 2001). These paintings of Tony–ranging from more classical, frontal portraits to a series of scenes depicting him sleeping (*Nude*, 2001)–reach beyond diaristic intentions. Like her portraits of celebrities, the pictures of Tony touch a collective chord.

In a recent interview, Peyton spoke directly about David Hockney, a key artistic source as well as an object of her affections. "I love that in the 70s, in the time of high dry conceptualism, Hockney was doing portraits, and he was really rendering them. (...) He believed in humanity, and humanism, and people–and he also looked fantastic. He was so aware of his image."[2] Conflating art practice and persona, David Hockney serves as the foundation for Peyton's artistic family tree that could include Alex Katz's cool yet precise sociological portraiture (particularly the lesser known "small paintings") or the perverse examination of bourgeois life by Edouard Manet.

Far from teenage girl obsession, Peyton attempts to elevate the petty idolatry and fleeting duration of celebrity into a timeless, painted image. Peyton transforms the "so-called retrograde language of figuration"[3] into a space that can make a pertinent commentary on the here and now while simultaneously allowing for a sense of visual pleasure rooted in the sentimental and the nostalgic.

Endnotes

1. Laura Hoptman, *Projects 60: John Currin, Elizabeth Peyton, Luc Tuymans*, (Exhibition pamphlet), Museum of Modern Art, New York, (June 24 – September 8, 1997).
2. Interview with David Shapiro. www.theblowup.com
3. Laura Hoptman, *op. cit.*

Excerpts from a conversation between Elizabeth Peyton, fellow New York artist Rob Pruitt, and writer Steve Lafreniere

On affect and historical time

Rob: I feel like all the idiosyncratic aspects of our society are documented in global electronic communication, and that our job [as artists] isn't just that important any more.

Elizabeth: We've had a glimmer of this talk before. I don't think it's about your time. I think at any given moment there's not so much great art, and that's why it's so amazing and totally magic when it works, and you feel its your time. It communicates to you, and it's really smart, and every other transcendental thing you'd want it to be.

Rob: Right.

Elizabeth: When you're living in your own time you don't get that remove the way you do with history. With music it's a lot easier.

Rob: So you really have a lot of hope for the idea of something going on and affecting people of a later era the way that we've been affected and spoke to by people from one hundred years ago.

Elizabeth: That's what oil paint is about. You know it will last forever.

On Portraiture

Steve: Elizabeth, what do you find so interesting in a photo of someone that makes you want to have that moment? That there is a certain candidness?

Elizabeth: That doesn't matter so much. I think the thing for me is just that the person's not there. At some point the photo's got to get lost.

Steve: The series of Tony asleep is remarkable. It's like romantic verité.

Elizabeth: Well, Tony was the first person who let me look at him that way and not feel violated or think it is strange. He just let it happen. It is a little weird, because I always feel like I'm getting so much.

Steve: Strictly speaking, would you consider yourself a portraitist?

Elizabeth: When cab drivers ask me what I do, I say, "I paint people." But then I always want to qualify it a little bit. I don't mind the portraiture thing, but I can't just paint anybody. I wish I had that skill, but I don't.

Rob: When was the first time you painted Napoleon?

Elizabeth: When I was really young, after this bad summer where I never went out. I read his biography and it somehow made sense of the whole world, that this one person changed everything. Let's make roads! Let's everyone go to school! [laughs] Plus he was gorgeous and had star quality.

Rob: There's the cliché about all portraits being self-portraits ...

Elizabeth: I don't know. It's like something I want to see in the world, and then I see it exists in another person. I get so excited that it actually is there. I don't know if it's self-identification as much as that's what I want every second to be like. When I was really young and just couldn't relate at all, and I was reading nineteenth century literature- that was my world. And then, Kurt [Cobain] That was the first time I ever painted an American from roughly my own time. It was such a revelation—it's here that thing I've been loving.

Rob: And very personally. Not in a detached, Warholian way.

Elizabeth: No, no distance at all. As in, this is what I want to live for. In a way, you can be much more intimate with people you don't know. But the fan thing conjures up that something's missing, that there is an inadequacy.

On Celebrity

Steve: Pop music stars are kind of more like friends than other celebrities.

Rob: Yeah, and one thing about pop music is that you can drag it back to the nest and be alone with it.

Elizabeth: It is like John Lennon, you hear his breath. And you can have it. And if you really love that person, then you take them into your life and you make it better with them. In a different way Kurt Cobain is a good example. It was just his own fucked up life, but how many millions of people related to it? It is a beautiful thing when a collapse occurs between our own personal needs and what's in the air.

On Beauty

Steve: Re-staging beauty does seem key to what you're doing. Bring it from the shadows.

Elizabeth: It's almost a nineteenth century idea that what's on the inside appears on the outside. Balzac was into the curve of your nose or mouth expressing some kind of inner quality, that it could be read on your face.

Rob: Warhol thought of beauty as a talent.

Elizabeth: I think for him it was almost enough. Wilde, for the first part of his life, was almost shallow about it. Beauty for beauty's sake – "Yeah, but let's have more of it." Later it seems he realized that it's at a cost. I like the idea of beauty coming from lots of things and that it's not easy to get there. Kind of what religion was doing at one time. This thing that everybody needs to find their way with. To believe in it, that it's possible.

Steve: Modernism had a beauty problem, and I think it's carried through to whatever era we're in now—this thing an artist is expected to work around.

Elizabeth: It's like they think it's their slutty side. Especially when we were coming in, in the 80s. It was such a no-no to have that.

First published in *Index*, July 2000, pp. 54-61.

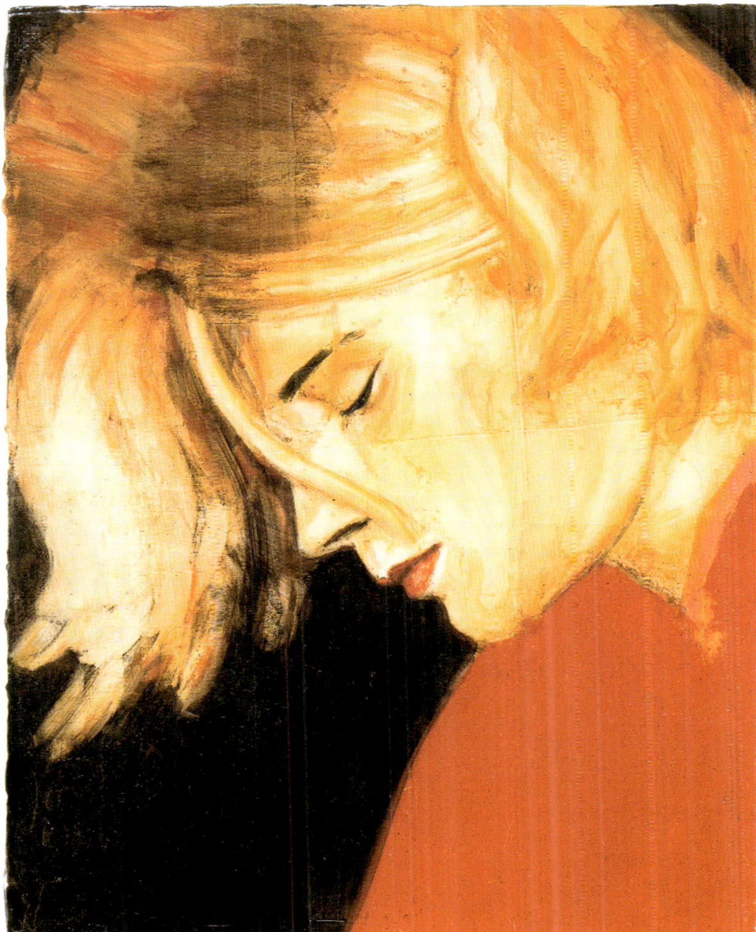

Elizabeth Peyton
Blur Kurt, 1995
35,6 x 27,9 cm
Courtesy David & Monica Zwirner, New York

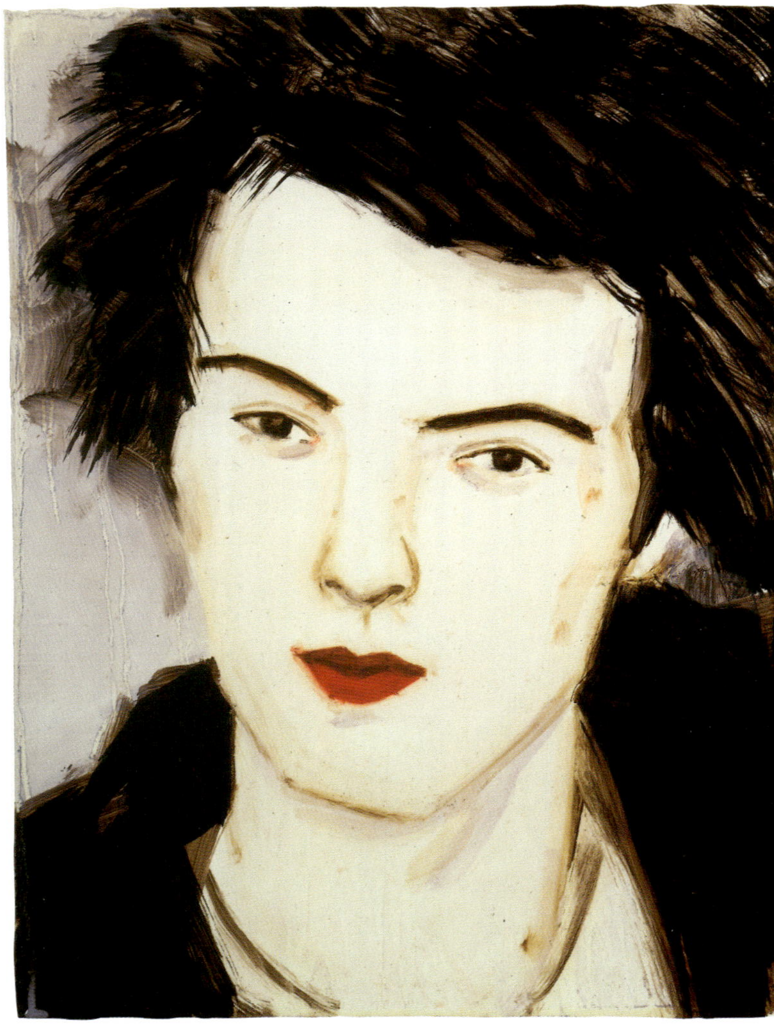

Elizabeth Peyton
John Simon Beverly Ritchie (Sid), 1995
30,5 x 22,9 cm
Museum of Fine Arts, Boston. Contemporary Collector's Fund 1995.120

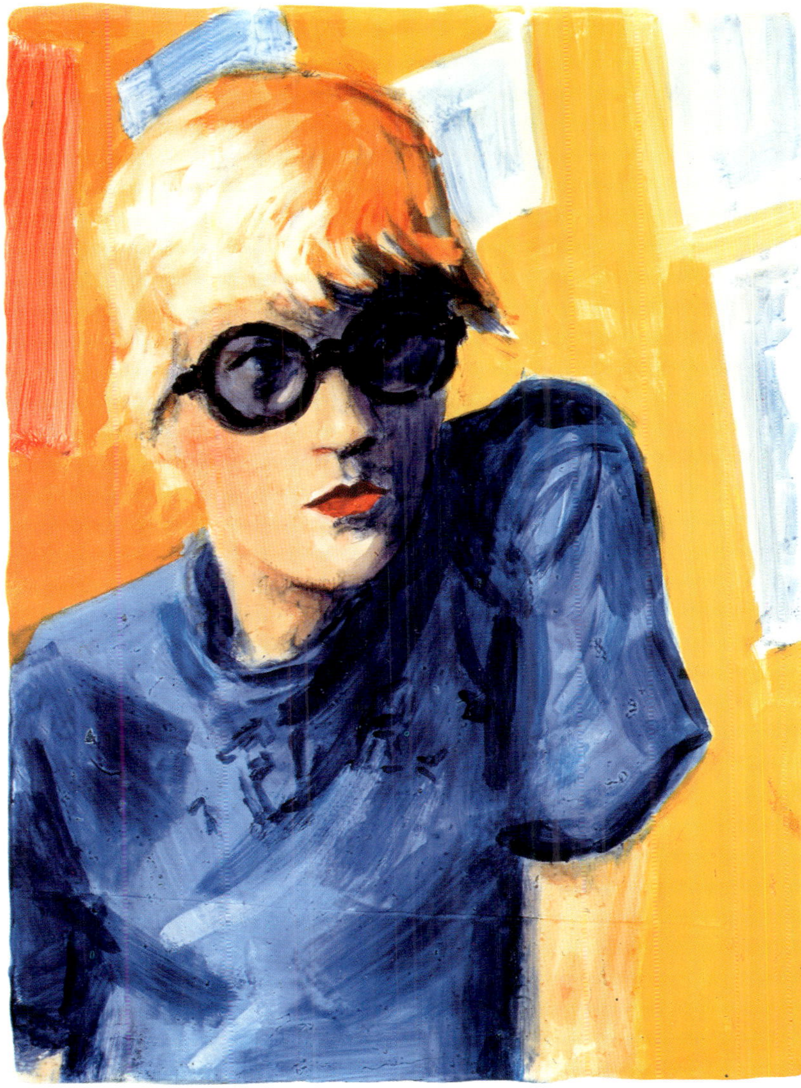

Elizabeth Peyton
David Hockney, Powis Terrace Bedroom, 1998
25 x 18 cm
Kunstmuseum Wolfsburg

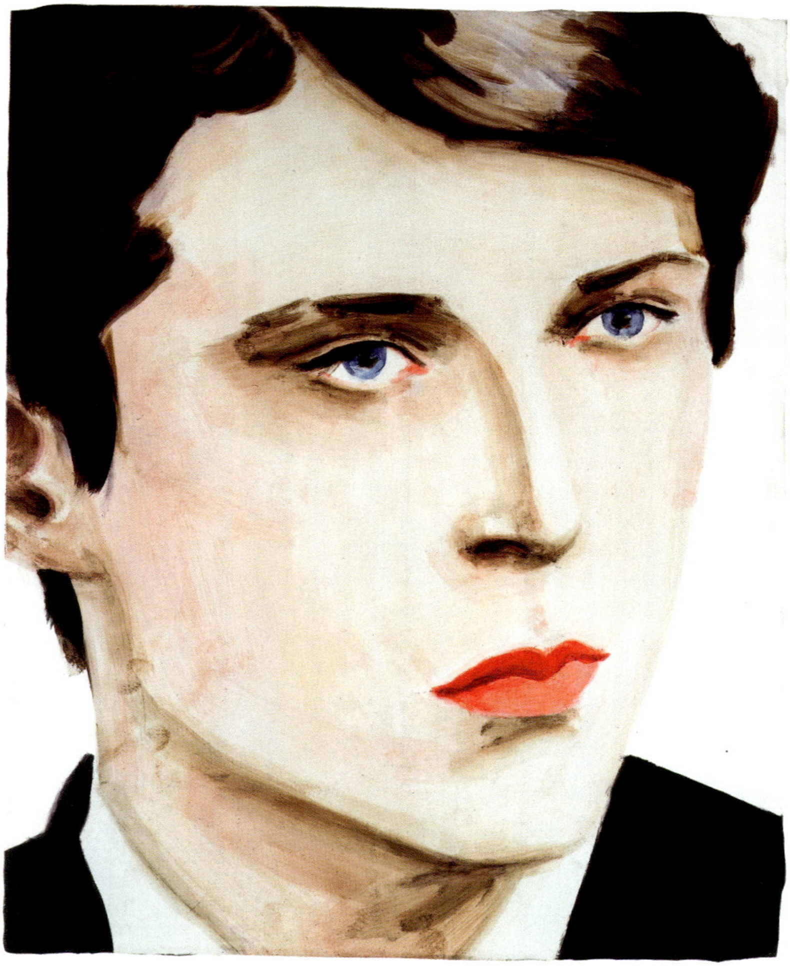

Elizabeth Peyton
Democrats are more beautiful (after Jonathan), 2001
25,4 x 20,3 cm
Collection Laura & Stafford Broumand, New York

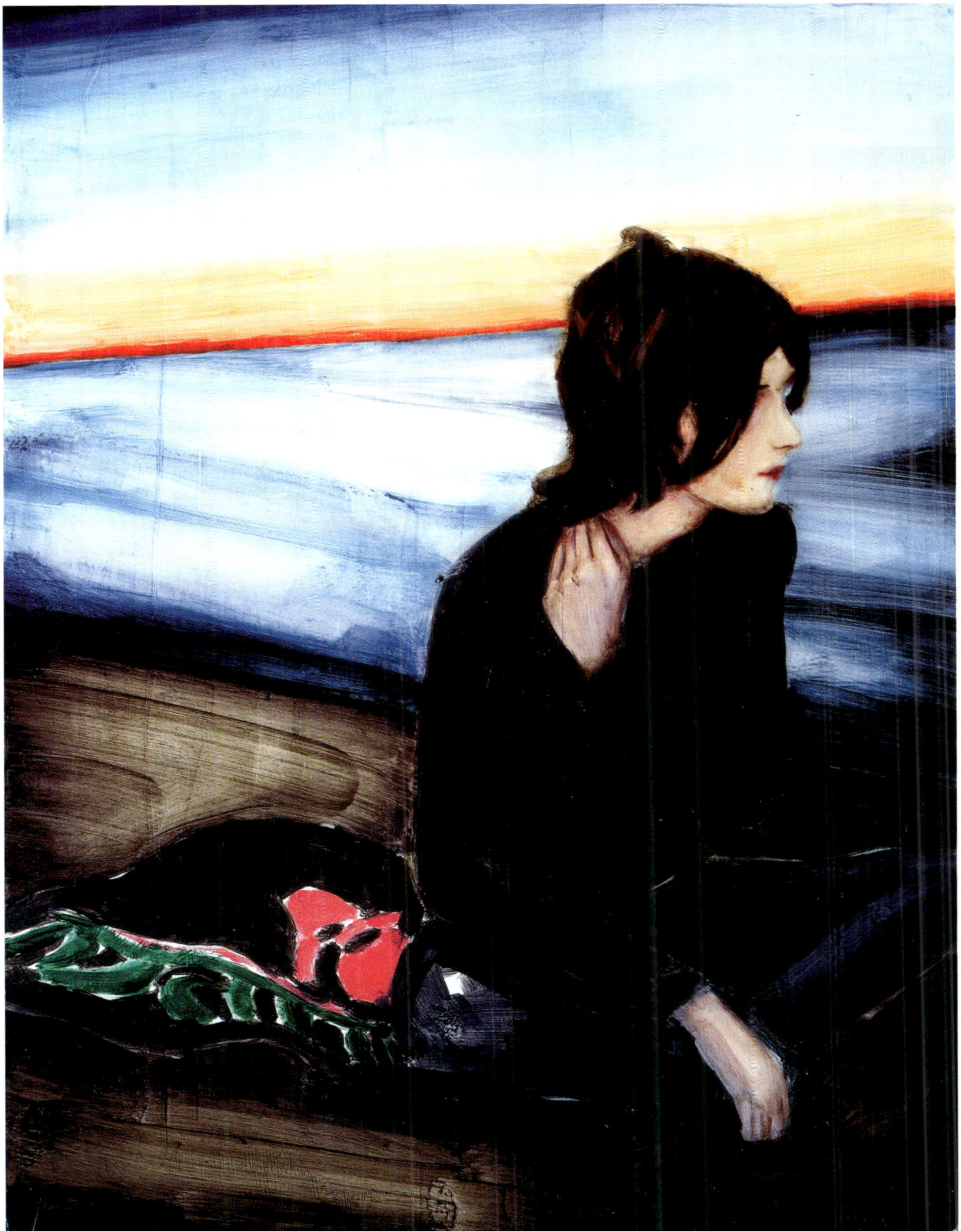

Elizabeth Peyton
September (Ben), 2001
30,8 x 23,2 cm
Collection particulière / Privatsammlung / Private Collection
Courtesy Gavin Brown's Enterprise, Corp., New York

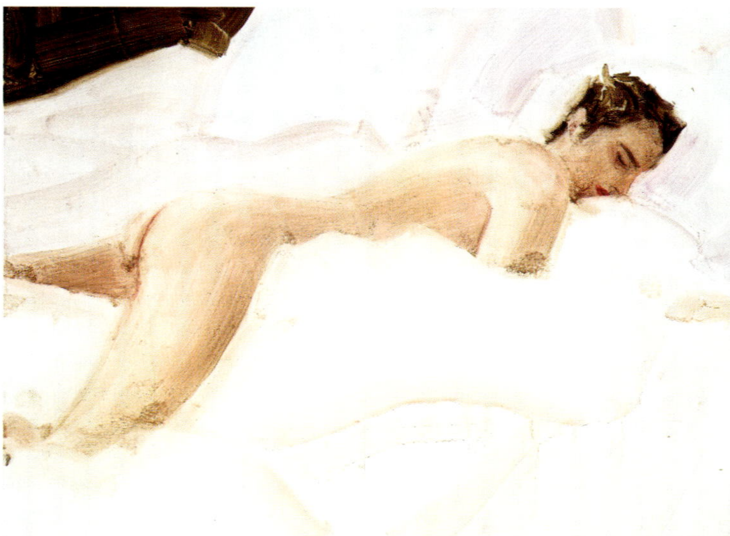

Elizabeth Peyton
Nude (Tony), 2001
15,2 x 20,3 cm
Collection Douglas S. Cramer, New York

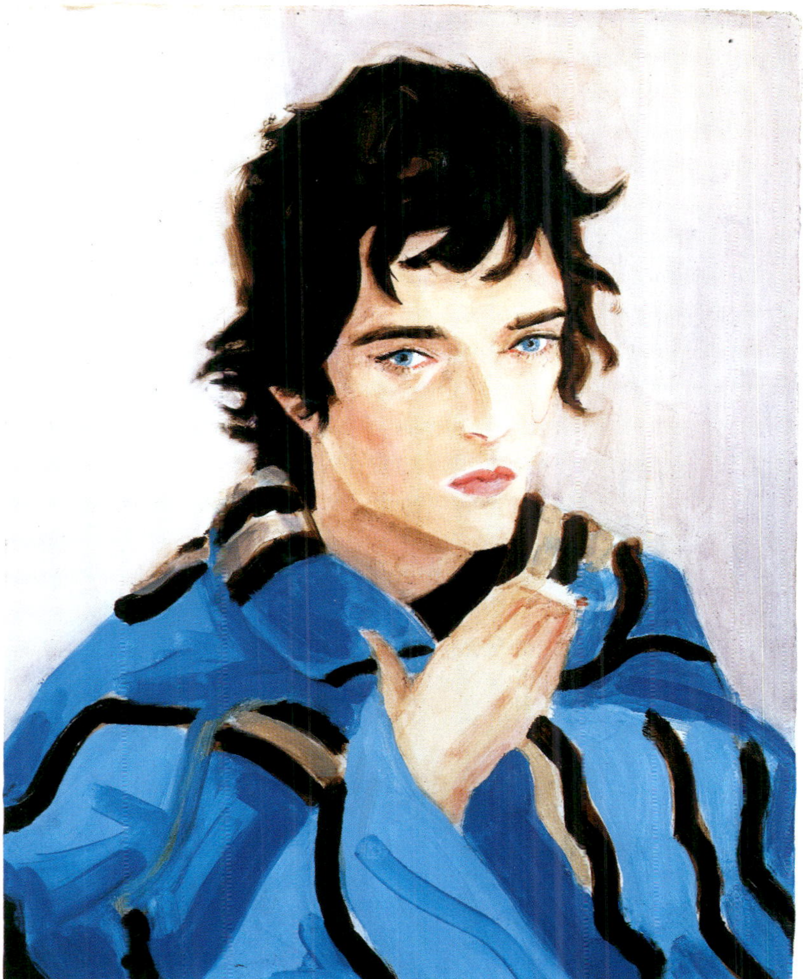

Elizabeth Peyton
Luing (Tony), 2001
35,6 x 27,9 cm
Collection Dianne Wallace, New York

Brian Calvin

Alison M. Gingeras

To the uninitiated eye, Brian Calvin might seem like the painter of some lazy, smoke-laced Bohemia, tucked away in the anonymous landscape of a Southern California suburb. Androgynous figures with long dirty hair, elongated faces, and cartoon-ish features populate his canvases. They smoke. They walk. They point. They stare forward vacantly. They make ambiguous gestures. They wear plain, casual clothes that might identify them as "slackers". When pictured in an outdoor setting, the background topography is rendered with an extreme economy: distant hills and bodies of water are delineated using a simple line, filled in with matte fields of color. Occasionally, a set of stairs or a cropped section of a chain link fence suggests a sense of spatial hierarchy, without betraying an overarching flatness that dominates both figure and setting. Interior scenes are equally as sparse. With the exception of a few domestic accouterments–a burning candle, a drinking glass, a painting–just simple line and color define the otherwise neutral rooms where his figures lounge, sit, stand or congregate.

The most obvious art historical comparison has connected Calvin's idiosyncratic world of suspended figures to the detached "social" portraiture of Alex Katz. Each painter shares a sense of extreme pictorial economy; each has a bare-bones sense of narrative; each employs color in flattened planes, using a matte, highly personal palette. A sense cool of born in 1950s New York in Katz's work meets a culture of *ennui* in the vast suburban sprawl of Brian Calvin's Los Angeles of the late 1990s.

Yet as Katz has proven over the past forty years, this seemingly overt simplicity is always deceptive. On the surface, Calvin's style and subject matter might seem easy or familiar–but underneath these cartoon-ish surfaces is a fundamental awkwardness. This pictorial and subjective unease comes not just from the non-narrative nature of the paintings but from the fact that each figure has subjected to an elaborate process of construction. Each one has been re-worked, flipped, "painted in or painted out"–an arduous process that is only apparent to a viewer who takes time to digest the visual complexity of each painting. The malaise present in each of Calvin's figures might be understood as a continual questioning of painting itself: its formal possibilities as well as its conceptual limits. This hypothesis seems to be echoed in Calvin's terse yet revealing titles. *Further On*, *Passing Through*, *Onwards* (2001)–these short words or phrases beg the viewer to move past the mere "illustrative" content to see the totality of the painting. A painting such a *Slow Burn* (2001) not only describes the mood of the painting (a figure passively watches a candle burning) but might also suggest the time necessary for the retinal "burning" of the image in the viewer's mind. Brian Calvin is a master of titling as well as a figurative painter who reasserts the primacy of visual thinking without returning to the cult of the formal in the Modernist tradition.

AG: Figurative painting is often read in a reductive manner, not extending beyond old debates pitting abstraction against figuration. Even today in the context of a much more heterogeneous field of art practices, figurative painting is often read as a mirror of its time: it reflects, records, and comments on the sociological, historical, or cultural context in which it is made. Are your human subjects actual people? Or are they typologies? Are they imaginary/fictive composites? Can your paintings of human subjects be considered within the traditional category of portraiture? Does your work embrace, resist, or is it indifferent to such classical genres?

BC: It's important to me that the figures in my paintings seem believable, but I don't worry whether they seem realistic or not. I'm not particularly interested in realism. I just want the figures to have specificity to them. I don't think about portraiture or genre at all while I'm working. I simply try to be observant of what is working and what isn't. I paint things in or I paint things out. Try to make a good painting.

AG: There seems to be a refusal of allegory in your work; a sense of narrative is always pared down to an austere minimum. Indeterminate or ambiguous hand gestures dominate certain paintings (*Onwards*, 2001; *Passing Through*, 2001). Single, simple activities are caught in a state of suspension: a figure smoking and climbing stairs (*Further Still*, 2001).

BC: I certainly didn't start painting to tell stories. I'm rarely interested in either narrative or allegory in painting. The way narrative is constructed within certain paintings can be quite exciting, but the narrative itself is usually anything but. I'm interested in the thought process painting provides. I don't want my paintings to break down into words, or at least into sentences, very easily. I hope to make work that is stubbornly visual.

AG: Another series of works deal with the figure of the artist or the painting of a painting (*Don't Be Denied*, 2000). Even in these self-reflexive works, the temptation to extract some kind of allegorical commentary about painting itself seems to be even more violently denied.

BC: Painting mystifies me. It is a very strange practice, just this side of alchemy. To me, all of my work is a contemplation of painting and it's possibilities, so it feels natural to sometimes make works involving the act of painting. I strive to think through painting, not to paint what I think. That would just be an illustration of the limits of my mind.

AG: Are you trying to strip figurative painting down to some kind of essential or rudimentary state? Figuration as an act of simple "showing" as opposed to "narrating", or "representing"?

BC: I want my paintings to feel self-contained when they are finished. I believe that each painting has it's own inner-logic, it's own thought process. Sometimes it seems interesting to include a lot of information, and sometimes I prefer to include very little. Recently my paintings look very simple, but I think that they are deceptively simple. It's quite complex to make a "simple" painting that doesn't just shut down or become overly iconic.

AG: Despite the sense of stillness and suspension, *ennui*, or "coolness" of your figures and their environment, it is striking to what degree they are evocative of the "cinematic." Living and working in Los Angeles, it seems evident that your daily experience must be completely saturated with images.

BC: I live and work at home. I find it suprisingly easy to ignore the outside world when it's necessary. As for the cinematic element, I don't really see it. It might be there but I primarily think about other painters and their paintings.

AG: In speaking with someone like Alex Katz, I ventured to ask him about his connection to cinema-especially the French films of the 1970s that attempted an insider examination of the bourgeoisie, like in the films of Eric Rohmer or Claude Chabrol. I was convinced that many of Katz's beach scenes recalled films such as *Le Genou de Claire* ('Claire's Knee", Eric Rohmer, 1970), in the way it was a very intimate portrait of a given class while guarding a calculated sense of distance or emotional detachment. Are you consciously drawing from cinema or other forms of photo-based image making?

BC: I tend to keep it all pretty separate in my mind. In general, I think about television more than cinema. I enjoy television's repetitive nature; it's strange anonymity and the flood of images. There's a lot to think about it. However, I'm a huge fan of Chris Marker's films and videos. You can feel the film thinking about itself ... very dense and yet open and playful at the same time. Absolutely inspirational and all very illuminating. I think William Eggleston does the same for color photography.

AG: As you know the exhibition is attempting to speculate about a certain strain of painting's ability to "digest" or engage with the "image" and its saturation of our everyday lives. Has this predominance of "image" (in the sense of its contemporary definition as being free-floating, disposable, detached, instantaneous, fleeting) dislodged more "traditional" concerns ascribed to figurative painting, such as representation and realism?

BC: I think figure painting's "traditional concerns" were dislodged well over 100 years ago, if not by Manet or Cézanne then certainly by all those that followed on their heels. It's been over 50 years since Pollock's heyday. I think a lot of people honestly believe that the drip paintings were the period at the end of a sentence. It certainly was an incredible breakthrough for

Pollock and for non-objective painting. Ironically though, it so quickly became the new image of modern art. I'm much more interested in artists who aren't looking for breakthroughs, but are simply trying to forge their own mode of communication.

AG: For many people who see your work for the first time, they immediately make a genealogical connection between you and Alex Katz. While certainly this connection is visible, I have been thinking about the deceptive austerity of your work in relationship to a certain European tradition that has fallen out of fashion, especially in France. Perhaps Katz is too obvious, too American, too rooted in a certain social class. In particular, I was thinking about the early paintings by Bernard Buffet that depict his ascetic existence in the immediate post war period, his isolation as an artist, his refusal of narrative/allegory, his early interest in bohemia and "outsiders". Are you familiar with Buffet's working, especially his early self-portraits? Another possible French antecedent could be Balthus, especially in regards to the interest you both seem to share for Italian quattrocento fresco painters (Piero della Francesca, Giotto).

BC: I don't know Buffet's work. It sounds interesting and I'd love to see some. I admire the eccentricity of Balthus and the frozen quality of his paintings, but never really felt a personal affinity between his work and my own. There are several painters whose work I spend a lot of time pondering and Katz is definitely one of them. Rarely will you find image and process so symbiotically linked. His work has a beautiful inner logic. As for French painting, my favorites aren't all that obscure. I constantly return to Manet, Bonnard and Matisse. I also love aspects of David, Géricault, Courbet, Cézanne and Vuillard.

AG: Are there other less obvious historical figures that are important to your work? Are these "genealogical" musings relevant, useful, or valid to your work?

BC: Piero della Francesca and Giotto are like planets to me. It was their work as well as that of Philip Guston and Andy Warhol that made painting really open up for me. Fra Angelico's frescoes in the Convent of San Marco in Florence completely blew my mind. Who else? Massacio, John Wesley, David Hockney, Sigmar Polke, Gerhard Richter ... These are the people who make me want to paint. They are all such deeply intelligent visual thinkers.

AG: Despite of the extreme two-dimensionality of your work, intensified by the matte use of color fields, there is a whiff of the sculptural embedded in the poses, gestures, and posturing of your figures.

BC: My technique is far from streamlined. I don't start with an image. I find my figures through a process that includes a lot of addition, subtraction and amending. Figures move around a lot, lose their arms or their heads, spin 90 degrees, are painted out, etc. I suppose that is where the "sculptural whiff" comes from. My work looks much more fast and graphic in reproduction. It's a problem for me.

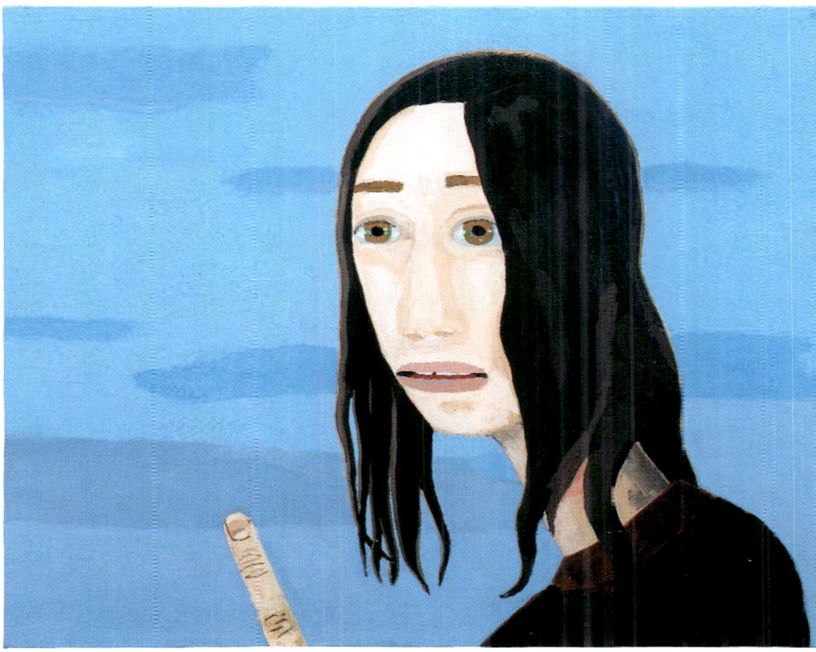

Brian Calvin
Onwards, 2001
45,7 x 58,4 cm
Collection Marc Foxx, Los Angeles

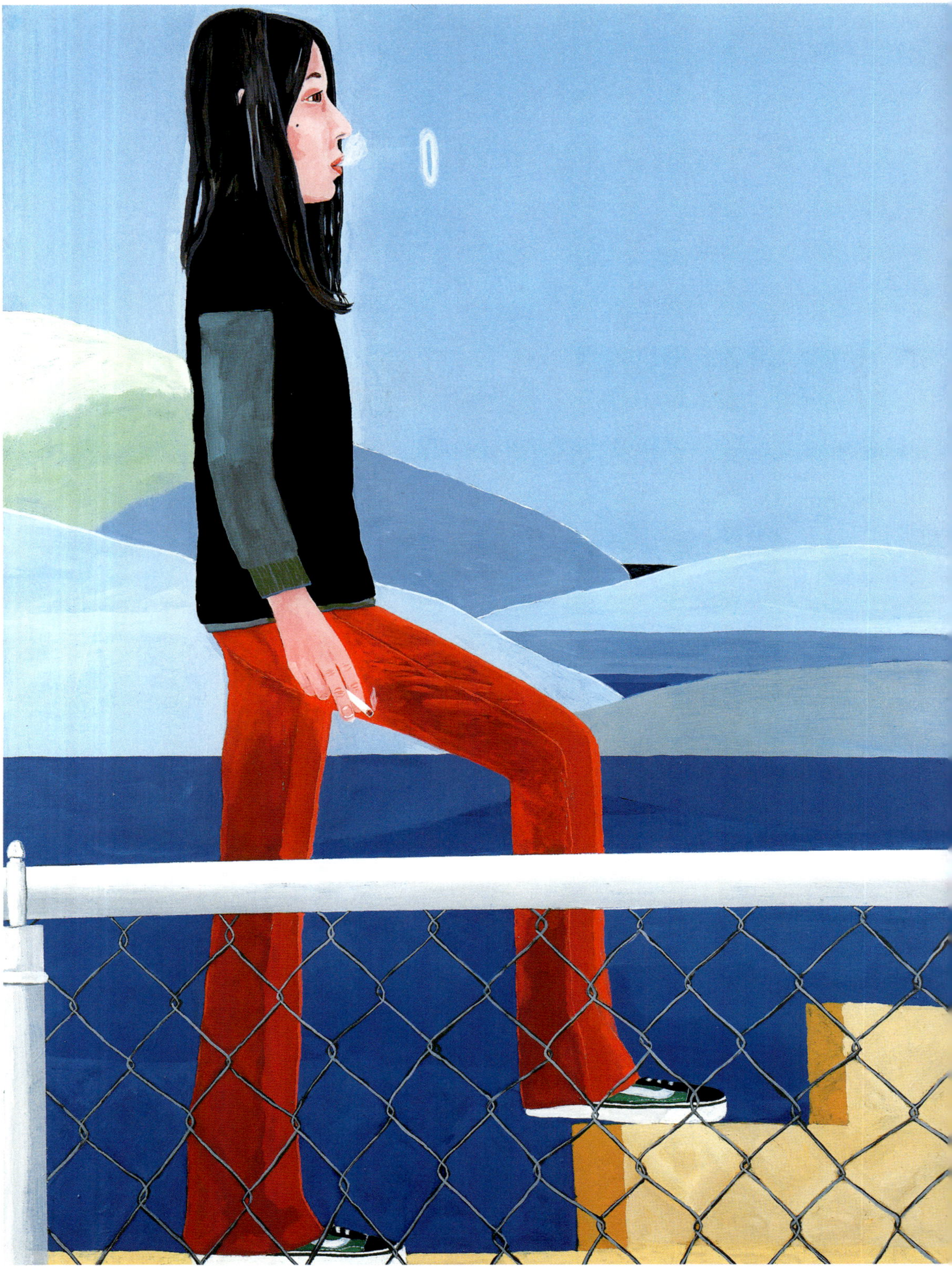

Brian Calvin
Further Still, 2001
123 x 92 cm
Collection particulière / Privatsammlung / Private Collection
Courtesy Corvi-Mora Gallery, London

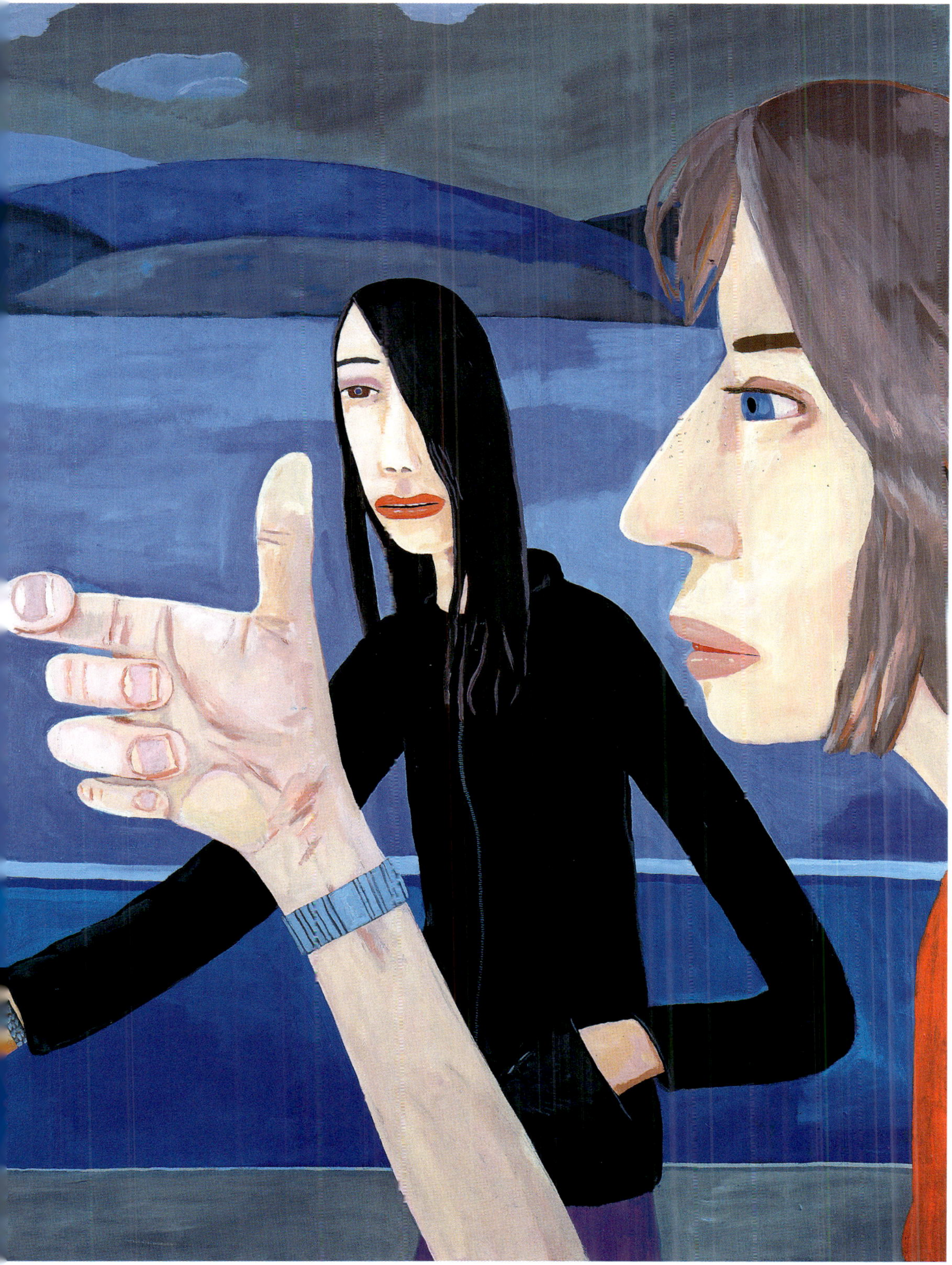

Brian Calvin
Passing Through, 2001
136 x 102 cm
Collection particulière / Privatsammlung / Private Collection
Courtesy Corvi-Mora Gallery, London

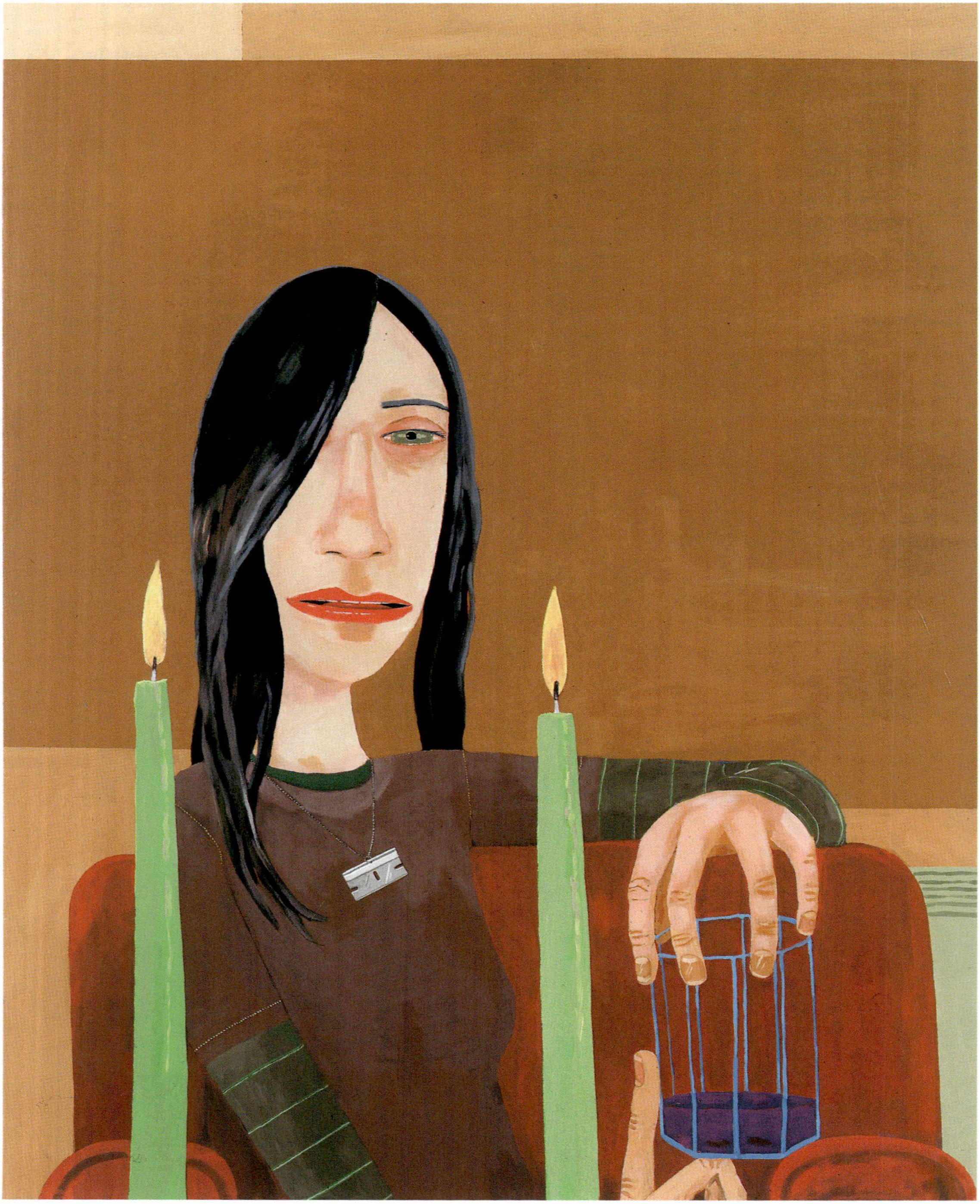

Brian Calvin
Slow Burn, 2001
152,4 x 122 cm
Collection Robert Harshorn Shimshak & Marion Brenner, Berkeley
Courtesy Marc Foxx, Los Angeles

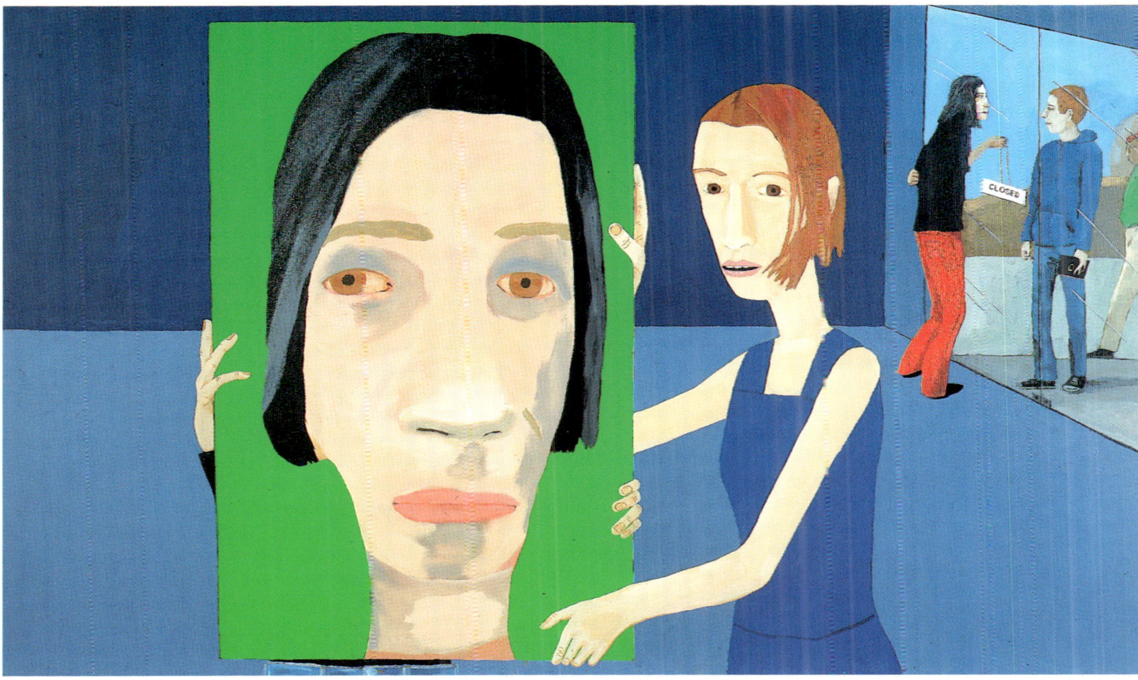

Brian Calvin
Don't Be Denied, 2000
91 x 152 cm
Collection Kenneth L. Freed, Boston
Courtesy Marc Foxx, Los Angeles

Sophie von Hellermann

Jemima Montagu

Sophie von Hellermann's solo exhibition in London last year had the enigmatic title "Vusering Hites". The words refer to the famous romantic novel by Emily Brontë called *Wuthering Heights*, as if pronounced with a German accent. This humorous title alone says much about the character of Hellermann's work. Brought up in both England and Germany, she is steeped in the cultural heritage of both countries. The reference to this nineteenth century novel betrays her close affiliation with the Romantic tradition–from the repressed passions of English writing to the lonely star-gazing in the work of German painters such as Caspar David Friedrich, one of Hellermann's acknowledged heroes. Growing up with her three sisters in the isolated English countryside, Hellermann personally identified with the lives of the Brontë sisters: without television they read books and fantasized about romantic encounters. But the jokey self-mockery of the German accented title gives the overall flavor of this artist's work which is glazed with an ironic humor.

Hellermann paints the scenes of her personal imagination: a fluid acrylic meltdown of images from books, films, art history, the media and her own life. Friends, lovers or simply people she has seen in the street, mingle intimately with literary, cinematic or art historical heroes–Catherine Deneuve, the characters of Edouard Manet's *Le Déjeuner sur l'herbe* ("Luncheon on the Grass", 1863), Maxim and Rebecca from Daphne du Maurier's classic novel *Rebecca* (1938). Even scenes that are further removed from identifiable sources seem to be drawn from a shared mass media archive–a generic "Leading Lady" in the painting by the same name, a DJ brooding in a recording studio, a couple wandering through a Hollywood set, or a girl collapsed in tears on the steps of a church. Describing her painting as "child's play–emulation, dream, game", Hellermann projects herself into these chosen scenarios and uses the filter of generic imagery to describe, and sometimes exorcize, her own personal experiences. Rather than see her painting in competition with images from mass media, she adopts these images as her own and so, despite the collective references, each painting is firmly rooted in her own subjectivity. Hellermann recognizes that she has been imaginatively molded by a world of images, both visual and literary, and that as a result they have become the markers for navigating her own experience.

Hellermann's uninhibited appropriation of historical or mass media imagery also relates to her participation in the artist collective Hobbypop. Founded in 1995 by a group of painters at the Düsseldorf Art Academy [1], the collective began as a series of exhibitions and parties which took place in abandoned industrial spaces across the city. Both intensely romantic and bitingly satirical, the group stage themed events that parody–and celebrate–inflated cultural phenomena such as fashion shows, sport competitions, space travel or the art world. *Foto-fashion-lovestory* (1999) recreated the banal but hyped world of fashion: against a background of large paintings and banners of text, the artists dressed up, handed out free cameras and created speech bubbles with empty chat such as "I slipped from one addiction to another" or "When I was in New York recently ...". Although their approach is fun and deliberately casual–the exhibitions are organized in-situ in the space of a few days–it disguises a serious wish to expose and critique the mechanisms of cultural consumerism. Hobbypop's anti-individual, informal and mocking strategies demonstrate a desire to combat the capitalist structures inscribed in art production and reception. They demonstrate a playful disregard for the traditional boundaries of high and low culture and their own use of appropriation mimics and mocks the cyclical repackaging of cultural capital. Hobbypop proposes that life is a game, and that this game is as serious and entertaining as life itself. As Hellermann says: "It's a bit *Absolutely Fabulous*." [2]

Hellermann's own work displays similar techniques of subversion. She freely fuses references to high and low culture - from her early series of "DJ" paintings to her recent preoccupation with literature. But while she frequently mixes together these different frames of reference, these phases also reflect specific moments in her own experience. Hellermann's disregard for traditional social and cultural boundaries was particularly evident in a recent Hobbypop collaboration with Markus Vater and Dietmar Lutz called *Hänsel and Gretel*. Lutz suggested that Vater and Hellermann adopt the roles of the notorious German terrorists Ulrike Meinhof and Andreas Baader, and paint a series of works imagining what the infamous pair might have done if they had not "committed suicide". In the paintings, each signed "Ulrike" or "Andreas", the couple are shown driving across the American desert or walking through a forest. The images are both a projection of personal fantasy ("everyone played at being terrorists when I was young" says Hellermann) and a deliberate provocation to conventions of good taste and sensitivity. For these artists such symbols are not taboos but aspects of their own past which are open to exploration.

Unlike artists of a previous generation, Hellermann's work seems refreshingly unburdened by the weight of the past, either artistic or historical. Although she describes her work as a "struggle", her paintings are imbued with an atmosphere of weightlessness and ease. Hellermann works fast and can often produce several canvases in one day. She uses fluid, loose brushstrokes against translucent washes of pastel colors and figures are depicted with great economy: swift outline strokes and a few careful touches of detail. Some areas of the canvas are almost always left bare. Painting's traditional associations of time-consumption and longevity are rejected in the simple sweep of her brush. Her style is perhaps the most challenging aspect of her work. Her apparently nonchalant attitude towards the appearance of technical skill reveals her own art historical roots. Like Martin Kippenberger, an artist she considers an important influence on her work, she moves freely between a demonstration of technical ability and a total rejection of it. Painting's value is not predicated upon virtuosity but upon its role as a manipulable tool for the artist.

Nevertheless Hellermann's nonchalance is coupled with an absolute faith and immersion in the act of painting itself. This is immediately evident in her handling of landscape, which inescapably reveals the Romantic notion of the "pathetic fallacy"[3]. In the touching painting *These things happened last winter, sir ...* (2001), a crying girl appears threatened by a brooding male figure who is obscured by the tangled branches of a tree. The autumn leaves fall like tears, or drips of blood. Despite the obvious differences in their approach to subject matter, the attraction to landscape as a space for emotional expression, as well as the simple romance of nature, recall the paintings of Peter Doig. Both artists use landscape as a projection of an inner psychological state. Hellermann's streak of Romanticism runs deep, but her images remain elusive: they suggest a glimpse or memory rather than something fixed indelibly in time.

Endnotes

1 Hobbypop is now based between Düsseldorf and London. Present members are: Thea Djordjadze, Sophie von Hellermann, Christian Jendreiko, Nick Laessing, Matthias Lahme, Dietmar Lutz, Andé Niebur, Marie-Celine Schäfer and Markus Vater.

2 A BBC television comedy series starring Joanna Lumley and Jennifer Saunders.

3 A literary term coined by John Ruskin in his work *Modern Painters* (1856). It refers to the attribution of human emotions or characteristics to inanimate objects or to nature.

JM: We were talking earlier about the work of Elizabeth Peyton, celebrity culture and about how she gives celebrity imagery an intimacy or familiarity. I was suggesting that this kind of imagery is often drained of meaning through the mass media, through their banality, but you were suggesting that glossy magazines act like mirrors to society.

SvH: Not mirrors, but because you are one of millions looking at the same cover photo of Gwyneth Paltrow, you can see in her eyes all the eyes of millions of other people, and I think everyone has this sense of a person being shared or held up in reflection. There are shared emotions, emotions shared by thousands about one thing.

JM: Before you were talking about media images as mirrors, as spaces for projection. Isn't there a difference between something you impose your own personal identity on and something that is a shared icon or collective symbol?

SvH: A girl on the cover of a magazine contains all the desires about how everyone would like to see themselves. She doesn't look like that, we don't look like that. It isn't even about looking like that, about beauty, or even about being on the cover. But it's a picture.

JM: Do you think that we want to own it, or possess it as an image?

SvH: It's forced upon us. Everyday there is a deluge of images.

JM: Do you feel a pressure, as a painter today, to compete with this deluge of images? There is TV, cinema and so many quick-fix, easy-access images and stories. Does your work try to compete?

SvH: I suppose I'm just open to this flood and somehow I recreate it in my painting. And then I just imagine or mix all the different references. It is enough to mix this week's events with last week's events to create something new. Like a trend factory.

JM: But your work is not just about quoting from mass media, there are also all the literary or art historical references. You mix literature, art history, mass media, high culture, low culture, friends, DJs,

Manet's *Le Déjeuner sur l'herbe*—all these different social and historical registers. Are you aware of this as a kind of leveling strategy? Are you imitating the deluge?

SvH: Yes, but it's also a portrayal of a state of being. A state of being—the here and now.

JM: Do you mean a reflection of your psyche, or imagination?

SvH: I am very aware that I am just one of millions. I am aware of painting as a very humble activity because it's so direct. I'm just really impressed by a lot of things I see, and it makes me want to paint. I try to locate a painting somewhere between this world of fantasy and reality, or the space somewhere in between.

JM: Thinking back to what you said earlier about projection, it seems to me that many of the people in your paintings seem like friends because they are very intimately portrayed. It's like an imaginary salon, you're thinking—"Ah, what would it be like to think of this person in this way or set against this other person". Is that space between reality and fantasy a personal space?

SvH: Yes, painting is a way of creating my own space. Like when I paint a personal situation, by making it fictional—because all my characters are fictional—I deal with the experience. I can invent something and by doing this I make it mine somehow.

JM: This seems something new. That painting today is able to address personal feelings again. This has been out of bounds in painting for a long time. Painting has been weighed down by its own history. Has something happened, or is there something special about painting itself, that allows you to feel that it is a space where you can express very personal things, or create a personal universe?

SvH: I could just write my experiences down or make some sort of direct response, but in painting it's very exciting to explore how little information is required. Only two brushstrokes are necessary to get a very specific image of something.
I used to get criticism a long time ago from tutors who said they could see in my paintings what had happened to me during the week. So many personal experiences are universal, and just by finding the right way to paint them they become personal experiences for everyone. It's a success when I paint something very personal and then someone else feels understood.

JM: To me a lot of your paintings look like scenes from films. This is partly because of the way they are painted—the wide angles and intimate, stage-set interiors. For example in *Leading Lady*, which you have said was inspired by the film *All About Eve* (Joseph L. Mankiewicz, 1950). Can you talk about these cinematic references, their way of creating a sense of familiarity, and how this works in relation to the personal content of your work?

SvH: The reason that I deliberately choose scenes from films to paint is because I know that my paintings are like storyboards, that I am somehow working on a fictional movie that is never going to be made. I also want to know what people feel. Painting is about communication: what I lack in rhetoric I try to make up for in my paintings. Still, I suppose I cannot escape mystery.
I don't think people need to know me to understand what is personal and what is not personal about the paintings. I enjoy the liberty of painting, I suppose.

JM: Liberty is a quality I also see in your work—it seems so free from historical weight. Even in the Hobbypop Baader-Meinhof series which you did with Markus Vater and Dietmar Lutz. At Lutz's suggestion you identified with the characters of Baader and Meinhof and then named the piece after the fairytale Hänsel and Gretel. You are German artists and this is a very serious political subject, but without taking away from the seriousness, you also feel free to inhabit and play with such weighty symbols.

SvH: It's actually a constant struggle to feel free, and to find an area in painting that is my own. Every time I paint I think of this painter or that painter; they just pop up in my mind. Or what someone has written or said about painting. Also I don't work alone in my studio but with Dietmar [Lutz] and Markus [Vater]. Whilst we consciously diffuse boundaries between our work, in some ways we are also fighting to be different from each other.
I think of painting like child's play—emulation, dream, games. In the Baader-Meinhof paintings we were playing at being children, acting out climbing Mount Everest or playing being terrorists. In all my paintings I'm pretending to be there. I imagine myself in the scene. Not necessarily part of the action, but more a question of "what would it be like if I were there", what would this room look like, what would the sounds in that room be like ... I try to recreate the experience as if it were my own.

JM: You must be aware that as someone very cultivated, you have a lot of high culture references at your fingertips. You play with these as much as you play with popular culture. Installations with Hoppypop are often very knowing or ironic, but in a very playful or easy way. Where does that ease with tradition come from?

SvH: I suppose it's like waiting for something to happen. It's about catching the elusive. We do not respect anything in terms in the pool of information—tradition, contemporary culture, history. More than anything else we do not make distinctions between things. We are aliens that have just landed on earth and say "Wow" or "How funny" at the same time. I have a strong sense of history and I am aware of where I come from, but it feels like Sartre's "The Games are Over" (*Les Jeux sont faits*, 1947). My "ancestors" are walking behind me but they cannot change what I do.

JM: There seems to be a difference between your way of playing with references to the past, your art historical vampirism and that of artists' you admire, like Sigmar Polke for instance. You refer to contrasting styles or subjects, but you inject them with genuine emotion. This seems to be a new territory for painting. A brave new world ...?

SvE: A *Brave New World*, yes, because I am not afraid of emotion and I do not stylize it. I genuinely believe that human emotions describe the universe and are as much linked to time and space as matter. I try to make painting necessary, as if it is absolutely necessary that I paint. My painting has to be convincing.

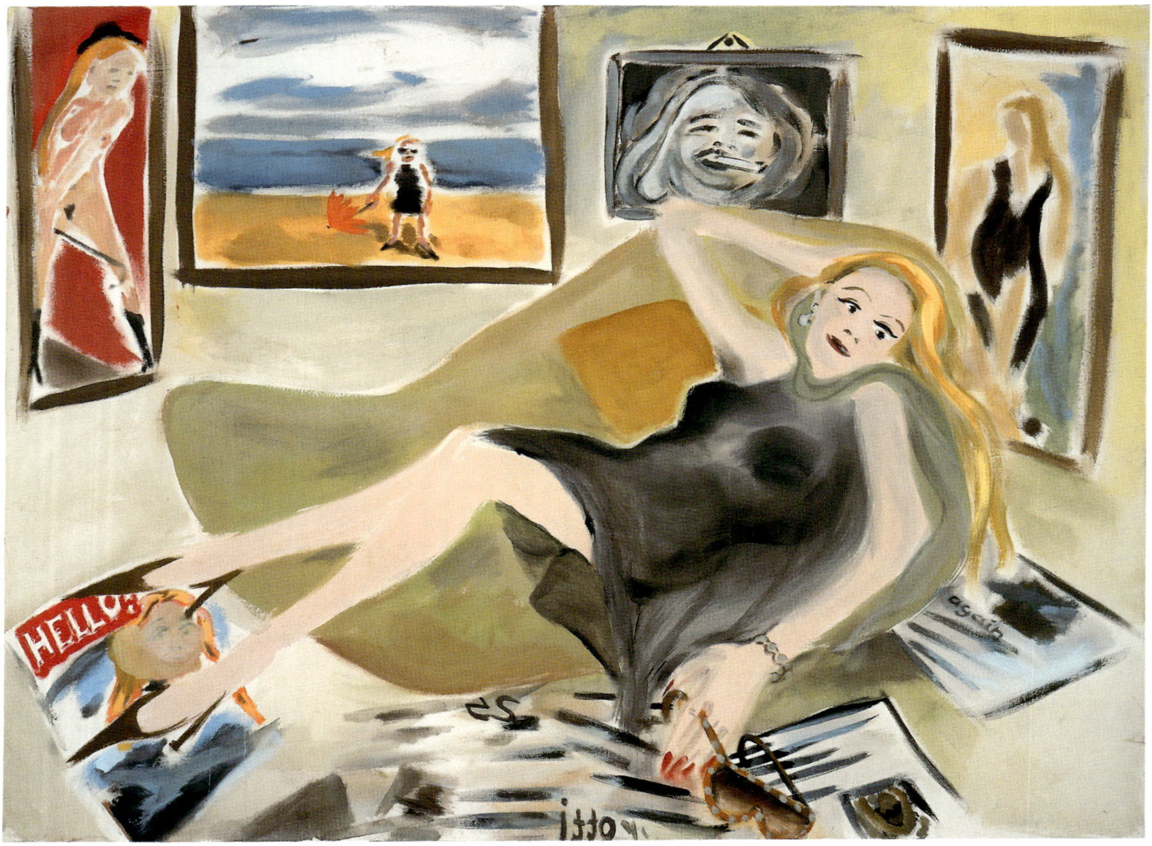

Sophie von Hellermann
Leading Lady, 2001
180 x 260 cm
The Saatchi Gallery, London

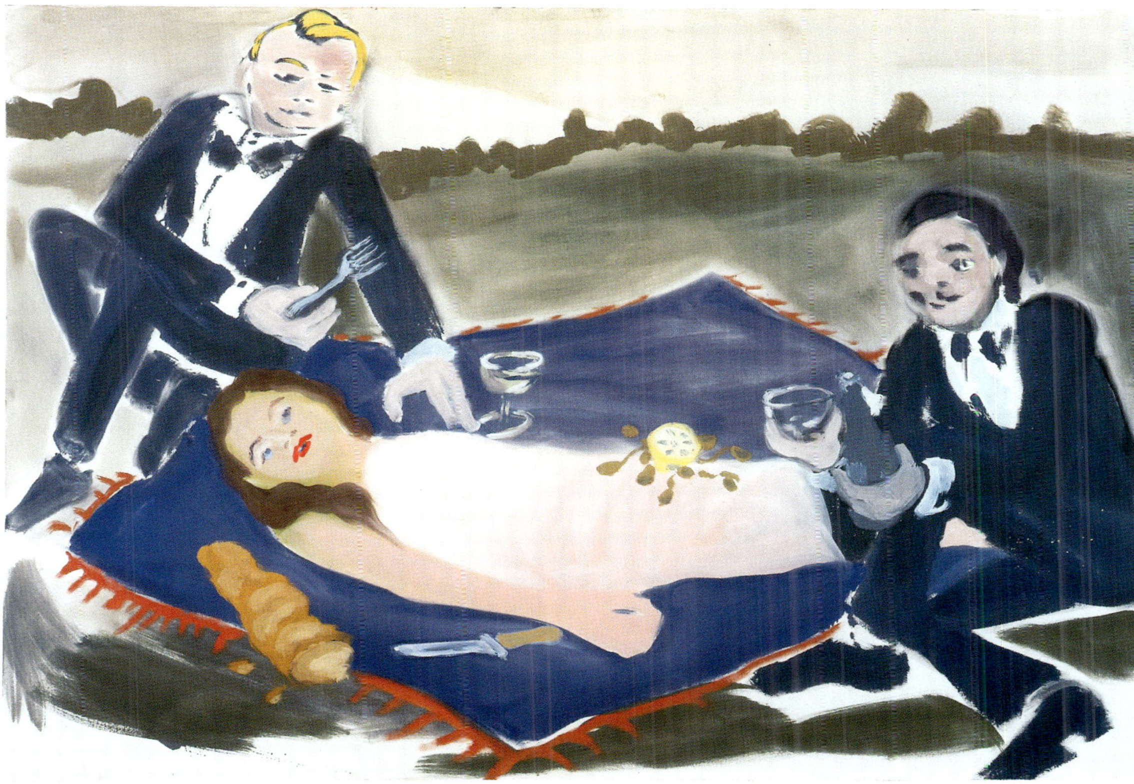

Sophie von Hellermann
When he came..., 2001
180 x 260 cm
The Saatchi Gallery, London

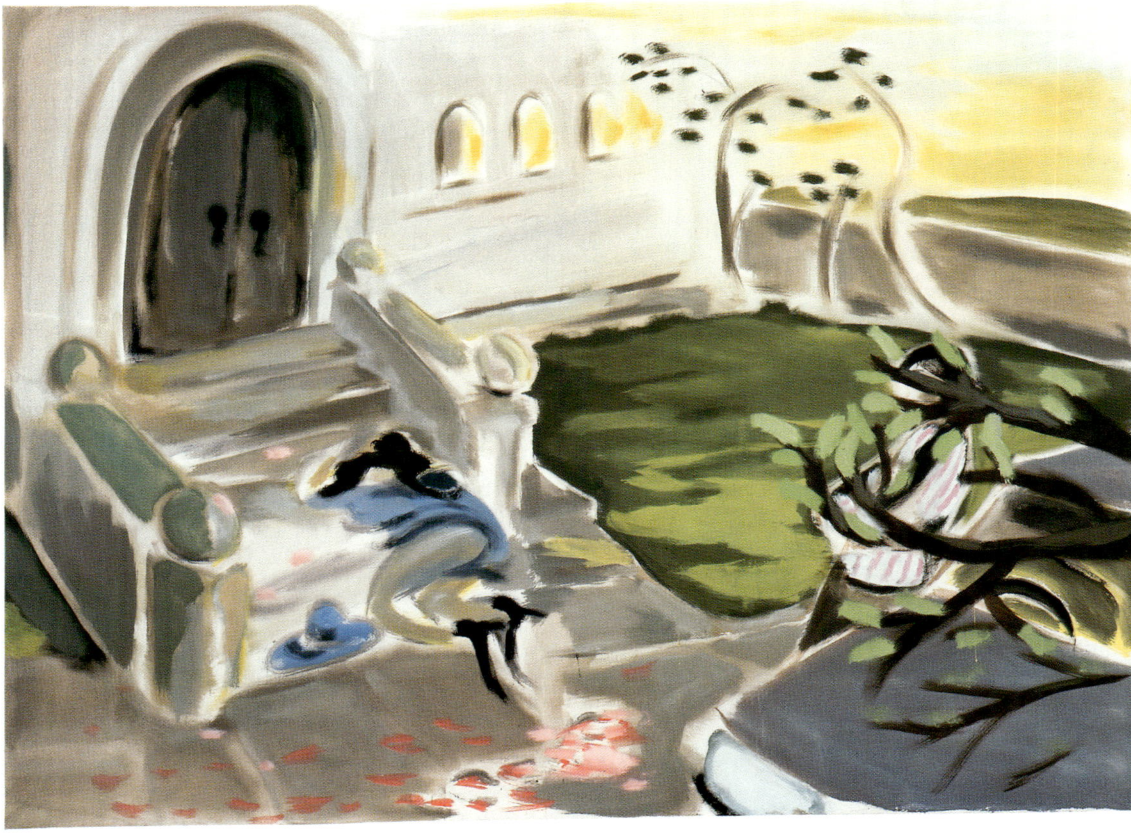

Sophie von Hellermann
These things happened last winter, sir, 2001
180 x 260 cm
The Saatchi Gallery, London

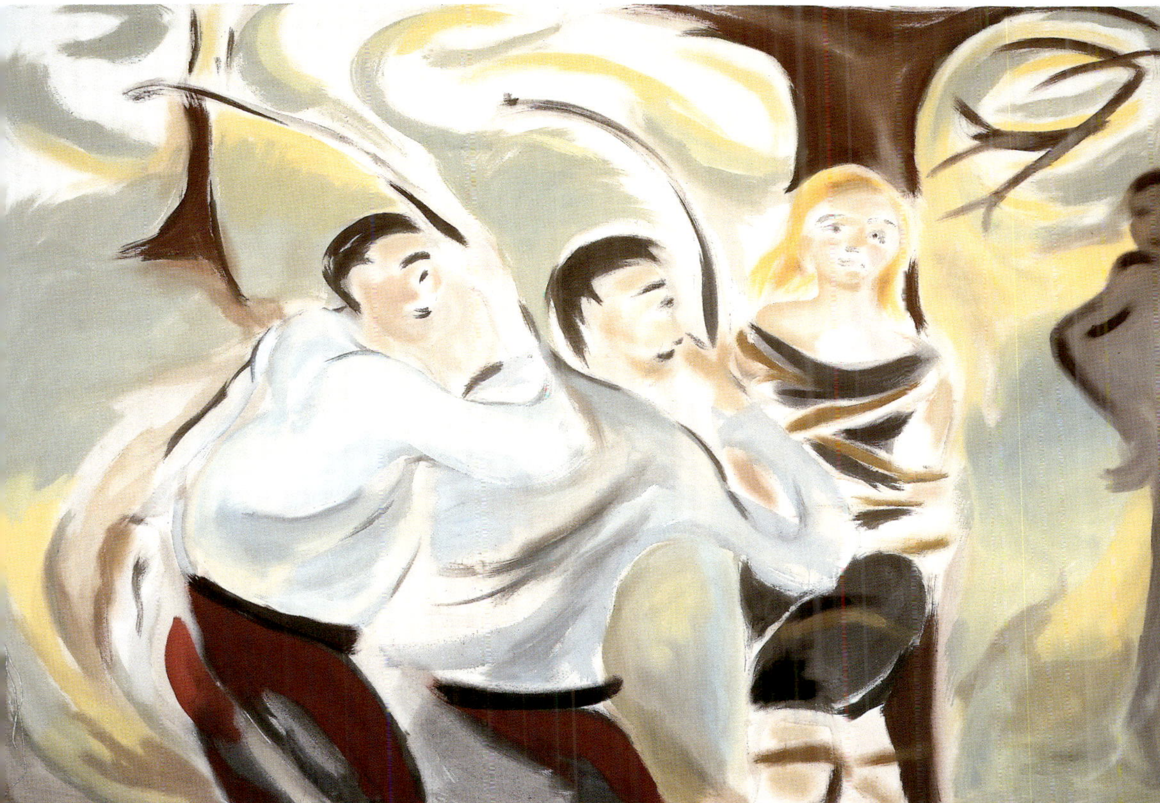

Sophie von Hellermann
Belle de jour, 2001
210 x 300 cm
The Saatchi Gallery, London

Peter Doig

Gabriele Mackert

It's about the idea of getting absorbed into them, so you physically get lost.

Peter Doig [1]

Peter Doig is a painter of the generation which always gets asked about its references to cinema and photography, to the pop idiom and various sub-cultures. Even though the discussion about the death of painting is now only distantly involved in this discourse, much analysis focuses on an interdisciplinary approach (for fear of engaging too much in hermeneutics) and shies away from a deadlocked scientific methodology. So descriptions of the obvious and unavoidable, such as the various aspects of the influence the entertainment culture has had on artistic practice and how the one is mirrored through the other, get endlessly bandied about. References to one's source material or preferences like one's record collection or sporting ambitions thus become an unexpected central connecting point between the worlds of one's life and one's work. Doig, however, does not quite fit into the pigeonholes reserved for those artists who live out their encounters with pop culture in their art. He uses his own photographs to paint from, and also found materials taken from newspapers, magazines, advertising or films. He views his collection of a thousand slides as his sketch books.

Doig's pictorial worlds are, however, fascinating primarily for their very immediate painterly creations and the receptional situations engendered by them. After all, one can, with the help of his pictures, renew the debate about abstract and figurative painting and so allow oneself to be entangled in the well-calculated game of contradictions within his pictures. Opposite poles, such as the near and the far, the shallow and the deep, the momentary and the permanent or just tradition and innovation define the tensions inside them. It is the richness of such facets that marks their expressiveness.

The characters that populate Doig's worlds renew a romantic theme, that of the relationship between the individual and nature. Primarily, however, they put well-known patterns to the test. They turn their backs on the viewer or lie down flat, in line with the pictorial plane, in nature (*Daytime Astronomy*, 1997-98), they get lost high-flying or shooting beyond the surface (*Olin MK IV*, 1995) as though the extension of the pictorial space here were not merely thematically metaphorical, as if, in fact, the exuberance of the sporting high spirits could really transcend even the pictorial, object-like limitations.

In *Blotter* (1993), the picture and its mirroring ice (or better: water) surface become one. Painting here is not just a mirror of divine nature or a reflective medium of the painter, it is also a projection screen for the viewer. Who, after all, has not experienced the challenge of poking sharply into layers of ice or the incredulous putting to the test of the ground while carefully groping one's way ahead on a frozen surface? Each probing step invites the same warning: Caution! Step on a crack and you won't come back! Painting may be flat, but it has treacherous depths of its own. You get in and break the waves at your own peril only.

Doig's landscapes serve neither to illustrate some meretricious ideal nor are they modelled from nature, but instead they are equipped with disconcerting effects of depth, inaccurate perspectives and hazy proportions. On *Figure in Mountain Landscape* (1997-98) Doig handles the image of his landscapes like some territory on a map. Mountains, as a strange craquele, generate an additional tilting effect of plasticity, some kind of wonky anamorphosis flipping between front view and plan view. The picture, on the other hand, which is in the process of being painted in *Figure in Mountain Landscape* is, in its turn, a rougher layer of the landscape's surface. Here the surface of the image in the picture functions, once again, as a classically-reflective reference.

Tranquility, timelessness and a fractured nostalgia shape the atmosphere. We are encouraged to take up our own space within them, when a detail jostles one of our recollections into action. The static image thus unexpectedly once again becomes a part of the history within which Doig's pictures function as open stages for thoughts and mental images, until at last all the biographical materials, previous experiences and narratives coagulate into an infinite snapshot. So these pictures simultaneously store collective memories, and there, in their generality, lies an uncanny precision. "The open quality of his paintings allows for various approaches. The figurative tells of things and occurences and enters into a direct dialogue with anyone who loves stories; at the same time, the narrative element is not overpowering and never takes away from the fact that we are looking at a painting."[2]

Doig captivates by the richness of his inventions, wild and sensitive, studiedly artificial and yet tailored towards a confrontation of the means, and absolutely enriched with sensational effects in the odd detail, his joy of experimentation sounding out all the surface opportunities of painting. In so doing, he refers back to the entire universe of art history, references can be found to Romanticism, Post-Impressionism, Expressionism and even Pointillism.

A sulphurous yellow, rusty tones of red, poisonous greens, for instance, determine the patch of lawn in *Daytime Astronomy*, an idyll featuring an individual staring up at the heavens. Centrally positioned and yet almost unnoticeable, this character also marks the borderline between foreground and background, lighter and darker zones, borne by an uncanny underworld, yet fully concentrating upon equally unknown heights. Through such horizontal rhythmic patterns Doig continues to inscribe his painting fast into the plane. Even the overland cable is used for this purpose. It becomes a line, reminiscent of the irregularities of computer print-outs: like a defective streak of white in a row of black letters.

This strip-like build-up is extended by an additional layer of bewildering elements in the foreground. They cloud the actual central object and add a dynamic quality to the gaze which is encouraged to follow its impulse of curiosity to seek an unobstructed visibility upon a building or a character and to leave the undercover concealment of the detective. In *White Out* from 1992 the incidence of snow flakes mentioned in the title is increased to twice its original amount through an indefinable precipitation of time and improper storage upon the surface of the picture into a homogeneous play of positive and negative blots and spots. In between all of this one can barely trace the outlines of a figure, which one can only suspect is moving, yet whose very direction is already lost in the turmoil of dots. Even conservative interpretations fare no better. The figure itself seems to float, like the snow flakes, somewhere upon the plane before a forest, which can be presumed to frame the upper, darker zone of the picture.

Doig's virtuosity is discreet, maintaining the painting and its motif in a state of balance. Both the object rendered and the means for doing so are defined as components, as a representation achieved through a process of work.

(translated from the German by Tom Appleton)

Endnotes

1 "I've never been canoeing on a toxic swamp. A conversation between Peter Doig and Adrian Searle", in *Peter Doig Blotter*, exh. cat. Berlin/London: Contemporary Fine Arts, Victoria Miro Gallery (1995), pp. 5-15.

2 „Foreword", in *Peter Doig: Blizzard Seventy-Seven*, exh. cat. London/Kiel/Nuremberg: Kunsthalle zu Kiel, Kunsthalle Nürnberg, Whitechapel Art Gallery (1998), p. 52.

GM: Peter, what was the situation like when you started painting? Comparing your first studies at St. Martin's School of Art (London) at the beginning of the 1980s to your later studies at Chelsea School of Art after your return to England, how were the conditions different? Was painting dominated by "wild", expressive gestures or by repeated mournings over the "death of painting" owing to the increasing influence of photography and the cinema on the arts?

PD: When I started painting in 1980 there was not much new painting that interested me to be seen in the London galleries. "Lyrical Abstraction" was on the menu—and I remember visiting New York a lot in those days and witnessing the emergence of graffiti into art. This was very exciting to see as a young student. At St. Martin's (1980-83) we had influential teachers in the "complimentary studies department": John Stezaker and Rosetta Brooks, who were introducing us to the works of artists coming out of New York as Cindy Sherman, Jack Goldstein, Richard Prince and others. These artists slowly started to show in London. This combined with the *New Spirit in Painting* exhibition at the Royal Academy, Guston and Beckmann at the Whitechapel, Basquiat and Fischl at the ICA, which made for a truly confusing whirlwind of painting influences. From a student's point of view at that point in time there was a lot of open territory—or so it seemed. A lot of bad work was made—but there was a genuine enthusiasm for the medium amongst painters at least. Not many British painters emerged out of all this. By the time I returned to study in 1989-90 there had been a huge shift away from any painting that wasn't either self critical, process-based or neo-minimal or Neo-Geo. Richter was now the *one* and there was a lot of blurring going on—1980s painting was seen as the kiss of death and not anywhere to be seen or discussed. Exhibition venues were extremely cautious of showing paintings. I think that it was a very good time to be a painting student because it gave you time to develop without too much attention—it seems nowadays everything happens extremely quickly. I think a lot of artists were making self conscious calculated paintings at this time. It seemed like a good time to look back to the past—to move forward into the future. There were a lot of artists dropping painting for other mediums like photography and film.

GM: I don't see your work so much as a reference to media, pop- or sub-culture, styles, art traditions or discussions, but more as a venture to create again and again a new relationship between painting as a process, painting as a physical object and—no less importantly—as a reality. You often use photographs, film stills, footage of current events, images found in newspapers, postcards, and such as a starting point for your rural or urban environments. Through the process of painting you shift from a concrete subject to a more atmospheric scenery. These images are not representing any place in particular—even though one may get detailed information on location, event or time of the photograph the painting is based on: this reality seems to be marginal and unreal, like a road that leads nowhere.

PD: Although the paintings are derived from the real world this is just the starting point. It is an entry or structure that is recognizable and familiar for the viewer and myself and therefore gives the painting a beginning that is tangible. This then allows the intangibles or the atmosphere of the painting to exist. I am never setting out to create a real space—only ever a painted one. This is what interests me. Maybe this is why there is never really a specific time or space (or sometimes season) in the paintings as such, even though, if one was to see the actual source, it would be "real".

GM: Your detour is rather to provoke a quiet sense of nostalgia reminiscent of one's past or to evoke an atavistic feeling of a forgotten moment, like an open scene, an invitation, where one may feel welcome and warm. Maybe that would best characterize the point of reference to the viewer's own experience. Most amazing is the amount of detail in your paintings; a great many of them are really impressive just by their very scale. Scale seems important to your seesaw of elements and views.

PD: The scale is important as a means of distorting or even subverting the subject.

GM: In what way?

PD: Sometimes the subject seems not worthy of anything more than a greeting card. By changing the scale and enforcing detail and time upon it you can change a familiar image into something that is less of this world. By this I mean less specific to its actual source.

GM: After digesting the themes in your work, the viewer is immediately confronted with a very sensitive and sensual variety and invention of combinations, like washes next to impasto, spots bathed in light and deep dark hollows, highlights of flashy artificial colors. These effects are heightened when they become partially concealed by a foreground of snowflakes or branches or leaves. And then there is this white which appears to be one of the "stars" of your painting. It is like a never-ending, constant white noise—be it snow, scratches, negative forms, lightning, flashes of light, or white cables, an all-over pattern of splashes, spots of dirt, cracks in the surface ...

PD: The snow was always a way of almost creating a negative space or a screen to be forced to look through or a distance from the subject within. It also has the ability to reflect and heighten color. It is also something that is rarely painted without associations of a cloyingly bad taste—I wanted to try it out on a large scale. I was completely surprised at how seductive it was to paint and also to look at and how it could create genuine atmosphere even though it is in some way such an abstract device.

GM: For your work *Blotter* you offered up two separate readings: On the one hand, the figure is submerged into the landscape and immersed in thought and within the painting. On the other hand, the title refers to how canvas absorbs paint. But still there is the playing with surfaces and, of course, the meaning of a spot in the landscape.

PD: The figure is relatively small and caught up within his own mind even though there is all this "landscape" activity happening all around him—he is a blot on and in the landscape but remains sort of oblivious to everything except for maybe the way his feet are melting into the ground. I think that there is a muffled atmosphere to the painting that is heightened by the puffiness of the clothes he is wearing.

GM: You are well-known for landscapes and urban scenes. Nevertheless there are small figures in these paintings which are of central importance. They do not usually face the viewer but turn away, they lie parallel to the painting's surface, or are lost in altitude. They seem closer to intellectual re-presentations than actual persons.

PD: I want the figures to act as ideas for figures or people so that the viewers have to bring their own experience to the painting rather than be told what exactly is going on. In this way a painting can have a life beyond the confines of what is depicted on and within its structure. I try to keep the expressions fairly open—leaving it to body shape and attitude rather than facial grimaces and such. In reality some of the figures are quite specific people—but this isn't important for the viewing of the painting.

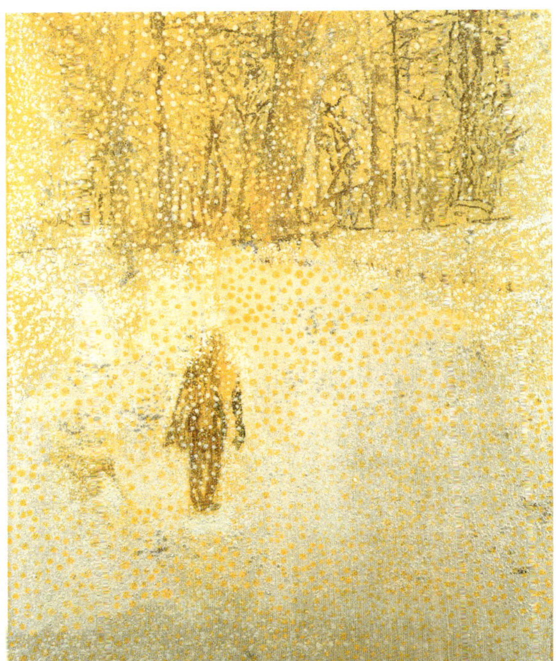

Peter Doig
White Out, 1992
145 x 114 cm
Collection particulière / Privatsammlung / Private Collection

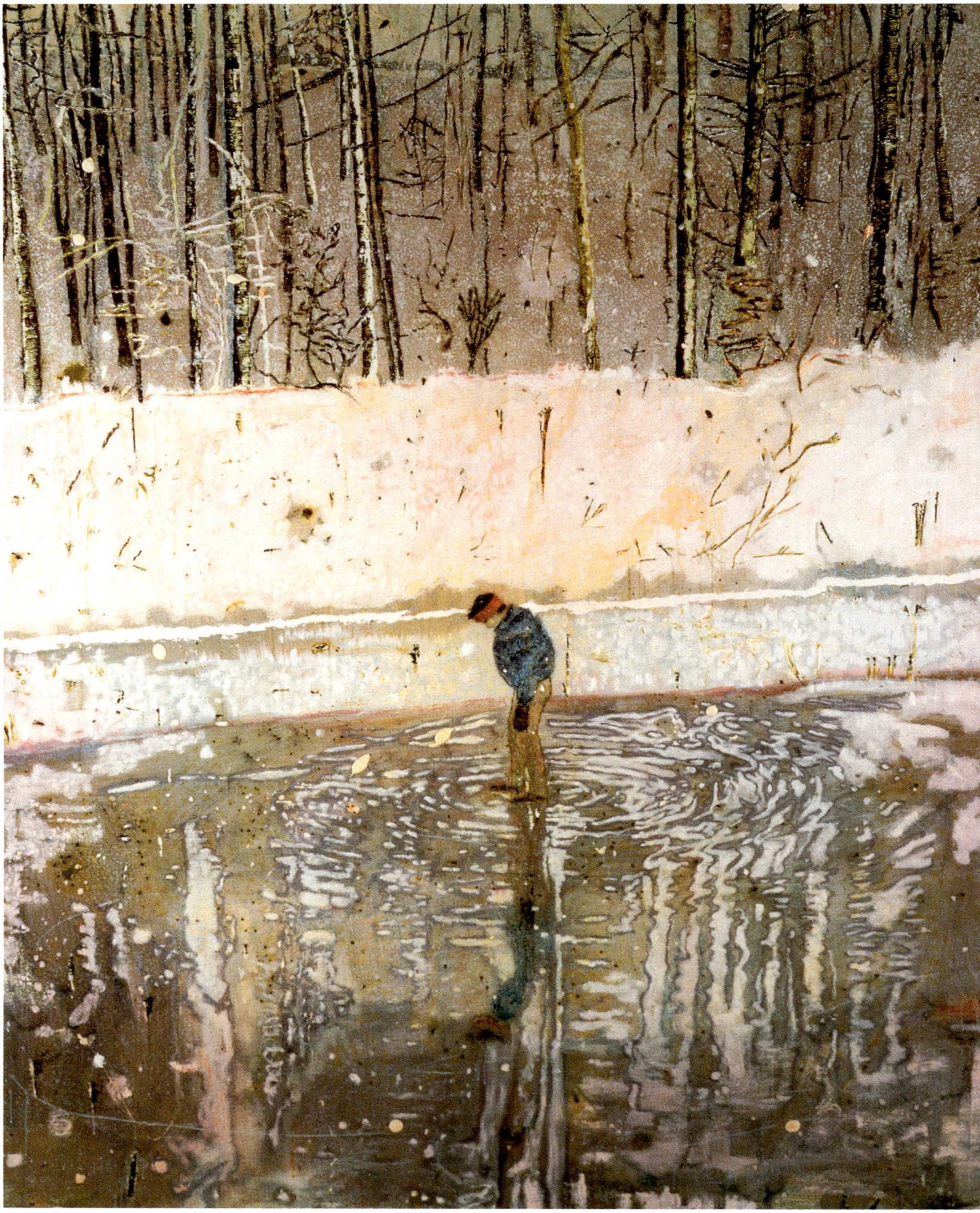

Peter Doig
Blotter, 1993
249 x 199 cm
Board of Trustees of the National Museums &
Galleries on Merseyside (Walker Art Gallery, Liverpool)

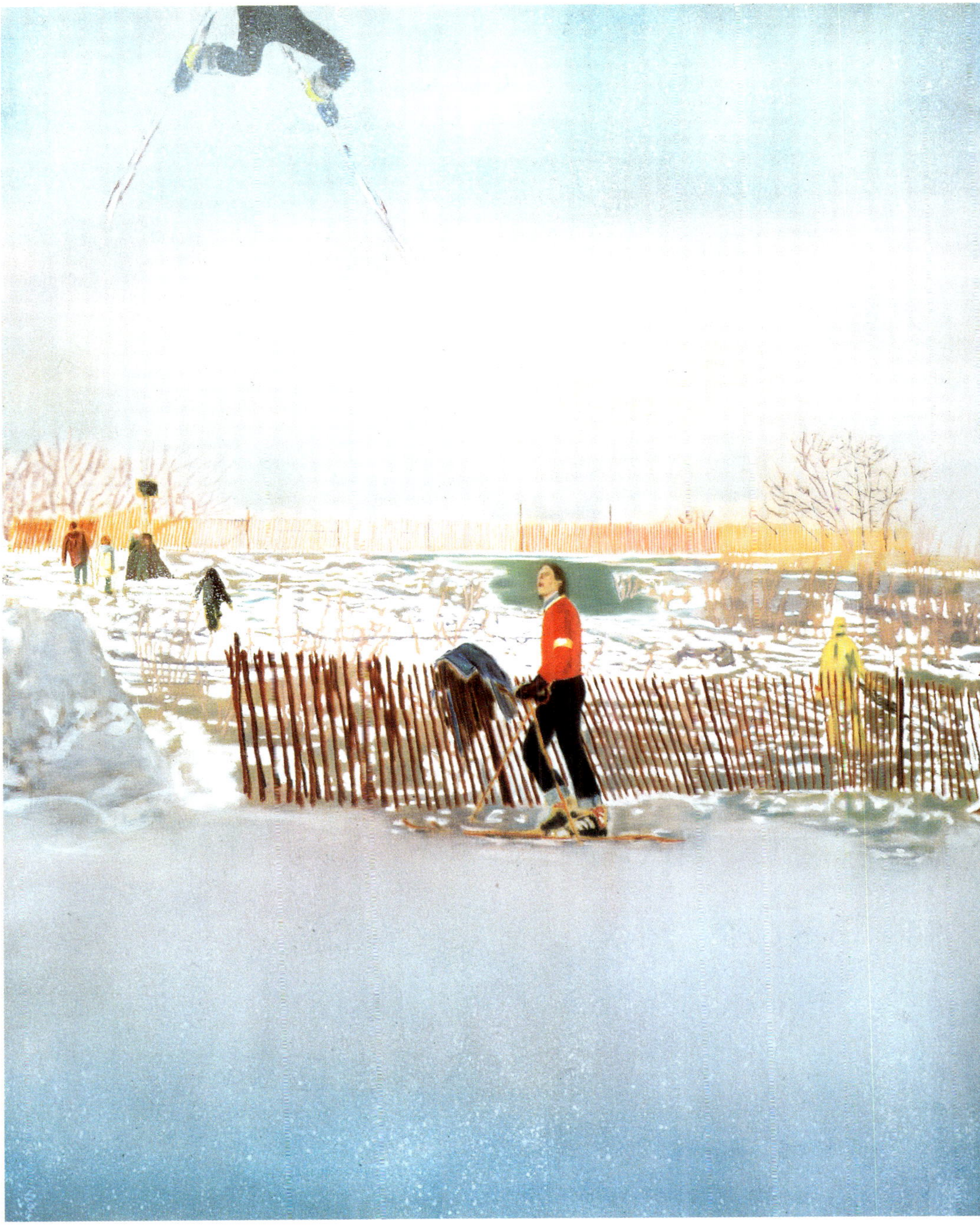

Peter Doig
Olin MK IV, 1995
250 x 200 cm
Collection Stephen Landwehr, Berlin
Courtesy Contemporary Fine Arts, Berlin

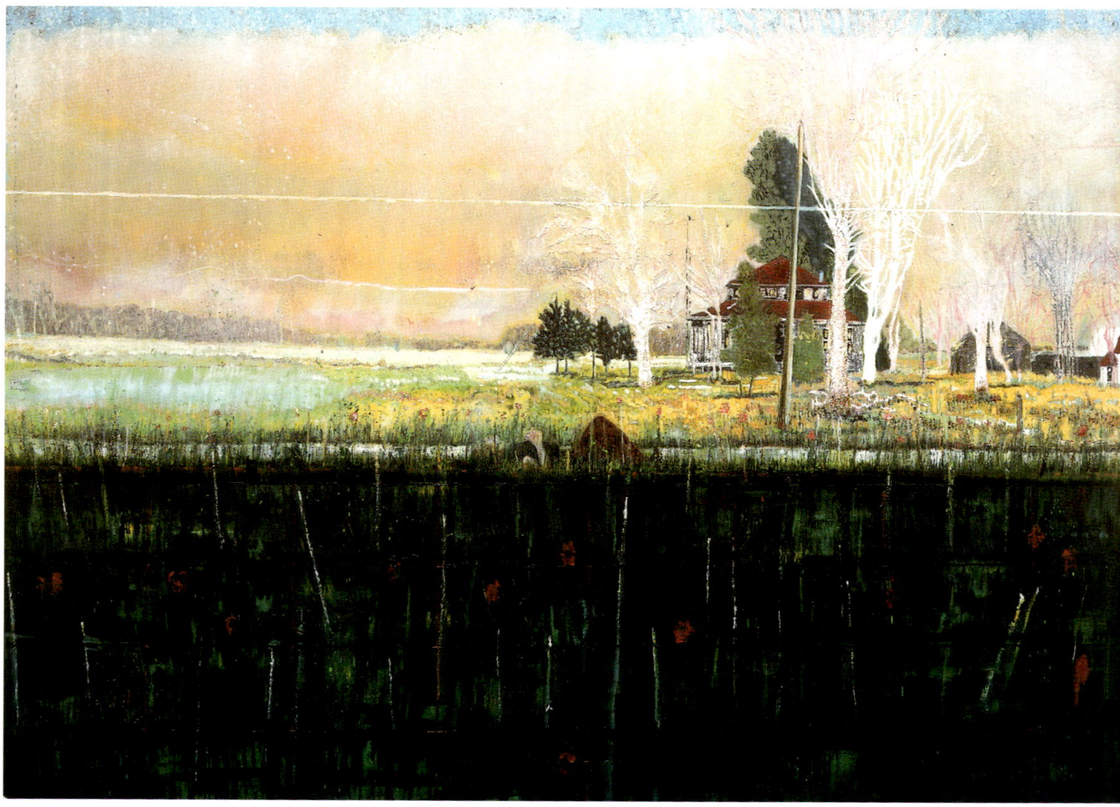

Peter Doig
Daytime Astronomy, 1997-1998
200 x 280 cm
Courtesy Warren & Victoria Miro, London

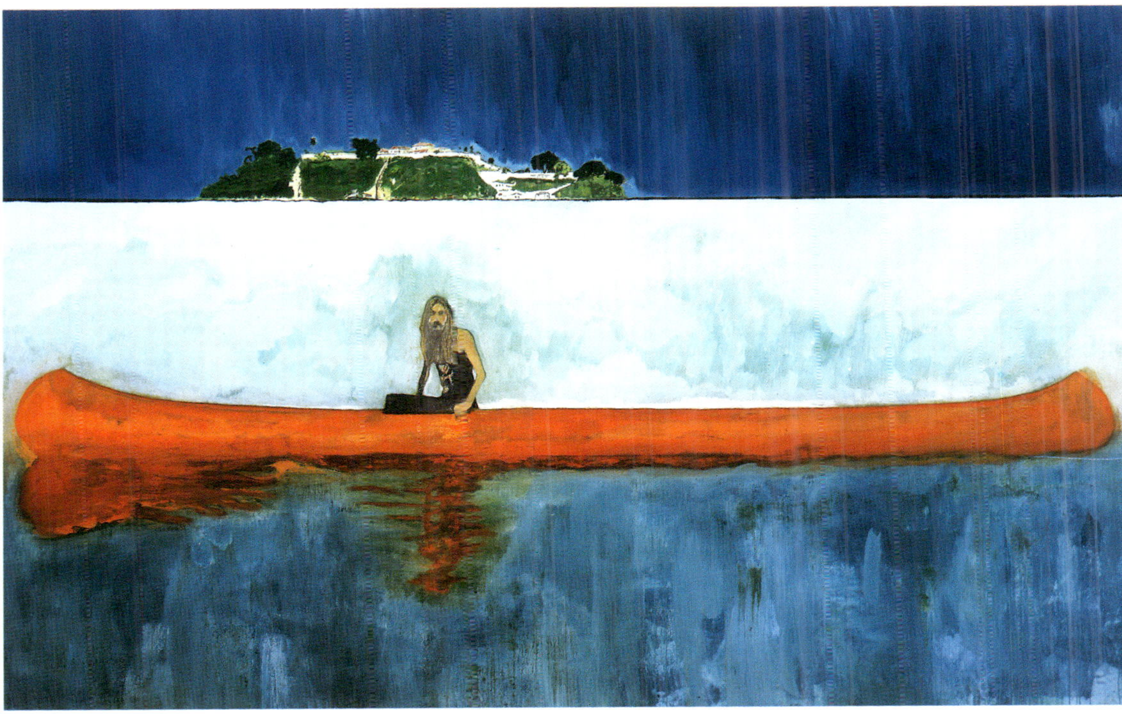

Peter Doig
100 Years Ago, 2001
229 x 358,5 cm
Centre Pompidou, Musée national d'art moderne, Paris

Artists' Biographies

Jemima Montagu

Kai Althoff

Kai Althoff was born in 1966 in Cologne, Germany, where he still lives and works. Althoff is artist and musician. He currently plays in his band *Workshop*. Althoff held his first solo exhibition at Lukas und Hoffmann, Berlin in 1993. He has participated in many international group exhibitions including: *Aperto '93*, Biennale di Venezia (1993); *Stonewall*, White Columns, New York (1994); *1. Fächerfest*, Graz (1995), *Wild Walls*, Stedelijk Museum, Amsterdam (1995); *Time Out*, Kunsthalle Nürnberg (1997); *ars viva 98/99*, Portikus, Frankfurt (1999); *oldnewtown*, Casey Kaplan, New York (1999); *German Open. Gegenwartskunst in Deutschland*, Kunstmuseum Wolfsburg (1999); *Produktivität & Existenz*, Künstlerhaus Bethanien, Berlin (2000); and *Deutsche Kunst in Moskau/ Nemeckoe iskusstvo v Moskve*, Central House of Artists, Moscow (2000). Althoff's solo exhibitions include: Galerie Daniel Buchholz, Cologne (1995, 1998, 2001); Galerie Christian Nagel, Cologne (1995, 1996, 1999); Robert Prime Gallery, London (1997); Galerie NEU, Berlin (1998, 2000); Galerie Ascan Crone, Hamburg (2000); Anton Kern Gallery, New York (1997, 2001).

Selected Bibliography

• *Kai Althoff. Gebärden und Ausdruck*, Frankfurter Kunstverein, Frankfurt/New York 2002
• Yilmaz Dziewior, 'Kai Althoff. Galerie Christian Nagel', *Artforum international*, v. 38, no. 9, May 2000
• Jörg Heiser, 'Bohemian Rhapsody', *Frieze*, no. 37, November-December 1997
• *Kai Althoff. Ja, Herrkenn mich genau*, (exh. cat.), Galerie Daniel Buchholz, Cologne 2001
• *Kai Althoff. Stigmata aus Großmannssucht*, (exh. cat.), Cologne 2000

Carole Benzaken

Carole Benzaken was born in Grenoble, France in 1964. In 1990 she graduated with her Diplôme Supérieur d'Arts Plastiques from the École Nationale Supérieure des Beaux Arts in Paris. In 1991 she was awarded the Albert Rocheron Award, and in 1995 she was given a scholarship for the artists' residency at the Villa Arson in Nice. Benzaken held her first solo exhibition at Pierre Lescot Gallery, Paris in 1991. Subsequent solo exhibitions include: Cartier Foundation for Contemporary Art, Paris (1994); Villa Arson, Nice (1995); Capc Musée d'art contemporain, Bordeaux (1999); Galerie Nathalie Obadia, Paris (1993, 1996, 1999, 2002); INMO Gallery, Los Angeles (2000); Annina Nosei Gallery, New York (2001). Selected group exhibitions are: Grancia d'Argento, Serre di Rapolano, Italy (1989); *KX Kunst auf Kampnagel*, Hamburg (1991); *Jeune Peinture*, Grand Palais, Paris (1991); *Fondation Cartier: A Collection*, National Museum of Contemporary Art, Seoul (1994); *Le Noir est une couleur*, Galerie Maeght, Barcelona (1995); *Kingdom of Flora*, Shoshana Wayne Gallery, Santa Monica (1996); *February in New York*, Nathalie Obadia Gallery, New York (1998); *L'œil et l'Esprit*, Museum of Modern Art, Gunma (1998); *Primitive Passion*, Palais des Papes, Avignon (1999); and *From Art to Fashion*, Christies, Paris (2000). In 1997 Benzaken was given an award by Association française d'Action Artistique to move to Los Angeles, where she currently lives and works.

Selected Bibliography

• Judith Benhamou-Huet, 'Contemporary Art: The New French Scene', *Les Echos*, April 2000
• Véronique Bouruet-Aubertot, 'Artiste du mois, Carole Benzaken', *Beaux-Arts Magazine*, no. 184, September 1999
• J.L. Pinte, 'Carole Benzaken', *Figaro*, April 28 1993
• *Carole Benzaken*, (exh. cat.), Capc Musée d'Art Contemporain, Bordeaux 1999
• *Carole Benzaken*, (exh. cat.), Villa Arson, Nice 1995
• *Carole Benzaken*, (exh. cat.), Fondation Cartier, Paris 1994

Glenn Brown

Glenn Brown was born in Hexham, England in 1966. Brown studied at Norwich School of Art from 1984 to 1985, and then at Bath College of Higher Education (1985-1988). In 1992 he completed a Masters in Fine Art at Goldsmiths College in London. Brown was selected for the *BT New Contemporaries* UK touring exhibitions in both 1990 and 1991. Brown has exhibited widely in United Kingdom, and internationally since the mid-1990s. His group exhibitions include: *Surface Values*, Kettle's Yard, Cambridge (1992); *Here and Now*, Serpentine Gallery, London (1994); *Brilliant: New Art from London*, Walker Arts Center, Minneapolis (1995); *Young British Artists V*, Saatchi Collection, London (1995); Galerie Ghislaine Hussenot, Paris (1996); *Ace*, Hayward Gallery, London and UK tour (1996-97); *The Jerwood Painting Prize*, Lethaby Galleries, London (1996); *Sensation*, Royal Academy of Art, London, Hamburger Bahnhof, Berlin and Brooklyn Museum, New York (1997); *Abstract Painting, Once Removed*, Contemporary Arts Museum, Houston (1998); *Examining Pictures*, Whitechapel Art Gallery, London (1998); *John Moores Painting Prize 21*, Walker Art Gallery, Liverpool (1999); *The British Art Show 5*, UK touring exhibition (2000-2001); and *The Turner Prize*, Tate Britain, London (2000-2001). Brown held his first solo exhibition at Karsten Schubert Gallery, London in 1995. Subsequent solo exhibitions include: Galerie Ghislaine Hussenot, Paris (1997); The Jerwood Gallery, London (1999); Galerie Max Hetzler, Berlin (2000); Centre d'art contemporain, Kerguéhennec, Brittany (2000); and Patrick Painter Inc., Los Angeles (1998, 1999, 2001). Brown lives and works in London.

Selected Bibliography

• Jennifer Higgie, 'Glenn Brown, Jerwood Gallery, London', *Frieze*, no. 47, July-August 1999
• Matthew Collings 'Higher Beings Command', *Modern Painters*, v. 12, no. 2, Summer 1999
• *Turner Prize 2000*, (exh. leaflet), Tate Britain, London 2000
• *Glenn Brown*, (exh. cat.), Centre d'art contemporain, Kerguéhennec, 2000
• *Glenn Brown*, (exh. cat.), Jerwood Gallery, London 1999
• *Glenn Brown*, (exh. cat.), Queen's Hall Art Centre, Hexham and Karsten Schubert, London 1996

Bernard Buffet

Bernard Buffet was born in Paris in 1928. In 1943, at the age of fifteen, he was admitted to the Ecole Nationale Supérieure des Beaux-Arts in Paris where he studied for two years. This was his only training. He exhibited his first painting in 1946 at the Salon des Moins de Trente Ans at the Galerie Beaux-Arts in Paris. In 1947 one of his paintings was selected for the Salon des Indépendants in Paris and in December of the same year he had his first solo exhibition at the Art Impressions book shop in Paris. Buffet's early style was influenced by Francis Gruber and his commitment to figuration was demonstrated by joining the group Homme-Témoin in 1949. In 1948 he was selected for the *Jeune Peinture* exhibition organised at the Galerie Drouant-David. Emmanuel David offered him an exclusive contract with his gallery, which was later shared by Maurice Garnier Gallery. The gallery has held an exhibition of Buffet's work every year since 1949. In 1948 Buffet was joint winner of le Prix de la Critique at the Galerie Saint-Placide, Paris. He moved outside Paris in the early 1950s, and his subsequent landscape paintings attracted the attention of critics such as Louis Aragon. In 1955 he moved to Aix-en-Provence which was his main residence until 1964. He was given his first retrospective exhibition in 1958 at the Galerie Charpentier, aged just 30. In 1961 Buffet painted a series of works depicting the life of Jesus Christ which are now on permanent display in the Vatican. He moved to Saint-Cast, Brittany, and from 1965-1971 he lived and worked between Brittany and Paris. In 1971 Buffet was awarded the Chevalier de la Légion d'Honneur and in 1974 he was elected a member of the Academie des Beaux-Arts in Paris. A museum devoted to his work was inaugurated in Surugadaire, Japan in November 1973; it was extended in 1988. Buffet remained a figurative painter throughout his career. He was extremely prolific and in addition to painting, he worked in lithography and engraving and also created the scenography for various theatrical or dance performances. Buffet's work has been exhibited in many exhibitions worldwide. Notable recent group exhibitions include: *Paris: Capital of the Arts 1900-1968*, Royal Academy of Arts, London (2002). In addition to his annual gallery exhibitions, Buffet's work has been the subject of a number of international solo exhibitions, including: Institute Françaises, Berlin (1955); Museum of Modern Art, Tokyo (1963); Postal Museum; Paris (1978); Seedam Cultural Center, Zurich (1983); The Odakyu Museum, Tokyo(1987); Pouchkine Museum, Moscow (1991); The Hermitage, St. Petersberg (1991); Hyundai Museum, Seoul (1991); Documenta Halle, Kassel (1994); and Odakyu Museum, Tokyo (1995). Most recent exhibitions include: Galerie Ursula Walbröl, Düsseldorf (2001); Art Thema Gallery, Brussels (2001); Galerie Rienzo, New York (2002). Despite his success internationally, Buffet has never been given a retrospective at a major French museum. He died in 1999.

Selected Bibliography
• *Bernard Buffet*, (exh. cat.), Galerie Ursula Walbröl, Düsseldorf 2001
• *Paris: Capital of the Arts 1900-1968*, (exh cat.), Royal Academy of Arts, London 2002
• *Bernard Buffet. Tableaux pour un musée 1950-1954*, (exh. cat.), Galerie Maurice Garnier, Paris 2002
• *Bernard Buffet. Tableaux pour un musée 1945-49*, (exh. cat.), Galerie Maurice Garnier, Paris 2001
• Yann le Pichon, *Bernard Buffet 1962-1981*, Galerie Maurice Garnier, Paris 1986
• Yann le Pichon, *Bernard Buffet 1943-61*, Galerie Maurice Garnier, Paris 1986

Brian Calvin
Brian Calvin was born 1969 in Visalia, California. As an undergraduate he attended the University of California, Berkeley, USA where he was awarded the James T. Phelan Merit Scholarship in Fine Arts in 1991. He completed a Masters degree at the School of the Art Institute of Chicago in 1994. Calvin's group exhibitions include: *New and Improved*, Worth Ryder Gallery, Berkeley (1991); *Discontents and Debutantes*, Center for Visual Arts, Illinois State University, Normal (1994); *X-Sightings*, Anderson Gallery, Buffalo (1995); *Meanwhile...*, Jan Cicero Gallery, Chicago (1999); *Collector's Choice*, Exit Art, New York (2000); Marc Foxx, Los Angeles (2000); *The Americans. New Art*, Barbican Art Gallery, London (2001). Calvin held his first solo exhibition at the Contemporary Art Workshop, Chicago in 1994. Subsequent solo exhibitions include: *God's Plot & John Wilkes Booth*, Zolla Lieberman Gallery, Inc., Chicago (1996); Gallery Side 2, Tokyo (1998, 1999); Marc Foxx, Los Angeles (2000); and Corvi-Mora, London (2001). Calvin currently lives and works in Los Angeles.

Selected Bibliography
• Jennifer Higgie, 'Brian Calvin: Corvi-Mora', London, *Frieze*, no. 61, September 2001
• Bruce Hainley, 'Openings: Brian Calvin', *Artforum international*, v. 39, no. 6, February 2001
• Christopher Knight, 'Art: Paintings Look at Our Cartoonish Nature', *The Los Angeles Times*, December 15 2000
• *The Americans. New Art*, (exh. cat.), Barbican Art Gallery, London 2001

John Currin
John Currin was born in 1962 in Boulder, Colorado. He trained at the Carnegie Mellon University, Pittsburgh, Pennsylvania from 1984 to 1986, and then completed an Masters in Fine Arts at Yale University in New Haven, Connecticut. Currin has been widely exhibited in group and solo shows since 1989. Recent group exhibitions include *Wild Walls*, Stedelijk Museum, Amsterdam and Institute of Contemporary Art, London (1995); *Projects 60: John Currin, Elizabeth Peyton, Luc Tuymans*, Museum of Modern Art, New York (1997); *Young Americans 2: New American Art*, Saatchi Gallery, London (1998). *Examining Pictures: exhibiting paintings*, Whitechapel Art Gallery, London (1999); *Malerei*, INIT-Kunsthalle, Berlin (1999); *Troublespot Painting*, MUHKA/NICC, Antwerp; Carnegie International, Pittsburgh (1999-2000); and the Whitney Biennial, New York (2000). Currin held 1989 his first solo exhibition at White Columns, New York. He has held solo exhibitions at Andrea Rosen Gallery, New York (1992, 1994, 1995, 1997, 1999, 2001); Galerie Monika Sprüth, Cologne (1995, 2000); Fonds Régional d'Art Contemporain du Limousin, Limoges (1995); Regen Projects, Los Angeles (1996, 1999, 2002); and Sadie Coles HQ, London (1997, 2000). A survey is currently being planned at the Museum of Contemporary Art, Chicago for 2002. Currin lives and works in New York.

Selected Bibliography
• Peter Schjeldahl, 'The Elegant Scavenger', *The New Yorker*, February-March 1999
• Keith Seward, 'John Currin: the Weirdest of the Weird', *Flash Art (international edition)*, v. 28, no. 185, November-December 1995
• Francesco Bonami, 'U.S. pair: New

American Figuration', *Flash Art*, May-June 1992
• Jerry Saltz, 'A year in the life: Tropic of painting', *Art in America*, no. 10, October 1994
• Barry Schwabsky, 'Picturehood is powerful. Three figurative painters on female subjects', *Art in America*, vol. 85, December 1997
• *Projects 60: John Currin, Elizabeth Peyton, Luc Tuymans*, (exh. pamphlet), Museum of Modern Art, New York, 1997
• *John Currin. Œuvres/Works: 1989-1995*, (exh. cat.), Fonds Régional d'Art Contemporain du Limousin, Limoges, 1995

Peter Doig

Peter Doig was born in Edinburgh in 1959, but grew up in Canada. In 1979 he returned to do an arts foundation course at the Wimbledon School of Arts in London (1979-80), followed by an undergraduate degree at St Martin's School of Art (1980-1983). He completed a Masters at Chelsea School of Arts, London in 1990. Doig has exhibited internationally since the early 1990s. His group exhibitions include: New Contemporaries, Institute of Contemporary Art, London (1983, 1985); *1st Prize Exhibition*, John Moore's Prize, Liverpool (1993); *Unbound: Possibilities in Painting*, Hayward Gallery, London (1994); *Here and Now*, Serpentine Art Gallery, London (1994); *Turner Prize*, Tate Gallery, London (1994); *Answered Prayers*, Contemporary Fine Arts, Berlin (1996), *Belladonna*, Institute of Contemporary Arts, London (1996); *About Vision: New British Painting in the 1990s*, UK touring exhibition (1996); *Peter Doig and Udomsak Krisanamis*, Arnolfini Gallery, Bristol and The Fruitmarket Gallery, Edinburgh (1999); *Twisted: Urban and Visionary Landscapes in Contemporary Painting*, van Abbemuseum, Eindhoven (2000); and *Cave Painting*, Santa Monica Museum of Arts (2002). His first solo exhibition was held at the Metropolitan Gallery, London (1984). Subsequent solo exhibitions include: Victoria Miro Gallery, London (1994, 1996, 1998, 2002); Gavin Brown's Enterprise, New York (1994, 1996, 1999); Whitechapel Art Gallery, London (1998); *Country Rock*, Contemporary Fine Arts, Berlin (1999); *Echo Lake*, Matrix, University of California and the Museum of Contemporary Art, Miami (2000). From 1995 to 2000 Doig was a Trustee of the Tate Gallery, London. He lives and works in London.

Selected Bibliography

• Leo Edelstein, 'Peter Doig. Losing oneself in the looking', *Flash Art*, vol. 31, no. 200, May-June 1998
• Anna Moszynska, 'Daytime astronomy', *tate magazine*, Summer 1998, pp. 30-35
• Jerry Saltz, 'Out of the Fog', *Village Voice*, 21 December 1999
• Alice Rawsthorn, 'Peter Doig-Scanning the post-conceptual landscape', *Elle Decor*, December-January 1999
• Daniel Richter, 'Dots on Doig', *Afterall*, Issue 1, February 2000, pp. 95-96
• *Unbound: Possibilities In Painting*. (exh. cat). Hayward Gallery, London. 1994
• *Peter Doig. Blizzard seventy-seven*. (exh. cat). Kunsthalle zu Kiel, Kunsthalle Nürnberg and Whitechapel Gallery, London, 1998
• *Peter Doig. Blotter*, Contemporary Fine Arts, Berlin and Victoria Miro Gallery, London 1995

Sophie von Hellermann

Sophie von Hellermann was born in Münich, Germany in 1975, but grew up near Oxford, England from the age of four. She completed an arts foundation course in Oxford in 1993, and went to study painting at the Düsseldorf Art Academy from 1993 to 1999. In 1999 she was given a DAAD award to study in London. She completed a Masters at the Royal College of Art, London in 2001. In 1995 she co-founded the artist collective Hobbypop with other students of Dieter Kreig at the Düsseldorf Art Academy. Hobbypop organised many exhibitions and parties around Düsseldorf throughout the 1990s, including *Eiskeller*, Artothek Karlsruhe & Wilhelmshöhe, Esslingen (1997); *Volkstümlich Malerei*, Kunstforum Rottweil (1998); and *Hobbypop Terror*, Kunsthalle Düsseldorf (1998). In 1998 they established a Hobbypop Museum and now exhibit under the title HobbypopMuseum. Their recent exhibitions include: *Angel Island*, NICC, Antwerp (2000), *Death to the Fascist Insect ...*, Anthony d'Offay Gallery, London (2001); *Hobbypop Museum*, Langton Arts Center, San Francisco (2001). Hellermann has also participated as a solo artist in group exhibitions such as *Troublespot Painting*, MUHKA/NICC, Antwerp (1999). In 2001 she held solo exhibitions at Vilma Gold Gallery, London and the Saatchi Gallery, (at Underwood Street), London. She lives and works in London.

Selected Bibiliography

• 'Sophie von Hellermann', *Hot Tickets*, January 2002
• Ulrike Knöfel, 'Jung, blond, böse', *Der Spiegel*, 10 December 2001
• William Preston, 'What's nagging Sophie?', *Art Review*, September 2001
• *Spiel des Lebens*, (exh. cat.), Hobbypop-editions, Düsseldorf 1999
• *Images that are nagging me*, (exh. cat.), Saatchi Gallery, London 2001

Alex Katz

Alex Katz was born in 1927 in Brooklyn, New York. He studied at the Cooper Union Art School, New York from 1946-1949, and also attended the Skowhegan School of Painting and Sculpture in Skowhegan, Maine. In addition to painting, Katz is also a dedicated print-maker. Katz has exhibited regularly since the early 1960s and has participated in group exhibitions across the world, including: *Young America 1960: Thirty American Painters under Thirty-Six*, Whitney Museum of American Art, New York (1960); *Two Decades of American Painting*, Museum of Modern Art, New York (1966); *Figures—Environments*, Walker Art Center, Minneapolis (1970); *American Drawings 1963-1973*, Whitney Museum of American Art, New York (1973); *New Images: Figuration in American Painting*, The Queen's Museum, New York; *America 1976: A Bicentennial Exhibition*, Corcoran Gallery of Art, Washington DC (1976); *30 Years of American Painting*, The Brooklyn Museum, New York (1976-77); *Contemporary American Realism since 1960*, Pennsylvania Academy of Fine Arts and tour to Lisbon, Madrid and Nuremberg (1981); *After Matisse*, Queens Museum, New York and touring (1986); *1991* Biennial, Whitney Museum of American Art, New York (1991); *American Realism and Figurative Art*, Miyagi Museum of Art, Sedai and touring Japan (1991); *By Night*, Fondation Cartier, Paris (1996); *Birth of the Cool*, Deichtorhallen, Hamburg and Kunsthaus, Zurich (1997); and *Carnegie International 1999-2000*, Pittsburgh.
Katz held his first solo exhibition at the Roko Gallery, New York in 1954. He was

given his first major retrospective by the Whitney Museum of American Art, New York in 1986, followed by a print retrospective at the Brooklyn Museum of Art in 1988. Other recent solo exhibitions include: *Alex Katz: American Landscape*, Staatliche Kunsthalle, Baden-Baden (1995); *Alex Katz*, I.V.A.M. Centre Julio Gonzalez, Valencia (1996); *Alex Katz: A Drawing Retrospective*, Munson-Williams Proctor Institute, Utica, New York (1996); *Alex Katz Under the Stars: American Landscapes 1951-1995*, P.S.1 Museum, New York and touring (1996-1998); *Alex Katz: Twenty-Five Years of Painting*, The Saatchi Collection, London (1998); *Alex Katz*, Galleria Civica Di Arte Contemporanea, Trento (1999); *Regarding Alex Katz*, Carnegie Museum of Art, Pittsburgh (2000); and *Alex Katz: Small Paintings*, Whitney Museum of American Art, New York and touring (2001-2002). In 1994 the Cooper Union Art School created the Alex Katz Visiting Chair after an endowment provided by the sale of paintings donated by the artist. Katz lives and works in New York.

Selected Bibliography

• *Parkett* no. 21, September 1989 (Bice Curiger, Brooks Adams, John Russell)
• Hilton Kramer, 'The Return of the Realists – And a new battle shaping up', *New York Times*, 25 October 1981, section C, pp. 1, 35
• Bruce Hainley, 'Alex Katz: Marlborough Gallery, New York', *Artforum International*, v. 35, September 1996, p. 109
• Barry Schwabsky, 'A conversation with Alex Katz', *New Art Examiner*, v. 27, no. 6, March 2000, pp. 16-19
• Roberta Smith, *Alex Katz in the Seventies*, (exh. cat.), Rose Art Museum, Brandeis University, Waltham, Mass. 1978
• Irving Sandler, *Alex Katz: A retrospective*, Harry N. Abrams, New York 1998
• *Alex Katz. Twenty-five Years of Painting*, (exh. cat.), The Saatchi Gallery, London 1997
• *Alex Katz*, (exh. cat.), Whitney Museum of American Art/Rizzoli International Publications, Inc., New York 1986

Kurt Kauper

Kurt Kauper was born in Indianapolis, USA in 1966. He studied Fine Arts at Boston University and completed a Master of Fine Arts at the University of California, Los Angeles in 1995. Kauper has exhibited widely in the USA and more recently has participated in exhibitions in Europe. His group exhibitions include: *Figures, Faces, and Body Parts*, Visual Arts Gallery, New York (1990); *Contemporary and Beyond*, The Armand Hammer Museum Gallery, Los Angeles (1994); ACME Gallery, Santa Monica (1995); *Painting From Another Planet*, Deitch Projects, New York (1998); *Transience and Sentimentality*, Institute of Contemporary Art, Boston (1998); *In Your Face*, New Langton Arts, San Francisco (1999); *Form Follows Fiction*, Castello di Rivoli, Turin (2000); *Casino 2001, First Quadrennial of Contemporary Art*, Stedelijk Museum Voor Actuele Kunst, Ghent (2000); and *Biennial Exhibition*, Whitney Museum of American Art, New York (2000). Kauper has held the following solo exhibitions: ACME, Santa Monica (1997); Jay Gorney Modern Art, New York (1997); ACME, Los Angeles (1999); and Deitch Projects, New York (2000).

Selected Bibliography

• Dominic Eichler, 'Casino 2001', *Frieze*, no. 64 January-February 2002
• Alison M. Gingeras, 'Kurt Kauper, Deitch Projects', *Art Press*, no. 260, September 2000
•Michael Kimmelman, 'A New Whitney Team Makes Its Biennial Pitch', *New York Times*, March 24 2000
• Christopher Miles, 'Kurt Kauper at ACME' *Artweek*, v. 28, July 1997
• *Form Follows Fiction*, (exh. cat.), Castello di Rivoli, Turin 2000

Martin Kippenberger

Martin Kippenberger was born in Dortmund, Germany in 1953. After an early interest in dance, Kippenberger went to work in a shoe store in 1968, followed briefly by a stint as a shop window dresser. In 1971 he moved to Hamburg and the following year he began studying at the Hamburg Art Academy (Hochschule für bildende Künste). Kippenberger abandoned his studies in 1976 and moved to Florence, where he hoped to become an actor. In Florence he painted his first canvases, including the series 'Uno di voi, un Tedesco in Firenze'. He returned to Hamburg in 1977 and held his first solo exhibition in Galerie Petersen, Hamburg. In 1978 he moved to Berlin and founded 'Kippenbergers Büro' ('Kippenberger's Office') with Gisela Capitain, and also became the manager of the famous S.O.36, a venue for film, concerts and performance. He organised exhibitions in the 'Office' and also founded a punk band called 'Die Grugas'. In 1979 he travelled to the U.S.A. and also commissioned the poster artist Hans Siebert to execute the series *Lieber Maler, male mir*. He also participated in films. In the early 1980s Kippenberger moved between Paris, Siena and Germany, working on writing and painting. During this period he met Franz West and collaborated on a number of works with Albert and Markus Oehlen, Martin Prinzhorn and Merlin Carpenter. In 1984 he began to experiment with sculpture and exhibited his first photographs at the CCD Gallery, Düsseldorf in 1985. As Kippenberger's reputation became established he began to exhibit regularly internationally, and also curated several exhibitions, including *Eurostroll I-III* in Cologne and Graz. In 1987 he collaborated with Albert Oehlen on an exhibition at the Villa Arson in Nice and exhibited in *Aperto* at the Biennale di Venezia in 1988. Kippenberger continued to travel regularly, living for periods of time in France, Spain, America, Germany and Austria. In 1990 he was made Guest Professor at the Städelschule in Frankfurt. In the 1990s Kippenberger worked on a variety of different projects, including a series of installations based on the public underground system. In 1991 he was given a major solo exhibition at the Museum of Modern Art, San Francisco. In his continued battle against the art establishment, in 1993 he set up the 'Kunstverein Kippenberger' at the Museum Friedricianium , Kassel and also established MOMAS (Museum of Modern Art Syros) in Syros, Greece. In 1996 he was awarded the prestigious Käthe Kollwitz prize. He died prematurely in Vienna in 1997, but his work was exhibited in several major exhibitions later that year. These include: *Documenta X* in Kassel; *Skulptur. Projekte*, Münster; and a retrospective at MAMCO, Geneva. There have been many solo exhibitions about Kippenberger's work, including: Galerie Gisela Capitain, Cologne (1987, 1989, 1990, 1997); Kölnischer Kunstverein, Cologne (1991); Centre Georges Pompidou, Paris (1993); Museum Boijmans Van

Beuningen, Rotterdam (1994); Hirshhorn Museum and Sculpture Garden, Washington, D.C. (1995); MAK Center for Art and Architecture, Schindler House, Los Angeles; Kunsthalle Basel (1998); and Deichtorhallen Hamburg (1999).

Selected Bibliography
• Reinhard Ermen, 'Martin Kippenberger : Die Sebst portrats, Kunsthalle Basel, Deichtorhallen Hamburg', *Kunstforum International*, no. 143, January-February 1999, pp. 422-423
•Manfred Hermes, 'Repetition, disguises, documents', *Flash Art (International Edition)*, no. 148, October 1989, pp. 96-103
• *Parkett*, no. 19, March 1989 (Bice Curiger, Diedrich Diederichsen, Patrick Frey, Martin Prinzhorn)
• *Martin Kippenberger: The Happy End of Franz Kafka's "Amerika"*, (exh. cat.), Deichtorhallen Hamburg 1999
• *Martin Kippenberger*, (exh. cat.), Kunsthalle Basel, Switzerland, and Deichtorhallen Hamburg 1998
• Roberto Ohrt. *Kippenberger*, Benedikt Taschen Verlag GmbH, Cologne 1997
• *Martin Kippenberger: Kippenberger sans peine avec des clichés de reconnaissance*, (exh. cat), Mamco, Geneva 1997
• *Martin Kippenberger: I Had a Vision*, (exh. cat.), San Francisco Museum of Modern Art, 1991

Enoc Perez
Enoc Perez was born in 1967 in San Juan, Puerto Rico. In 1990 he moved to the United States to study Fine Art at the Pratt Institute in Brooklyn. He began a Masters in Fine Art at Hunter College in New York in 1992. Perez has been exhibiting in group exhibitions since 1991. His earliest exhibitions include: *Invitational Show*, Sala Alternativa Galeriá de Arte in Caracas (1993); *Pequenos Formatos*, Luigi Marrozzini Gallery, San Juan (1993); and *Update 1993*, White Columns, New York (1993). Other group exhibitions include: *Quinta Bienal de la Habana*, Havana, Cuba (1994); *Annual Benefit Exhibition*, White Columns, New York (1995); *V Bienal Internacional de Pintura*, Cuenca, Ecuador (1996); *Road Show '97*, Bronwyn Keenan Gallery, New York (1997); *Encyclopedia 1999*, Turner & Runyon, Dallas, Texas; *Message to Pretty*, Thread Waxing Space, New York (1998); *Home & Away*, Gavin Brown's Enterprise, New York (1998); *At Century's End*, Museum of Contemporary Art, Lake Worth, Florida (1999); *The S-Files: The Selected Files*, El Museo del Barrio, New York (1999); *Two by Two for AIDS and Art*, Dallas, Texas (2000); and *Annual Benefit Exhibition*, White Columns, New York (2000). Perez solo exhibitions include: White Columns, New York (1993); Galeria Uno, Caracas (1993); *Winter*, Bronwyn Keenan Gallery, New York (1999); *Daydreaming*, Turner & Runyon, Dallas (1999); *The Secret*, Galerie Michael Janssen, Cologne (2001); and Dee / Glascoe, New York (2002). Perez lives and works in New York.

Selected Bibliography
• Joseph Wolin, 'Enoc Perez', *Art Nexus*, no. 35, February-April 2000
• Sarah Schmerler, 'The Art of the Dealer', *Time Out. New York*, 4-11 November 1999
• 'Message to Pretty. New York: Thread Waxing Space, 1998', *The New Yorker*, 21-28 September, 1998
• Bill Arning, *Enoc Pérez: New Works*, (exh. cat.) Leanora Vega, New York 1994
• *Enoc Pérez* (exh. cat.), Galeriá Leonara Vega, San Juan 1993

Bruno Perramant
Bruno Perramant was born in Brest, Brittany in 1962. Perramant works as a painter and occasionally, a writer. From 1980-1982 he studied at the Ecole des Beaux Arts in Brest, and then at the École des Beaux Arts, Quimper. He also spent three years at the Ecole de Beaux Arts in Avignon from 1983-1985. Perramant first exhibited in a group exhibition at the Galerie Porte-Avion, Marseille in 1988, and in a solo exhibition at ODC, Aix-en-Provence. Perramant spent 1994-95 in Tokyo doing the Marunuma Residence and spent 1999 doing the Ville Medici Residence, supported by Association française d'Action Artistique, in New York. Perramant's recent solo exhibitions include: Centre d'Art Contemporain, Brétigny/Orge (2001); and Galerie Ferdinand van Dieten-d'Eendt, Amsterdam (2001). Selected group exhibitions include; *Un écran, le tableau*, Centre d'art contemporain, Pougues-les-Eaux (1999); *Trouble Spot*, MUKHA/NICC, Antwerp (1999); and *Mimetic Power*, Galerie Ferdinand Van Dieten d'Eendt, Amsterdam (2000). Solo exhibitions at the Fonds Régional d'Art Contemporain, Auvergne, Clermont-Ferrand and In-SITU, Paris are planned for 2002. Perramant was recently awarded the International Cité Studio Grant 2002. He currently lives and works between Paris and Brittany.

Select Bibliography
• Evence Verdier, 'Bruno Perramant', *Art Press*, July 2002
• Bruno Perramant, 'Autoportrait', *Tema Celeste*, January 2001
• Cyril Jarton, 'La peinture générique', *Art Press*, no. 235, May 1998
• *Bruno Perramant. Sun*, (exh. cat.), Centre d'art Contemporain, Brétigny Orge 2001
• *Trouble Spot Painting*, (exh. cat.), MUKHA/NICC, Antwerp 1999
• *Un écran, le tableau*, (exh. cat.), Centre d'art contemporain, Pougues-les-Eaux, Nièvre 1999

Elizabeth Peyton
Elizabeth Peyton was born in 1965 in Danbury, Connecticut. She studied at the School of Visual Arts, New York from 1984 to 1987. Peyton has been included in many group exhibitions internationally, including *Okay Behaviour*, 303 Gallery, New York (1994); *Campo*, Venice Biennale (1995); *Wunderbar*, Kunstverein, Hamburg and Kunstraum, Vienna; *Projects 60: John Currin, Elizabeth Peyton, Luc Tuymans*, Museum of Modern Art, New York (1997); *Young Americans*, Saatchi Gallery, London (1998); *Auf der Spur*, Kunsthalle, Zürich (1998); *Examining Pictures*, Whitechapel Art Gallery, London (1999); *Greater New York*, PS1, New York (2000); *Longing and Memory*, Los Angeles County Museum of Art, California (2001); *Abbild Recent Portraiture and Depiction*, Landesmuseum Joanneum, Graz (2001). Peyton held her first solo exhibition at Althea Viafore, New York in 1987. Since then she has had solo exhibitions at the Kunstmuseum Wolfsburg and Museum für Gegenwartskunst, Basel (1998); Gavin Brown's Enterprise, New York (1993, 1995, 1996, 1997, 1999, 2000, 2001); Sadie Coles HQ, London (1998, 2000) and the Deichtorhallen, Hamburg (2001). Peyton lives and works in Orient, Long Island.

Selected Bibliography
• Elizabeth Peyton, *Prince Eagle*, Powerhouse, New York and Turnaround, London 2002
• *Elizabeth Peyton*, (exh. cat.), Deichtorhallen, Hamburg 2001
• Jerry Saltz, 'Getting Real', *The Village Voice*, 20 April 1999
• *Parkett*, no. 53, 1998 (Linda Pilgrim, David Rimanelli, Philip Ursprung & Lisa Leibmann)

Francis Picabia

Francis Picabia was born in 1879 in Paris. In 1895 he went to study at the École des Arts Décoratifs in the ateliers of Humbert and Wallet. From 1899 he began to exhibit regularly in the official salons. In 1903 he discovered Impressionism, and was taken up by the Galerie Haussman, Paris. In 1910 Picabia met Marcel Duchamp and experimented with various avant-garde styles, including Fauvism, Cubism and Orphism, before moving towards abstraction. He went to New York in 1913 where he exhibited in the landmark *Armory Show* and also held an exhibition at the 291 Gallery. During this period Picabia was immersed in the radical activities of the pre-war avant-garde and was close friends with Guillaume Apollinaire. He spent the First World War between Paris, New York and Barcelona, where he established the review *391* and promoted Dada activities. From 1917-1919 he published two volumes of poetry and co-produced the journal *Dada* with Tristan Tzara, before co-founding a Paris Dada group in 1920. The group disbanded in 1922 and Picabia held an exhibition of machinist paintings and drawings at the Gallery Dalmau, Barcelona. In the 1920s Picabia was vehemently opposed to Surrealism and took up figurative painting again. He also continued to make Dada collages. In 1927-28 he developed the *Transparences* series and painted after Old Masters such as Titian, Veronese and Boticelli. The first retrospective of his work, *Picabia, Trente ans de peinture*, was held at Gallery Léonce Rosenberg, Paris in 1930. Picabia's style shifted again in the 1930s towards naturalism and drew on classical and mythical motifs. He work was included in the survey exhibitions *Cubism and Abstract Art* (1936) and *Fantastic Art, Dada and Surrealism* (1936) at the Museum of Modern Art, New York. Picabia held exhibitions of his 1930s work at Galerie Duverney, Cannes and Galerie de Beaune, Paris but his colorful, figurative paintings were received with muted critical response. Picabia spent most of the Second World War in the south of France during which time he painted realistic, figurative works based on photographs from erotic magazines. In 1945 he returned to Paris and experimented with biomorphic abstraction, exhibiting these works at the Salon des Surindépendants (1945). Picabia's reputation became increasingly established in the post-war period and he held survey solo exhibitions at the Kunsthalle, Basel, and Galerie Denise René, Paris (1946). A major retrospective of his work, *491, 50 ans de plaisir*, was held at Galerie René Drouin, Paris in 1949. From 1950 Picabia's health declined and he died in 1953. A retrospective of his work is planned at Musée d'Art moderne de la Ville de Paris in Autumn 2002.

Selected Bibliography
• Carole Boulbès, *Picabia. Le Saint masqué*, Jean-Michel Place, Paris 1998
• *Francis Picabia. The Late Works 1933-1953*. ed. Zdenek Felix, (exh. cat.), Hatje, Ostfildern 1998
• *Francis Picabia. Les Nus et la méthode*, (exh. cat.), Musée de Grenoble, 1998
• *Francis Picabia. Anthology*, (exh. cat.), Centro Cultural de Bélem, Lisbon 1997
• *Francis Picabia. Nudes*, (exh. cat.), Panicali Fine Art, New York 1989
• Maria Lluïsa Borràs, *Francis Picabia*, Albin Michel, Paris and Thames and Hudson, London 1985
• *Francis Picabia. The Later Work*, (exh. cat.), Michael Werner/Mary Boone Gallery, New York 1983
• *Francis Picabia, fleurs de chair, fleurs d'âme: Nus, transparences, tableaux abstraits*, (exh. cat.), Galerie Hauser & Wirth, Zurich and Oktagon Verlag, Cologne 1997

Sigmar Polke

Sigmar Polke was born in 1941 in Oels, Silesia (now Olesnica, Poland). In 1945 his family moved to Thuringia, East Germany and finally, in 1953, to Düsseldorf, West Germany. Initially Polke trained as an apprentice glass painter, but from 196[illegible] to 1967 he studied painting at the Staatliche Kunstakademie, Düsseldorf. Among his fellow-students were Gerhard Richter and Konrad Lueg (later Fischer). Polke's first public exhibition was in a store in Düsseldorf in 1963, where he exhibited with Richter, Lueg and Manfred Kuttner. In the same year he co-founded the movement 'Capitalist Realism' with Lueg and Richter. Polke has exhibited widely internationally since 1963. Group exhibitions include: *Demonstrative Ausstellung* Ladenausstellung, Düsseldorf (1963); *Neodada, Pop, Décollage, Kapitalischer Realismus*, Galerie René Block (1964); *Junge Generation: Maler und Bildhauer in Deutschland*, Akademie der Kunste, Berlin (1966); *Deutscher Kunstpreis der Jugend: Malerei*, Staatliche Kunsthalle, Baden-Baden (1966); *Neuer Realismus*, Haus am Waldsee, Berlin (1967); *Jetzt. Künste in Deutschland heute*, Kunsthalle, Cologne (1970); *Prospekt '71 &'73*, Kunsthalle, Düsseldorf (1971, 1973); *Documenta 5*, Museum Fridericianum, Kassel (1972); *Amsterdam-Paris-Düsseldorf*, Solomon R.Guggenheim Museum, New York (1972); *XIII Bienal de São Paulo* (1975) ; *Aspekte der 60er Jahre*, Nationalgalerie, Berlin (1978); *Avanguardia-Transavanguardia*, Mura Aureliane, Rome (1982); *A New Spirit in Painting*, Royal Academy of Arts London (1982); *Magiciens de la terre*, Centre Georges Pompidou, Paris (1989); *Brennpunkt Düsseldorf 1962-1987*, Kunstmuseum, Düsseldorf; *Pop Art*, Royal Academy of Arts, London (199[illegible]); *Der zerbrochene Spiegel. Positionen der Malerei*, Deichtorhallen, Hamburg (1993); *Stiftung Froehlich*, Tate Gallery, London (1996). Solo exhibitions include: Galerie René Block, Berlin (1966, 1968, 1969); Galerie Konrad Fischer, Düsseldorf (1970, 1971, 1973); Galerie Michael Werner, Cologne and New York (1972, 1973, 1974, 1975, 1990, 1995); *Sigmar Polke. Original + Fälschung*, Westfälischen Kunstverein, Münster (1973); *Sigmar Polke. Bilder, Tücher, Objekte: Werkauswahl 1962-1971*, Kunsthalle, Tübingen, Städtische Kunsthalle, Düsseldorf and Stedelijk van Abbe-Museum, Eindhoven (1976); *Sigmar Polke*, Musée d'Art Moderne de la Ville de Paris (1988); *Sigmar Polke*, San Francisco Museum of Modern Art (1990); *Sigmar Polke Photoworks. When Pictures Vanish*, Museum of Contemporary Art, Los Angeles (1995); *Sigmar Polke. Die Drei Lügen der Malerei*, Kunsthalle, Bonn & Hamburger Bahnhof (1997-98); *Sigmar Polke. Works on Paper 1963-1974*, Museum of Modern Art, New York (1999). In 1970 Polke was appointed Guest Professor at the Academy of Fine Arts, Hamburg and later took up the role of Professor (1977-1991). Polke has been given many awards for his work; including the Grand Prize, Biennale di Venezia (1986) and the Carnegie Prize (1995). In 1978 he moved to Cologne, where he now lives and works.

Selected Bibliography

• *Parkett* no. 26, 1991 (Bice Curiger, Dave Hickey, Thomas McEvilley)
• *Sigmar Polke: Die drei Lügen der Malerei*, (exh. cat.), Kunst- und Ausstellungshalle der Bundesrepublik Deutschland, Bonn and Museum für Gegenwart, Berlin 1997
• *Sigmar Polke: Bilder, Tücher, Objekte: Werkauswahl 1962-1971*, (exh. cat.), Kunsthalle Tübingen, Stedelijk Van Abbemuseum, Eindhoven and Städtische Kunsthalle, Düsseldorf, 1976
• *Sigmar Polke: Works on paper, 1963-1974*, (exh. cat.), Museum of Modern Art, New York and Hamburger Kunsthalle, 1999
• *Sigmar Polke*, (exh. cat.), Kunsthaus Zürich; Die Kunsthalle, Cologne 1984
• *Polke! Polke!*, (exh. cat.), Gesellschaft für moderne Kunst am Museum Ludwig, Cologne 1992
• *Sigmar Polke*, (exh. cat.), Musée d'Art Moderne de la Ville de Paris, Paris 1988
• *Sigmar Polke. Original + Fälschung*, (exh. cat.), Städtisches Kunstmuseum, Bonn 1974.

Neo Rauch

Neo Rauch was born in Leipzig, in the former German Democratic Republic, in 1960. From 1980 to 1986 he studied Fine Art at Hochschule für Grafik und Buchkunst Leipzig, in the class of Professor Arno Rink. He continued with post-graduate studies from 1986 to 1990 under the Professor Bernhard Heisig. Rauch first exhibited in *Junge Künstler im Bezirk Leipzig* at the Staatliches Lindenau Museum in Alternburg in 1986 and held his first solo exhibition at the Galerie am Thomaskirchhof, Leipzig in 1989. Rauch has been exhibiting internationally since the mid-1990s and has participated in the following group exhibitions: Goethe House, New York (1995); *Der Blick ins 21ste*, Kunstverein, Düsseldorf (1996); *Vitale Module*, Plauen, Dresden, Prague, Ludwigshafen, Wrozlaw (1997); *Die Macht des Alters*, Deutsche Historisches Museum; Berlin; Kunstmuseum, Bonn (1998); *The Golden Age*, Institute of Contemporary Arts, London (1999); *After the Wall*, Moderna Museet, Stockholm (1999); *Contemporary German Art*, Goethe Institute, Bombay, Bangalore, Calcutta, New Delhi (2000); and in the Italian Pavilion, Biennale di Venezia (2001). His solo exhibitions include: Galerie Schwind, Frankfurt (1991); ImKabinett Galerie, Berlin (1993); Dresdner Bank, Leipzig (1995); David Zwirner Gallery, New York (2000, 2002); and Galerie EIGEN + ART, Leipzig (1993, 1995, 1997, 1998, 1999, 2000); *Randgebiet*, Galerie für Zeitgenössische Kunst, Leipzig; Haus der Kunst, Munich, Kunsthalle, Zurich (2000-2001); and Deutsche Guggenheim, Berlin (2001). In January 2002 Rauch was awarded the Vincent Van Gogh Biannual Award for Contemporary Art at the Bonnefanten Museum, Maastricht, where he will be given a solo exhibition later in the year. An exhibition of his work on paper is also planned at the Museum of Modern Art, New York in 2002. From 1993 to 1998 Rauch was an assistant lecturer at the Hochschule für Grafik und Buchkunst, Leipzig. He currently lives and works in Leipzig.

Selected Bibliography

• Gregory Volk, 'Neo Rauch at David Zwirner', *Art in America*, May 2000
• Roberta Smith, 'Neo Rauch', *New York Times*, 10 March 2000
• U.C., 'Morgen in New York: Die Eigenart des Neo Rauch', *Frankfurter Allgemeine Zeitung, Berliner Seiten*, 18 February 2000
• Thomas Mayer, 'Etwas Rauch über den Wolkenkratzern', *Leipziger Volkszeitung*, 3 March 2000
• *Neo Rauch. Manöver*, (exh. cat.), Galerie EIGEN + ART, Leipzig/Berlin 1997
• *Neo Rauch. Randgebiet*, (exh. cat.), Galerie für Zeitgenössische Kunst, Leipzig 2000
• *Neo Rauch. Sammlung Deutsche Bank*, (exh. cat.), Deutsche Bank AG, Leipzig 2000

Luc Tuymans

Luc Tuymans was born in Mortsel, Belgium in 1958. From 1976 to 1979 Tuymans trained at the Sint-Lukas-instituut, Brussels, followed by a year at the École Nationale Supérieure des Arts Visuels de la Cambre, Brussels. He moved to Antwerp in 1980 and spent two years at the Koninklijke Academie voor Schone Kunsten. From 1982 to 1986 he studied at the Vrije Universiteit in Brussels. His first solo exhibition was held at the Palais des Thermes in Ostende, Belgium in 1985. Tuymans has exhibited widely internationally, and was chosen to represent Belgium at the Biennale di Venezia in 2001. His group exhibitions include: *Der Zerbrochene Spiegel*, Kunsthalle, Vienna (1993) ; *Luc Tuymans and Francis Picabia. Paintings*, David Zwirner Gallery, New York (1995); *Face à l'Histoire*, Centre Georges Pompidou, Paris (1996) ; *Project 60. John Currin, Elizabeth Peyton, Luc Tuymans*, Museum of Modern Art, New York (1997); *Future, Past, Present*, Corderie, Biennale di Venezia (1997); *Troublespot Painting*, MUHKA/NICC, Antwerp (1999) (curated by Tuymans); *Apocalypse*, Royal Academy of Art, London (2000); *The Beauty of Intimacy*, Gemeentemuseum, The Hague (2001); *Luc Tuymans: Mwana Kitoko (Beautiful White Man)*, Stedelijk Museum voor Actuele Kunst (S.M.A.K.), Ghent (2001); *The Painting Room*, Kaiser Wilhelm Museum, Krefeld (2002); and *Documenta 11*, Kassel (2002). Tuymans' solo exhibitions include: Creux de l'Enfer, Centre d'art contemporain, Thiers (1991); *Superstition*, David Zwirner Gallery, New York and touring to Frankfurt, Toronto and London (1994-95); *Luc Tuymans. Premonition*, capc Musée d'art contemporain, Bordeaux, University Art Museum, Berkeley, and Kunstmuseum, Bern (1997-98); Kunstmuseum Wolfsburg (1999); Salzburger Kunstverein, Salzburg (1999); *Luc Tuymans - Sincerely*, Tokyo Opera City Art Gallery, Tokyo (2000); *Signal*, Hamburger Bahnhof, Berlin (2001); Belgian Pavilion, Biennale di Venezia (2001); David Zwirner Gallery, New York (1994, 1996, 1998, 2000); Gallery Zeno X, Antwerp (1990, 1992, 1993, 1994, 1995, 1996, 1997, 1999, 2000); and White Cube, London (2001, 2002). Tuymans lives and works in Antwerp.

Selected Bibliography

• Daniel Birnbaum, 'More is Less', *Artforum international*, vol. 4, no. 1,

September 2001
• *Parkett*, no. 60, December 2000 (Laura Hoptman, Gerardo Mosquera, Hans Rudolf Reust)
• Frank Frangenberg, 'Luc Tuymans. The Purge', *Kunstforum*, no. 147, September-November 1999
• *Luc Tuymans: Mwana Kitoko (Beautiful White Man)*, (exh. cat.), Stedelijk Museum voor Actuele Kunst (S.M.A.K.), Ghent, 2001
• *Signal*, (exh. cat.), Hamburger Bahnhof, Berlin 2001
• *Premonition. Luc Tuymans. Dessins, Drawings*, (exh. cat.), Kunstmuseum Bern 1997
• Ulrich Loock, Juan Vicente Aliaga and Nancy Spector. *Luc Tuymans*. Phaidon London 1996

Exhibition Checklist

Kai Althoff
Ohne Titel, 1993
['Untitled']
Pasteboard, crayon, watercolor, lead pencil on cardboard
100 x 135 cm
Collection of the artist, Cologne
Courtesy Galerie Christian Nagel, Cologne
Reproduced on page 111

Ohne Titel, 1998
['Untitled']
Crayon and lead pencil on paper
35.2 x 47.2 cm
Sammlung Alexander Schröder, Berlin
Reproduced on page 112

Stern, 1999
Feltpen on resopal
84.4 x 74.9 cm
Sammlung Alexander Schröder, Berlin

Aleph, 2000
Felt pen, watercolor and color pencil on paper
68.5 x 55.8 cm
Collection Dean Valentine and Amy Adelson, Los Angeles
Courtesy Galerie Daniel Buchholz, Cologne
Reproduced on page 113

Ohne Titel, (aus der Serie *Impulse*), 2001
['Untitled' from the series 'Impulse']
Synthetic resin drawing with seeds
70 x 64 x 4 cm
Collection Susan & Michael Hort, New York
Courtesy Anton Kern Gallery, New York
Reproduced on page 117

Ohne Titel, (aus der Serie *Impulse*), 2001
['Untitled' from the series 'Impulse']
Marine lacquer, watercolor and varnish on canvas
40 x 40 x 4.5 cm
Sammlung Karola Grässlin, Cologne
Courtesy Galerie Christian Nagel, Cologne
Reproduced on page 115

Ohne Titel, (aus der Serie *Impulse*), 2001
['Untitled' from the series 'Impulse']
Marine lacquer, watercolor and varnish on canvas
50 x 70 x 8 cm
Private Collection, Chicago
Courtesy Anton Kern Gallery, New York
Reproduced on page 116

Ohne Titel, (aus der Serie *Impulse*), 2001
['Untitled' from the series 'Impulse']
Marine lacquer, watercolor and varnish on canvas
50 x 50 x 4.2 cm
Collection Ivelin & Craig Robins, Miami Beach
Courtesy Anton Kern Gallery, New York
Reproduced on page 114

Carole Benzaken
Rouleau à peintures, 1989 – ongoing
['Roll of Paintings']
Acrylic on paper
5 x 4500 cm
Collection of the artist, Paris
Courtesy Galerie Nathalie Obadia, Paris
© Adagp, Paris 2002
Reproduced on page 144-146

Sol (Fragment I), 2002
['Floor (Fragment I)']
Ceramic, oxides and metal on lava tile
475 x 640 cm
Realised by Carole Benzaken in the studio of Jean-Claude and Pascal Laristan, Beaugency, with the support of Daniel & Florence Guerlain; the subscribers to F.R.A.C., Alsace
Collection Daniel & Florence Guerlain, Les Mesnuls
Courtesy Galerie Nathalie Obadia, Paris
© Adagp, Paris 2002
Study reproduced on page 147

Glenn Brown
The End of the Twentieth Century, 1996
Oil on board
79 x 57 cm
Collection Byron Meyer, San Francisco
Reproduced on page 92

Seligsprechung, 2000
Oil on board
85 x 67.5 cm
Collection Bob Rennie, Vancouver
Courtesy Patrick Painter, Inc., Santa Monica & Galerie Max Hetzler, Berlin
Reproduced on page 91

The Suicide of Guy Debord, 2001
Oil on board
58.5 x 46.7 cm
Courtesy Patrick Painter, Inc., Santa Monica & Galerie Max Hetzler, Berlin
Reproduced on page 94

The Rebel, 2001
Oil on panel
84.5 x 70 cm
Collection Leopoldo Villareal Fernandez
Reproduced on page 93

It's a Curse, It's a Burden, 2001
Oil on board
105 x 75 cm
Collection Thomas Dane, London

Ride with the Devil, Sympathy for the Poor, 2001
Oil on board
62.5 x 46 cm
Sammlung Scharpff, Stuttgart
Reproduced on page 95

Joseph Beuys, 2001
Oil on board
96 x 79.5 cm
Collection Bobbi & Walter Zifkin, Los Angeles
Courtesy Patrick Painter, Inc., Santa Monica & Galerie Max Hetzler, Berlin
Reproduced on page 90

Bernard Buffet

Nu(e) debout, 1949
['Standing Nude']
Oil on canvas
192 x 95 cm
Musée d'Art Moderne de la Ville de Paris
© Adagp, Paris 2002
Reproduced on page 42

Portrait de l'artiste, 1949
['Portrait of the artist']
Oil on canvas
92 x 65 cm
Musée d'Art Moderne de la Ville de Paris
© Adagp, Paris 2002
Reproduced on page 43

Annabel en T-shirt, 1960
['Annabel in a t-shirt']
Oil on canvas
130 x 81 cm
Annabel Buffet, Paris
© Adagp, Paris 2002
Reproduced on page 47

Annabel en blue-jeans, 1960
['Annabel in Jeans']
Oil on canvas
130 x 97 cm
Annabel Buffet, Paris
© Adagp, Paris 2002
Reproduced on page 46

Femme couchée (de la série *Femmes déshabillées*), 1965
['Reclining Woman', from the series 'Women Undressing']
Oil on canvas
200 x 300 cm
Annabel Buffet, Paris
© Adagp, Paris 2002
Reproduced on page 44-45

Brian Calvin

Don't Be Denied, 2000
Acrylic on canvas
91 x 152 cm
Kenneth L. Freed, Boston
Reproduced on page 173

Onwards, 2001
Acrylic on canvas
45.7 x 58.4 cm
Collection Marc Foxx, Los Angeles
Reproduced on page 169

Further Still, 2001
Acrylic on canvas
114 x 91 cm
Private Collection
Courtesy Corvi-Mora Gallery, London
Reproduced on page 170

Passing Through, 2001
Acrylic on canvas
136 x 102 cm
Private Collection
Reproduced on page 171

Slow Burn, 2001
Acrylic on canvas
152.4 x 122 cm
Collection Robert Harshorn Shimshak & Marion Brenner, Berkeley
Courtesy MARC FOXX, Los Angeles
Reproduced on page 172

John Currin

Girl in Bed, 1993
Oil on canvas
96 x 122 cm
Collection David Teiger

The New Guy, 1994
Oil on canvas
40.5 x 30.5 cm
Private Collection
Reproduced on page 82

Dogwood, 1997
Oil on canvas
27.9 x 35.5 cm
Private Collection, New York
Reproduced on page 79

Jaunty & Mame, 1997
Oil on canvas
121.9 x 91.4 cm
Lorinda Ash Fine Art, New York

Sno-bo, 1999
Oil on canvas
121.9 x 81.2 cm
Private Collection, New York
Reproduced on page 80

The Hobo, 1999
Oil on canvas
101.6 x 81.2 cm
Museum of Contemporary Art, San Diego, purchase Contemporary Collectors' Fund
Reproduced on page 81

Minerva, 2000
Oil on canvas
71.1 x 55.8 cm
Collection David Teiger
Reproduced on page 83

The Moroccan, 2001
Oil on canvas
66 x 55.8 cm
Centre Pompidou, Musée national d'art moderne, purchase 2002
Reproduced on page 85

Angela, 2001
Oil on canvas
55.8 x 40.6 cm
Collection Ninah & Michael Lynne, New York
Reproduced on page 84

Peter Doig

White Out, 1992
Oil on canvas
145 x 114 cm
Private Collection
Reproduced on page 185

Blotter, 1993
Oil on canvas
249 x 199 cm
Board of Trustees of The National Museums and Galleries on Merseyside
(Walker Art Gallery, Liverpool)
Reproduced on page 186

Olin MK IV, 1995
Oil on canvas
250 x 200 cm
Stephan Landwehr, Berlin
Courtesy Contemporary Fine Arts, Berlin
Reproduced on page 187

Daytime Astronomy, 1997-1998
Oil on canvas
200 x 280 cm
Courtesy Warren & Victoria Miro, London
Reproduced on page 188

100 Years Ago, 2001
Oil on canvas
229 x 358.5 cm
Centre Pompidou, Musée national d'art moderne, purchase 2002
Reproduced on page 189

Sophie von Hellermann

Leading Lady, 2001
Acrylic on canvas
180 x 260 cm
The Saatchi Gallery, London
Reproduced on page 178

When he came ..., 2001
Acrylic on canvas
180 x 260 cm
The Saatchi Gallery, London
Reproduced on page 179

These things happened last winter, sir, 2001
Acrylic on canvas
180 x 230 cm
The Saatchi Gallery, London
Reproduced on page 180

Belle de jour, 2001
Acrylic on canvas
210 x 300 cm
The Saatchi Gallery, London
Reproduced on page 181

Alex Katz

February 5:30 P.M., 1972
Oil on canvas
183 x 366 cm
Collection of the Artist,
Courtesy Galerie Thaddaeus Ropac
© Adagp, Paris 2002
Reproduced on page 62-63

Thursday Night #2, 1974
Oil on canvas
183 x 366 cm
The Saatchi Gallery, London
© Adagp, Paris 2002
Reproduced on page 60-61

Summer Picnic, 1975
Oil on canvas
198.1 x 365.8 cm
Courtesy of Marlborough Gallery, New York
© Adagp, Paris 2002
Reproduced on page 64-65

Saturday, 2002
Oil on canvas
264.1 x 284.4 cm
Courtesy Galerie Thaddaeus Ropac
© Adagp, Paris 2002
Reproduced on page 59

Kurt Kauper

Diva Fiction #11, 1999
Oil on birch panel
215.9 x 121.9 cm
The Dakis Joannou Collection, Athens
Reproduced on page 152

Diva Fiction #12, 1999
Oil on birch panel
223.5 x 120.7 cm
Collection Jeffrey Deitch, New York
Reproduced on page 153

Cary Grant #1, 2001
Oil on birch panel
228.6 x 142.2 cm
Collection Dean Valentine and Amy Adelson, Los Angeles
Reproduced on page 154

Cary Grant #2, 2001–02
Oil on birch panel
Diameter 119.3 cm
Courtesy of ACME, Los Angeles; Deitch Projects, New York
Reproduced on page 155

Martin Kippenberger

Bekannt durch Film, Funk, Fernsehen und Polizeirufsäulen, 1981
['A celebrity in film, radio, television and police stations']
Mixed media
21 parts, each 60 x 50 cm
Sammlung Grässlin, St. Georgen
Reproduced on page 70

Ohne Titel (aus der Serie *Lieber Maler, male mir...*), 1981
['Untitled' (from the series 'Dear Painter, paint me')]
Acrylic on canvas
300 x 200 cm
Nachlass Martin Kippenberger, Cologne
Courtesy Galerie Gisela Capitain, Cologne
Reproduced on page 71

Ohne Titel (Selbstporträt), 1988
['Untitled, (Self-portrait)']
Oil on canvas
241 x 202 cm
The Dakis Joannou Collection, Athens
Reproduced on page 72

Ohne Titel (aus der Serie *Das Floss der Medusa*), 1996
[Untitled from the series 'The Raft of the Medusa']
Oil on canvas
150 x 180 cm
Private Collection
Reproduced on page 73

***Enoc Perez**
Sarah, 1998
Oil on canvas
144.5 x 124.5 cm
Courtesy Galerie Michael Janssen, Cologne
Reproduced on page 138

Catherine, 1999
Oil on canvas
124.5 x 144.5 cm
Courtesy Galerie Michael Janssen, Cologne
Reproduced on page 137

Someone else's girlfriend, 2000
Oil on canvas
106.5 x 152.5 cm
Courtesy Galerie Michael Janssen, Cologne
Reproduced on page 136

The Love that Got Away, 2001
Oil on canvas
152.5 x 172.5 cm
Courtesy Galerie Michael Janssen, Cologne
Reproduced on page 139

Bruno Perramant
Dessous dessous maintenant/toujours plus, 1997
Oil on canvas
5 paintings: 3 x (92 x 73 cm); 2 x (90 x 130 cm)
Overall dimensions: 182 x 415 cm
Collection Fabienne Leclerc, Paris
Reproduced on page 131

Matrice, 1997-98
Oil on canvas
9 paintings, each 73 x 92 cm
Overall dimensions 276 x 219 cm
Courtesy Galerie In-situ, Paris
Reproduced on page 132

Stacks of Time (Selection Alison Gingeras; Arrangement Bruno Perramant) 2002
Oil on canvas
16 paintings, dimensions variable
Monsieur & Madame Agostini, Paris; Joanna Chevalier-Sèvres, Paris; Gilles Fuchs, Paris; and Galerie In-Situ, Paris
Reproduced on page 133

Elizabeth Peyton
Blur Kurt, 1995
Oil on masonite
35.6 x 27.9 cm
Collection David & Monica Zwirner, New York
Reproduced on page 159

John Simon Beverly Ritchie (Sid), 1995
Oil on masonite
30.5 x 22.9 cm
Museum of Fine Arts, Boston. Contemporary Curators' Fund 1995.120
Reproduced on page 160

Piotr, 1996
Oil on MDF
22.9 x 12.7 cm
Collection of the artist
Courtesy Gavin Brown's Enterprise, Corp., New York

Jarvis 1996
Oil on board
28 x 35.6 cm
Susan & Michael Hort, New York
Reproduced on the cover

David Hockney, Powis Terrace Bedroom, 1998
Oil on board
25 x 18 cm
Kunstmuseum Wolfsburg
Reproduced on page 161

Democrats are more beautiful (after Jonathan), 2001
Oil on board
25.4 x 20.3 cm
Laura & Stafford Broumand, New York
Reproduced on page 162

Nude (Tony), 2001
Oil on board
15.2 x 20.3 cm
Douglas S. Cramer, New York
Reproduced on page 164

Luing (Tony), 2001
Oil on MDF
35.6 x 27.9 cm
Dianne Wallace, New York
Reproduced on page 165

September (Ben), 2001
Oil on board
30.8 x 23.2 cm
Private Collection
Courtesy Gavin Brown's Enterprise, Corp., New York
Reproduced on page 163

Francis Picabia
Modèle nu(e) debout, 1941
['Naked standing model']
Oil on paper and cardboard
106.5 x 76.5 cm
Flick Collection
© Adagp Paris 2002
Reproduced on page 35

La brune et la blonde, 1941
['The Brunette and the Blonde']
Oil on cardboard
104 x 75 cm
Flick Collection
© Adagp, Paris 2002
Reproduced on page 37

Femme nue devant la glace, 1941-42
['The Mirror']
Oil on canvas
106 x 76.5 cm
Collection David & Monica Zwirner, New York
© Adagp, Paris 2002
Reproduced on page 36

Nu de dos, 1940-42
['Nude from the Back']
Oil on cardboard
105 x 76 cm
The Dakis Joannou Collection, Athens
© Adagp, Paris 2002
Reproduced on page 33

La femme blonde/La blonde, 1942
['Blond woman']
Oil on cardboard
106 x 76 cm
Sammlung Hauser & Wirth, St. Gallen
© Adagp, Paris 2002
Reproduced on page 34

Portrait d'un couple, 1942-43
['Portrait of a couple']
Oil on board
105.7 x 77.4 cm
The Museum of Modern Art, New York, purchase, 2000
© Adagp, Paris 2002
Reproduced on page 38

Sigmar Polke
Engel, 1962
['Angel']
Oil on canvas
49 x 60 cm
Karin Polke
Reproduced on page 52

Der Wurstesser, 1963
['The Sausage-Eater']
Emulsion on canvas
200 x 150 cm
Flick Collection
Reproduced on page 53

Liebespaar, 1967
Varnish and ball-point pen on canvas
170 x 130 cm
Sammlung Speck, Cologne
Reproduced on page 55

Neo Rauch
Unerträglicher Naturalismus, 1998
Oil on wood
160 x 105 cm
Sammlung Ruth
Courtesy Galerie EIGEN+ART, Leipzig/Berlin
Courtesy David Zwirner Gallery, New York
© Adagp, Paris 2002
Reproduced on page 101

Die Wahl 1998
Oil on canvas
300 x 200 cm
Sammlung Ruth
Courtesy Galerie EIGEN+ART, Leipzig/Berlin
Courtesy David Zwirner Gallery, New York
© Adagp, Paris 2002
Reproduced on page 102

Sturmnacht, 2000
Oil on canvas
200 x 300 cm
Sammlung Goetz
© Adagp, Paris 2002
Reproduced on page 103

Grat, 2000
Oil on canvas
200 x 300 cm
Private Collection
Courtesy Galerie EIGEN+ART, Leipzig/Berlin
© Adagp, Paris 2002
Reproduced on page 104

Niederung, 2001-02
Oil on canvas
250 x 210 cm
Private Collection
Courtesy Galerie EIGEN+ART, Leipzig/Berlin
© Adagp, Paris 2002
Reproduced on page 105

Luc Tuymans
Sealed Rooms, 1990
Oil on canvas
Triptych, each painting: 36 x 38 cm
Courtesy David Zwirner Gallery, New York

Der diagnostische Blick I, 1992
['Diagnostic View I']
Oil on canvas
53 x 48 cm
Private Collection
Courtesy David Zwirner Gallery, New York
Reproduced on page 122

Der diagnostische Blick III, 1992
['Diagnostic View III']
Oil on canvas
62 x 40 cm
Collection van Cauwenberghe-De Man, Bachte Maria Leerne

Der diagnostische Blick IV, 1992
['Diagnostic View IV']
Oil on canvas
57 x 38 cm
Courtesy Zeno X Gallery, Antwerp, long-term loan to De Pont Stichting voor hedendaagse kunst, Tilburg
Reproduced on page 123

Der diagnostische Blick V, 1992
['Diagnostic View V']
Oil on canvas
58 x 42 cm
Private Collection
Reproduced on page 124

Der diagnostische Blick VI, 1992
['Diagnostic View VI']
Oil on canvas
75 x 48 cm
Collection Debra-Houtsaeger,
De Panne
Reproduced on page 125

Der diagnostische Blick VIII, 1992
['Diagnostic View VIII']
Oil on canvas
68.5 x 39.5 cm
Sammlung Peter & Heidi Aaen,
Neustadt
Reproduced on page 126

Der diagnostische Blick IX, 1992
['Diagnostic View IX']
Oil on canvas
49 x 57 cm
Sammlung Hauser & Wirth,
St. Gallen

Der diagnostische Blick X, 1992
['Diagnostic View X']
Oil on canvas
48.5 x 55.5 cm
Jean-Paul Jungo, Geneva
Reproduced on page 127

All titles have been translated
where possible.

* Artist presented only at the
Schirn Kunsthalle Frankfurt.

Printed in July 2002
on the presses of
Snoeck-Ducaju & Zoon,
Ghent, Belgium.

Photographic credits

ACME, Los Angeles, p. 154, 155.
Gavin Brown's Enterprise, New York, p. 159-165 and front cover.
Galerie Gisela Capitain, Cologne, p. 71.
Corvi-Mora Gallery, London, p. 170.
Deitch Projects, New York, p. 153.
Galerie EIGEN+ART, Leipzig/Berlin, photos Uwe Walter, Berlin, p. 101-105.
Fayer, Vienne, p. 55.
Galerie Jennifer Flay, photo Marc Domage, Paris, p. 82.
Marc Foxx Gallery, Los Angeles, p. 172.
Galerie Maurice Garnier, Paris, p. 44-47.
Galerie Michael Janssen, Cologne, p. 136-139.
The Dakis Joannou Collection, Athens, p. 33, 72, 152.
J. Littkemann, Berlin, p 34, 36.
Marlborough Gallery, New York, p. 64-65.
Victoria Miro Gallery, London, p. 185-189.
The Museum of Modern Art, New York, p. 38.
Galerie Christian Nagel, Cologne, p. 111-115.
Pace Wildenstein, New York, photo Ellen Page Wilson, p. 59.
Patrick Painter, Inc., Santa Monica, p. 90-95.
Photothèque des Musées de la Ville de Paris/Jean-Yves Trocaz, p. 42-43.
Centre Pompidou, Paris, photos Georges Meguerditchian, p. 73, 131-133, 144-147.
Andrea Rosen Gallery, New York, photo Oren Slor, p. 84, 85 ; photos Fred Scruton, New York, p. 79-83.
The Saatchi Gallery, London, p. 60-61, photos Stephen White, p. 178-181.
Peter Schälchi, Zurich, p. 35.
Oren Slor, p. 62-63.
Zeno X Gallery, Antwerp, photos Felix Tirry, Antwerp p. 120-127.